PIANO MAN

PIANO MAN

A Life of John Ogdon

CHARLES BEAUCLERK

**SIMON &
SCHUSTER**

London · New York · Sydney · Toronto · New Delhi

A CBS COMPANY

For Richard

First published in Great Britain by Simon & Schuster UK Ltd, 2014
This paperback edition published by Simon & Schuster UK Ltd, 2015
A CBS COMPANY

Photographs kindly supplied by the following people and organizations:
1, 3, 5: Philippa O'Hara; 2, 4: Richard Ogdon; 6, 12, 13, 14, 15, 17, 25:
Brenda Lucas Ogdon; 7: Marjorie Stevenson; 8: Schott Music Ltd; 9: Rodney
Friend; 11, 24: C.J. Spencer-Bentley; 16, 22: Clive Barda/ArenaPAL; 18: Daniell
Revenaugh; 19, endpapers: Royal Manchester College of Music; 20: P.I. Tchaikovsky
Museum, Klin and the Tchaikovsky Competition Organizing Committee; 21:
Warner Music; 23: Chris Rice.

1 3 5 7 9 10 8 6 4 2

Simon & Schuster UK Ltd
1st Floor
222 Gray's Inn Road
London WC1X 8HB

www.simonandschuster.co.uk

Simon & Schuster Australia, Sydney
Simon & Schuster India, New Delhi

A CIP catalogue record for this book
is available from the British Library

ISBN: 978-1-84983-177-2
ebook ISBN: 978-0-85720-012-9

Typeset in the UK by M Rules
Printed and bound by CPI Group (UK) Ltd, Croydon, CR0 4YY

CONTENTS

Preface

A PERSONAL NOTE

I got to know John Ogdon through my friendship with his son Richard, who was the first person I met at prep school when we were a couple of eight-year-olds in stiff shorts and tweed jackets. That was back in September 1973, not long before John suffered his breakdown, and we have been friends ever since. I had the privilege of meeting John many times during the sixteen years between 1973 and his early death, and heard him play both informally and in concert.

To the eight-year-old who first encountered him at his Regency home on Chester Terrace John was a baffling and rather scary figure. I remember surreptitiously entering a darkened room one sunny afternoon while playing hide-and-seek with Richard and his sister Annabel, and concealing myself behind a clothes rack. Peeping through the coats and dresses I was shocked to see a large bespectacled figure lying on the bed blowing smoke from his nostrils. I was so terrified at this unexpected presence, not to mention the feeling of brooding intensity that surrounded it, that I crawled out instantly, no longer caring whether I was caught or not. Little could I have imagined that one day I would be the biographer of that shadowy figure.

To the young man in his twenties, John was affable, shambolic and inspiring – a prodigal pearl-caster, who seemed to hover between earth and other more spritely dimensions (though he never lost his passion for food). I remember him being deeply excited by ideas and wonderfully receptive to new thoughts: it was impossible to conceive of him *not* understanding something. I once gave him a copy of a 900-page tome on the authorship of Shakespeare's plays. He read it straight through over the course of a weekend. On the Monday the doorbell rang; it was John's wife Brenda with a suitcase in each hand, looking absolutely shattered – she had just returned from the States. John stood in the doorway, blocking her path. 'Have you heard, Brenda?' he asked breathlessly. 'Heard what?' she replied, eager to be let in but at the same time hopeful of good news. 'Well . . . there's this remarkable new theory about Shakespeare. It's awfully compelling!' The last time I saw him was in Exeter in July 1989, where he played the *Emperor* Concerto just weeks before he died. It was a deeply poignant account of the piece that made one realize that he only spoke deeply about himself at the piano and that his everyday reticence made artistic sense. We spoke briefly after the concert.

Brenda Ogdon was always a charming hostess who put on a brave face. Of course I had little or no idea what she was going through in the 1970s, but her sufferings must have been tremendous. The frank portrait of her in this book owes much to her own honesty and capacity for self-criticism, both in the book she wrote with Michael Kerr in 1980 and in the recent interviews she accorded me. She may appear harsh at times, but much of what she lived through with John was extreme and would have driven less formidable folk to give up altogether. In her own way Brenda kept faith with John, even when all seemed lost – that is to be admired, as is the way she fought with great tenacity for the welfare of her son and daughter: two more reasonable and good-natured people you could not hope to meet.

Ultimately, this is a book written with affection and admiration for its subject, and in a spirit of non-judgement. I am grateful to the Ogdon family for its encouragement, support and forbearance, and above all for the freedom to write the book as I saw fit. I trust that they recognize in my portrait of John the touching, eccentric and superbly talented man they loved and revered.

Charles Beauclerk,
October, 2013.

Foreword

HALF PIANO, HALF MAN

*In his intimate contact with his instrument he appeared to
me like a new centaur, half piano, half man.*

Bruno Walter on pianist Eugen d'Albert

On the evening of Thursday 14 July 1988 one of the most exceptional piano recitals in the history of music-making took place
at London's Queen Elizabeth Hall. The programme announced a
single piece of music, more than four hours in duration, to be played
straight through with two short intervals. There were around 400
people in the audience, the hall being a little over half full. The weight
of expectation was palpable, with people sensing that what they were
about to witness was less a concert than a rite of passage. The music
they had come to hear was uncharted territory; to play it would
require a huge act of faith on the part of the artist. Surely many
would have seen the composer's dedication to the work, prominently
displayed in the programme, and recoiled at the blasphemous aplomb
with which he extolled 'the everlasting glory of those few men blessed
and sanctified in the curses and execrations of those many, whose
praise is eternal damnation'.

The same uncompromising spirit permeated the music itself. On
the day he completed the work the composer wrote to a friend:

The closing four pages are as cataclysmic and catastrophic as any-thing I've ever done – the harmony bites like nitric acid and the counterpoint grinds like the mills of God to close finally on this implacable monosyllable:

'I am the spirit that denies!'

There was little chance that the ninety-five-year-old Kaikhosru Shapurji Sorabji would attend the concert – though the organizers must have counted themselves fortunate that he had granted his per-mission for it to happen at all, for he had for more than half a century discouraged public performance of his works. A diminutive man of fiercely reclusive habits, Sorabji was now the resident of a nursing home in the Isle of Purbeck, Dorset, where he had suffered a stroke only the previous month. He was of Parsi and English heritage and for many decades had lived an ivory-tower existence on the edge of Corfe Castle. He had named his house 'The Eye', after the Eye of Horus: the divine child of Isis who, as the god of war and silence, took the form of a falcon.

There, in the home of this hermetic-hermitic composer, was a hoard of the most colossal scores ever penned. The very few privi-leged to open these unpublished volumes were confronted by a forest of staves festooned with dizzying runs of hemidemisemiquavers and harmonic complications of such soaring and swooping intricacy as to scare off all but the most dauntless of musical explorers. It was hard-core black on black. According to one critic, the scores were the creations of a 'megalomaniacal character the like of which has rarely been encountered in the annals of musical history'; another described the composer as 'a one-man musical apocalypse'.

Almost no one had heard of the composer, let alone heard his music. His concessions to the music-going masses could be summed up in the

blandest of all monosyllables: nil. 'Utterly out of the fashion, aren't I?'
he wrote impishly to the Scottish poet Hugh MacDiarmid in the
1930s. '*And glory in being so!*' He was a forbidding figure who shrank
from contact with the public and poured scorn on anyone presuming
to understand his work or person. Like the sole Arabian bird, he sat
upon his pyre in inconsolable intensity. Composition was his religion –
or rather he made a cult of his own work, of which he was both priest
and communicant. His genius was *sui generis* and to outsiders the
expression of an Olympian misanthropy, yet to those who befriended
him he was a sensitive and generous man. The usual pleasures and distractions of modern life held no appeal for him; he dedicated every
ounce of his energy to bringing his lonely gifts to flower.

The piano stood centre stage, a mysterious flying craft with folded
wings: a Steinway Model-D Concert Grand, just shy of nine feet
long. Wedged into its music stand was the spaceship's manual, a gargantuan score awaiting a navigator of supreme ability. Off to the side
was a chair for the evening's co-pilot, the valiant page-turner. At six
thirty a silence descended on the hall; after what seemed an eternity
the house lights suddenly went down, leaving the piano cocooned in
an oval of light. A heartfelt cheer went up with the odd strangled
'Bravo!' as onto the stage shuffled a bulky, bespectacled figure of a
man, hunched less with age than buckled fury, his furrowed brow sur-
mounted by a thick bank of wavy white, nicotine-stained hair. His
head was bowed, a yellowish-white goatee bobbing on his chest as he
gave rapid little half-bows and scurried towards the piano with his
page-turner in his wake like Falstaff with his loyal page[1]. His gait was
crablike, almost sideways on, and mechanical-looking as he hurried
stiffly forwards, his forehead beaded with sweat. A reticent smile
played upon his lips – blissfully unaware, it seemed, of the frown
inscribed above it. Once his hand touched the deck of the piano,
however, his whole body relaxed. He turned to face the audience and
gave a long low bow – bending forward from the waist, as if operated

1 Says Falstaff to his page in *2 Henry IV*, I.ii.9-11: 'I do here walk before thee like a
sow that hath overwhelm'd all her litter but one.'

by wires – followed by a couple of perfunctory bobs and nods. The eyes behind the frosted spectacles reflected the same disturbing balance of gentleness and strife that marked his face as a whole. If a sun shone in his countenance it did so from behind a ridge of dark clouds. When finally he sat down at the piano it was as though he had plugged himself into a vital energy supply.

This was of course the fifty-one-year-old John Ogdon; it could have been no one else. He had come to play the longest piano piece ever published, Sorabji's 270-minute *Opus Clavicembalisticum*, composed in 1930. The inspiration behind the work was the twelve-part *Fantasia Contrappuntistica* of Busoni – itself a homage to the master of the fugue, J. S. Bach. There are four gigantic fugues in Sorabji's piece, some with five voices, which to many have the feel of a monotonous landscape extending endlessly towards some undefined horizon. The musically literate have called them 'grindingly cerebral', better savoured on the page than in performance, but it is clear that John Ogdon thought otherwise. 'The first thing to be said about *OC*,' he wrote, 'is that it is a tuneful piece. I say this because its proliferation of notes can sometimes obscure its melodic feeling.' He talked lovingly of the architecture of the composition – its overarching structural dimensions – as if it were some desolate palace from the *Arabian Nights*. He understood the fugues to have a meditative function and to exert a calming influence, allowing the audience to relax and the performer to take a 'mental breather'. They might even induce a trance-like state, and this may be what he had in mind when he once compared Sorabji's music to the acid-house or rave music popular in the 1980s. In the same vein, he felt that the piece would give the performer energy if he could orient himself correctly to the music.

John understood the work in spiritual terms. Writing in the late 1980s, he expressed it this way:

It ends with a religious blessing and may be said, like Messiaen's *Vingt Regards*, to embody a religious experience and perception. Its main tonality I believe is C-sharp major, which is achieved through a passage of conflict with, principally, the keys of G-sharp minor and D-sharp minor. It may be that the minor tonalities express the

darker feelings through which one must struggle to achieve a perception of religious light.

He also referred to the *Parsifal*-like solemnity of Sorabji's finest passages, and it could be said that *OC* not only expresses a Grail-like quest
but *is* the quest itself – with its terrors, frustrations and revelations.
Another metaphor for *OC* might be that of *Moby-Dick*, a work that
engrossed Ogdon his whole adult life. There isn't much of a story (or
horizontal melody-line) to *Moby-Dick*, but there is great depth. It is all
harmony and counterpoint – a symbolic down-weaving into something
inhumanly deep and strange. There are countless passages on whale-
lore, the doctrines of sea-life, the almost mystical rituals associated
with whale-hunting, the butchery of whales, the extraction and storage of the oil and spermaceti, the fashioning of a foreskin cassock
from the circumcised monster, the appalling whiteness of Moby Dick
himself, and of course the endless moods and movements of the ocean.
These descriptive stretches are broken up by the sudden drama and
perverse majesty of the whale-hunts themselves. The fugues in Sorabji's
OC resemble the perpetual motion of the waves; the 'multiform trans-
verse scurries across the keyboard' the underlying currents or
submarine movements of the whales; and the 'thunderous shattering
crashes' the sudden murderous attacks of Moby Dick. As D. H.
Lawrence wrote of the novel, 'There is scarcely a taint of earth – pure
sea motion.' One could also say that the cetological passages in *Moby-
Dick* find a parallel in long passages of *Opus Clavicembalisticum* that
appear to probe the history and evolution of keyboard music – hence
the name. The piano stands duty for the whale. Like the *Parsifal* story,
Moby-Dick in its dreamlike phantasmagoria describes an inner journey – only this is a journey towards not redemption but annihilation.
Both Herman Melville and Sorabji employed a high-flown, densely
wrought art that feels like a shield against chaos and raw feeling. Again
and again they raise the banner of the intellect with scintillating passages of bravura writing. Sorabji, for instance, revels in the
'devilish-clever' textures of Paganini, plying five staves at once with
more ideas than they can hold or two hands can express. Melville,
meanwhile, uses erudite digressions and virtuosic descriptions of the

sea as a way of distracting himself and the reader from the roving malice of the albino whale. The formless in both works is experienced
through the incessant water imagery. Ronald Stevenson has stressed the
aquatic nature of much of *OC*, and Sorabji himself included expression
marks such as *scorrendo, lisciamente e liquido* ('scrolling, smoothing and
fluid'). There are eerie moments of half-silence, too, that are nonetheless fraught with menace. Again, these sinister atmospheres find
parallels in Melville's masterpiece, as in this sudden lull in one of the
whale-hunts:

> As the three boats lay there on that gently rolling sea, gazing down
> into its eternal blue noon; and as not a single groan or cry of any
> sort, nay, not so much as a ripple or a bubble came up from its
> depths; what landsman would have thought, that beneath all that
> silence and placidity, the utmost monster of the seas was writhing
> and wrenching in agony!

The penultimate image afforded by *Moby-Dick* – that of the *Pequod*
sinking beneath the waves, an eagle nailed to its mast – is every bit as
godforsaken as the life-denying chord at the end of *OC*.

The monomaniacal Captain Ahab once lost a leg to Moby Dick
and now stands upon an ivory prosthesis, 'fashioned from the polished
bone of the sperm whale's jaw'. A man of austere reserve, Ahab sinks
into profound periods of self-communion in which he broods upon
the malice of the whale that mutilated him. He is eaten by dark
thoughts, and made callous by the long loneliness of his obsession.
This is the story of a man who dries up inside, crucified by his own
mind, while the massive incarnation of his rejected libido – that
prodigy of the Moon, Moby Dick – rises to destroy him. It is a tale of
the havoc that is wreaked when the mind makes war on the blood.
Ahab's whale-jaw leg symbolizes his mysterious oneness with Moby
Dick. It is as if the whale is the captain's destructive genius. An eerie
reflection of this dynamic is found in Ogdon's relationship with the
keyboard, which served as his ivory limb as well as the sounding
board of all his darkest feelings.

*

That July night, after a tentative start, John delivered a performance of great power and vision. Carrying the audience with him by dint of his unremitting stamina and musical imagination, he seemed to rise from the piano in a state of spiritual refreshment. Nor did the audience appear wearied by the length of the recital, for there is a curious time-warp effect in Sorabji's immense pieces – evidence perhaps of an oriental dimension to his music – whereby a six-hour concert can appear to be a third of its actual duration. This strange temporal retrenchment was mirrored throughout by the pianist's economy of movement at the keyboard, which allowed him to process page after page of the most complex music without exhaustion.

According to Nigel Scaife, his page-turner that night, John could be hard to follow in places – especially during the fugues, when he would switch to automatic pilot. It was at such moments that he could lose his place or fluff a line of crotchets – an elementary error that left Nigel aghast. While he might stumble in the less adorned, more mechanical passages, though, there was no denying the leonine relish with which he rounded on the technically hair-raising sections. Indeed, the thicker the notes bristled on the page the more engaged he became. The decorative interludes, with their filigree figurations bearing the shimmering hallmarks of Ravel, Scriabin and Szymanowski, were also enchantingly brought to life by Ogdon, who in defiance of his physique proved marvellously adept at weaving diaphanous veils of sound.

To the question 'Why climb Everest?' George Mallory famously replied, 'Because it's there.' There is no doubt that Ogdon similarly revelled in the knowledge that he could scale this musical peak. Towards the end of the concert, as he reached the summit, he appeared to be breathing a purer air – and his elation communicated itself directly to the audience. Richard Morrison wrote in the following morning's *Times*:

John Ogdon, giving the first complete performance [of *OC*] in England, was simply astonishing. Extract any 10-minute segment from the work and you could find enough technical improbabilities to dissuade any average virtuoso from performance. Ogdon conquered them, one after another, with magnificent resource and sheer guts – the epic chordal cascades, the frenetic chromatic lines racing five ways simultaneously, the complex chains of emphasis needed to make even partial sense of the fugues. Four hours after starting, he seemed to be playing more brilliantly than ever. Finally, a somewhat stunned audience rose in euphoric acclaim.

The standing ovation began at 11 p.m. and lasted a full eleven minutes.

Backstage, meanwhile, pots of pills bore eloquent witness to the internal wars to which Ogdon was heir, and the heroic effort required of him simply to step out onto the stage. In the green room after the concert, the music critic Felix Aprahamian was overcome with emotion. Embracing John with tears in his eyes, he congratulated him on his performance. John stood nodding sweetly and drenched in sweat, like a rare fish that had found itself translated from its natural element. 'Would you like me to play it again?' he replied, his voice earnest and sing-song.

HAUNTED HOUSE

Scorpion fights against the Sun
Until the Sun and Moon go down . . .

T. S. Eliot, 'East Coker'

In 1947, when John Ogdon was ten years old, his father, Howard, had a book published called *The Kingdom of the Lost*. The first chapter, entitled 'A Lunatic at Large', opens with the words, 'I am an escaped lunatic. This is the true story of a man who went sane.' The book is Howard's account of his severe mental breakdown in July 1938, his subsequent committal to local asylums and his protracted struggle to understand what had happened to him. John was aged just eighteen months when six burly officers arrived one summer morning and removed Howard from the house. After that, John's mother would take him with her on her Saturday-morning visits to the asylum, travelling the sixteen miles from Mansfield Woodhouse to Nottingham by bus. Although Howard, in the early days of his lunacy, was allowed out for short stretches, it would be a full six years before he returned home for good. His confinement, which lasted the better part of three years, was cut short by an audacious escape in August 1941.

Howard Ogdon, whose full name was John Andrew Howard

Ogdon, was born in the small Derbyshire town of Wirksworth in December 1899. Before it became Derbyshire's principal stone-quarrying town, Wirksworth was renowned for its lead mining, which had been a local industry since pre-Roman times. On his father's side, Howard's family had been settled in Wirksworth for centuries. The Church of St Mary the Virgin there contains many memorials to the Ogdon family, including one to Howard's father, William Francis Ogdon, who was an articled clerk in a solicitor's office. He died of throat cancer at the age of thirty-seven, when Howard was just eight years old. William's father, another William, was innkeeper of the Royal Oak, as was *his* father (Howard's great-grandfather) – except that he was also a butcher, like his own father and namesake. (Aptly enough, the Ogdon residence was Oak House, the name Ogdon deriving from the Old English *ac denu*, meaning 'oak valley'.) Finally we arrive at one John Ogdon, born in 1718, the pianist's great-great-great-great grandfather, who in common with many of his forebears was a lead miner.

Howard Ogdon's father married Ethel Brown of Coalville, Leicestershire, whose own father, Charles, was assistant foreman at the local mine. They had two children – Howard and his sister Kathleen – born four years apart. A few years after Howard's birth, with his father already ailing, the Ogdons moved from Wirksworth to Coalville. When their father died Howard and Kathleen moved with Ethel into her parents' home there. Howard's maternal grandfather died a year later, in 1909, and his paternal grandfather in 1910, so in the space of two years the boy lost all the male figures in his life. He and his sister were brought up by Ethel and her mother Elizabeth Brown. Later on, they were joined by their Ogdon grandmother, Sarah, widow of William Ogdon of the Royal Oak, who came to live with them from Wirksworth, where she had been a hat-maker. Nothing is known of Howard's father beyond his profession and the long illness that put an end to his short life. His mother, however, was known for her superb singing voice and used to sing solo at concerts as a young woman. It is said that when her husband died she vented her anger on her eight-year-old son, even to the extent of telling him that she hated him.

Howard was a nervous, sensitive child of precarious health and precocious intellect. He had rheumatic fever when he was four, around the time his father first fell sick, which branched out into chorea (St Vitus' Dance) at the age of eight, the year his father died. He attended the Ashby Grammar School for Boys at Ashby-de-la-Zouch, from where he won a scholarship to University College, Nottingham. Even as a fourteen-year-old schoolboy he was a heavy cigarette smoker. Before he could take up his university studies he was drafted into the army for the final year of the Great War. He served from January 1918 to February 1919 with the 5th Duke of Wellington's (62nd Division) on the Western Front, where he was blown up at the Battle of Havrincourt. The trauma of his shell-shock was never treated, but accompanied him back into civvy street, its horrors eating away beneath the surface normality of his life. Howard described it as a 'war neurosis', which he managed to hold in check – 'neatly submerged' – for twenty years. Today he might have been diagnosed with post-traumatic stress disorder; he would certainly have received some form of therapy.

After demobilization at Clipstone Camp, near Mansfield, Howard pursued his studies at University College Nottingham, reading English and gaining his Board of Education certificate (awarded by the University of London). The fact that he achieved only a third-class degree may suggest a mind destabilized by war; either that or his unconventional way of thinking was not to the taste of the examiners. He followed this up with teacher training at a secondary school down in Callington, southeast Cornwall, where he taught English, French and PT. It was in Callington that he met the nineteen-year-old Dorothy Mutton – the youngest daughter of William Mutton, a master boot-maker, and his recently deceased wife, Philippa Honeychurch. On both her father's and her mother's side Dorothy's family was Cornish to the bone, and lead mining was as much a feature of her ancestry as it was of Howard's. In a newspaper column in the early 1960s entitled 'Meals my mother cooked me', John Ogdon was quoted as saying, 'My mother is Cornish, and I've never tasted Cornish pasties like hers – it seems to be something that only Cornish people know how to make.' Howard courted Dorothy for a year before they eloped in September 1922 (she had just turned

twenty), and they were married at the registry office in East
Stonehouse, near Plymouth, that same month, with Dorothy three-
and-a-half months pregnant. Her age on the marriage certificate was
falsified to twenty-two.

Shortly after the wedding the couple moved back to Howard's
mother's place in Coalville, where a daughter, Philippa, was born in
March 1923. Howard took jobs as a supply teacher, first at the
Leicestershire County Council Elementary School, then at Palmers
Boys, a secondary school in Grays, Essex, where he taught English,
French and Latin. Essex was a very long way from home, however,
and he resigned from Palmers after just two months, when he was
appointed to the staff of the Queen Elizabeth Grammar School for
Boys in Mansfield, Nottinghamshire, to teach English. He took up
the post in September 1924, having bought late that summer a small
semi-detached house in Catherine Street in Mansfield Woodhouse,
a large village to the north of Mansfield proper. Howard taught
English and French, and occasionally Latin and art, but English was
his principal subject. On his teaching card his interests are listed as
literature, music, aesthetic theory, philosophy (Schopenhauer, Hegel,
Nietzsche), and educational theory. Under 'games' is written
'temporarily disabled', while 'poultry breeding' is given as his only
hobby.

Woodhouse (or 'Wooduz' as the locals call it) was Nottinghamshire's
principal quarry town and home to Sherwood Colliery. It is an attractive town in undulating countryside, about halfway between
Nottingham in the south and Sheffield in the north. In the old days, on
what is now the site of a haunted spot called Hallam's Grave, stood a
scythe-and-sword factory renowned for the quality of its steelwork.
Mansfield Woodhouse was the administrative centre of Sherwood
Forest and even in the Ogdons' time was a town of foresters and quar-
rymen. Despite the activity their presence implies, the place has a
dreamy quality to it. Certainly Howard must have cut quite a figure
striding to school over Pheasant Hill with his black gown billowing out
behind him.

In the following six years three further children, two sons and a
daughter, were born to Howard and Dorothy Ogdon: Paul in 1925,

Ruth in 1929 and Karl in 1930. Howard's passion for music, in particular Wagner, was reflected in the names he chose for the boys: Paul Siegfried Wolfgang and Karl Tristan Donnertrager – 'the thunderbearer' – Ogdon. Howard was a small, wiry man, with closely cropped hair, who described his pleasures and constitution as 'ascetic'. His thoughts, however, were grandiose – and when he describes Hitler as 'an ascetic genius with a taste for the magnificent' one detects an element of self-portraiture. Dorothy, on the other hand, was large and comely, with dark hair and dark eyes. She was a modest, hard-working woman, an excellent cook and talented dressmaker, who for all her nervous energy kept her demons securely kennelled. When her temper did flare, she could slap – and slap hard. Although not bookish, she was intelligent, creative and freedom-loving and it was her fascination with Howard's writing that first drew her to him. She was one of four sisters, two of whom – Bessie Perry and Nance – came to live in nearby Mansfield as middle-aged widows.

It seems that Howard and Dorothy's marriage was not a naturally comfortable one, with husband and wife quickly resorting to separate beds. Howard was austere and remote with his family and had his own little study downstairs in which he spent most of his spare time. Sunday lunch was one of the few occasions on which he mixed with the family. A highly strung man with unusual ideas, he was not known to suffer fools and would spend whole days locked in his sanctuary, drinking dandelion tea and smoking roll-ups while he filled notebook after notebook with his thoughts and inspirations. Sometimes the mighty strains of Wagner or Berlioz could be heard issuing from under the door. (In the 1970s one of John's pupils at Indiana University recalls him getting up during a performance of the overture to Wagner's *Flying Dutchman* and leaving the auditorium, visibly shaken. He later told her that the music had terrified him.)

There were frequent upheavals at home. Philippa and Paul were often sent away to stay with Grandpa Mutton in Cornwall or Grandma Ogdon in Coalville, while Ruth and Karl were farmed out to Howard's sister Kathleen or the two Mansfield aunts, Bessie and Nance. Dorothy's father, William Mutton, had a large flat in Callington over his shoe shop. He was a true Cornishman, with snow-white hair and piercing blue eyes. In addition to his cobbling activities he was a Wesleyan preacher, though he refrained from preaching to his grand-children because he knew it riled their father.

Howard had literary ambitions, and spent a good deal of his non-professional life writing poetry and stories. He would periodically destroy his work, however. It is unlikely that he ever had the peace of mind or sustained concentration to bring his talents to fruition; or, if he did, his nervous eruptions swept everything away. None of his fic-tional writing has survived except for a 400-line poem entitled 'The Camp', published in *Life and Letters* in 1930. In all his photographs there is the signature row of pens glinting in his top pocket, like a line of exquisite daggers.

In addition to the interests listed on his school record, Howard was deep into Eastern mysticism, witchcraft and psychology. Seventeenth-century literature, with its heady blend of spiritual and esoteric investigation, was a particular passion, Robert Burton, Joseph Glanvill and Sir Thomas Browne being high on his list of best-loved authors. He revered the Brontë sisters and was also an aficionado of French lit-erature, in particular the Symbolist poets Baudelaire and Émile Verhaeren. After literature his most enduring enthusiasm was music and the psychology of music. Here Berlioz, Wagner and Debussy were his heroes. All three wrote highly sensual music and were pro-foundly influenced by literature and the occult. Howard had a vast collection of gramophone records, which he delighted in playing for-tissimo. Although he wasn't a musician in the strict sense of the word, he could read music and had the gift of what he called 'visual-auditory transfer' – meaning that he could hear a work in his head as he read the score. He also had extremely sensitive hearing. In 1931 *Life and Letters* published his article on Berlioz's sense of the macabre, 'Berlioz: The Earlier Phase'. It is a brilliant and wide-ranging piece that weaves profound thoughts on music, literature and psychology, and contains an extended analysis of Berlioz's *Symphonie Fantastique* (1830), which Howard describes as 'the supreme achievement of the macabre in music'. The author revels in technical and *outré* words such as 'diathe-sis', 'retractation', 'intitulation', 'Bassaridic', 'infructuously', 'conation' and 'autopsychopathology'.

By his own admission Howard had always had a 'strong and deep-seated taste for the macabre'; he kept a human skull, which he named Hubert or 'the grinning Death', above the mantel in his study. The word 'macabre' comes from the Aramaic *maqqaba* meaning 'sledge-hammer' (Judas Maccabeus was famed for his prowess in war), and the connection with war and death has lingered. Berlioz himself wrote in his journal, 'My subject is, and always has been, war.' Howard Ogdon's battlefield experiences, no less than his father's illness and early death, attuned him to the macabre. Indeed, in his case, the intellect itself was fashioned into an implement of war, his tongue whetted in preparation for the cut and thrust of philosophical debate.

Howard's interest in psychology extended to autohypnosis, mesmerism and channelling. Far from being merely academic pursuits, they constituted some of his more exotic dancing-grounds. Communing with the dead was clearly an important element in the life of a man who had lost his father as a boy. There is no better description of a haunted house in literature than Henry James's *The Turn of the Screw*, if by 'haunted house' one means the deep psychological effects (amounting to demonic possession) of early loss on the psyche of a child. Like Howard Ogdon, James's father was an amateur scholar with a deep interest in and susceptibility to the metaphysical. He once saw the devil, or so he said, and for several years was pursued by a 'perfectly insane and abject terror' in the form of a damned figure that used to squat beside him. Henry's brother William suffered in much the same way as their father, and his sister Alice had suicidal tendencies. Henry James himself, who was one of John Ogdon's favourite authors, was acutely responsive to horror throughout his life. In both the James and Ogdon families the children were brought up in an atmosphere of supernatural speculation.

Not only tetchy and withdrawn, Howard was by all accounts a tyrannical father, who never processed his war experiences and found a release for his anxiety and aggression by persecuting his family. He bullied and browbeat his children to such an extent that all of them suffered from some form of neurosis. Paul became an invalid with many strange illnesses and bouts in hospital, suffering a heart attack in 1973 at the age of forty-eight. Karl developed a violent and debilitating stammer, almost as if he was choking, which was caused by a particu-larly severe thrashing he received at the hands of his father that at the time left him speechless. Howard, far from showing sympathy, taunted him about his speech impediment. Karl and his sister Philippa (who was described as a 'high neurotic' and speaks at quite a gallop) emigrated to Australia in their twenties, and Karl died out there at forty-one from a heart attack. Howard kept battery hens as a hobby and once forced John's sister Ruth to watch him strangling a chicken. In an interview with his psychiatrist at the Maudsley Hospital John confessed that all his father's children – excepting himself (!) – had been damaged by their father's cruelty.

Though all very bright, the children had disrupted educations. Philippa won a scholarship to Nottingham Girls' High School but gave it up – transferring instead to the local secondary school in Mansfield Woodhouse, which she left at sixteen. (Shortly after her father's breakdown she persuaded her mother to let her quit without her school certificate.) Ruth attended the same school, and was only fifteen when she left home to train as a nurse in a children's hospital. Both girls took piano lessons, while Paul learned the trumpet. Paul was a day scholar at the Queen Elizabeth Grammar School, where Howard taught. These were not happy years for him, as Howard's expectations of academic brilliance placed an onus on his eldest son that left him feeling depressed and unfulfilled. He was intelligent but could never be bright enough for Howard; nor did he share his father's literary interests. Paul was charming, very good-looking and well-liked by his classmates, one of whom remembers the general sympathy that his difficult relationship with Ogdon Senior aroused in them. At the time of Howard's breakdown, when he was thirteen, Paul missed four whole terms of school. He left in July 1942, shortly after his sev-enteenth birthday, and went to work for the D'Arcy Exploration Company in Eakring, which was developing England's first commer-cial oilfield. At eighteen he was called up and joined the Fleet Air Arm, seeing action off Scotland. After the war he studied to be an architect but gave it up. He then worked in a mental hospital, where he met his future wife – who was a nurse. Philippa and Ruth also became psychiatric nurses early in their working lives.

Karl, who was the closest in age to John and the nearest to a kindred spirit, was disruptive in school and frequently ran away from home. He ate horse manure to impress his friends at the Oxclose Lane School and thanks to his amateur cheese-making activities there was an appalling smell each time he lifted the lid of his desk. Neighbours recall him climbing trees in the old cemetery across from the house and scaring passers-by with his ghoulish wailing. He suffered from emotional problems and in 1944, aged fourteen, was sent to Red Hill, near Maidstone in Kent, a special school for 'difficult' children of high intelligence – in Karl's case exceptionally high intelligence. The school was run by Otto Shaw, who provided a sympathetic and humane environment for the fifty-five children under his care, even offering radical psycho-analysis to those who wanted it. The children were free to stay there during the holidays, so little was seen of Karl at home between the ages of fourteen and eighteen. The youngsters at Red Hill were allowed to smoke and, though classes were not compulsory, they were expected to involve themselves in the running of the school through the student court and committees. Many of the kids came from foster homes and were funded by their local authorities.

Howard projected his own dreams of literary glory onto Karl, and was irked that his son showed an obstinate propensity towards music. (Even as an adult Karl received letters from his father telling him to give up music, because John was the musician, and devote himself instead to literature.) Karl not only played the piano and the guitar but also composed, and it would seem found his own way in all three disciplines. The following passage from Otto Shaw's book *Maladjusted Boys* refers to Karl Ogdon:

We can only record one pupil who has seriously and insistently tried to compose his own music. His interest was undoubtedly connected with a very serious vocal impediment, and his studies were mainly in the form of highly involved compositions for piano. They took up a great deal of his spare time.

It was rare for parents to visit the school. The children were usually accompanied back and forth by an officer of the Child Guidance clinic

for the relevant county, which for Karl was Nottinghamshire. Nor did
Shaw encourage parental visits, especially where early trauma was so
clearly the cause of a child's delinquency. Karl was described by one of
his fellow pupils at Red Hill as 'a bit of a loner, totally immersed in
his music'. There was no formal music instruction at the school,
but one of the maths teachers, Paul Pollak, a Jewish refugee from
Czechoslovakia, played the piano and encouraged those with talent. In
addition to having musical prowess Karl was a formidable chess player
and a gifted painter. Some of his pictures were exhibited at the Cooling
Galleries in London in 1946 (*The Temple* and *The Butterfly*) and 1948
(*The Whirlpool*, *The Phantom Ship* and *The Dark Side and the Bright Side*).
Later in life John would refer to Karl's IQ in reverential terms. Like
Paul, Karl was dark and handsome and shared his brother's slim,
muscular frame. Like his father, he started smoking at fourteen and
continued to do so heavily for the remainder of his short life.

Howard's mother, Ethel, though she put on a good deal of weight and
became something of an invalid in her late middle-age, was a regular
visitor at Catherine Street. She died in 1935 at the age of sixty, and it
was shortly after this that the family of six moved to a more spacious
property at 5 Welbeck Road. Auckland House, as it was known, was
just down the street from St Edmund's Church and directly opposite
the cemetery with its leaning graves and ancient linden trees. It was a
detached three-storied Victorian house with two large attics and an
old coach house at the end of the driveway. It had a large garden with
a considerable apple and pear orchard, where Howard kept his inten-
sive poultry stock. Ruth was sent down most mornings to collect the
eggs and take her father his breakfast in bed (he insisted that his boiled
egg have a brown shell). The house had been built in 1865 by the
local doctor, and when the Ogdons bought it it was inhabited by the
vicar of St Edmund's, who was too old to climb up to the vicarage on
the hill opposite. The steep field down from the vicarage was – and
remains – common land and the Ogdon children used to sleigh down
it in winter. Auckland House was adjacent to the National School and
stretched most of the length of School Lane, the alley separating the
two properties.

The Ogdons kept themselves to themselves in Wooduz, where they were seen as outsiders; there were even rumours locally that they were Jews. It is unlikely that the local greeting of 'Ey'up m'duck!' was met with anything other than blank astonishment from Howard & co. The year of John's birth, 1937, brought with it premonitory tremors of the war that would tear apart the whole European continent. England herself was still in the throes of the abdication crisis, and an uncrowned king with a fearful stammer sat on the throne. To the horror of his friends and family – and the delight of his pupils – Howard Ogdon celebrated the new year by purchasing a trombone, which he played very loudly (and with questionable competence), possibly to drown out the mounting pulse of war, or maybe to sound a fanfare for the birth of his fifth and final child at Auckland House on 27 January.

At the time of his son's birth Howard was undergoing a series of depressions that he described as 'almost unbearably heavy'. Over the course of that year he gave up his 'studious habits' and shut his ears to the charms of music, which he claimed had always been the first of his interests. He also gave up his hen-breeding operation and sold his equipment. Instead, he acquired 'a powerful and very wasteful car', in which he drove around the country lanes in search of fresh distractions. He found it increasingly difficult to concentrate and a growing callousness of soul and nerves, not untypical of the schizophrenic, led to an inordinate capacity for alcohol. There were drunken binges when he would be out until 3 a.m., consuming enough beer and neat spirits to floor an elephant. These were followed by bouts of insomnia and dreams of war. The days were passed with chains of cigarettes and endless cups of tea.

It is not surprising that the approach of the Second World War should have triggered Howard Ogdon's psychosis, as the Great War had shaken him to the core. His hypersensitive antennae picked up the potential horrors of the new conflict long before it occurred. The old dread and uncertainty returned, and with them a hurried retreat from reality. He began to feel as if he were a shadow divorced from his true life; and in this shadow world, ruled by the pitiless Moon, an unhealthy proliferation of meaning engendered itself. The most commonplace action, such as putting one foot in front of the other, was dogged with significance, as if the fate of the seven stars depended upon it. The result was a total paralysis of the will. All distinction between literal and symbolic dissolved, and Howard found himself living in a metaphorical world that no one else inhabited. The reins of consciousness had been taken up by an alien, hallucinatory self.

It was through sound rather than sight that Howard Ogdon was chiefly haunted. How fitting then that in one of his dreams he should have swallowed Hermann von Helmholtz's mighty volume of 1863, *On the Sensations of Tone as a Physiological Basis for the Theory of Music!* Howard himself was a bell-ringer and shortly before his confinement began to feel persecuted by the bells of St Edmund's, reading fatal messages into their tolls. On one occasion they instructed him to go upstairs and throw himself out of the attic window. 'Go, go, go!' came roaring from their iron throats. It was a close-run thing, but in the end Howard managed to reach the refuge of his study and drown out the sound by yelling out the titles of the books on his shelves at the top of his voice, followed by the frenzied repetition of the words 'National Gramophonic Society!'

The summer of 1938 was particularly hot and oppressive, but it didn't stop Howard from lighting fires in the house and sealing all the windows. On Friday 22 July he was sitting at his desk, marking pencil in hand, staring blankly at a pile of examination papers when he suddenly experienced a profound and terrifying disengagement from his life. It was as if he had died, and yet was conscious that part of him was living on. He managed to pull himself back from 'some ineffable remoteness' and get to his GP, Dr Preston, who looked frightened at what he saw.

The next morning Howard was driven to the Nottingham suburb of Mapperley for an interview with David Hunter, Medical Superintendent of the Coppice Lunatic Hospital, who arranged for him to be admitted on the Monday as a voluntary patient at the cost of two guineas a week. Hunter was in no doubt that Howard was in a severe delusional state and required professional care. Though displaying a complete lack of will in the outer world, inwardly

Howard was in control of a vast empire whose smooth running required constant mental exertion. At the time of his first admission to the Coppice, as it was known, he had just recruited the Chinese Nationalist leader Chiang Kai-shek as one of his lieutenants. Other allies and aliases during his confinement included Peter Abelard, Albertus Magnus, Francis Bacon and Haile Selassie. On the afternoon of Monday 25 July a taxi arrived to take Howard the twenty miles to the asylum on Coppice Road – only this wasn't your average taxicab but a 'sumptuous funeral coach'. Cyril Welch, the local undertaker, ran a taxi service and on this occasion it seems the only vehicle available to him was a hearse – a macabre twist of fate that must have set the threadbare nerves of Howard Ogdon a-jangle. For many years afterwards the letters and numbers of the car's licence plate were for him synonymous with death.

The Coppice had opened in 1859 for patients of the upper and middle classes, and accommodated 100 patients in all, equally divided between the sexes. There were a number of rate-aided patients, of whom Howard was one. The great red-brick Victorian Gothic building stood on a bold projection and was surrounded by seventeen acres of grounds, including well-stocked orchards and gardens. It was lavishly furnished and had its own chapel. Patients were closely monitored by grey-suited attendants bearing sheaves of keys. The food was wholesome, with fruit and vegetables grown on the premises, and sports such as cricket, tennis and cycle polo were played in the grounds, often to comic effect. Howard signed his own admission form that Monday afternoon. His religious persuasion was given as 'nonconformist', and the principal cause of his breakdown as 'prolonged mental stress'.

Howard's megalomania proceeded apace. Everything around him was drafted into the World State he was building, whether it was the fork slipped into his pocket at lunchtime (a stalwart ally he!) or a neighbour at table whom he took for the rich Chinese merchant Chu Chin Chow. Others, because they rubbed him up the wrong way, had to make do with scavenging posts on the outskirts of the Empire. Then there were the ever-proliferating mental inhibitions. Infected letters and numbers made reading books or newspapers a

hazardous undertaking, with words readily split into syllables and rein-
terpreted. To illustrate the 'tyranny of fatal letters', Howard in his
book gives the example of the letter C. If C is ill-omened, then S,
which can sound identical, becomes contaminated, as do all words in
which either of these two letters occur. Thus Monday and Friday
become the only safe days for action. As C is the third letter of the
alphabet, the number 3 is infected, as are its neighbours 2 and 4, not
to mention B and D – and so the complex quickly reaches its tentacles
into all corners of life, eliminating the remaining days of the week and
disabling the will. Or rather the will becomes the servant of the complex, devoting all its energy to feeding the subject's displaced sense of
reality. It is not just letters and numbers that become infected but
people, too, by a process of morbid suggestion. Hence the dangers to
Howard's wife and children were he to return home.

Howard's initial stay at the Coppice lasted a matter of days. He was
unhappy and depressed, and spent much of his time prowling the
grass verge nearest the road. He was sent home for the August Bank
Holiday but his brief sojourn at Auckland House was a nightmare for
everyone. He locked himself in his study, grabbed hold of some of
his choicest books and turned on them 'in an access of pyrolatrial
fury'. Having ripped them up and tossed them into the grate, he uri-
nated on them then set them ablaze. A number of his own
manuscripts augmented the pyre. Writing a decade later, he observed
that he had unwittingly enacted a ritual quickening of the Kundalini
Shakti.

The book-burning, suggesting as it does an unconscious rebellion
against the dominion of the intellect, goes to the heart of Howard
Ogdon's psychosis, for here was a man who from boyhood had used
his mind and scholarship as a bulwark against the pain of lost intimacy
and the dread of war, and now as a weapon against his own vulnerability and the high spirits of his children. As a result, he had come
to identify consciousness with reason alone and so fortified himself
against the power and intelligence of the unconscious by arming
the mind. His teacher's gown and the asylum of his study, with
the great intellects that lined its walls, kept his fiction of mental
supremacy alive for decades, but eventually the dam burst and the

waters of the unconscious overwhelmed the outposts of his embattled ego.

Howard returned to the Coppice but on Christmas Eve 1938 was allowed home for the weekend accompanied by a burly male nurse, 'a massive elderly man with a grievance'. It was a gloomy few days, with Howard himself as melancholy as a gib cat. He went back to the Coppice on 27 December, this time staying only four days before signing himself out and going home on New Year's Eve. The reason for this departure is not known: his admission and discharge records have been ripped out of the Hospital Register. It could be that it was too expensive, even with aid from the local authority. His week at home was punctuated by visits from doctors and medical officials, as well as a carload of tearful relatives. By the end of it he had signed himself in to the Nottinghamshire County Asylum, a public institution about eight miles east of Nottingham, between Radcliffe-on-Trent and Saxondale.

The Saxondale Hospital, as it was known, was a far cry from the gentlemanly refuge of the Coppice. Here there were some 700 inmates – 350 each of men and women – all of whom were strictly regimented ('herded like swine') and made to wear the same uniform ('I cannot adequately describe these sartorial horrors' writes Ogdon). At night they were put in identical long twill nightdresses and looked for all the world like 'a parcel of Julius Caesars'. One lavatory served for the forty men on Howard's ward. Though the place was attractively situated on a hill and surrounded by 130 acres, including a 100-acre farm where they kept livestock, Howard described it as bleak and barrack-like, sparsely furnished and badly lit, more like a prison than a hospital. It had been used during the Great War to care for shell-shocked soldiers; now it housed lunatics, neurotics, epileptics and low-grade defectives as well as being 'a refuse dump for the unwanted and the aged'.

When, after a fortnight, he signalled his intention to leave, Howard was threatened with certification. He held his ground, and signed himself out on 21 January. This time he kept his freedom for four months – though he was firmly convinced that being at home hindered his recovery, and that if only he could keep moving from place to place his various complexes could be dislodged. Family life was stressful to him and he freely confessed to being 'allergic' to certain close relations. Consequently he made frequent trips to stay with relatives further afield, many of whom were lulled by his bland exterior into believing him cured.

Behind Howard's inscrutable mask, however, the old turmoil was unabated. He could not pick up a paper without reading himself into the headlines. He was seized by a mania for cycling; the faster he cycled the more lethal his thoughts became. He could not cut the grass without feeling he was committing genocide, nor feel secure without touching a certain rock in the garden. To add to his misery he developed a fixation about crosses. Like the jaunty badges pinned to a tramp's hat, the fetishes stuck to his restless brain.

More dangerously, Howard took it into his head to murder his wife with an axe – but was cheated of this consummation by his eldest son, Paul, who blocked him on the stairs. It was shortly after this episode, on 24 May 1939, that one of the local GPs, who was a magistrate, turned up unannounced and issued a certificate of insanity; his partner arrived within the hour, examined him and asked some strange questions, such as 'Do you prefer poultry or drugs?' Later six hulking men arrived at the house – three entering by the back door, three at the front. Howard recognized one of them as a local policeman. He was kept talking while one of them went to fetch the reception papers for his readmission to Saxondale under certification. On the forms it stated that he was 'potentially dangerous'. He was driven the twenty-two miles to the asylum in a Black Maria at breakneck speed, the officers keeping their hands firmly on the door handles and window levers.

Both the routine and complete lack of sentiment at Saxondale reminded Howard of the army, which suited his stoical outlook. He was a tough man, without a shred of self-pity, who never expressed regret at being away from his family or friends. Furthermore, he appears always to have been conscious of his predicament, even at the height of his lunacy. Instead of therapy the nurses relied on drugging and most inmates were reduced to what Howard called 'compulsory stagnation', which consisted of 'aimless wandering, aimless standing, aimless sitting'. There was a weekly dance, a weekly cinema of silent movies (popular with the low-grade defectives) and an annual sports day at which the lunatics were given a bag of sweets, a stick of chocolate and an orange. 'Our appreciation of time,' writes Ogdon, 'was oriental in its spacious negligence.'

Howard worked in the storeroom for two years and was granted a raft of privileges – including his own room in the Villa Ward, where he kept his illegal typewriter and portable gramophone. He managed to write two short stories as well as a letter to the MP Sir Ernest Graham-Little, who asked a question in Parliament on his behalf. He was given a later bedtime, excused from court rambling ('mooching and marching', as he called it) and granted estate parole, which meant he was at liberty to wander the institution and its grounds. As the idea of escape took shape in his mind, he walked between six and ten miles every night. Although he felt the regressive pull of the complex – his dining companions included Delius, Galsworthy, Montgomery and Rommel – Howard took up his studies once more, following the steep path of Gautama, Schopenhauer and Nietzsche.

Most vitally, he resolved to master the practice of Hatha yoga with a view to curing himself of his disease and leaving the asylum. To this end he concentrated on the four essentials of diet, posture, breath and mantra. With his self-trumpeted iron resolution Howard achieved 'the perfect seat', known as Siddhasana. He also delved deeply into the mysteries of Pranayama and while his fellow inmates slept spent many night hours learning to control his pulse, heart rate and breathing. He was woken twice in one week by a concerned night nurse because he didn't appear to be breathing. Eventually he was able to achieve an auto-hypnotic state.

Howard's yoga seems to have breathed life into his feeling nature, as one poignant episode reveals. In his brief book *Darkness Visible* the novelist William Styron recalls how hearing a sudden, soaring passage from Brahms's *Alto Rhapsody* one night cut through the crippling depression of years and woke up his dormant heart. Similarly, on the afternoon of Good Friday 1941, Howard Ogdon was sitting in the dayroom of the Villa Ward when someone switched on the wireless and he heard Alexander Gretchaninov's *Liturgia Domestica*.

I found my eyes strangely flushed with tears [...] Not while my mind was going piecemeal, and I stood watching it; nor when I was in the pit of despair, nor while I was in death's own toils; not even when I was dragged from my own hearth could I find a murmur of reproach or wring a tear of regret. And now the music of a strange litany filled me with tears and yearning.

And disgust. The reaction was immediate. I realized clearly what we were – forgotten waifs in the Kingdom of the Lost. My full resolution was instantly reinforced for quicker, more determined action. This music, that entered the threshold as a sob, became an instant spur.

Howard left the dayroom and made straight for the engine-yard, where he fashioned an old nail-file into a screwdriver. As with the yoga, everything was directed towards a single idea: escape. As he made preparations for the big day he went more frequently into the one-pointed meditative state in which the ego merges itself in the circumfluent Self and found as a result that for long periods he was invisible to other people in the asylum, even when walking about in 'clanking' shoes. Either he was vibrating at a frequency imperceptible to his fellows, or some form of mass hypnosis was taking place. *Or* Howard Ogdon was in some way deluding himself.

According to Howard he made his escape openly, in broad daylight, without attempting to screen his movements:

I sauntered slowly through the main hall of the Male Villa. I was dressed for escape, with bulging pockets, and carrying a leather shopping bag stuffed full. I wore no hat. I stood for a minute at each window nearest the fireplace. There were up to forty patients in and around the hall. They gazed blankly through me.

On the way out I looked at the clinic. One attendant was in, one was just outside the door. They both looked through me vacantly. I stood for a moment in the doorway. A group of men went by to the staff cricket match. I knew most of them. None of them saw me. On my way out of the town I met a number of people who knew me well. I was not observed. Only one, a woman, spoke – or rather replied. And she also admitted, many months later, that she couldn't remember having seen me.

This was on 2 August 1941. Howard managed to hitchhike his way south to Hampshire, where he was hidden out by his friends George and Ethel – first in their garage and then in the house. It was wartime, with increased security and identity checks, so there were many close calls with the law as he ventured out onto the streets, usually at night. Finally the statutory fortnight passed, and he was automatically decertified. Now he could move about as he wished, without fear of arrest. He stayed in his friends' 'busy little town' for more than a year, until the autumn of 1942, making no effort to return home to his wife and children in Nottinghamshire. He approached the Labour Exchange for some light work in the national interest, and was given the job of inspector in a munitions factory. On 23 April 1942 he was declared civilly competent and his civil rights fully restored. At the beginning of the following year he resumed teaching in a grammar school near Portsmouth and took lodgings at a nearby boarding house.

Howard admits that his schizophrenia was at its peak at the time of his escape, and for two years afterwards he remained in the grip of the 'heroic phase' that saw him controlling world affairs through the supervision of his empire. He continued to practise Hatha yoga, but now that he had achieved his goal of escape his self-discipline slackened. For all his fresh interests and activities, the old illness was still toiling away in the background. Rooting out the sort of deep-seated mental disease that afflicted him could probably have been achieved only had Howard persisted with his yoga. Instead he used the mind to fight the mind, which is little more than shadow boxing. He declared war on the unconscious, equating it with darkness, chaos and the forces of regression, hence his persistent references to it as 'the wily unconscious', which it was his duty to fight.

One cannot discount the possibility that Howard's grandiose mind embellished and distorted the true narrative of his escape. We have only his word for the miraculous nature of his getaway, and the strain of self-justification and *braggadocio* that runs through *Kingdom* should at

least put us on our guard. Towards the end of his book he makes the
following startling assertion:

> I think I can claim to be the only person who has, consciously, on
> planned methods, tackled this disease from the inside, groped
> within its depths, arrested its progress, and driven it back from its
> encroachments into that nuclear position it may occupy in any
> 'normal' mind.

Howard did not return home to Mansfield Woodhouse until the
beginning of 1944, two and a half years after his escape. His absence
had haunted the house as fully as his presence, and in no mind had he
loomed larger than in that of his youngest son. The very walls were
infused with the memory of Howard's schizophrenic fantasies and
inhibitions, his self-crucifying thoughts, not to mention the morbid
grandiloquence of the music that passed under his study door. After
his escape, his family would not have known from one day to the next
when he might turn up – nor in what state of mind they might find
him.

2

JOHN RACHMANINOFF OGDON

You see, for me my piano is what his frigate is to a sailor or his horse to an Arab – more indeed: it is my very self, my mother tongue, my life.

Franz Liszt

John Ogdon was born at home at Auckland House on 27 January 1937, sharing his birthday (albeit 181 years later) with Mozart. Photographs of John aged two show him to have been a chubby child with tight blond curls (soon to turn dark) and a serious, inquisitive face with a look of faraway concentration about it. He was the youngest of his siblings by almost seven years. Curiously, he was given the exact same names as his father – John Andrew Howard Ogdon. Although he was never baptized, one is left with the uncomfortable feeling that Howard was displacing more than just a name onto his youngest born.

With war following on the heels of Howard's madness, a considerable burden was placed on John's mother, Dorothy, who periodically sent his brothers and sisters to stay with relatives. She took in lodgers, four in all, and moved the children to the two big attics at the top of the house. Her housemaid, Margaret Fletcher, also lived in for a while, making it a busy household. Dorothy supplemented her income from the boarders by working as a part-time secretary at Sherwood Colliery.

The family had a Weber Duo-Art pianola in the front room, which could be used as a standard upright or to play piano rolls. The rolls were played either by pedalling or electrically (like an organ). Dorothy used to place John in a highchair in front of the keyboard while she worked about the house. As he listened to the music he watched the rolls rotating and the keys moving. She did this as soon as he was able to sit up, so probably from the age of six months. Before long he was focusing on the perforations in the piano rolls and making an intuitive connection between their length, position and frequency and the notes being depressed on the keyboard. This could well have been the origin of John's extraordinary sight-reading gift, which never ceased to astonish even his most talented colleagues. The pianola was not only his nanny but also his first music teacher – it is extremely rarely that a prodigious musical talent such as John grows up without a parent who also plays proficiently. (Howard's dyspeptic blasts on the trombone would, if anything, be a disincentive to pursue music.) Another thing the pianola bequeathed him was a beautiful, velvety tone.

On *The South Bank Show*, aired in March 1989, just four months before he died, John Ogdon recalled that his parents had owned a piano roll of Percy Grainger playing 'Shepherd's Hey'. He remarked on the strong impression that the pictures at the side of the roll made on him and 'how fresh and fine' they looked. 'I got fascinated with the way the pianola made notes depress,' he went on. 'I think that started me off exploring the piano a bit, and I started notating music in a pianola notation under the impression that that *was* musical notation!' Indeed, while John was a student at the Royal Manchester College of Music (RMCM), Dorothy told Harrison Birtwistle that she found him one day as a child of three or four sitting on the floor with a large piece of brown paper, utterly absorbed in the task of cutting little holes in it. When she asked him what he was doing he replied without hesitation: 'Composing.' Howard, too, in a June 1953 letter to Sir Frederic Cox, then principal of the RMCM, refers to John composing in this 'quaint perforation-style', and mentions that the boy pedalled the instrument with one foot as soon as he was tall enough. This is confirmed by John's eldest sister, Philippa, who recalls him aged two holding onto the flap where the control levers were and pedalling with one foot while she put the rolls in for him.

Perhaps John's reverence for texts took root at this precocious age. He certainly focused on the piano rolls as devotedly as a Tibetan Lama gazes on his prayer wheel or a Rabbi scrutinizes the sacred scrolls of the law. And it was via the piano rolls that he got used to vertical reading, which made it second nature for him to take in a whole page of music at a glance. This is because when you follow a piano roll you don't so much read from left to right as you do from north to south. This verticality weaves itself into the concept of harmony, as opposed to the more horizontal movement of melody, and goes some way to explaining John Ogdon's instinctive grasp of musical structure. He naturally viewed scores as if they were piano rolls. That's one of the reasons he could sight-read orchestral scores, all the way from the flutes to the double basses, reducing them instantaneously for the keyboard. It is also why Sorabji's highly involved passages (with the music on five staves instead of two) presented no problems for him. He was a vertical structuralist who looked first and foremost to the architecture of the music.

Dorothy Ogdon soon became aware of another facet of John's musical talent: his extraordinary memory. Over time, as she listened to her three-year-old son experimenting with the keys of the pianola, she began to recognize some of the piano-roll tunes that she had played for him when using the instrument as a babysitter. He was also picking out refrains from the Wagner operas he'd heard coming from his father's study.

In recorded interviews the pianola is the only thing to feature in John's recollected memories before the age of eight. He seems to have shut out everything else. In a sense it became a symbol or talisman of the happy family life he never had. 'My sisters and brothers and myself used to spend many happy hours round the pianola,' he says with bowed head in his *South Bank Show* interview. 'Home was a very happy place with the pianola,' he adds. He speaks with some fervour, but when he looks up at the end of the sentence there is a haunted look in his eyes. His idyllic recollection is not shared by his sisters. It was John alone who seized on the pianola from an early age, single-mindedly playing all the music he could lay his hands on, and his parents approved his zeal. He was the pianist in the family, and playing the piano was what he was meant to be doing. Yet it was obvious to his sisters that John was a lonely, vulnerable boy who didn't have any real friends.

When he wasn't at the keyboard John was wandering around the garden looking for insects – a pursuit that held a peculiar fascination for him, just as it had done for the young Béla Bartók. To a solitary, overweight boy with an awkward gait, his run never much more than an accelerated shuffle, insects offered the promise of metamorphosis. Spiders were no less of an enthusiasm; and not just the British varieties but tropical spiders, too, which he studied in books and whose Latin names he mastered. He was also an avid reader who devoured anything that came his way, including children's encyclopaedias.

Naturally for one so precocious, John spent most of his childhood in the company of adults. One particularly fateful meeting took place at his aunts' house in Mansfield in the summer of 1940. Dorothy, as was her wont, had dropped John off at Layton Avenue to spend the day with her widowed sisters, Auntie Nance and Auntie Bessie. Their neighbours on this rather august avenue of Victorian villas were Mr and Mrs James Wood, a retired couple whose daughter, Marjory, a vivacious girl of twenty-five, was an art teacher at Teversal Primary School, near Sutton-in-Ashfield, where she also played the piano for Miss Tucker's Choir. On this particular afternoon Marjory could hear the old, out-of-tune piano next door being played for hours on end. This made her curious: she had never before heard the sound of music from her neighbours' house. Peeping through the bay window at the front of the house she was astonished to see a plump, curly-headed little boy playing from some tattered old sheets of music. As she relates it in her book, *The Young John Ogdon*:

He was reaching up to the keyboard, walking back and forth to play the treble keys or the bass, while trying to use the pedals without losing his balance, quite an accomplishment for a three-and-a-half-year-old. I hurried round to the back door to ask his aunts who he was, and they told me he was their sister Dorothy's little boy from Mansfield Woodhouse. Mrs Fox added, 'He's just amusing himself on our old piano – he loves to play.'

Marjory realized immediately that she was witnessing something extraordinary, for the boy was sight-reading pieces by Chopin. Not only was he straining to make his small hands stretch to encompass the big chords; he was also paying attention to the expressive markings, including tempo and dynamics. At the end of the piece John turned to his audience of three and said in his grave lisping voice, 'Those pieces were from Chopin Opuses.' For the benefit of their visitor he added, 'I could play when I was two, but not when I was one.' At the end of the afternoon John's eleven-year-old sister Ruth arrived to take him home. Like a little mother hen, she made sure that his coat was properly buttoned before leading him off by the hand. She told Marjory that their elder sister, Pippa, had taught John the notes and that he read music before he could read words, and played the piano before he could speak.

Marjory Wood fell in love with the little genius and arranged for him to come next door to her house to play on her newer, well-tuned instrument, and so began a very special relationship that lasted from 1940 to 1945. She was John's friend and benefactress, his childhood muse even, but not his teacher – for when it came to the piano John was in a different league. Marjory knew that the Ogdon family was under strain, and that she was doing Dorothy and her sisters a favour by taking John under her wing, but that's not why she did it. She was fascinated by the boy himself. John would spend hours playing her piano and exploring the many volumes of music in her house. When he was still very small he sat on her knee to play while she pedalled and turned the pages for him. His stamina and concentration at the keyboard were unflagging, even at such a young age; the piano focused his attention completely. The one thing that frustrated him was the size of his hands. His fingers were strong and double-jointed but could stretch only a sixth; he desperately wanted to span an octave. He would stop playing, look at his hands and ask Marjory if she could stretch them for him.

John was a frequent visitor at the Wood home, his arrival signalled by the rattling of the letterbox as he was too short to reach the bell. He was often accompanied by a stray black-and-white cat, which hid in the laurel bushes by the front door ready to dash in after him. John christened it Rondo and it became known as his cat. If music was John's first love, food came a close second and often on his arrival he would make a beeline for the pantry. Although it was wartime, with a grey compound known as 'axle grease' replacing butter, there was usually some decent fodder to be found – and John didn't much mind what it was so long as he could eat it. Despite the rationing, Mrs Wood managed to conjure up a range of treats. Raspberry-jam tarts, made with fresh fruit from Mr Wood's allotment garden, were John's favourite: a plateful could disappear before his fellow trenchermen had time to reach for one. Through the long, lean years of rationing John never looked anything other than thoroughly nourished! As for the sirens and blackouts, he played through all the interruptions of war with zealous abandon. Nothing could keep him from the piano: even in the cold of winter he would play with a hot-water bottle on his lap.

Marjory Wood, or 'Mith Wood' as John lisped her name, was taking piano lessons from Nellie Houseley – the eldest of a quartet of spinster sisters (the others being Ethel, Mabel and Gladys), all of whom were pillars of the artistic and educational life of Mansfield. Ethel ran the local choir in Mansfield and gave singing lessons from home; Gladys and Mabel were both schoolteachers; Nellie's domain was the piano. The sisters lived together with their father at 1 Layton Avenue, just down the road from Marjory Wood and the Ogdon aunts. Nellie was in her early fifties, a diminutive black-haired lady of the old school who could terrorize her pupils into playing quite well. She was an accomplished musician and a true martinet. You did as she said, or you'd be sure to feel the sharp edge of her tongue – and woe betide any pupil who came to the lesson unprepared or badly turned out! Girls were not allowed to wear nail varnish and boys were expected to have clean hands.

When Marjory told Nellie Houseley about John's remarkable gifts the older woman readily agreed to hear him. An audition was arranged at her home in late 1940, while John was still three. John's mother was delighted at the prospect and, having arrayed him in his best outfit and flattened and parted his unruly curls, delivered him to the waiting Miss Wood, who walked him down to Houseley's House of Music. The door had no sooner opened than John looked up into the startled, bespectacled face of his future teacher and announced himself: 'I'm John Rachmaninoff Ogdon!' There were gasps and chuckles from the two women. Once inside, John inspected the piano by walking cautiously around it; he had never seen a boudoir-grand before. On it was a piece by Scarlatti, which he opened and began to play while still standing. Miss Nellie, as she was known to her pupils, stopped him and placed some cushions on the piano stool so that he could sit down. As John rattled his way through every piece from Scarlatti to Liszt, using his own homespun technique and fingering, amazement flamed upon the normally implacable brow of Nellie Houseley. From time to time she would offer a little instruction but John was too engrossed in the music to pay heed. Even at three his typical posture at the piano was to be hunched bearlike over the keys, as if to cow the notes into submission. 'He wanted to exhaust himself (if that were possible),' wrote Marjory Wood. What had begun as an audition became a full-length recital, without intermission! In the end, his fingers had to be prised from the keys.

Astonished though she was by the boy's talent, Nellie Houseley advised waiting until John's hands were slightly bigger before starting formal lessons. These began when he was four and a half, in the autumn of 1941, and took place at her studio above Kent & Cooper's music shop in Mansfield. Writing to a friend in 1970, Miss Nellie recalled that 'the first piece [John] brought to me was the *Warsaw* Concerto. He could play the notes but of course without any idea of correct technique. He had a remarkable ear and could read a piece of difficult music (not playing it) and know how it would sound.' The *Warsaw* Concerto is a single-movement work written by Richard

Addinsell for the 1941 movie *Dangerous Moonlight* (also known as *Suicide Squadron*). Despite its weak narrative and mawkish excesses, the film met with considerable success on account of Addinsell's music. John might well have seen the film; that being the case it may have inspired his lifelong passion for the cinema and film music.

Millicent Roberts, who was a teenager at the time, well remembers John's first appearance at Nellie Houseley's studio – because it happened to be *her* lesson that day that was interrupted. As she describes it, a young girl (Ruth Ogdon?) 'literally burst into the room. She had a small curly-haired boy with her, with the *Warsaw* Concerto under his arm. Miss Nellie protested, but I was pushed out of the way and the child sat down and began to play.' Once she heard John, Millicent vowed that she would never play again. But she did, and John shared her lessons for the next month before being given his own slot on Saturday mornings. Despite their prolonged contact, she never once heard him speak.

Nellie Houseley taught her best students from home on her mellow-toned Broadwood boudoir-grand. One such student, Mike Hays, remembers John arriving for lessons with a matchbox containing some form of insect life to be presented to Miss Nellie's father, George Houseley. Often a string of girls would be waiting for their lessons. If the phone rang Miss Nellie would go to the hall to answer it, and the girls would dive into the music cabinet, grab the blackest piece they could find and put it up on the piano for John to play – which of course he did without the least hesitation. Another Houseley pupil, David Chamberlain, who became musical director of the Mansfield Choral Society, remembers staying behind after his lessons so that he could listen to John play. David was seventeen to John's eight, yet John could play all David's pieces perfectly at sight.

Technique was everything to Nellie Houseley. Her emphasis on rotation and 'sinking' into the notes to produce what she called 'a musical tone' was a hallmark of her instruction. 'Dip and roll, dip and roll,' she would chant, even to her youngest pupils – and dip and roll they did. To play a piece without 'sinks', however correct the notes, was in her eyes to play mechanically. For arm-weight practice she recommended raising the arm well up, nail joints firm and knuckles hard, as if clasping a fat ball, and then dropping onto notes up and down the keyboard with the middle fingers. John Ogdon's dipping and rolling hand became a distinctive feature of his playing, as did his beautiful tone, and his use of body weight to influence the sound he made was apparent in the way he would arch over the keyboard.

In addition to his uncanny sight-reading ability John was blessed with perfect pitch. You could sit on the keyboard and he'd tell you every single note in the chord. He had a blind man's keen discrimination of tone, as if the keys under his hands were Braille. Often it was his fingers that would remember a piece for him (through touch memory) rather than his eyes or ears. In this regard he was as natural and instinctive a musician as there has ever been, the Art Tatum of the classical world. The piano was for him a kind of sixth sense. Little wonder, then, that he would feel withdrawal symptoms if he spent a day away from the keys. Even as a small child the dramatic contrast between John at the piano and John away from it was noted. At the keyboard he was fluent, expressive and confident; away from it he was diffident and frequently withdrawn. The disparity widened as he grew older, though there were periods, especially at college, when he was more generally high-spirited.

It is striking that 'baby Johnty', as his siblings called him, should have identified with Rachmaninoff. The Russian composer was famed for his melancholy, a condition that had its roots in a serious childhood illness that claimed the life of his sister Sophia. Rachmaninoff's preoccupation with death and the macabre grew out of this experience and was deepened by his exile from his native land. As Robert Rimm writes: '[...] in spite of his great success all over the world and the devotion of his audiences, Rachmaninoff lived shut up within himself, alone in spirit and everlastingly homesick for his Russia.' The theme of the *Dies Irae* (or *Day of Wrath*) from the Catholic Requiem Mass became something of a musical signature for the Russian. His symphonic poem *The Isle of the Dead* is a particularly evocative example of his uncanny sensitivity to the inward-circling rhythms of death.

John would wander about the house and garden in Mansfield Woodhouse, lost in thought, and at such times a sombre mood seemed to descend upon him, as if he was communing with the sorrows of the world. His melancholy disposition is well illustrated by an anecdote his mother told Marjory Wood. One day, unable to find John anywhere in the house or garden, she ran out into the street to see a funeral cortège passing, with black horses pulling the hearse, and behind the hearse the grieving family and friends. Bringing up the rear was her own six-year-old son, his head bowed in solemn condolence. One of the earliest pieces he composed, written aged seven, was a funeral march for an American soldier called Manny who used to bring candy and chocolate for him. John had got it into his head that Manny and Marjory Wood were going to marry, and when the wished-for union didn't happen he wrote a funeral march. Shortly afterwards Manny left for D-Day.

Even as a small boy John's attitude to music was one of high seriousness, and his usual sweet temper could be riled if it was not accorded due respect or if he considered it frivolous. Marjory Wood recalls him arriving at her house, dashing to the piano, picking up the first piece of music he could find (it happened to be highlights from *Snow White and the Seven Dwarfs*) and launching into it. He played the introduction without blinking, but when he came to the first song, 'Someday My Prince Will Come', he stopped playing, clapped the music shut and flung it across the room. To soothe his outrage Marjory gave him a book of Chopin pieces (mazurkas, preludes, nocturnes and waltzes) and equanimity was restored as he began to play through them. But when he came to the Waltz in A flat his agitation returned and quickly grew to anger. Marjory had crossed out a number of the repeat bars, and in John's eyes this was tantamount to sacrilege. The texts of the masters were sacred and not to be tampered with. 'You never, never, never do this!' he kept repeating in his disbelief – and this was a seven-year-old boy talking to a twenty-nine-year-old woman! In general, John's saturnine temperament was a foil to the incorrigibly sunny outlook of Marjory Wood, who rarely allowed a cloud to cross her horizon. On another occasion they went to the Empire in Mansfield to see the movie *Meet Me in St. Louis*, a romantic comedy starring Judy Garland. John began grumbling about the music and when Garland launched into the infamous 'Trolley Song', with 'Clang, clang, clang went the trolley . . .' he leaped up from his seat and shouted angrily, 'Why do grown-up people thing thuch thilly thongs?' his lisp becoming more pronounced in his exasperation.

With his siblings largely absent – effectively leaving him to grow up as an only child – and being isolated from his peers by his outsized talent, John found himself largely in the company of his seniors. Marjory Wood once walked in on an eccentric tea party in the piano room of their Mansfield home. At a beautifully decorated table, with embroidered tablecloth and dainty chinaware, groaning with cucumber sandwiches and raspberry jam tarts, sat a delightfully offbeat trio: Marjory's mother, Mrs Wood (dressed as Mrs Methuselah), Miss Emily Lewis, the elderly children's poet, and Master John Ogdon – alias John Rachmaninoff Ogdon or, for his messiness, John Pell-Mell Ogdon – the curly-headed piano prodigy. Before they sat down Mrs Wood had performed her monologue, Miss Lewis had recited several of her poems, including 'The Little Millionaire', and John had given a stirring recital – to which sheets of music scattered over the floor bore lively witness.

John would spend hour upon hour playing through whole volumes of the classics (from Mozart to Rachmaninoff), building up his phenomenal repertoire from a very early age. Once he had played a piece it seemed to become locked into his memory. This habit of playing through pieces one after the other at speed, as if he wanted to get through as much music as possible, stayed with him as an adult; baffled critics would sometimes note a reckless haste on the concert platform as John zoomed through Chopin's Op. 25 études without so much as a pause between the pieces.

Marjory Wood wasn't content simply to provide John with a peaceful place to practise: a talent of such exceptional brilliance required more active nurturing. Certain things they could do for virtually nothing, such as listening to BBC Symphony Orchestra concerts on the wireless; other things, such as buying sheet music, could be managed within the limits of Marjory's income (John would sometimes have a sixpence to contribute). In order to attend first-class classical concerts at the Albert Hall in Nottingham, however, something more was required. She decided to set up a 'John Fund'. To this end she sold some of her own paintings and took to making gloves, handbags and stuffed toys to sell to local stores. Each concert outing to Nottingham with John would cost at least twenty-five shillings, so she had her work cut out. But the thought of John's future greatness spurred her on, as these extraordinary words from her book attest:

> As I spent hours and hours 'thonging' away in my attic workshop, I would picture John and me sitting hand in hand at the Albert Hall in Nottingham, listening to and applauding wonderful pianists, dreaming that one day my loving little sweetheart, John Ogdon, who I knew would be a great pianist, would outshine and surpass them all.

In 1943, when John was six, Marjory took him to his very first concert: a piano recital by Louis Kentner. Although she cannot recall the repertoire, she well remembers John's rapt attention throughout (he was 'in visible ecstasy') and his delighted applause after each piece. On their way out of the hall John turned to Marjory and said, 'When I get home, I'm going to practise and practise – how to bow like Louis Kentner.' Back home, after playing several pieces to Marjory and her two sisters, John got them to stand in three stations to mark the different parts of the hall – the central banks of seats and the two wings – then, with their applause still ringing in his ears, he bowed to each in turn, holding his stomach with his left hand (which Kentner did not do!) and making a flourish with his right, doing his best not to topple over as he bent forward. From this moment forth John had no doubt that he would be a concert pianist; the recital had inspired a vision of himself to which he held fast throughout his school years. Little did John know then that one day he would study with Louis Kentner's first wife, Ilona Kabos, before the Tchaikovsky Competition in 1962 and eight years later would join Kentner in writing the section on Liszt's music for solo piano in the book *Franz Liszt: The Man & His Music*.

John and Marjory attended many other concerts together, including the following year a performance of Beethoven's *Emperor* Concerto, conducted by Sir Adrian Boult, with whom John himself would perform. The soloist was John's future friend and teacher Denis Matthews. The concert ended with a performance of the Symphony No. 7 in C major by Sibelius, whose 'wondrous' music remained a lifelong favourite of John's. They also heard the Hallé Orchestra under John Barbirolli give a memorable performance of Beethoven's Fifth Symphony, which John already knew from a piano arrangement. He was excited to see all the instruments of the orchestra ranged together – in particular the brass section, as his father's instrument was the trombone. In the summer of 1944 he and Marjory went to two performances of the International Ballet, at which they saw *Coppélia* with music by Léo Delibes, *Les Sylphides* (Chopin) and *Twelfth Night* (Grieg). Again, John was familiar with the music and had played sections of the Delibes and Chopin, as well as passages from Tchaikovsky's *Nutcracker* Suite and *Swan Lake*. Among the other British pianists they heard were Cyril Smith and Solomon.

The John Fund was also used to purchase sheet music. John and Marjory would stop off at Wilson Peck's music store and showroom on the way back from the Albert Hall to the bus terminal. With his sixpence in his pocket, John would make for the most expensive volumes – complete works or sequences of works, rather than single pieces – and Marjory would indulge him by paying the difference, however substantial. On one occasion he found an album of Liszt's works for seven and sixpence and with Marjory's blessing rushed over to the nearest piano to try out the pieces, but one of the salesmen, who had been eyeing the scene, got there first and closed the lid before John could place his fingers on the keys. 'Madam,' he said to Marjory, 'we do not allow children on our pianos. Please keep your child away from them.' John was mortified by this rebuff; Marjory never once saw him cry in the five years she spent with him but she saw him come very close now. Amends were made on a future occasion, however, when the salesman's back was turned and Marjory quickly ushered John to a waiting piano. He had chosen a large album of Beethoven sonatas and no sooner had he begun to play than a crowd (including the officious salesman) gathered round to listen. Each time John paused between pieces there came a burst of applause, but he seemed oblivious of the stir he was creating. Once when he stopped he seemed confused and anxious to see all the faces around him and called out, 'Mith Wood?'

John often used his sixpence at Wilson Peck's to buy manuscript paper: he was already an enthusiastic composer and had compiled a youthful set of pieces entitled *Gems of Ogdon*. On their way back to Mansfield one day, a ferocious storm blew up that forced the bus driver to pull over to the side of the road. As the wind and rain pounded against the windows Marjory began to hum Chopin's *Raindrop* Prelude while John tapped out the beat of the downpour against the streaming panes. 'I'm going to write a thunderstorm prelude,' he suddenly exclaimed, 'and I'm going to do it now.' He had manuscript paper to hand but nothing to write with so Marjory dove into her handbag and found an eyeliner pencil. Soon John was busy notating. The music tumbled out of him, as Marjory observed:

> The speed with which he worked and his intense concentration were unbelievable. He did not hesitate, ponder, look around or chew the end of his pencil, but wrote with the most assured confidence and deliberation [. . .] Some notes were on high ledger lines, some on low, and others on extended staff lines, which he roughly sketched in to the edge of the paper. To keep within the confines of the five staff lines was far too restricting for John [. . .] he did not need a piano while he was composing, only when he had finished. He heard every note in his mind. I am sure he composed music much more rapidly than his little hands ever had time to write down – such a long, tedious job even for skilled adults. Many times during the previous year or so, I had been fascinated by the method John had devised for writing music. After writing in the treble and bass clefs, sharps or flats key, and the time fraction or C, he would write all the notes as semibreves, mark in the bars, then backtrack, making the semibreves into minims, crotchets, or quavers by adding stems, filling them in, and completing them accordingly.

Back at Marjory's house John finished the prelude – which resembled a storm on the page, with its thick dark clusters of notes – then performed it for his adoring female audience, aunts included. He had to play it standing up to reach the extremities of bass and treble but the ovation was worth all the effort and drew from him many an elaborate bow. Across the top of the paper John had drawn a row of composers' heads, all with long hair, including his own at the end. Marjory wrote their names in for him, and 'Ogdon' – John insisting on the surname alone – duly took its place beside Beethoven, Brahms, Rachmaninoff, et al.

In addition to the purely musical activities they shared, John spent a lot of time with Marjory up in her attic rummaging through the old trunks while she worked on her crafts to raise money for the concert fund. Together they compiled an album of composers, pasting in pictures and biographical snippets. Schubert and Beethoven took pride of place, though the album opened with a picture of the infant Mozart reaching up to touch the keys of the harpsichord. On one page they wrote out a quote from Beethoven in large calligraphic letters: 'My miserable hearing does not trouble me here. In the country it seems as if every tree said to me, "Holy! Holy!"' When Marjory told John that Beethoven had gone deaf he paused thoughtfully then said, with childish gravity, 'Beethoven should have had his hair cut.'

With his own father languishing in the Notts County Asylum John found a surrogate parent in Marjory's father. A retired policeman, James Wood played the piano by ear and was an enthusiastic gardener. He and John used to stick old spade handles in the ground as feeding perches for the robins; when the birds alighted they'd throw worms to them. While Mr Wood was digging Marjory and John would busy themselves picking baskets of fruit and vegetables to take back to the house. While a good many of the raspberries and other small fruits found their way into John's mouth, he never neglected to think of his mother and always set aside a portion of his pickings as a gift for her. Sometimes Marjory would string the hammock between the apple and pear trees and John would clamber happily into its nylon folds.

John proved to be a treasured companion for both the Wood parents. He would play for Mrs Wood while she sat by the fireside reading poetry, or for Mr Wood as he sat at the bay window sketching in pen and ink. Sometimes Mrs Wood would read aloud to John from her *1001 Gems of English Poetry*, and on one occasion explained to him that she was an elocutionist. The next time Dorothy came to collect John she told the Woods that John had confided to her, not without a tremor, that Mrs Wood was 'a wonderful executionist'! The motto in the Wood household was 'Satan finds mischief for idle hands to do', but John's hands were rarely idle, for he interpreted the world around him through the keys of the piano. He once gave an impromptu recital at Teversal School, where Marjory taught, and afterwards one little girl came up to him and said, 'John, you play like magic!' Despite these idyllic interludes, though, the shadow of war never wholly lifted. In the summer of 1942 Marjory's twenty-one-year-old brother, Jimmy, was killed in action and John, who had occasionally played for him, stayed away from the house for weeks. When finally he returned his playing provided a source of comfort to the bereaved family.

John attended St Edmund's Primary in Mansfield Woodhouse, which was next door to the Ogdon home. He seemed shyly affable towards everyone at school and sometimes invited boys back home to play. One of these was Raymond Clark, who remembers playing cowboys and Indians in the long garden. In the barn at the bottom of the lawn was an old Red Indian-style canoe in which they'd pretend to paddle for their lives. They also played hide-and-seek in the orchard. John didn't run so much as lumber; according to Raymond, everything about him was thick and heavy. When John had to go inside for his hour's piano practice Raymond would sit outside the door and wait for him to finish. John never tried to avoid his practice: he would dash in immediately he was called. When he went over to Raymond's he didn't go inside the house; instead the two friends sat on the wall outside and talked. Raymond assumed that John was an only child because none of his siblings were in evidence at Auckland House.

Keith Beastall, another friend, does remember John's elder brother Karl joining in their play sessions. The Tarzan films with Johnny Weissmuller were all the rage at the time, and Karl would run up and down the garden in a loincloth making the famous ululating cry of the ape-man. He even had a couple of ropes rigged up down by the barn and would swing from one to the other. Keith and John would scrump for apples in an orchard to the other side of the school. John, he said, had the most beautiful head of thick, curly hair and was 'a wonderful lad, full of life, plump and unassuming'. Karl, on the other hand, was 'a bit of a crackpot, and uninhibited in a mad sort of way'. He found Howard strange and highly strung, not at all normal. He would say hello but that was the extent of his involvement with the children and their friends.

In 1944, aged seven, John began to suffer from severe headaches. When these were followed by a fever and hallucinations he was taken to Mansfield General Hospital. Meningitis was suspected. From there he was transferred to Nottingham General, where it was discovered that he in fact had mastoiditis. A double mastoid operation was performed but John was left virtually deaf in his right ear. Once the worst was over and he was allowed to get out of bed, he said to the nurse, 'I've got to have a piano now.' He also spent some of his three weeks in hospital sitting up in bed composing. On one visit Nellie Houseley collected up John's 'effusions', as his father dubbed them, and sent them to the music master at Worksop College, who found that sixty-seven bars from Beethoven's lesser-known sonatas had been reproduced from memory in these juvenile efforts. On his return home John had several more weeks off school to convalesce.

In June 1945 Edward J. Mason, director of education for Nottinghamshire County Council, arranged an audition for the eight-year-old John at the Royal Academy of Music in London. There he played before the principal, Sir Stanley Marchant, the warden, Dr Thatcher (formerly deputy director of music at the BBC), and the conductor Clarence Raybould, founder of the National Youth Orchestra of Wales. They were all deeply impressed with the boy and offered the necessary scholarships should his family decide to send him to London. The Ogdons, however, preferred to remain in the north. Consequently Sir Stanley wrote to the principal of the Royal Manchester College of Music, R. J. Forbes. The letter was dated 22 October 1945:

My dear Forbes,

I have to-day written to a Mr. Ogdon suggesting that he should seek your advice with regard to the guidance of his son, aged about seven.

I found the boy to be quite phenomenal and a very interesting character. It is quite clear that between us we must look after a boy with such talent. I am sure you will do anything you can to suggest a sensible teacher for him.

My love to you,
Yours ever,
Stanley Marchant

The summer of his audition John took part in the Under-18 Piano Sight-Reading competition at the Beeston Musical Festival, near Nottingham, and was awarded Second Prize with a mark of 81 out of 100: a remarkable result for an eight-year-old (one imagines that the size of his hands kept him from the top prize). This was the first and only time during his childhood that he entered a music festival or, for that matter, took any kind of music exam. At this stage in his life his father described John's playing as 'that of an imperfect infant prodigy – a fate that he narrowly missed'.

In the autumn the family moved to Prestwich in the Manchester suburbs when John was offered a special scholarship (or 'junior exhibition') at the Royal Manchester College of Music. He was the youngest person ever to be granted admission.

3

SCHOOL OF ONE

*Conversation enriches the understanding, but solitude is the
school of genius.*

Edward Gibbon

Howard Ogdon began in his teaching post at Purbrook Park
County High School, north of Portsmouth, in January 1943
and remained there for sixteen months. Having spent more than a year
as a munitions inspector, he was rejoining his chosen metier; and
eventually his thoughts turned towards the home and family he'd left
all those years ago. From Purbrook he applied for a job at the
Southwell Minster Collegiate Grammar School in Nottinghamshire,
a post he took up in May 1944. As he drew closer to home his movements were guarded and cat-like. At Southwell, where one of his
favourite poets, Byron, had kept a house, Howard was only fifteen
miles from Mansfield Woodhouse. It's clear from his attitude in
Kingdom of the Lost that he believed his mania was exacerbated by
proximity to his family. His wife and children got under his skin, and
he would suddenly find himself on a knife edge. For now the errant
life suited him better. Civil rehabilitation was a slow and expensive
process – in Howard's case it involved legal and medical costs (three
Harley Street and two provincial specialists) – and he had no savings.

A decade later, in a letter to Frederic Cox at the RMCM, Howard laments that he is 'only just beginning to pull out of the morass'.

It is not known when Howard returned home but it was probably sometime in the summer of 1944, not long before John was hospitalized. Even then he may have lived at home only on weekends: he kept his teaching post at Southwell through to the summer of 1945. Nevertheless, the impact on the seven-year-old John of the reappearance of this rogue patriarchal element was bound to be critical. That John came out of hospital with his hearing permanently impaired suggests a kind of sealing off from the harsh discords of domestic strife. It is said that Beethoven's tyrannical father contributed to his son's subsequent deafness through violent beatings to the head. While John's experience did not replicate this literally, the violence in the air could have had the same effect – plunging him ever deeper into the world of music. At seven most children become more conscious of the wider world, through school and visiting friends' homes; they encounter authorities other than their parents and begin to develop a greater sense of perspective. Making mental comparisons between themselves and their peers, they often feel the shame of being different or disadvantaged in some way. John's unorthodox home life and the stigma of his father's madness must have added to his torments at this age and forced him to repress and dissemble. It's a short step from repressing one's feelings to losing touch with them altogether.

John's severe illness in 1944 was like a rite of passage into a premature adulthood. The following year he was auditioned at the Royal Academy of Music and his path to the RMCM was cleared. His sense of self was now firmly rooted in his musical prodigy. Because of illness and absence Howard had missed the first seven years of John's childhood. Even on his return Dorothy remained the dominant presence in John's life, though her love came at a price. She was the guardian of John's genius, and took care of his everyday needs so that he could channel all his energies into the piano. Her ambition for him became his ambition and, with no emphasis on self-reliance, she helped turn the boy into an obese and unkempt youth who couldn't tie his shoelaces. Howard, meanwhile, took a keen interest in his son's education, because educational theory was one of his passions. He was a strong intellectual influence on John, who picked up every scrap that fell from his father's austere table. Besides Dorothy, John was Howard's sole audience as he held forth on the subjects that absorbed him: literature, music, psychology and the occult. In their own ways both parents were controlling figures who made little allowance for self-expression in their offspring. For love and the freedom to be who he was, John turned to Marjory Wood – but this relationship was about to end.

In the early autumn of 1945, with the war finally over, the Ogdons moved up to Prestwich, which, together with neighbouring Whitefield, was home to a large Jewish community. Howard had been appointed to the post of senior English master at Stand Grammar School with immediate effect. As a temporary measure they found rented accommodation in Sunnyfield Road on the edge of Heaton Park, a vast green sanctuary that had once been the estate of the Egerton family, Earls of Wilton. John attended Lady Wilton's CE Junior School in Simister, a village to the north of the park surrounded by small farms. John, who was gauche and very quiet, was teased and bullied at the school because of his size. He used to charge his tormentors, with his head down, which earned him the nickname 'the bull'. He was called upon to play the piano in assembly but his musical brilliance, far from winning the admiration of his peers, simply became fuel for their taunts.

John's scholarship at the RMCM required his release from school for one day every week but initially the local authority would not allow it. In the meantime, in an attempt to bring a measure of discipline to his musical education, his parents put him onto some theoretical studies and he would obediently take down chords from dictation. Eventually, after what Howard Ogdon described as a 'brawl', the Lancashire Education Committee relented and John was free to attend the college from 1 May 1946. He attended on Wednesdays, his scheduled day, but also spent most Saturdays there. It was around this time that Marjory Wood married an American serviceman and went to live in New Jersey. John still wrote to her, and his letters – addressed to 'Mrs Kasen' – are a touching mixture of childish formality and devotion. In one he tells her that the only animal he has left in the soap zoo she gave him is the polar bear 'because somebody took the lion'. He signs off 'Millions of kisses and tons of love, your loving sweetheart, John'. Any physical affection John had received in his childhood came from Marjory. Whatever gap she now left in his life – and it must have been immense – he filled with music.

At the end of October 1946, on Howard's initiative, John gave a short recital at Stand Grammar. Howard sent a boy from his class to collect John from the bus stop. There he found a tubby young fellow in shorts, with round-rimmed glasses beneath his school cap, who looked inquisitively about him as they made their way to the school. Remarkably the recital took place in front of all the year groups, with the boys seated on the floor of the assembly hall. John, who had been billed as a child prodigy, walked on stage to muffled titters, bowing stiffly before he sat down at the piano. He proceeded to play three pieces by Chopin (Prelude in G minor, No. 22; Polonaise in A major, Op. 40, *Military*; and Nocturne in A flat, No. 10), Grieg's 'An der Frühling' (from *Lyric Pieces*, Op. 43), and his own Suite in Four Movements (I. *Preludio*, II. *Menuetto*, III. *Gavotte*, IV. *Gigue*). The sight of this chubby little boy presiding over such brilliant and fleet-fingered flurries of notes created general merriment in the audience and there was some ill-stifled laughter. The concert lasted about twenty-five minutes in all and at the end John bowed three times to the different sections of the hall, just as he had rehearsed after the Louis Kentner recital. A euphoric Howard invited three of his English students back to his house and impressed upon them what a privilege it had been for them to have heard John that afternoon.

Stand Grammar School was on Church Lane, Whitefield, just a couple of miles up the road from the Ogdons' new home. It was founded in 1688, though not on that site, and claimed Clive of India as its most illustrious old boy. When Howard joined the English staff there were 480 boys at the school. Among the famous pupils he inspired with his idiosyncratic teaching were the author and journalist John Heilpern and Booker Prize-winning novelist Howard Jacobson. The school had a sizeable contingent of Jews and

Howard Ogdon was one of the few masters who wasn't anti-Semitic. Many of his former pupils at Stand have described his classroom as a haven of civilized conduct in what could be a brutal and bigoted school culture.

From 1947 to 1952 Howard edited the school magazine, the *Standian*. Also in 1947 he took on the presidency of the school's Music Society, turning what had been a sleepy, rather stuffy little club into a dynamic and growing circle of music lovers that by 1950 boasted a membership of eighty-eight. He organized evenings at the Hallé Orchestra and overnight trips to the Royal Opera House at Covent Garden (supplying notes on the ballets and operas himself). When the Covent Garden production of *Lohengrin* came to Manchester's Palace Theatre, Howard arranged for his group to attend. He also instituted a lecture series for which he gave a number of illustrated talks. His subjects included Berlioz and French Romanticism, Wagner's *Ring* and *Flying Dutchman*, and Music & Drama, illustrated by music and scenes from Berlioz's *Roméo et Juliette* and Grieg's *Peer Gynt*.

Joe Bog, as Howard was known by the boys, was a bizarre figure in the school's gallery of pedagogues, even in an age of pedagogic eccentricity, but was generally valued by the pupils as a kindly, studious man who did his best to instil a sense of the value of reading thoughtfully and writing well. His methods were a curious mixture of conservative and avant-garde. The first thing he did with a new class was to test everyone for colour blindness because he was searching for links between colour perception and learning ability. He would also get the boys to analyse sentences in coloured boxes and would wax lyrical about the way in which different authors punctuated their works. He was keen on reading aloud and getting the boys to memorize large chunks of literature. He made them keep vocabulary books while they read, and urged them on during his own disquisitions with what became his catchphrase: 'Take copious notes, boys.' Where he could he brought his own literary passions to the fore. Being an aficionado of the Brontë sisters, for example, he organized a sixth-form trip to Haworth Parsonage.

Howard's appearance would generally startle the boys until they got used to him. Peering round the door at the beginning of a lesson, he would stare silently at the rows of faces then suddenly bellow out, 'Hey nonny, nonny!' To class he wore his academic gown (other teachers didn't) over a green tweed suit, dark-mauve shirt and university tie. His bicycle clips remained attached to the ankles of his trousers throughout the day. He had a crew cut (the equivalent of a nose ring in those days) and wore a large alchemical-looking ring on the middle finger of his left hand. One day in 1949 he arrived at school with a completely shaven head following some sort of religious conversion. Shaven heads were rare back then – but not as rare as spending the entire morning break in a headstand position against the classroom wall!

On his wanderings through the corridors or about the school grounds Howard could be seen acting out roles from Shakespeare. Sometimes he would accost a boy and urge him to imbibe the wonders of nature and write down his feelings on the subject. In class he was a diligent and skilful trapper of insects, a fascination he shared with his youngest son. The flies he snared were stowed in his desk, so that by the end of the school day his drawers were audibly buzzing. He smoked in class during break then sprayed the room with perfume to cover his tracks, leaving behind a rather sickly incense-like smell. He made no bones about the fact that he had been in a lunatic asylum. If anything he seemed to revel in the memory of it, regaling the boys with tales of his breakdown, committal and supernatural escape. He told them that at least he had a certificate to prove his sanity – theirs had to be taken on trust.

In April 1946 Dorothy Ogdon wrote to Marjory Wood just before she set off to begin her new life in America. Word of John's scholarship to the RMCM had got about and they'd had a reporter at the house. There were articles about him in both the local and national newspapers, including the *Manchester Evening News*. The *Daily Mail* ran a piece entitled 'A Chopin at 9', which began:

In Prestwich, Lancashire, nine-year-old John Andrew Ogdon of Mardale Close is regarded as a 'modern Chopin'. He is a composer of some merit, and his piano recitals have aroused the interest of many well-known musicians.

'Now he has something to live up to!' writes Dorothy. She says that John's playing has improved considerably in spite of his not having had lessons for such a long time, and that he has been to hear the Russian pianist Iso Elinson playing the complete cycle of Beethoven sonatas in Manchester. Later in the letter she mentions that John has injured his right hand playing football. At first they thought his little finger was broken, but it turned out to be no more than badly bruised. The hand was bandaged by the doctor, who gave strict orders that John was not to use it. Nevertheless, he would not be banished from the piano and continued his practice by attempting to play both parts of his pieces with the left hand alone.

The nine-year-old John, in his stiff shorts and cap, must have presented an extraordinary sight at a college full of young adult students and distinguished old professors. But to the boy himself entry to that august temple of music seemed perfectly natural; he was like a fish in water. For this was a world – perhaps the only one – in which he felt assured. Where music was the lingua franca he could happily converse with kings. As John himself described it in an interview on his fiftieth birthday:

As a young boy I never stopped to think about difficulties which I might encounter. Fortunately, at that age I lived so much in the present, I was so busy studying and playing the instrument I loved, that I never had any doubts. I was immersed in music, and that was an enriching experience.

John was treated by his colleagues as 'one of them', despite the glaring disparity in age. In a letter to Marjory Wood shortly after he started at the college, John wrote to say that the other students had been very kind to him. Ronald Stevenson had bought him Grieg's *Album Leaves*, Brahms's *Clavierstücke* and three concertos by the German composer Louis Spohr, while John Hopkins had made a gift of Chopin's sonatas. Stevenson, Scottish composer and pianist, who was eighteen at the time, would become a lifelong friend; Hopkins, a cello student, became college librarian and, eventually, conductor of the BBC Northern Orchestra. Earlier in the same letter John mentioned that he had joined the Henry Watson Music Library and had bought Liszt's *Transcendental Studies* and Archibald Jacob's *Musical Handwriting*. Of the former, one of the most forbiddingly difficult works in the piano literature, he wrote with artless modesty: 'It is only Book 1, next time I will get Book 2.' He then listed all his teachers at the RMCM: Iso Elinson for piano, Richard Hall for composition, Gordon Green for ensemble and Dr Norman Andrew for harmony.

John had not been admitted to the RMCM because he showed promise for his age; his pianism was already such that he could be ranked with the best of the full-time students twice his age. Yet he himself never thought of it in terms of age or precocity. He was simply getting on with what he loved best. On *Desert Island Discs*, recorded just months before he died, there was this delightful exchange between him and the host, Sue Lawley:

> **Ogdon:** And I went a bit to the Royal Manchester College of Music when I was about eight years old, as a junior exhibitioner.
> **Lawley:** Good heavens above! That was quite a precocious talent, surely.
> **Ogdon:** [*squirming*] Well, relatively, I suppose.

Ronald Stevenson recalls the first time he heard the nine-year-old John play on the college's concert platform. He performed Chopin's big A-flat polonaise, the *Heroic*, an immensely challenging piece, requiring the full resources of a keyboard master. Yet if you closed your eyes, says Stevenson, and concentrated on the music, you could have had no doubt that you were listening to a fully-fledged virtuoso. The adult students were amazed by the performance, as no one could play the piece as well as John. Another student at the time, the pianist and teacher Harold Taylor, was roaming the top corridor of the college one day in search of a practice room when he was stopped in his tracks by the eruption of the violent octave trills in the first movement of the Brahms D-minor concerto coming through a half-open door.

Curious to find out which of the college's top performers was scaling this particular Everest, I gingerly opened the door and peeped inside. The piano was playing itself! My first instinct was to retreat in disorder, but reason prevailed and I advanced cautiously into the room. I discovered no phantom at the keyboard, but a thoroughly solid little boy with black curly hair and thick-lensed glasses, who had been hidden behind the score on the music rack. He was so absorbed in his performance that he didn't notice me and I tiptoed out, somewhat shaken, but also stirred by the manifestation of genius which I had witnessed.

As Taylor later wrote, this was no mere sight-reading in the sense of someone feeling their way through a new piece, but 'a *performance*, with all the technical and musical accomplishment that the word implies'.

The first encounter between John Ogdon and Ronald Stevenson was highly significant, and speaks to another dimension of Ogdon's musicianship. As Stevenson recalls it, this was the day on which he had discovered the full score of the mammoth Busoni Concerto at the college library. He was practising the piano part in one of the studios on Oxford Road and had arrived at a passage marked *quasi con brutalita* – 'as if with brutality', a most unusual marking – when he became aware of a presence in the room. He turned to see a plump, shy-mannered boy with a serious look on his face. 'What was that you were playing?' John asked in a piping treble voice. 'How remarkable,' exclaims Stevenson now, 'that a nine-year-old boy should have been interested in the Busoni Concerto!' John himself harked back to the event in an interview some forty years later:

Yes, I vividly remember that day. I wanted to become a pianist and study composition so that I could fulfil my dream of being able to write music like that which I had just heard. Ronald was very kind; he lent me some piano pieces by Busoni and, in spite of their complex structure I struggled through, page after page, in my simple and determined way. Surprisingly, I was not deterred by their enormous technical difficulties. All that mattered was my excitement, my joy of hearing myself playing pieces with extraordinary richness of sounds and textures.

Those who tell this story talk of John being infused with the desire to play Busoni's music. But that's not what he says. Hearing Ronald Stevenson that day inspired John to *write* music of this kind. John's dream was to become a pianist-composer in the tradition of Liszt and Busoni, and he already had an acute ear for what his contemporaries were writing. Stevenson remembers playing his first sonatina for John around this same time, and decades later receiving a letter from him in which John quoted the first four bars from memory – though he hadn't played or heard the piece in the interim!

John took lessons in composition from Richard Hall, an Anglican minister who had a passion for Scriabin and would later become the guru of the New Music Manchester group. John was remembered by one fellow student of Hall's as being rather wrapped up in himself and doodling in class. He would bring in little sonatas or album leaves that he'd written and Hall would sit down with him and correct them or make suggestions. Later, when Hall went to the canteen for his break, he'd find that John had transformed these sheets of music into paper aeroplanes and was flying them around the room. Others recall him playing marbles on the floor of the college hall until the principal put his foot down.

Stevenson was aware of John's composing at this time, and realized that he had been at it for some considerable while. Any composer will tell you that the notion of learning composition is questionable; you can learn *about* certain facets of it, such as counterpoint, but the impulse and ability to vary sound seem to be instinctive. 'John was certainly composing from improvisation,' says Stevenson. 'He was a very good improviser.' Stevenson also noted the influence of Russian music on John, even at that age. Iso Elinson was exasperated by John's refusal to practise classical pieces and follow a step-by-step approach. His headstrong desire to arrive in the company of the great Romantic composers with a single vaulting leap led Elinson to complain to Dorothy Ogdon that he couldn't do anything with her son. 'Please take him away!' he cried.

Elinson was something of a marathon man who relished the challenge of playing Bach's 48 Preludes and Fugues or Beethoven's 32 Sonatas in public, a feat he had first attempted in his native Russia as early as 1927 as part of the celebrations of the centenary of Beethoven's death. Elinson was born in White Russia in 1907 and was taught piano by his mother, a pupil of Anton Rubinstein. He later studied piano and composition at the Petrograd Conservatory with Felix Blumenfeld and Alexander Glazunov respectively. Elinson took up his appointment in Manchester in 1944. He was a broadly cultured man, with many literary and artistic enthusiasms, who encouraged his students to find out all they could about the history and inspiration behind the pieces they played. Ogdon described him as a Renaissance man and said that studying with Elinson had been 'an extraordinary adventure'. Though responsible for introducing Scriabin's music to Manchester audiences, Elinson has been criticized by some of his pupils for being overly conservative in his choice of repertoire and feeding them an exclusively classical diet: Bach, Mozart, Clementi, Beethoven, Schubert and Brahms (Liszt he called 'old socks'). Yet to the study of these classics he brought great depth. He introduced John to several different editions of Beethoven's sonatas, including those of Tovey, Dukas and Czerny, and urged him to seek out others. And it was Elinson who put John onto the Brahms D-minor concerto – or rather John himself seized upon it when he heard his teacher practising it for a Promenade concert in September 1946.

Elinson was noted for the restraint and purity of his playing. He impressed upon his students the need to 'take' the keys, as he called it, rather than strike them – in other words to stroke the keys with varying degrees of pressure. That way the pianist may achieve penetration of sound and avoid obscuring the clarity of the notes with the extra noise made by hitting the keys. (This became typical of John's style of playing: he caressed the keys, sinking into them when he required greater volume; he was not a basher.) Elinson's economical use of the sustaining pedal helped clarify his textures even further. He was in many ways a pianist's pianist, more suited to the salon than the modern concert hall. According to Ronald Stevenson, he *exuded* music, and embodied that characteristically Russian blend of mirth and melancholy. His wife, Hedwig Stein, also taught piano at the RMCM.

Destruction was etched on the face of the Manchester to which the Ogdons moved at the end of the war. The Palace Theatre, the Free Trade Hall and Manchester Cathedral had all received direct hits from German air raids. Piles of rubble marked the sites where buildings and homes had once stood. The suburbs had also been affected. Initially the Ogdons had rented a two-up, two-down 1930s semi-detached house from which John had written to Marjory in August 1946 complaining how very small it was. They were, he said, only just getting used to Manchester. By the autumn they had moved round the corner to Mardale Close, which wasn't much bigger but at least had a decent garden at the back which gave out onto an open expanse of playing fields. This would be their home for the next ten years.

They created the same sort of set-up they'd had in previous houses, only this time the family was much smaller. Pippa and Paul had left home before Manchester, though Pippa did return for a while after the war when she worked as a teleprinter operator. Being fourteen years John's senior, she had never been a close companion. Karl was away at Red Hill and Ruth, who had left school aged fifteen, in 1944, had gone to train as a nurse at a children's hospital in Southport. At seventeen she got pregnant by an American soldier who had a wife back home. Her parents sent her to a mother-and-baby home in Surrey, where she gave birth to a son, Paul, who was put up for adoption and renamed John. She returned home in 1947 and took work first as a weaver in one of the Lancashire mills and then as a mental nurse in Prestwich Hospital – a job she left after being attacked by a patient. There was a rumour in the family (now known to be untrue) that Ruth wasn't Howard's daughter. Karl certainly believed it, and it might well have set John pondering his own paternity. Howard, as was his wont, holed himself up in a specially requisitioned downstairs sanctum, piled high with books and records, and with Wagner set to triple forte worked himself up into a Faustian lather. Now when he wasn't at school he was working feverishly on the manuscript of *The Kingdom of the Lost*, for which he had a contract with The Bodley Head. Dorothy was roped in as word counter and typist; it was all hands to the deck as 'Daddy' – as Dorothy called her husband – used every available minute to hammer the work into publishable form. Howard had persisted with the trombone, as a release from all the mental strain, and John used to accompany him on the piano in classic pieces such as the overture to Rossini's opera *William Tell*. Howard also played in the Besses o' th' Barn Band, one of the oldest brass bands in the world.

Had John been Russian, like Ashkenazy, he would have gone to Moscow's Central Music School at eight, the feeder school for the Moscow Conservatory, and for the following ten years been taught by some of the finest musical pedagogues in the Soviet system, such as Heinrich Neuhaus and Alexander Goldenweiser, before moving onto the Conservatory itself at seventeen or eighteen. Music would have been the centre of his scholastic life, and the training unapologetically rigorous. He would have been marked down from the start as a potential great, a talent to be cultivated with the full resources of the State.

The situation in England was very different. Although John's parents were keen for him to continue his studies at the RMCM when he went off to grammar school, the education system at the time did not permit it. On leaving the Lady Wilton school in 1947 John won scholarships to Stand, Bury and Manchester grammar schools and chose Manchester, the largest – it had 1,400 pupils – as well as the most distinguished of the three. (At that time, MGS won more Oxbridge scholarships than any other school in the country, leaving the likes of Eton, St Paul's and Dulwich trailing in its wake.) At ten John was young to be entering the school. In the entrance exam he placed eighty-first of the 210 boys admitted in his year (there were 1,000 applicants in all) and was made a foundation scholar. The high master of the time, Eric James, was adamant that John must adhere to the full school timetable; there would be no opportunity for him to scurry across town for piano lessons. So John duly left the RMCM in July 1947 and the door was shut on his formal musical education.

Extraordinarily, John had no music lessons whatever between the ages of ten and sixteen. Christopher Elton, head of piano at the Royal

Academy of Music, has said that a pianist's technique needs to be developed by the age of fifteen or sixteen. That being the case, it is hardly surprising that John's later teachers were concerned about his lack of keyboard discipline and the strain of unruliness that marked his playing. Manchester Grammar School had no music department, and no master in charge of music: in fact the role of music in the life of the school was virtually non-existent. If it was not frowned upon then it was tolerated, but no more. There was a choir, run by a geography teacher called Dickie Radford, but its main purpose was to provide the chorus for school productions. Radford, a gifted and enthusiastic choirmaster, had taught generations of children to sing 'Nymphs and Shepherds,' but was perhaps not the man to shepherd the raw, colossal talent of Ogdon. There was a modern-languages teacher, however, Cyril Maguire, who was a very good pianist and all-round musician, and he encouraged John and to a certain extent took him under his wing. Maguire organized informal lunchtime concerts in the Memorial Hall, which were announced at morning assembly. They didn't attract large audiences – people tended to drift in out of curiosity – but they were showcases for a handful of talented pupils, including the violinist Michael Davis. John was the most outstanding and the most regular performer. John Harvey, who was John Ogdon's junior by several years and a pianist himself, recalls being shaken to the core by a performance Ogdon gave of Bartók's *Allegro Barbaro*. Ogdon was fifteen at the time, and to hear the piece played with such demonic intensity by a boy not much older than himself was an electrifying experience for Harvey. He hadn't realized that the piano could be played like that. Others remember John's exploration of Liszt's music, which was a tremendous passion with him even then, and their astonishment at how swiftly and delicately those large pudgy hands could move over the keys.

The school was divided into two groups: Classical and Modern. Both learned French, but whereas the Moderns studied German the Classics learned Latin. The Classical division was perceived to be more civilized and tolerant and John was in this set. In fact he was very good at Latin, and in his third year was one of only two boys in his class who embraced Latin poetry. For his first two years John was placed in the Alpha division, which was the highest in any given year, but he languished towards the bottom. His form master in the first year thought he was handicapped by his deafness, which, he said, made him very nervous; his form master in the second year confined himself to the single remark, 'I fear he is not of Alpha type.' So for his third year he dropped down into the Beta class, where he came top. He was always first in English, French and Latin, at which he excelled, and occasionally science. For maths they were placed in separate sets. His form master Philip Hill, aware of his short sight and hearing problems, brought John to the front of the class. Hill described him as 'a very keen and steady worker', not exactly shy but one who kept himself in the background. Although Hill was himself a pianist, who used to play Clementi sonatas in the Memorial Hall, he never realized that John played. He confessed himself 'staggered' when twelve years later he learned of his former pupil's victory in the Tchaikovsky competition!

Other teachers were more observant, noting John's keen interest in music and entomology (particularly butterflies). After the third year several commented on his self-assurance, while one of his classmates described him as possessing 'a certain secretive confidence, as if he knew something that no one else did'. It was noted that each year when he went up to collect his form prize in front of 1,500 people at the Free Trade Hall, he would walk very purposefully up the steps and across the stage with his head held slightly back and an air of 'Well, chaps, whatever you may think of me, I've succeeded!' He could so easily have become a target of more bullying: with his round-shouldered frame, rolling gait, partial deafness – for which he wore patches of cotton wool behind his ears – and short sight (item: one pair of pebble-lens spectacles), he was a sitting duck. He also still had a slight lisp and experienced difficulty in pronouncing certain conso-nants, such as 'R', though these handicaps were offset by a sweet sing-song voice, very soft and pleasant to listen to, with the mildest of northern accents. His voice was quite high for his age; he didn't reach puberty until his first year at college, when he was seventeen. He was rarely to be seen at games, and when he was it was as part of the 'Remnants' – the five or six boys who were not in one of the two form teams and so had to make do with chasing an uneven-shaped ball around a bumpy patch of ground. He did occasionally appear for gym classes: one boy remembers him looking particularly awkward in his tight white gym shorts. Bearing in mind that even teachers were a good deal less sensitive about making personal remarks in those days (John's history teacher in the Remove described him on his report card as 'ponderous and ungainly') it is something of a miracle that John passed the pikes of his contemporaries largely unscathed.

Then of course there was the Howard factor. The Bodley Head had just published his crowing account of his madness (it came out the month after John arrived at MGS), and there wasn't anyone, friend or stranger, whose ear Howard wouldn't bend about his antics behind asylum gates. As one enters secondary school a parent is embarrassing enough without wearing a big shiny badge with the words 'I am an escaped lunatic' emblazoned across it. John must also have wondered if the demon that had afflicted his father would spring onto his own back any day soon. Would he too be bundled off in a Black Maria one fine morning?

The reason John escaped the hostile notice of his fellows was perhaps something to do with his essentially amiable and tolerant nature and his habit of looking up to everyone, whether they deserved it or not. Though quiet and shy in a crowd, he could be jovial and fun-loving in a small group. He was an ardent collector of *Beano* and *Dandy* comics; and, in as much as he bumbled through school with a shy grin on his face and guffawed in an exaggerated manner when he was amused, he was something of a cartoon character himself, whose idiosyncrasies were generally perceived as benign. Everyone called him 'Oggy', and overall the attitude towards him was one of amused affection. Though slow to anger, on the rare occasions that he was provoked John really let fly – screaming and shouting and lashing out with his school bag, which he whirled above his head like a battle axe.

The school day started comparatively late, at 9.30 a.m., because many of the boys had far to come. John's trips to and from Prestwich would have taken him an hour by bus each way; it would have been around 5 p.m. when he was reunited with his beloved piano. Evenings, no less than the weekends, would be taken up with his self-devised course of musical studies, including exercises by Beethoven's student Carl Czerny. John enjoyed exploring the treasures of Forsyth Brothers, Manchester's largest music store and showroom, and spent countless happy hours foraging at the Henry Watson Music Library in the town centre as well. He borrowed piano transcriptions of the Beethoven symphonies, as well as Sibelius's Fifth and César Franck's D-minor symphonies. Writing to R. J. Forbes at the RMCM in June 1953, Howard Ogdon related how John had, since 1947, constantly borrowed from the library not only scores but also biographies of composers, theoretical works and gramophone records, 'covering in this way a range of studies abnormal even in a full-time student!' Howard himself contributed to John's musical education by taking him to concerts, mainly through the Stand Music Society. These were symphonic and operatic concerts rather than piano recitals. For instance, when John was fourteen Howard took him to see Benjamin Britten's *Peter Grimes* at the Palace Theatre, with Peter Pears in the title role and Sir Geraint Evans as Captain Bulstrode. John was also a founder member, in 1946, of the Prestwich Music Club.

In August 1951 Howard had a meeting with Eric James at Manchester Grammar to see if John might be permitted to resume music lessons at the RMCM in the sixth form. James gave his assent on two conditions: one, that the timetable permitted John's absence on certain afternoons (he had by this time been excused games altogether); and two, that his new form master was in agreement. James wrote a brief memo to himself about the meeting, which begins:

Saw father (rather unpleasant man). Has been in mental institutions and written a book about it. [Re John:] Because of physical defects a number of careers ruled out. Thinks of bank or something like that where could do his music in spare time. This seems a good idea.

The bank was Howard's suggestion, not John's. If they were all thinking of him as a potential banker, why even entertain the possibility of sending him back to the Royal College? It's all strangely dysfunctional. The chemistry teacher Solomon Clynes found himself sitting next to John on the bus home one day and said, 'Well, my boy, what are you going to do when you leave school?' John replied that he was thinking of qualifying as a librarian, adding with typical under-statement, 'But I'm also very interested in the piano.' 'Oh no!' exclaimed Sol. 'It's all very well having a knees-up round the old Joanna on a Saturday night but I advise you to stick to your library work!' In the end, all talk of an early return to the RMCM proved academic: the college principal was against the idea, considering it important for John to concentrate on his school exams for now.

John was happy to dissemble in order to please his superiors but his mind had been made up long before. According to an article in the *Prestwich & Whitefield Guide* John was in such a hurry to get back to the RMCM that he took the unusual step of sitting his O levels and A levels at the same time, when he was sixteen. For A level he took history, Latin and English Literature, scoring his best marks (the equiv-alent of an A grade) in English Literature. This was hardly surprising: John, inspired by his father, was a prodigious reader and a fine writer who had developed a mellifluent and nimble prose style studded with distinctive, gem-like phrases. Fellow student George Richardson, who once borrowed John's Shakespeare essays, was struck by his deep insight into the characters and motifs of the plays. John was, he says, a clever and original thinker. History and film were other lifelong enthusiasms that took root at MGS, where he joined the school's Film Society. His sister Ruth worked for a while as an usherette at the Manchester News Theatre and she used to let John and George in through a side door so they could watch the programmes for free. It was also at this time that John became a fan of Manchester United Football Club.

Even in the sixth form John continued to win the form prize, as a reward for which his parents bought him a new piano when he was fifteen – an upright, but an advance on the old childhood pianola. John never seemed bothered about the quality of the pianos he played; though he appreciated a really excellent instrument, he would cheer-fully make do with what was available. He also possessed the enviable ability to concentrate on creative tasks no matter what was going on around him. This was just as well in the cramped and often noisy households of his childhood. A friend of Karl Ogdon, Keith Wright, remembers visiting his old school chum in 1950 when he was on leave from RAF Padgate in Cheshire:

> They lived in a tiny modern house in the suburbs. I was introduced to the young boy who was John [he was thirteen], and he volunteered to play something for me. I asked for Chopin's Ballade No. 4 in F minor, and John performed it very competently. At some stage of the visit Karl produced a collection of French press cuttings about his father (who at the time was at work). My French was very rudimentary, but I gathered that they were about this Englishman called Ogdon who had escaped from a French mental institution in Paris. When their father was due home the cuttings were hastily assembled and put away. I didn't see any mother. As the time of the father's arrival drew near, the boys started becoming agitated and I was ushered from the house.

If Wright's account is correct, it would suggest that Howard Ogdon was institutionalized in France during the First World War – some twenty years before his breakdown. This seems unlikely.

Karl Ogdon at this time was doing clerical work in Manchester but (much to his father's irritation) spent all his spare time playing the piano and guitar and composing. He was already an extremely well-read self-taught musician with a particular zeal for Beethoven. In 1951 he was examined by the medical staff of the Northern Command, Manchester, and excused national service on the grounds of unstable mental health. This was on the recommendation of Otto Shaw, who sponsored his former pupil as a desirable migrant to Australia. Before Red Hill Karl had had long periods of clinical treatment at home, and the two doctors involved corroborated Shaw's assessment that military service would provoke a recurrence of his old insecurities. Karl, who was twenty-one, duly emigrated to Australia in 1952 as a 'ten-pound pom' under an assisted-passage scheme operated by the Australian government to boost the country's population. He never returned to England. Had John's career as a concert pianist not taken him to Australia in the 1960s he would never have seen his brother again. As it was it would be twelve years before they were reunited. Their sister Pippa had gone out to New Zealand several years earlier to work as a psychiatric nurse at Kingseat Hospital, Auckland, before moving to Wellington and finally over to Australia. She had settled in Darwin, where she met her future husband.

There is a photograph of the fourteen-year-old John on holiday in Cornwall with his parents. They are standing in front of what looks like a mammoth dolmen, or burial chamber. White-haired Dorothy stands in the middle in a white dress, holding a black handbag and looking vastly older than her forty-eight years. On her right, in a jaunty cap and pale suit with open-neck shirt, holding a camera and wearing a pair of binoculars round his neck, stands Howard, looking for all the world like an elderly American tourist; while on her left, in a tightly buttoned black suit (probably his school uniform) with open-neck shirt and round-rimmed spectacles, stands goofy John under his mop of curly black hair. Looking more like their grandson than their son, he has the air of a cuckoo that has grown up to find itself inhabiting a reed warbler's nest.

The Manchester Grammar School had been quite a lonely place for John, being in musical exile. Nevertheless, it was this period of exile that shaped him as a musician – for it allowed him free rein to range over huge expanses of the repertoire, much of it esoteric, in a spirit of open-minded exploration. His seemingly infinite capacity to absorb music served him in excellent stead for these forays to the wilder shores of the keyboard literature. And where he encountered technical obstacles, it was up to him to find a way through. He may have developed some bad habits along the way, but in return he created a style and technique that were *sui generis* and tailor-made to his own physical and energetic requirements. This period of uninhibited musical reconnaissance also stimulated his development as a composer. Talking in 1988 for *The South Bank Show*, John reminisced about these early days:

When I was at Manchester Grammar School I got a lot of volumes of music from the Henry Watson music library, including some Alkan, the Busoni Concerto and also many of Ravel's works, and I suppose they influenced me in a number of childhood compositions which I wrote between eleven and seventeen, mainly sonatas and one or two shorter pieces.

When Marjory Wood crossed the Atlantic in the summer of 1952 she paid a visit to the Ogdons in Manchester. It was seven years since she had seen John and heard him at the piano. Having been through the childhood ritual of having his hands stretched to measure his span, John produced a manuscript book containing seven pieces he'd written for Marjory, three waltzes (in D minor, E major and E minor), a prelude, a *fantaisie macabre*, an intermezzo and – at twelve pages by far the longest piece – a sonata in C-sharp minor in the style of Rachmaninoff, which he played for her. There is a picture from this visit of John with Marjory, Howard, Pippa (over from Australia) and Marjory's daughter, and once again one is struck by the formality of John's attire. He is wearing a dark double-breasted suit with V-neck sweater and tie.

In June 1953, as he was preparing for his O and A levels, John took his scholarship exam at the RMCM. For his works by heart he chose Liszt's Ballade No. 2 in B minor and the opening movement of Beethoven's *Appassionata* Sonata, two large-scale virtuosic works. There was also a sight-reading test, which he rattled off with his usual aplomb. MGS still wanted John to stay on and try for Oxford – there seemed little doubt that he could have read English there to a very high standard and pursued an academic career had he so wished. The RMCM, however, was by now keen to have him back. 'How can we see he is not wasted?' asks the examiner. 'He is definitely talented and unusual.' He concludes by noting that Howard Ogdon will ask MGS if they can provide John with some sort of scholarship to the RMCM, while he himself will try the local council. There was clearly a lot of pressure on available awards. In the end, John was granted the Percy Heywood scholarship by the RMCM as well as a Lancashire County scholarship. Howard wrote to the principal of the RMCM to accept the award on John's behalf, devoting most of his letter to the subject of his breakdown, committal and escape and the costs of rehabilitation.

John, meanwhile, was back in his element.

Interlude

THE DRAMA OF THE
GIFTED CHILD

You can drive the devil out of your garden but you will find
him again in the garden of your son.

Johann Heinrich Pestalozzi

You could be forgiven for thinking that you were looking at a
picture of Piggy from *The Lord of the Flies* taken on the island
before things turned ugly. Actually it's a photograph of John Ogdon,
aged twelve or so, in a Boy Scouts uniform, khaki shirt and khaki
empire builders, grinning broadly under his unruly curls. He's wearing a pair of round-rimmed wire-frame glasses and is one of only two
boys in uniform; the others are in casual shorts and tops. There are
wigwam poles at their feet, and trees and hills are visible in the background. The image of Piggy is not altogether inappropriate – not
simply because of the physical likeness to Ogdon but also because he
is the guardian of the conch, the symbol of law and order that helps
maintain a standard of civilization among the stranded boys. The
conch is also a symbol of music and harmony. When it smashes Piggy
dies. Reared by an aunt, Piggy has an unparented way about him:
as if he comes from another planet – one without families – and for

all his faith in order and harmony he casts a dark shadow. The rotting pig's head covered in flies, put out to feed the Beast, is a grotesque image of Piggy himself, whose over-reliance on conventional auntly wisdom is all too liable to call forth the savagery he abhors.

From the moment Ogdon touched its keys the piano became a means of establishing order in his life, and of channelling some of the darker spirits that inhabited his childhood home. It was his conch. He, like Piggy, lacked the warmth of a loving relationship with his parents; instead his youthful ardour and affection were lavished on his chosen instrument. Its responses, unlike those of his parents, were predictable and harmonious, obedient to the touch. As for Liszt so for Ogdon, the piano grew to be his 'very self'. Ultimately, however, despite his huge psychological investment in it, this self was a projection, a magical, tinder-box self, a metaphor for something else. The piano became a bastion against the world, which made it progressively harder for John to relate to others. It cast a dark shadow of its own. The Grimm brothers' fairy tale *The Wonderful Musician*, in which a travelling minstrel lures animals through his playing then ties them up and goes on his way, leaving them in a fury, speaks to this rather deceptive and illusory quality to music. It seems to warn us that music – indeed, all art – can aid in repressing the instincts while appearing to give them voice. It provides a kind of magical assistance which nevertheless bypasses the true self and fails to bring healing. If relied on too heavily it can prove a cruel mirage. At its best art may be a bridge to truth, but it is not truth itself.

John, let us not forget, was a child of insanity. Born as Howard was plunging towards madness, he took the lightning stroke of his father's perverse inspiration. He also partook of the older man's traumatic rebirth by being made to share his name. It was as if the senior English master had marked John down for a special part in his own private soul-drama. Both Howard and Dorothy must have looked on John as a kind of redeemer born from the ashes of their despair. Dorothy no less than Howard seems to have been a creative spirit, fired with adventure and longing, who before she knew it found herself saddled with the burdens and responsibilities of running a family. This was the Cornish girl who at twenty had eloped from her Methodist father to marry an eccentric thinker and writer, and who gave birth to her first child before she came of age. She surely hadn't run away to find entrapment under the rod of another man! Appearing almost seven years after her last child, and at a time when her marriage had dried up, John was clearly not planned – at least not by human agency. He was a mysterious gift, quite different to the other offspring in looks and physique, and as his extraordinary talent began to manifest itself Dorothy must have wondered whether the madness of John Andrew Howard Ogdon Senior hadn't been transformed into the genius of John Andrew Howard Ogdon Junior.

As for John, what did he feel? He too must have wondered where he came from. Was he a changeling? Was his father a mad uncle? Howard disappeared when John was eighteen months old, yet even before this he was an alien soul barricaded behind his study door – more audible than visible, at most a figure in a long black gown glimpsed hurrying schoolwards of a morning or swooping down in a rage on one of the children. From a child's point of view there were few overt clues to his decline: the muttered imprecations or sudden violent gusts of Wagnerian passion (both heard from behind the study door) gave but slight body to the phantom. Then the study fell silent and the rows of tobacco-scented books and gramophone records resigned themselves to the monotonous gaze of Hubert the skull. Howard's sudden reappearances, with a male nurse in tow, only deepened the mystery of 'father'. In the Gothic novels that John relished, the hero or heroine seeks to discover what lies behind the locked door at the heart of the decrepit mansion. In John's case it was his father's study door, and what lay behind it was ultimately his own impounded soul. Instead of opening the locked door John turned away and sought refuge at the piano.

Mysteries, ghost stories, tales of vampires and the macabre: this was the literature which John devoured both as a child and in his maturity. It was around the house in great profusion, for Howard was himself a fan of all things Gothic. His fascination with the Brontë sisters, which became a big project for him in the 1950s, strongly communicated itself to John, and a lively element of the Gothic runs through *Jane Eyre* and *Wuthering Heights*. All these books are concerned with the repression of an early instinctual life force, often signified by a young girl who is either shut away or severely restrained. This feminine force in both men and women seems to symbolize the natural unfolding of the soul. When blocked, all sorts of obsessions and quirks of character take root. In John's case the delayed puberty is a particularly vivid and literal example of such an inhibition.

Significantly, the Gothic novel had its heyday during the madness of King George III, who attacked his eldest son by trying to smash his head against a wall. In this instance it was the father of the nation who was locked in his cabinet while the mystery and horror of his affliction seized the collective imagination. The Gothic novel was like the spike driven into the king's head to relieve the pressure of his oppressive thoughts. By following the path of John Ogdon's literary enthusiasms one can at least hold some sort of communion with his inner life and begin to understand the emotional labyrinth in which his soul wandered. The musical world he entered fulfilled the same function as Gothic fiction; it provided a mirror in which he could glimpse reflections of the demons that had usurped his life. The precedents are as old as human experience. Perseus, for instance, could not look directly at the Gorgon: he used his polished shield as a glass.

The piano was John's mirror. He hunched over it in what became a classic pose, as if peering intently into its depths. In its sound world he discerned the soul-flowering that is so rudely uprooted in the Gothic imagination, and heard an echo of his own soul singing from the depths. Yet however much he played, it was still only a tantalizing echo. Like Narcissus, he was spellbound by a reflection. The magic of his art may have drawn the animals from deep in the forest, but it always left them in a state of suspension. All too often it became a drug, a compulsion, rather than a means to the centre.

When John was a very young child sitting in front of the pianola while his mother got on with housework the tones and harmonies of the instrument replaced the maternal voice, creating a safe harbour and healing embrace. The piano became a surrogate mother. To begin with the relationship was entirely sonic. Later, when John learned to create the sounds himself, and felt the keys under his fingers, it became tactile as well. When he touched the keys he felt the mother's pulse in their vibrations. Bone for flesh, but so warm and tuneful that the loss was hardly felt. The strident tones of family disharmony were dissolved in the harmonious body of the piano.

John laid all his sorrows and joys at the altar of the keyboard; he watered it with his tears and sunned it with his smiles. In return it gave him great facility over itself, an exhilarating gift, and before he knew it a transfer had taken place: his soul had taken up its lodging under the shiny black rafters. The piano had become a proxy self, an external hard drive where all his feelings were stored. Until he plugged himself into its current he could often seem disengaged.

Of all the arts music is closest to the unconscious; by diving into its depths at such an early age John remained connected on a very deep level to the universal matrix; it gave him extraordinary powers of memory and imagination, but prevented any real differentiation and ego development. He remained relatively unformed on the level of personality. One thinks of Lancelot who, when his father fell in a swoon in fleeing his burning kingdom, was whisked away by the Lady of the Lake to her palace beneath the waters where he was brought up in the company of women and faery-like mermen and developed formidable skills. Lancelot, however, did not manage to attain the Grail; he was always pulled back into the regressive waters of the unconscious. John inhabited the same kind of underwater palace.

John was an inquisitive boy, thoughtful and affectionate, who learned from an early age to bury his feelings and cultivate his intellect. Naturally impressionable and wax-like (with a photographic memory), he always reflected what he thought others wanted to see and hear. Any attempt to understand John's psychology as a child must begin with the fact that he was a prodigy, with all the challenges common to that species. His parents didn't relate to him as a boy, but as a talent; and not being loved for himself meant that his ability to relate to others was atrophied. It was inevitable that his sense of self – as soon as it emerged – would be vested in his prodigious gift. As a child John experienced both parental deprivation (as a kid hungry for love) and overvaluing (as a prodigy). Approval was voiced for one thing only: the cultivation of his gift. This was a profoundly alienating experience. Even Marjory Wood, who showed him physical affection, responded first and foremost to John's genius. It was a confusing thing this genius, winning him 'love' yet preventing intimacy. Not being seen for who he was created a deep sense of isolation in John, making it hard for him to relate to children his own age. To keep the everyday world of shadows at bay a false or adapted self (in John's case, a super-placatory self) grew up around his genius. This was his 'yes, yes' self. John's deepest longing was to be accepted and loved for who he was as a person, but his only way of seeking this love was through his genius.

One can think of many other celebrated concert pianists who experienced similar personality problems to John's. Horowitz, for instance, was nervous and aloof and did not mix easily with people. He carried a deep sense of loneliness around with him. His eldest brother, Jacob, was killed as a youth in the Russian Revolution, while his other brother, George, was emotionally unstable and in and out of institutions. His father, Simeon, died in one of Stalin's labour camps. The pianist Eduardus Halim, who studied with Horowitz, described him as 'a sad man, happy only at the piano'.

When Howard finally returned home 'sane' in 1944 John was the little man of the house, his mother's companion, and probably felt crushed by this intruder with whom he did not have the strength to fight. His severe illness that summer may have been something of an Oedipal crisis, made doubly acute by the fact that he had never really known his father. At the age when a child begins to move away from the mother as sole care-giver and reaches out to the father for guidance in how to meet the world, there had been no father. In John's case that role was taken by Marjory Wood and her focus was almost entirely the piano. He remained caught in the maternal matrix.

As Bruno Bettelheim has convincingly shown, most fairy tales are about the challenges of growing up and separating from the parents. Witches and ogres are mothers and fathers who won't let go of their children, or else the fearful and over-dependent child's mental image of his or her omnipotent parents. The transition from oral fixation to phallic power is not the final step in a boy's passage to adulthood. He must find a deeper and more individual form of assertion and expression. In *Jack and the Beanstalk* Jack, having climbed the giant beanstalk, arrives at the house of an ogre and his wife. The ogre is out, so his wife gives Jack something to eat then hides him in the oven when they hear the fearsome giant returning. Here we see the child's Oedipal fear that he will not be a welcome presence when his father returns home from work. In order to challenge the power of the ogre-father and come into his own Jack must appropriate certain objects (a bag of gold, a hen that lays golden eggs and a magic harp that plays itself). The third time, as Jack is making off with the harp, the giant wakes and pursues him down the beanstalk, but his mother fetches him an axe and he manages to hew it down just in time, sending the ogre tumbling to his death. Now if we were to retell the story with young Jack Ogdon as the hero, things would turn out very differently – for he would have stayed in the ogre's house playing the magic harp and being fed by the ogre's wife. In other words, by not challenging the ogre he would have remained in the mother's world (in a state of oral fixation). This is essentially what happened. John kept his rage at his parents bottled up and failed to assert himself; in essence he gave up the struggle to achieve maturity. When he did lose his temper it erupted in sudden violent tantrums, a form of 'global' rage rather than individual self-assertion. He remained the prodigal child, winning the mother through his magical playing, but not gathering the will to defy the father.

4

NEW MUSIC MANCHESTER

In his sight-reading John got behind the notes. He was far, far more talented than any of us, and in that regard more talented than anyone I've ever known.

Sir Peter Maxwell Davies

John had led a very sheltered life before arriving at the Royal Manchester College of Music as a full-time student, and one suspects there had been no experience of alcohol, women or rock and roll. His drug of choice was the piano and his teenage kicks lay in offbeat music by abstruse composers such as Alkan and Moszkowski. Meanwhile Dorothy continued to feed him mountains of food – even supplying batches of honey butties to consume on the bus to college. Among his fellow students his pie-eating prowess quickly earned him the nickname 'Six-Pie Oggy'. He was a shambolic figure, widely remembered for his odd socks, trailing laces and ill-fitting undarned clothes. His signature garment was a huge battered black oilskin coat with a large ink stain on the left side, not unlike the foreskin cassock worn by the mincer on the *Pequod* in *Moby-Dick*. John did indeed resemble a great fish as he pushed his way through the double doors of the main entrance hall to the RMCM, his old leather music case bulging with scores.

The college that John was entering was rooted in the European Romantic tradition of Chopin, Liszt, Brahms and Tchaikovsky. Its founder, Sir Charles Hallé, the originator of the famous Manchester orchestra that bears his name, was born in Germany (as Karl Halle), where he studied under the composer Christian Rinck in Darmstadt. Later he moved to Paris, where he befriended Chopin, Berlioz and other leading composers. He was a fine pianist and conductor and earned his living through both when he moved to England in 1848. He was the first pianist to play the complete cycle of Beethoven's piano sonatas in England. When he established the Royal Manchester College of Music in 1893 it was the first full-scale English conservatory outside London. (Before that, students who decided against studying in London invariably chose the Continent.) Hallé became its first principal as well as the chief professor of pianoforte. Other members of the piano faculty included pupils of Clara Schumann and Anton Rubinstein. Hallé's pedagogic ambition for the RMCM was very clearly stated: he wanted to provide a comprehensive musical education that would make artists of its students.

Hallé died in 1895, just two years after founding the college, and was succeeded by the violinist Adolph Brodsky, to whom Tchaikovsky had dedicated his violin concerto. William Dayas, a pupil of Liszt, became the new head of piano. When he died unexpectedly he was replaced by Arthur Friedheim, a pupil of both Liszt and Anton Rubinstein, and the former's secretary for many years. His successor, the great Beethoven interpreter Wilhelm Backhaus, was himself succeeded by Egon Petri, whom Busoni considered his pianistic heir. So, far from being a provincial backwater, Manchester attracted notable musicians from the cultural heart of Europe.

When John arrived there in 1953 it was rather conservative in its musical outlook, and had turned its back on the Modernist movement – in particular the Second Viennese School of Schoenberg, Webern and Berg and its acolytes. Even Mahler was little appreciated. On the one hand its teachers paid homage to the native English lyrical tradition of Delius, Stanford, Vaughan Williams, Holst and Bax, which had its roots in folk and Church music, and on the other to Busoni, who had been something of a cult figure at the college since

Egon Petri had brought his music to Manchester in 1906. (The Henry Watson Music Library in Manchester, founded by the RMCM professor of that name, contained an unrivalled collection of Busoni scores.) Busoni, the pianist-composer *par excellence*, is impossible to pigeonhole, in part because he eschewed schools of thought and perceived no division between classical and modern, tonal and atonal. His study of microtonality led him to realize that major and minor tonalities can 'shimmer and coalesce indistinguishably'. Reflecting deeply on what had gone before and peering eagle-eyed into the future, his best work has a strongly visionary quality. He was in many ways the Ralph Waldo Emerson of music.

Busoni himself played many times in Manchester before his death in 1924, and Brodsky commissioned works from him. In the 1920s and 1930s several of the piano staff at RMCM had been pupils either of Busoni or of Egon Petri. Lucy Pierce, who joined the faculty in 1912, had been a Busoni pupil at both the Weimar and Vienna masterclasses, while Gordon Green and Claud Biggs had been pupils of Petri. All of them would have used Busoni's fingerings. Pierce taught Ronald Stevenson in the 1940s and it was Stevenson who was carrying the banner for Busoni at the college when the nine-year-old John Ogdon stole into his practice room to listen to the Busoni Concerto. Ogdon himself helped keep the flame alive in the 1950s, while he and Stevenson were largely responsible for the Busoni revival in Britain during the 1960s. When Ogdon died, the director of the Centro Studi Musicali Ferruccio Busoni in Empoli wrote that 'no other pianist has contributed as much as he did to the knowledge and understanding of this composer'.

According to Alexander Goehr, the two composition classes at the RMCM – those of Thomas Pitfield and Richard Hall – represented discrete, mutually exclusive worlds. The scorn in which the Hallites held the Pitfieldites is still fresh in Goehr's decades-later dismissal of Pitfield's group as 'a Nadia Boulanger class', and their compositions as 'sub-French'. They were, he says, admirers of Stravinsky and the French musical culture of Ravel and Debussy. (Pitfield's mentor had been Vaughan Williams.) The Hall group, on the other hand, were anti-Stravinsky and were attracted to the more theoretical and experimental composers of the Second Viennese School, as well as to figures such as Paul Hindemith and Olivier Messiaen. It was out of the Richard Hall class that the New Music Manchester group emerged, led by Goehr.

The group comprised students from both the RMCM and Manchester University. Alexander Goehr and Harrison Birtwistle were in Richard Hall's class, while Peter Maxwell Davies and Elgar Howarth studied under Humphrey Procter-Gregg (a pupil of Charles Stanford) at the university. They were joined by the cellist John Dow, who played in the Hallé orchestra, and John Ogdon, who was in Pitfield's composition class. All six men were composers but most of them kept their compositions to themselves. It was Goehr and Maxwell Davies, the king and crown prince respectively, who were the leading lights of the group. Both spoke German and read German literature, and both were linked into the Darmstadt School of Boulez, Stockhausen and company and closely followed its developments. They were fascinated by the twelve-tone music being composed in Germany and France by the European avant-garde and were always searching out innovative scores for performance at the college and university.

Sandy and Max, as they were known to their friends, were in boisterous rebellion against the establishment; Sandy in particular delighted in challenging the professors in his deep, baritone voice with its de-li-be-rate, slightly Continental enunciation. Middle class and cosmopolitan, he had had a different upbringing to his unsophisticated northern colleagues. His father, the conductor and composer Walter Goehr, had been born in Berlin (as had Sandy) and had studied under Arnold Schoenberg. Goehr senior indirectly influenced the group and approved of its activities. Sandy was very much the leader and demanded respect for his superior knowledge – and he did know more than the others by dint of the cultured surroundings of his youth and the scores and literature available to him at his father's home in Putney. He brought a middle-European awareness of the importance of not just Schoenberg but also the school of experimental composers who acknowledged the brainy Austrian as their guide. The other four members were somewhat in the shadow of Sandy and

moved towards compositions, such as the *Fantasia Contrappuntistica*, which were written as *absolute* music rather than music for this or that instrument or combination of instruments. In his essay *A New Aesthetic of Music* he wrote:

> Let us take thought, how music may be restored to its primitive, natural essence; let us free it from architectonic, acoustic and aesthetic dogmas; let it be pure invention and sentiment, in harmonies, in forms, in tone-colours [...] let Music be naught else than Nature mirrored by and reflected from the human breast.

It was from the purity of this musical spring that John drank. His quest to get behind the notes to what the composer was hearing in his mind owed much to Busoni's philosophy. His carefree attitude to musical fashions was due in part to Ronald Stevenson's influence. Stevenson, like Ogdon, harked back to the nineteenth- and early twentieth-century tradition of the pianist composer, and his independent stance and refusal to bow to the 'derriere-garde', as he called the avant-garde, was an inspiration to the younger man trying to find his voice as a composer. Stevenson's assessment of Busoni's uniqueness offers a profound clue as to why John might have been drawn to the Italian master:

> Busoni's music was the only music that expressed fear unto death and its opposite, serenity. These two things characterize the 20th century: the threat of total annihilation (nuclear war) and the crying need for peace. These qualities were uniquely in Busoni's music.

These poles of experience describe Howard Ogdon's journey from war trauma to Hatha yoga. John's literary obsessions (Melville, Poe, Golding) also bespeak a man who had inherited his father's 'fear unto death', through witnessing childhood violence, and who sought serenity through music. Another fellow student at the RMCM, composer and pianist Keith Cole, recalls that Edward Dent's biography of Busoni (a gift from Stevenson) made a deep impression on John, who began to model himself after the great man. Busoni never talked about his childhood but had an irascible, domineering father and an over-protective mother.

What John found at the RMCM was a new family of musician friends who helped him move out from under the shadow of his parents. John treated this new family with touching respect and affection, if not devotion, and overflowed with praise for his colleagues. On Peter Maxwell Davies' twenty-first birthday John presented him with the complete works of Heine in German. His letters to Max betray a youthful exuberance and are full of references to not just music but films and literature as well. He gives himself composite names made up of different composers, as when he signs a telegram 'Kaikhosru Boulez', and letters and envelopes are peppered with outrageous chords with extravagant markings (for example, 'for 5,000 trombones') or sudden dutiful shouts of joy, such as 'Viva Nova Musica Mancunipunttistica Alexandri Goehrii!' He even alludes to his address with Tolkeinian glee as 'the Ogboggeries'.

In his essay on Liszt's late piano music John expresses his high ideals of creative fellowship, and in the following words gives a premonition perhaps of his own social fate: 'Both Melville and Liszt engaged in the dangerous ideal of total artistic friendship; in both cases these were at first fruitful, but later disappointing.' The friendships referred to were with Nathaniel Hawthorne and Richard Wagner respectively, and John describes them as descending from soul-sharing to watchful calculation. The one quality in John which struck his friends most forcefully was his humility, which Stevenson described as 'all but Franciscan'. It is clearly a quality that he valued in others, too, as this startling passage from the coda to his Liszt essay makes clear:

> [Liszt's] music shows an avant-garde attitude to the problems of composing which was without parallel in the nineteenth century. But what I think I admire most about the aged Liszt is his continuing humility in the face of so splendid an achievement. He lived out his extraordinary life as if guided by the words that William Golding was to write eighty years later: 'There's a kinship among men who have sat by a dying fire and measured the worth of their life by it.'

The probing mystery of the last sentence is quintessential Ogdon. His ideals of total friendship and humility are perhaps the most brilliant and unexpected jewels of a highly complex and self-enguarded soul.

In a letter of the time Dorothy Ogdon described her son as 'about six feet and very big' (adding that he looked good in his dress suit). His handshake, on the other hand, was like a lettuce leaf (it wilted in yours) and his voice was sing-song and soft, with its own shy music. Gentle, kind and vulnerable though he was – a kind of simpleton on some levels – there was no doubting that you were in the presence of a penetrating intellect. Keith Cole told John that he reminded him of Prince Myshkin, the hero of Dostoyevsky's *The Idiot*. He was thinking principally of the prince's modesty and simplicity, though he might have added innocence, charity and unbounded perception to the list. John got himself a copy of the book and read it. The next time he saw Keith, he said, 'You paid me a compliment, didn't you?'

John carried an aura of loneliness, but in the right company he could come alive and give voice to a ribald sense of humour. On the other hand he could just sit there with a slight frown on his face, and just when everyone thought he'd nodded off he'd come up with an insight into music or literature that would set the whole conversation on its ear and have everyone racing to catch up with his thought processes. To those unused to John's sudden interventions, what he said could appear a complete non-sequitur. The wheels of thought were always turning, and at a great depth.

Even in this new family John was the baby. When he arrived at the RMCM he was sixteen, while most of the others were eighteen or nineteen; Sandy Goehr, the only one of them with a girlfriend, was twenty-one. Nevertheless John was at the centre of the matrix because it was principally through him that the new music was heard and tested. In the famous photograph of the group John is in the centre in an armchair while the others are on the floor around him. All are touching him; it is as if he is the sun and they are his satellites.

New Music Manchester was in the business of cocking a snook at the professors. There was, according to Alexander Goehr, a great deal of posturing and playacting, but John was not sophisticated enough to playact. They made literature as well as music their province, and encouraged each other in their reading of modernist works. Max was mad keen on James Joyce's *Ulysses*, and in particular fascinated by the way he wrote in fugue form, for example in the chapter entitled 'Sirens'. Soon they were all reading and studying it, and in their daily perambulations across Manchester imagined that they were walking through the slums of Dublin. 'Being James Joyce when we weren't being Schoenberg was all part of the act,' says Goehr. In a letter to Max, John ends with a jaunty 'Saluti', before signing himself 'Benven-uto Giovanni OgBoschysses' (with nods in the direction of Busoni, Palestrina and Joyce). John also followed his own literary star and in one letter he sends Harry to the library to get him Charles Williams' *Shadows of Ecstasy* and Frederick Rolfe's *Hadrian the Seventh*.

The group's unofficial headquarters was Sandy Goehr's flat in Withington, to the south of the city. John, Max and Gary still lived at home and Harry, whose father was a farmer in Accrington, was peri-patetic, so Sandy was the only one with his own place. He and his artist girlfriend, Audrey Baker (later his wife), were generous hosts, and she would cook supper for everyone. They would eat and drink a good deal and sit up into the early hours (which sometimes meant till dawn) talking about music and literature. John occasionally seemed a little puzzled by what was going on, though he took everything in. Very much his own man in a stealthy way, his head, according to Max, was full of rather chaotic musical ideas. John was gloriously unrefined in his table manners and was quite capable of picking up a whole fish and putting it in his mouth. He would sometimes get drunk (which he couldn't do at home) and end up staying the night. He was rather like the tiger who came to tea – only he didn't disappear into the night once he'd eaten and drunk everything in the flat. The others would roll him up in a carpet, where he'd sleep until they unrolled him again the following morning; then off he'd amble towards college, his brain still teeming with impertinent thought.

John was in many ways a lovable oaf in the eyes of his fellows, a bit of a grunter, always nodding, always agreeing with everything you said, yet curiously stubborn. Harrison Birtwistle recalls that there was a little Jewish restaurant in Salford called Black's, which sold salt-beef sandwiches with Vimto or black tea served in glasses. Whenever he went there with John, John would ask for a pork pie. Harry tried to explain to him that the Jews didn't eat pork, but to no avail. No sooner had they got through the door than John would turn to him and say, 'D'you think they'll have a pork pie?' Harry, who was a bit of a dresser in those days and wore a fishing fly in his hat, was appalled by John's 'terrible' clothes and advised him on where to get a suit cut. The violinist Rodney Friend's father, who was a tailor in Bradford, pitched in and made clothes for John when he came to stay at their house. Not even John's concert attire was guaranteed to offer sartorial respectability. On one occasion the whole NMM group went over to Sheffield to hear John play the Tchaikovsky First Piano Concerto with the Hallé under George Weldon. John shuffled onto the stage looking a bit startled. He sat down and seemed preoccupied with his trousers. For a moment it looked as though he wasn't going to come in with those crashing opening chords. He did, though, and the performance was a great success. They all went backstage to congratulate him and he said, 'Bloody 'ell, I sat down and looked down and I'd left m'flies wide open! Oh well, at least I knocked three minutes off Monique de La Bruchollerie's performance.'

In the autumn of 1956 the Ogdons moved from Mardale Crescent to a two-up two-down on the Bury New Road, the main road connecting Manchester to Bury. Their new house was in Besses o' th' Barn, an area of Whitefield, to the northwest of Prestwich. Here they were closer to Stand Grammar, Howard's workplace. Both Howard and Dorothy had been suffering from heart problems and, although Howard was still only in his mid-fifties, Dorothy had talked the previous year of the unlikelihood of their moving because old age was against him. The house was very small, semi-detached – like a council house – and neither Howard nor Dorothy were keen on it. Dorothy no longer worked outside the house, but helped the assiduous Howard (whom she described as 'a glutton for work') by typing and retyping his thesis on the Brontës, which was the centrepiece of an MA in psychology he was taking at Liverpool University. She also had to count his nouns, verbs, pronouns, adjectives and other parts of speech for four hours a day! He still had his sanctuary downstairs, but that now had to compete with John's music room, which was piled high with scores and books alongside the upright piano with its broken strings. Dorothy and Howard were generous hosts to John's friends from New Music Manchester, and John later recalled a long conversation over tea between Howard and Sandy Goehr on the subject of Jung's *Psychology of the Unconscious*.

Rodney Friend became a good friend of John's when he arrived at the RMCM in 1956 aged fifteen. He remembers having to wander through teetering columns of novels in order to reach the kitchen, where Dorothy kept her abode and sanity – marooned as she was between the two strange geniuses that governed her life. John, who was frequently late into college, would spend his mornings in bed reading the novels. Friend occasionally spent the weekends at John's place and had cause to discover that both John and his father were night owls. Friend woke up one night in the early hours and, hearing strange noises downstairs, sat bolt upright in bed. Thinking there had been a break-in, he crept across to John's room to find him sitting up in bed reading scores. 'John, what the hell's going on?' he said. 'You've got a burglar downstairs.' 'Oh no,' replied John, barely looking up, 'that's just Dad channelling.' Apparently Howard would chant and go into a trance and had devised a special method using tape recorders that snapped him out of it at just the right moment. 'I was too young at the time to absorb this craziness,' says Friend. 'It was all too much for an ordinary Jewish boy from Leeds!' In the mornings everyone would be downstairs eating stacks of toast and Marmite. Somehow Dorothy Ogdon remained tranquil, at least on the surface. She was, according to Friend, 'very calm and worshipped John in a very calm way', though her letters reveal that she was worried he was trying to do too much too quickly.

John's fellow students all remember his passion for films. When John Huston's *Moby Dick* came out in the summer of 1956, starring Gregory Peck as Captain Ahab, John went to see it every day that it was playing. He also read the book about seven times that week. It became a total obsession with him. John perhaps identified Captain Ahab with his father, Howard, for Howard's neurotic, all-consuming search for the roots of his insanity mirrored Ahab's monomaniacal quest for the White Whale. Disturbingly, John himself was being drawn into the more obsessional corners of his father's psychology and used to talk a good deal about Howard's book. John was also very keen on Westerns and after he'd seen a film would play variations on the theme music. Harrison Birtwistle remembers John doing just that after they'd seen *The Sheepman* (with Glenn Ford and Shirley MacLaine). The films had double bills and were continuous, so John and Harry would often go in to the cinema at 1 p.m. and not emerge until seven thirty or eight, having seen four movies in a row. *High Noon* with Gary Cooper and *Shane* with Alan Ladd, both released in the early 1950s, were particular favourites with John and continued to delight him decades later.

John was sent with Rodney Friend to study violin sonatas with the RMCM's former principal R. J. Forbes, who had played with Kreisler, Ysaÿe and other great violinists. With the aid of the college they were booked for concerts locally, mainly in small towns in Lancashire and Cheshire, receiving the tidy sum of two guineas each plus bus or train fare. John was 'bonkers keen' on the Busoni E-minor sonata, which they played everywhere. On one occasion, well remembered by Friend, they arrived at the venue to find that John had forgotten to bring the piano parts. 'What's on the programme, Rod?' he asked Friend. It was the Brahms D-minor sonata, Bartók's *Romanian Dances* and Paganini's *Le Streghe*. 'Oh, I know them,' said John, 'we played them a month ago' – and he performed them all faultlessly. They basically played what they wanted, and in most of the concerts there was a mixture of solo piano pieces and violin sonatas. John would usually play solo for the first half, and that could go on for ninety minutes! 'Sometimes I wouldn't get a go until late on,' says Friend. John was a fan of the Szymanowski First Violin Concerto and convinced Friend that it was a great piece. His musical enthusiasms were difficult to resist.

Like the others, Friend was in awe of John's gifts, especially his phenomenal ability to learn and perform a piece after a single run-through:

I had never seen anything like it. It was awesome, frightening. Whether it was a Mahler symphony or a Bartók quartet he could read and reduce it at sight. He was a lonely boy, a genius, around whom there was this halo of tragedy. He was physically unattractive, but when he sat down at the piano and that brain kicked into gear, he became one of the most magnificent creatures on this earth. It was too much to deal with almost. And yet he seemed totally unaware of his own talent.

Karl Ogdon's name kept cropping up on Friend's visits to John. He was aware that there was this brother in Australia, the black sheep of the family, who had gone to live with the Aborigines to learn their music. John was fascinated with Karl and it was obvious that he loved him as well as followed his life with keen interest.

In 1955, when John was eighteen, Peter Maxwell Davies had stumbled across one of a limited edition of hand-printed watermarked copies of Sorabji's *Opus Clavicembalisticum* on a barrow in front of a second-hand bookstall in Shudehill, Manchester. The copy was No. 19 of 23 and had originally been given by the composer to the work's dedicatee, Hugh MacDiarmid. The signatures of both men graced the frontispiece. It cost one pound, a princely sum for a student in those days. It was a rare find and Max, having bought it, went straight to the Ogdon home in Prestwich and presented it to his brilliant young friend. John took it, sat down at the piano and sight-read the whole thing from start to finish! It was a stunned Maxwell Davies who wandered out into the night some four hours later. 'The music blazed from the printed page,' Ogdon later wrote.

Although none of his Manchester colleagues shared his enthusiasm, John was immediately hooked. On the back of one letter to Max, John wrote his name as 'K. S. Sorabji'; on another he gave the following address:

77 Bury New Road,
Whitefield,
Nr. Manchester,
In the middle of primeval slimy oozy ogre-infested vampire-ridden
Splogoghaunted Sorabjicountry.

John's fetish for Sorabji had its roots in his vision of the Parsi composer as the spiritual heir of Busoni. John, who described Busoni's *Fantasia Contrappuntistica* as the 'geodesic statement' of *Opus Clavicembalisticum*, possessed an inborn affinity for Sorabji's complex, super-virtuosic music. It certainly influenced his own compositional art, which according to Max was, in those early days at least, 'always rather chaotic'. (Goehr described it more impishly as consisting of 'masses of dissonances alternating with Hymns Ancient & Modern in F sharp'.) John loved the moderns who were without any faddish sense of being modern, who sought the grail of a new transcendent tonality and were rooted in the nineteenth-century Romantic tradition: composers such as Alkan, Busoni, Scriabin, Szymanowski, Reger, van Dieren, Sorabji, Medtner and Stevenson. What mattered to Ogdon was not innovation but the quality of the musical ideas – the imagination – though as a young man he was naturally attracted to pieces that challenged his fabulous technique. Sorabji did that of course, but he did more. He drew John into his solipsistic world. As Alexander Goehr has wryly remarked, 'Max didn't do John a good turn by giving him the Sorabji score.' In a letter of 8 August 1955 John wrote to Max, 'I want to write a piano concerto to really work out all my virtuoso instincts ONCE in a fantastic 200-page Piano Concerto. After that I could settle down to a life of profound and devotional simplicity!!!'

Elgar Howarth remembers that a parcel for John arrived at the college from Germany one morning in a cylinder. He opened it in front of a group of students to find a sonata-length fantasie for piano by a young German composer called Elmer Seidel, a pupil of Messiaen. Alexander Goehr had got to know Seidel in Darmstadt and had asked him to send it to John. 'I'll go and read it through,' he said excitedly, and Elgar went along to turn pages for him. It was a ferociously convoluted work, with certain sections written on four staves. But John played it through as if it was *Chopsticks*. 'Although the music was all over the piano,' says Howarth, 'his hands were always in the correct place.'

John played everything but that didn't mean he liked everything. One afternoon Peter Maxwell Davies and Sandy Goehr were sitting at a piano in the Ducie Street building of the RMCM trying to make head or tail of the Boulez Second Sonata for piano – a huge, complex piece and very accomplished – and not making much progress, when in blundered John in his inimitable manner and with an 'Ooh, what's this?' pushed them aside and sight-read the piece with no problem whatever. It's a four-movement work lasting about thirty minutes, and horrendously difficult to read. (Yvonne Loriod burst into tears when faced with the prospect of performing it.) When John had finished Sandy said, 'That was extraordinary. My father could get you a good date in London to play that in public,' to which John replied, 'I don't want to play that. I don't like it.' Undeterred, they decided they would programme it at a Manchester University concert. The professor there, Humphrey Procter-Gregg, insisted on privately auditioning everything that was to be played in his concert hall. So the three cavaliers duly trooped down to his office, where John was seated at the piano and the score propped up for him. Procter-Gregg almost had a fainting fit as Oggo sweated his way through the heretical score, for this was music way outside his comfort zone. In the silence that succeeded the final note, John looked round with a frown and said, 'Hmm, it's a funny piece.'

That particular concert didn't take place, but another provides a similar illustration of John Ogdon's unconditional musical self-belief. One Wednesday morning the pianist David Wilde was chatting with John in the college hall when in walked Max with a large score under his arm and an anxious look on his face. He came straight up to them and asked if either of them knew Messiaen's *Vingt Regards sur L'Enfant-Jésus*, as the guest pianist for Friday's Modern Music Society concert had pulled out at the last moment. Neither of them knew it, but without even looking at the score John said, 'I'll play it.' 'But don't you want to see it first?' asked Max. 'No, it'll be OK,' said John. He knew he could play it no matter what was written on the page. So in two and a half days he learned one of the most testing pieces ever written for piano. *Vingt Regards* is more than a piece: it's an entire piano cycle, comprising twenty pieces and lasting over two hours. Alex Ross has described it as an 'immense sacred landscape'. More than simply an evocation of the birth of Jesus, it probes the symbolic and metaphysical essence of Christianity, its emotional language ranging from the exaltedly devotional to the surreal.

By far the biggest NMM concert in terms of publicity and all-round notoriety was at the Arts Council drawing room in London on 9 January 1956. The programme consisted of Anton Webern's Piano Variations, Op. 27, Alexander Goehr's Fantasias for piano and clarinet, Op. 3, Nikos Skalkottas's Sonatina for piano and *Tender Melody* for cello and piano, Peter Maxwell Davies' Sonata for trumpet and piano, Op.1, Elmer Seidel's Fantasie for piano, and Richard Hall's Sonata for cello and piano. As required, Harrison Birtwistle played the clarinet, John Dow the cello and Elgar Howarth the trumpet. John, though, played in every single piece (including three solos), and was described by Donald Mitchell in the *Musical Times* as 'omniscient' and 'a pianist of exceptional gifts'. He was still only eighteen. The reviewer didn't care for the new pieces brought from Manchester, though he had kind things to say about Goehr's fantasias. Max's piece was considered too fierce for the drawing room, while Seidel's fantasie was lambasted as 'a fashionable piece of primitivity without much to commend it but for a certain hysterical dynamism'. A critic from one of the major newspapers wrote, 'If London does tomorrow what Manchester is doing today, God help us!' The concert certainly created a hubbub in the London classical music world. If the reviews are anything to go by it was John, rather than the new composers, who made the greatest impression.

The young Manchester Turks played their Arts Council programme for Walter Goehr in his Putney drawing room. When it came to the Seidel fantasie John threw himself over the keys as if he was stirring half a dozen saucepans at once on a scalding-hot stove, sweat spraying from his furrowed brow, while his host sat in stony silence. At the end of it Goehr senior stood up and said, 'Does he spell Fantasie with an "F" or a "Ph"?' and walked out. In a letter to Max the previous December, before he'd seen the score, John wrote that both Sandy and Harry considered the Seidel piece 'simply magnificent, super-Messiaen', while John himself paid tribute to Richard Hall as the spiritual father of their new music revival. 'We will show some people yet,' he bubbles over, 'that New Music will not be shut out indefinitely by obscurantist philistinism!'

Shortly after the London concert John's piano teacher Claud Biggs counselled him not to play that sort of music because it could be bad for his career. But it was not the music that had drawn John in (according to Max, he would play atonal music under sufferance, if Sandy Goehr had a word with him), but the artistic camaraderie. John was largely defiant to begin with, but by the spring of 1957 he was refusing the opportunity to play Max's trumpet sonata at the York Festival and at Dartington, leaving Max himself to play the piano part. In a letter of 13 April 1957 John wrote to Max:

> After much thought I have come to the conclusion that I must withdraw from 'New Music Manchester' [...] partly because I am very much behind in the matter of building up a repertoire, to which I feel I must devote more time, and partly because I now basically feel myself in disagreement with the policy and aims of the group. I have written to Sandy telling him of my decision. There are also personal reasons for it of which you may not be entirely unaware.

The customary sign-off 'love, John' is now 'yours sincerely, John'. The personal reasons alluded to may have involved a falling out with Sandy Goehr: it's clear from John's next letter to Max that Sandy had accused John of withdrawing 'dishonourably' from the York concert, but John, who had given three months' notice, begs to differ. He has written to Sandy explaining his position. 'I hope he sees what I am getting at,' he writes to Max. 'Somehow, although I tried to put him right (to my mind) as regards his notions that I am against him in some mean way, I don't think he will.' Max was really the driving force behind NMM at this late stage, and John may also have been feeling some resentment towards him. According to Goehr, Max was a martinet-cum-medieval fascist in his early twenties and soon ran NMM into the ground. He and John would give concerts at Stockport and the like, following which John – having played everything on the programme – would be tired, but Max would insist that they walk the several miles home instead of getting a taxi.

If John was omniscient he was also omnipresent, being the accompanist for nearly everyone's examinations at the RMCM – no matter what instrument they played. Predictably, he was still a regular at Forsyth Brothers on Deansgate, which had been selling sheet music for almost a century. He rarely bought anything, however; he was known to go in, look through a score, then hurry back to college to play it, the music already secure in his note-perfect mind.

Emmie Tillett of Ibbs & Tillett, the foremost musical agency in the world at that time, had begun to take an interest in John and was helping arrange a period of study abroad. Her interest would no doubt have helped focus his mind on his professional life and the need to develop his classical repertoire. She and the college were now casting around for teachers of the highest repute with whom John could continue his studies; he had already auditioned for Solomon, who had given his opinion that John was destined for an international career. In the summer of 1957 he gave his first BBC broadcast, for the North of England Home Service, a brief recital of works by Rachmaninoff and Liszt for which he was paid seven guineas, and he was now in demand for recitals at local music clubs. His performance of Beethoven's *Hammerklavier* Sonata at a student concert at the RMCM in March 1956 received a glowing review in the *Manchester Guardian*, and is still remembered by fellow students today.

There had been another jolt from the outside world in May 1956 when John took part in the prestigious Queen Elisabeth International Competition in Brussels. In a letter to Max barely a week beforehand he is talking about the possibility of winning and asking Max to get some scores out of the library for him: works by Satie, van Dieren, Sibelius, Nielsen and Busoni. There were almost seventy entrants in what was to prove one of the most talented competitions ever held. If John was nervous he certainly didn't show it, and performed with his usual conviction. In the first round he played Handel's Suite No. 6; Chopin's Etude in A minor, Op.25, No. 11; Liszt's Etude *Ab Irato*; Debussy's Etude in Thirds; and Balakirev's *Islamey*. His playing of the virtuoso pieces caused a sensation among both audience and critics, but he came unstuck in the Handel and there was a general feeling that he tended to play too fast. He was unhappy about the Handel himself and later wrote to Max that he had never played it so badly. He had, he wrote, missed notes and mordents 'owing largely to a rather stiff piano'. He ends the letter, 'God damn Handel, God bless Balakirev (and John).'

Just twenty-four entrants would remain for the second round. John's choices included Liszt's *Dante* and B-minor sonatas; Beethoven's *Hammerklavier* Sonata; Brahms's Paganini Variations, Book 1; and Alkan's Etude for the left hand, Op. 76, No. 1 (plus compulsory works by Bach and two Belgian composers, Jongen and Franck) – a mammoth virtuoso feast! For the finals he chose the Brahms D-minor concerto. He wrote urgently to Max right after the first round, asking him to get the Alkan out of the Henry Watson library and send it on to him, as it occurred to him that he ought to have the music there. But, alas, he didn't make it through. John had also written to his mother between the first two rounds, expressing his unqualified admiration for an eighteen-year-old Russian pianist, Vladimir Ashkenazy, who he said was 'in a class apart'. He wishes he wasn't in the same competition as him, but wouldn't have missed hearing him play. He calls him 'a great master' and compares him with Dinu Lipatti.

John wrote to Max as soon as he heard the news that he'd been knocked out, complaining how unfair it all was. In his letter he talked openly of corruption, wondering how on earth five Belgians managed to get through, as well as an Austrian (Hans Graf) who'd had two 'thundering big memory lapses' in the Handel. Then there was a Japanese girl who *murdered* the *Mazeppa* Etude. 'What Liszt – my well-beloved Liszt – would have said I do not know,' he writes. Expressions of disbelief are scattered liberally through the letter. 'As you see I am a very bad loser,' he moans, '*unless* I am genuinely (without false modesty) not so talented as I thought.' He was as quick to praise as he was to damn, however, and was indignant that the 'superbly musical' Florence Margue-Wong did not get through. He found a kindred spirit in the Polish pianist Andrzej Czajkowski, to whom he wrote a letter of congratulations praising his performance of the Beethoven Op. 109 sonata in the second round, which opened his eyes to much in it that he'd not seen before; Busoni's Sonatina Seconda and Alexander Goehr's piano sonata were enclosed for his perusal. The top six prize-winners from Brussels that year read like a *Who's Who* of distinguished concert pianists: first, Vladimir

Ashkenazy (USSR); second, John Browning (USA); third, Andrzej Czajkowski (Poland); fourth, Cécile Ousset (France); fifth, Lazar Berman (USSR); and sixth, Tamas Vasary (Hungary).

There must have been some soul-searching when John returned to Manchester. Brussels had opened a window on the world in which he would have to compete if he was to fulfil his ambitions as a pianist – and it was a world that provided much more rigorous training than Manchester had proved capable of doing. John's teachers at the RMCM were nervous of spoiling his natural gifts and for the most part, therefore, neglected to tame his excesses. They may also have been rather in awe of his talent. Claud Biggs, a Bach and Scarlatti expert who even at the age of seventy could play Bach's 48 Preludes and Fugues from memory, declared that John played octaves faster than Horowitz. One fellow student recalls Biggs sitting in the concert hall listening to John playing Alkan's Etude for the left hand, music which had been forgotten for 100 years, and saying to everybody: 'How does he do it? I don't know how he does it!' In his report of June 1956 Biggs wrote of John, 'He is a delight to teach as he possesses that modesty and power of self-criticism which so often attends real genius [...] He is already equipped as a solo performer of a very high order.' John had a gigantic talent that seemed to exceed the possible – but if you listened carefully his playing was all over the place, hopelessly undisciplined. The question was where to start. No one wanted to take away what he had, but something had to be done.

Not only had NMM taken John off his path as a concert pianist, but he was also no longer finding it a safe and pleasant environment in which to explore and exchange ideas on composition. Though loath to admit it, he had felt hectored and browbeaten by the leading lights of the group and out of tune with their often cliquey and dogmatic approach to music. He felt much safer with students such as Keith Cole, Gerald Hine and David Wilde. He also admired David Ellis, who organized the Christmas parties at the college, John McCabe, and the Wigan-born composer Hugh Wood. Cole was a younger composition student who John would search out at the beginning of each term, asking for his timetable. He would always want to see what Keith had written and used to experiment along the same lines. They had discussions about serialism, a largely cerebral technique that they both rejected because of the lack of creative control. In his end-of-year report for 1956 Thomas Pitfield wrote that Ogdon composed almost exclusively for the piano and that he felt his range was not being extended in the orchestral or vocal realms. 'Composes with both relative ease and a sense of emotional liberation,' he commented by way of conclusion.

David Wilde, a former pupil of Solomon, had been considered the RMCM's pianistic star when he went off to do his two years of national service in 1953. When he returned in September 1955 for a refresher course he found that a new prodigy, in the form of John Ogdon, had stepped into his shoes. All talk at the college was now of John. Wilde found it hard not to like his usurper, whose awkwardness and modesty were the perfect foil for his enviable talent. John, he says, was a fascinating conversationalist late at night with a glass of wine in his hand; the rest of the time he was just very nice and very quiet and agreed with everything you said. He invited John to his twenty-first birthday party in Manchester. When John arrived he saw the score of Schoenberg's melodrama *Ode to Napoleon* on the piano and said, 'Is it a good piece?' He then sat down and reduced it at sight for two hands. When he'd finished he looked shyly around and said quietly, 'Yes, it is a good piece.'

John graduated in July 1957, making off with all the prizes – including the Dayas gold medal for pianoforte and his ARMCM, again with gold medal. He was still very much under the wing of the college, however; and, having been deemed unfit for national service by the medical board, was now free to search out new teachers, either in England or abroad. Though he was assisted by Emmie Tillett and Frederic Cox it was no easy task, for since the war the recognized international teachers had, as Cox lamented, 'been scattered to the four winds'. Many had ended up in the USA. They considered Marcel Ciampi in Paris, Bruno Seidlhofer at the Musikakademie in Vienna and Friedrich Wührer in Mannheim (Wührer had been an associate of the Second Viennese School and had founded the International Society for Contemporary Music in Vienna). Ogdon himself was strongly in favour of Ciampi until it was discovered that Egon Petri had returned to Europe from California and was teaching at the Basel Conservatory of Music. All agreed that he must be the first choice and John was over the moon at the prospect. Petri, however, had been let down by the conservatory (the masterclass he'd been promised hadn't materialized) and was set to return to America within a couple of months; he could squeeze John in for only six weeks of private lessons at his apartment. It was still considered worthwhile and, with the necessary money raised from foundations and scholarships, John was soon installed at the Hotel Baslerhof. Later he stayed with Madame Ganz, the niece of Rudolph Ganz, who had been a pupil of Busoni in Berlin and to whom Ravel dedicated *Scarbo*. In a letter to Max, who was coming to stay with him over Christmas, John wrote, 'the woman who owns this flat is away so we can have the free run of the place, which includes a good Blüthner grand which she has kindly let me use – I have gone very lightly on it so far, but God knows what'll happen when she's away.' Madame Ganz was a member of the International Society for New Music and got John free tickets for three Schoenberg concerts. He was impressed with much of the music, but the *Ode to Napoleon*, which he had thought a marvellous piece when he sight-read it at David Wilde's party, was a big disappointment in performance. He had seen 'all sorts of fantastic canons and counterpoints' which were nowhere to be heard in concert.

It's not known how John felt about being alone in a foreign town for the first time, but Dorothy certainly felt his absence. She wrote to Marjory Wood, 'We shall miss him terribly of course – he has been such a source of joy and pride to us, and is such a good companion.' John probably didn't mind in the least. With music as his passport he would have flown to the moon, providing there was something there resembling a piano. We know that he was charmed by the seventy-six-year-old Egon Petri, who insisted on showing him around Basel the day after he arrived and allowed him to practise at his apartment. He was equally generous with his lessons, which sometimes ran to three hours. Petri, like John, was a champion of Alkan and an accomplished composer. His interpretations of Busoni naturally carried enormous authority. He was greatly admired in Russia, where he had been the first Western musician to perform after the Revolution.

John studied the Busoni Concerto with Petri, who had given the English premiere in 1909 under the baton of Busoni himself. In a letter to Sir Adrian Boult, once he had returned to America, Petri couldn't help mentioning the pupil from Manchester whom he'd just taught: 'He is really astonishing, quite a pianistic genius and only 20 years old. He played the "Concerto" absolutely faultlessly with the greatest naturalness and ease, so that I hardly had anything to say or criticize [...] he should make a name for himself very soon.' John did not take the score of the Concerto to Petri: he had memorized it; and when Petri stopped him he was astonished to see that John could start again in the middle of a demisemiquaver. With Petri John also studied the *Hammerklavier* Sonata, the Busoni Sonatina Seconda and Elegies, the Brahms Paganini Variations, Liszt's *Dante* Sonata and Mephisto Waltz and a number of Chopin studies. Petri's principal criticisms were the excessive speed of John's playing (especially in the Mephisto Waltz) and a lack of precision and clarity in finger work, including a tendency to flag at the end of phrases. John was worried that he came hopelessly unstuck in the Chopin studies, and felt that they contained 'the crux' of his finger weakness. In a letter to Max on his return to England, he wrote:

> One curious result of the lessons [with Petri] is that I have become very interested in technical exercises, as an indirect result of Petri's close watch on economy of hand movement, finger independence and so forth. It is indirect, because as I told you he is much against technical exercises – I feel, with discrimination and used for weaknesses, it should be alright though.

Later in the letter John confesses to feeling very depressed (despite doing pretty well materially) and spiritually he wonders if he has lost or is losing what depth he had. 'At the moment I feel rather like throwing it up and trying to go on the music halls as the man who broke the octave barrier or something of that sort,' he adds wryly.

John's life in Basel was focused entirely on his music, and absorbed as he was in it he lived a life of simple, almost monastic routine. When not practising or discovering new scores (he raves, for instance, about Tausig's transcription of *The Ride of the Valkyries*), he foraged for food. 'Bread is cheap here,' he wrote to Max, 'so I am afraid I eat bread.' Butter was too expensive, but he did have honey, milk and eggs. In his letters to Max John fails to mention one very important meeting he had in Basel. It was a chance encounter but would prove to be one of the more enduring and significant friendships of his life. John used to practise in a poky little room above one of the music shops in town. One morning he was playing his own cadenza for the Beethoven Third Piano Concerto and had overrun his time when a fellow student of Petri's arrived to use the room. John apologized and was about to get up when the tall, dark-haired, sombre-eyed young man, who spoke English with an upper-class accent, gestured to him to continue playing. He played Liszt's Mephisto Waltz and then anything the stranger asked him to play. The young man was Alexander Charles Robert Vane-Tempest-Stewart, the Ninth Marquess of Londonderry, known as 'Alistair', and an exact contemporary of John's. He was also Earl of Londonderry, Earl Vane, Viscount Castlereagh, Viscount Seaham of Seaham, Baron Londonderry and Baron Stewart of Stewart's Court and Ballylawn – not that either of them cared a fig for all of that. Alistair was so fascinated by John's playing that he just kept asking him to play the next thing that came into his head. 'I had never seen real virtuosity up close before,' he says. 'I was a piano buff, not a serious student like John. My talent was in my head, not my fingers.'

Alistair rescued John from his bread and honey, and in the coffee houses of Basel they discovered a shared interest in jazz and horror movies. For the most part Alistair found John to be 'Mr Taciturn' – though when he did talk his father's ideas and writings were often on his lips, and it wasn't long after their return to England before Alistair was reading a copy of *The Kingdom of the Lost* and even found himself corresponding with Howard about it. Alistair's own life had been marred by tragedy from an early age. He had been a sensitive, modest, slightly reclusive child who developed a stutter and found comfort in music and books. His mother contracted cancer of the mouth and died when he was fourteen (her illness was kept a secret from the children); following her death his father fell into a deep, alcohol-fuelled depression, succumbing to liver failure four years later. Alistair would also suffer bouts of depression throughout his life, locking himself in his study for days on end. His self-deprecating manner and clownish sense of humour masked large deposits of undigested grief. He may have reminded John of his brother Karl and even mirrored hidden elements of his own melancholy nature.

About four weeks into his lessons with John, Petri wrote to Frederic Cox to give his impressions of his new student. These are worth quoting in full:

> I can now say quite definitely that I have rarely met such musician-ship, technical ability, ease and achievement, besides wide knowledge, in one so young. For me as a teacher he is quite dis-arming, because there is so little for me to tell him. All he needs is to curb his temperament – he often plays much too fast – to go right through the keys, especially in *piano*, to make all passages absolutely rhythmically controlled, in short to go more into detail. Learning too easily has its disadvantages – one is led to believe that everything is done already, whereas the final correctness and polish are still wanting.
>
> Having had all this pointed out to him, he is, I think, intelligent enough to enable him to work out these ideas by himself. He does not really want regular lessons and even if we lived in the same city, I would refuse to give him those. But a little control from time to time with a good artist would be advisable, I feel. Otherwise he should play in public as much as possible, hear good music per-formed by fine players, meet them, talk to them and in general develop and mature. Life will take care of that.
>
> As he is not very communicative, I find it difficult to draw him out. I wonder whether he is not too exclusively interested in music – but I may be wrong [...] He certainly has a very sweet nature and seems to be quite modest. I am very grateful to you for sending him to me.

The summer before going out to Petri John had taken his Licentiate of the Royal Academy of Music (LRAM), submitting the first two movements of *Opus Clavicembalisticum* as the piece of his choice – 'with results of death and devastation to all and sundry', he remarked in a letter to Max. By now he was already engaged upon quite an extensive performing career. Even at twenty he was in demand for concerts all over the north of England and was quite a regular with the Hallé and increasingly with the BBC North of England Home Service. He captivated audiences with the sheer facility of his playing – so at odds with his bemused, slightly shell-shocked demeanour. But Frederic Cox was surely wide of the mark when he wrote to the BBC Television *Music for You* programme suggesting that they might find in the twenty-one-year-old Ogdon a TV personality! In fact, many in the BBC had strong reservations about Ogdon at this early stage of his career. Writing to a colleague in July 1957, Paul Huband of the BBC music department in Manchester described Ogdon as 'so badly taught that I fear his talent will be wasted unless something is done pretty quickly'.

The lack of any piano tuition between the ages of ten and sixteen was evident to the trained ear. The 'Ogdon problem' was still simmering the following spring when it was decided to go ahead with the television audition that Frederic Cox had suggested. Gordon Thorne of the BBC, who had heard John play a number of times, wrote a memo to colleagues saying he wasn't sure what to recommend:

He is definitely outstanding, and can play absolutely everything – perhaps that is the trouble and the reason why, to me, his playing tends to be a little superficial and not always compelling. He scored quite a success with the Royal Liverpool Philharmonic last week in Liszt's *Totentanz*. Also last week I heard him in the Royal Manchester College of Music's Review Week, playing Ravel's *Gaspard de la Nuit* and the *Kreutzer* Sonata with one of the student violinists, and there is no doubt that following his recent coaching from Egon Petri he has become more sensitive [...] He is certainly interesting to look at – he is not unlike a young edition of Charles Groves, fairly rotund and with a mop of black hair, but without the force of character which I feel sure Charles had even when he was 21.

John had commented to Harry that he wanted to become a provincial Busoni, maintaining his base and sphere of action in the north of England, but those around him had other ideas. The RMCM was keen for John to go abroad again, and a number of teachers were mooted. John himself fancied studying in Russia, and had his eye on two people: Sviatoslav Richter (though John was unsure whether he took students) and Lev Oborin, Ashkenazy's teacher at the Moscow Conservatory. When considering Oborin, John was thinking of Ashkenazy's wonderful clarity and control in complex finger work. In the end John stayed at home and through the auspices of Emmie Tillett began to take lessons with Denis Matthews, who was renowned for his luminous playing of Beethoven and the classics and was a considerable musical scholar. They first met at Steinway's in London, where Matthews gave John a two-hour lesson on the Beethoven Third Concerto, which he was due to broadcast with the BBC Northern Symphony Orchestra. In the lesson report he sent to Emmie Tillett, Matthews mentioned that he had come across Ogdon in 1955 when the eighteen-year-old played part of the Busoni Concerto at a National Youth Orchestra audition. When asked to play something different he had launched into the fugue of the *Hammerklavier* Sonata! Ogdon's choice, wrote Matthews, demonstrated his quality, adding that 'he plays in the grand style'. As for the Beethoven Concerto, Matthews came away with the impression that John had studied the work 'rather quickly', especially considering that he was to play it in public so soon. The cadenza John had written for the first movement 'proved an intellectual exercise in the Busoni tradition', and Matthews felt that it was 'more "impressive" than stylistically or structurally satisfactory'. He found John 'most cooperative in accepting advice'.

Frederic Cox was still in two minds about how to 'improve' John's technique. He wrote to Matthews that he was 'very frightened that in trying to eradicate the faults (which may be engrained in his artistic nature) his talent may be destroyed'. Matthews replied that, since Ogdon's talent would not come to fruition without clear discipline, it was their duty to bully him! His job was to tame the bear, not turn it into a marmoset. John was and always would be a very un-English pianist who had much more in common with the Russian tradition of pianism – especially that of Anton Rubinstein, with his colossal tone and large conceptions. So John began to see Matthews on a regular basis at the older man's home in Henley-upon-Thames, where he was given rigorous schooling in the art of Bach, Mozart and Beethoven. He was not permitted to zoom off on the super-Romantic highway; though when asked during his first lesson to play something by Mozart he launched into Liszt's *Don Giovanni* fantasie. Matthews himself had an enormous repertoire, not only of piano music but other scores too, and was an occasional composer of merit. John admired his deeply thoughtful approach to music, and thought it a shame that he couldn't devote more time to composition.

John had been engaged by the Royal Liverpool Philharmonic under John Pritchard to play the Busoni Concerto at the end of November 1958 – a rare honour for one so young. This was music that had not been heard in Britain since the glory days of Egon Petri and Mark Hambourg, and the occasion marked something of a Busoni revival. John's old mentor Ronald Stevenson read a notice of the concert in the *Times* and shortly afterwards, as if by telepathy, received a letter from John via the BBC asking if he could visit him to discuss his interpretation of the work. They arranged to meet in Edinburgh at one of the BBC studios. Stevenson went to collect John at Waverley Station but twelve years had passed since their last meeting and he had no idea what he looked like now, so he kept his eyes open for someone carrying a music case. Sure enough there was a man wandering up and down with just such an article, but he was gigantic and looked like the heavyweight champion of the world. Stevenson peered at him in profile and immediately noticed the resemblance to the nine-year-old boy he had known, but he refrained from slapping him on the back just in case he *was* the heavyweight champion!

They played the concerto together on two pianos, with Ronald playing the orchestral reduction. They played through the first two movements, then in the third, slow movement (which is very complex with different tempi) Stevenson came unstuck; he couldn't really do it. So John played the orchestral part from memory to show him how it went. Stevenson was flabbergasted. Despite the vastness of the work,

John knew both the solo and the orchestral parts from memory. It was the start of an important musical friendship between the two composer-pianists and John became a frequent visitor to Townfoot House, Stevenson's home in West Linton on the Scottish borders. They swapped notes on composition and interpretation and John championed many of Stevenson's major works for piano, making key suggestions for changes while they were still in the forge – the Prelude, Fugue and Fantasy on *Doktor Faust* being a good example. John repaid Stevenson's inspiration by offering huge encouragement to the older man. He even wrote a letter to the *Times* pleading for 'more frequent hearings of the music of a younger British composer of genius, Ronald Stevenson'.

Stevenson was in many ways the polar opposite of chaotic, shambling John. He was always stylishly attired, usually with a bohemian twist (he had a fondness for bolo ties), and all that issued from his stern, refined countenance was scrupulously articulate and beautifully spoken, as if it were music. His presence was almost bardic, and he had the lilting, oracular voice to give credence to such a persona. His handwriting was precise and calligraphic and he was master of a sculpted, lyrical prose. But his meticulousness was never at the expense of warm-heartedness. He was a deeply hospitable and humane man, and a lifelong pacifist. There was something rather mysterious about him, something cloaked that can't be captured in words. It would for instance be easy to imagine that he was a practising alchemist with a homemade laboratory at the end of the garden.

John first visited Townfoot House in February 1959. He went straight to the piano, sat down on Ronald's antique piano stool and broke it. All twenty stones of him were sprawled on the floor. Stevenson's daughter, who was about four at the time, ran to her father and whispered, 'Daddy, John Ogdon eats pianos!' John was accepted as one of the family and liked nothing better than to tuck into mounds of Marjorie Stevenson's cooking after a morning spent in Ronald's music room. His letters to Ronald, frequently requesting the return of items of clothing and music left in his house, are remarkable for the profound creative bond evinced between the two men. John had not only found a musical mentor in Stevenson – he had found a soul mate, someone worthy of the Lisztian ideal of total artistic friend-ship. In December 1959 he wrote to Stevenson:

> So many things have been made possible only through your kindness and your enthusiasm has opened so many doors to me that I always feel the full extent of my debt to you can never be measured: if I had not known you at the Royal Manchester College when I was 8, would I still have played the Busoni Concerto when I was 21? It must be doubtful. The guiding hand of an enthusiast at so early an age was invaluable and has never been – will never be – forgotten by me.

He mentions that he is writing the letter very late at night and imagines his friend sitting up composing something himself; he won-ders what it might be. In another letter he wrote, 'Need I say how inspiring I find it to be in spiritual communion with a mind of the quality and greatness that yours evinces?' Many times John signs off 'with my deepest love', or 'all love to you, dear Ronald', and he never fails to mention Marjorie and all the children by name.

John described his visits to Ronald as 'milestones' in his artistic life. One of these milestones was laid down on 1 December 1959 in Stevenson's music room, when John was invited to play Sorabji's *Opus Clavicembalisticum* for its dedicatee: Scots poet Hugh MacDiarmid. It was the first time MacDiarmid had heard the work, although it had been dedicated to him nearly thirty years earlier. The Edinburgh pho-tographer Helmut Petzsch captured the occasion. We can see young Oggy, slope-shouldered, grinning deferentially, his tent-like trousers pulled halfway up his chest, standing half gormlessly beside the great poet. The performance was a vintage four-hour marathon with the Og so much in his element, sweating Vulcan-like at his musical forge. Several years later he, Stevenson and MacDiarmid would gather again at Townfoot House to record a symposium on Sorabji's music – a transcription of which was included in MacDiarmid's 1966 book, *The Company I've Kept*. Ogdon's contribution gives evidence of his wide-ranging if slightly quirky musical erudition, which is lightly worn and expressed with philosophic dispassion.

*

John was still very much a part of life at the RMCM and in the autumn of 1958 he returned there to teach two days a week. In addition to his fortnightly lessons with Denis Matthews in Henley, John began to study with Gordon Green in Liverpool. Green had been a pupil of Petri at the RMCM and was a man of wide culture who was as likely to recommend a novel he'd just read as he was a new score. His home at 33 Hope Street, just down from the Philharmonic Hall, was a place of refuge for travelling artists from all over the world – Richter and Gilels among them. His wife, Dorothy, ran a club and restaurant on the same street called the 23 Club, which was also a musicians' and artists' haunt. A modest, genial man with a marvellous fund of anecdotes, his white goatee shimmering through the halo of pipe smoke that invariably surrounded him, Green taught John to listen carefully to his own playing and thus brought a deeper quality of self-awareness to his performances. He was, in a way, teaching him how to be his own mentor. John's remarkably sensitive pedalling, in which he used not only half pedals but quarter pedals too – almost like notches on the harpist's pedals – came from Gordon Green but originated with Busoni, who described the pedal as 'a ray of moonlight'. It was through Gordon Green that the process of artistic maturation in Ogdon's playing began, while Denis Matthews worked more specifically on ironing out problems of technique.

John was paid twenty guineas for his Busoni Concerto in Liverpool. It was a huge performance in every sense, and by the end of it his collar and studs were flying in all directions! Sorabji had written to Ronald Stevenson two months earlier:

Mr. Ogdon has already written me about his forthcoming performance of the greatest and grandest piano concerto ever written. What a brave fellow he is! WHAT torrents of abuse he is going to receive from the Grub-Street hacks who scribble what they (but no one else in his senses would) call 'musical criticism.'

Even where critics failed to appreciate the piece, however, there was unstinting praise for the pianist. The *Scotsman* appreciated both, and wrote of Ogdon:

During these dark years for British pianism, when such pianists as Solomon and Cyril Smith have been tragically incapacitated, it is comforting to know that there is a rising pianist, John Ogdon, whose two hands may recreate and even eclipse the lost glories. At 21 he lacks serenity, but almost reconciles us to its lack by his promethean energy and colossal virtuosity.

What the reviewer didn't know is that John had practised so hard for the concert that he had injured the pads of his fingers. For days before his performance his hands had to be bandaged to protect the swelling. He'd take them off to practise and his mother would put them back on when the pain became intolerable. It was a heroic performance, fully befitting the scope of the piece. The Italian pianist Pietro Scarpini wrote of the concerto that 'Busoni meant this work to be nothing less than the history of man's soul'.

John struck up a good relationship with John Pritchard, who was a fellow champion of contemporary music through his Musica Viva series at the Liverpool Philharmonic. Less than two months after the Busoni, Pritchard called on Ogdon to fill in at twenty-four hours' notice for a soloist who'd fallen ill. The piece was Brahms's massive four-movement Piano Concerto No. 2 in B-flat major, which is harder to play than the more frequently performed first concerto. In the late 1980s, shortly before both men died, Pritchard recalled the incident:

John played the work to the manner born. It was a big beautiful sound. John always had what they call an orchestral sound and this piece is like a piano symphony. It was a remarkable triumph for him. But while I was conducting I did notice that when the turner over was a little bit late perhaps in turning the page John was peering round to see what the next bar was, and my suspicions were aroused. He got through everything fine, but afterwards I said, 'John had you really studied and played the Brahms B flat?' 'No,' he said, 'but I knew the music alright, I'd heard it many times.' So in twenty four hours or less he'd been able to encompass this phenomenally difficult work.

In a letter to Ronald Stevenson acknowledging the latter's telegram of congratulations, John described his performance as 'rather rough!!'

In May 1959 John entered his second major competition, the Liverpool International Piano Concerto Competition, a one-off sponsored by the Royal Liverpool Philharmonic Society. Among the jurors were Solomon (principal), Cyril Smith, John Pritchard, Herbert Menges and Gordon Thorne (BBC Music). There were forty-eight entrants, of whom twelve, including Ogdon, made it to the penultimate round. John was uncharacteristically nervous beforehand in the knowledge that losing on home turf could damage his reputation. For the final concert the twelve were winnowed down to three: John Ogdon (UK) playing the Liszt E-flat concerto, Aldo Mancinelli (USA) playing the Tchaikovsky B-flat minor concerto, and Joaquin Achucarro (Spain) playing Rachmaninoff's Rhapsody on a Theme of Paganini. At twenty-two, John was the youngest by a considerable margin. In the end he was placed second to Achucarro but the jury made it clear that it was by 'the narrowest margin'. Solomon, who had had the last word, felt that John, for all his virtuosity, lacked that last degree of finish. The next morning's reviewers, however, gave John their votes and were clamorous in his praise. Colin Mason in the *Manchester Guardian* wrote that

> from the very first phrase Ogdon gave the impression of an outstanding and creative sensibility and of total musical command. He played the lyrical parts with beautifully controlled legato phrasing and great subtlety and variety of dynamic shading, including ravishing pianissimos almost of the quality of Richter's.

He also praised his unfailing watch on the conductor's beat, something his fellow finalists had lacked. Ogdon's attentiveness and superb timing, he said, acted as an inspiration to both conductor and orchestra. So John missed the first prize but scored a real triumph in winning over not only the critics but also the very large audience who attended the final concert. Other competitors had included Thorunn Tryggvason (the future Mrs Ashkenazy), and Brenda Lucas (the future Mrs Ogdon), both of whom made it into the final twelve.

Much flowed from John's Liverpool success. He was formally signed by Ibbs & Tillett and that summer gave his first Promenade concert at the Royal Albert Hall. He played the Liszt E-flat concerto with the London Symphony Orchestra under Basil Cameron. He was standing in for the Dutch pianist Cor de Groot, who had hurt his hand. 'I admire the form of the work very much,' he wrote to Ronald Stevenson; 'there is such a marvellous sense of control and direction in it, particularly in the last movement: a wonderful feeling of effortless composition which I feel is something fine.' It was an unforgettable experience for John, taking his bows before such a vast audience and looking out into the cavernous hall with its tier upon tier of crimson stalls and boxes. The London critics were equally roused by his performance. The *Times*' reviewer didn't feel that he could judge the pianist's musicianship by the Liszt Concerto, but 'in so far as prestidigitation and sheer physical exuberance were concerned, Mr. Ogdon passed his test with flying colours'. Other pianists on Mrs Tillett's books at the time included Claudio Arrau, Wilhelm Kempff, Clifford Curzon, Eileen Joyce, Shura Cherkassky, Benno Moiseiwitsch, Myra Hess, Rudolf Serkin and Denis Matthews. John's childhood idol Rachmaninoff had also been with the agency.

John's Wigmore Hall debut came at the end of September and was sponsored by Lord 'Alistair' Londonderry. It was a typically challenging and gargantuan programme, with works by Bach, Beethoven, Brahms, Liszt, Balakirev, Busoni and Ogdon. Three weeks before the concert John wrote to Londonderry expressing unease about the critics' quotes included on the programme, as he felt he hadn't a ghost of a chance of living up to them. His nerves were soothed by being invited to stay at Alistair's Eaton Place home four days before the recital. There he practised in peace under the benevolent and reassuring eye of his friend and patron. There was no doubt that this would be John's most cultured audience yet but he needn't have worried: he gave the performance of a lifetime and was called back for encore after encore. Neville Cardus, no less, wrote in the *Guardian*, 'I don't remember hearing a pianist as richly endowed as Mr. Ogdon at 21 since I first listened to the boy Claudio Arrau.' Though he was of the opinion that Ogdon was 'a shade too formidable as a pianist', he was ready to acknowledge that his bravura was 'informed by a remarkably keen musical intelligence: there was thought in the fingers' ends, no matter how drastic the strength of wrists and shoulders'. The *Times* chided the young man that in some of the Brahms variations he must have 'beaten all existing speed records – though in unnecessary speeding he did sacrifice a certain measure of accuracy'.

John's parents had travelled from Manchester for the occasion, as had Brenda Lucas – who was by now his fiancée. After all the hubbub in the green room had died down, John and his betrothed were whisked off to Belgravia for a lavish reception and buffet supper to which John's parents were also invited. They were overawed by the surroundings and the elegant sophistication of the guests, but John himself seemed quite unaffected by it all. He nodded and smiled, revelling in the attentions of Alistair's cultured and aristocratic friends and those of Alistair's wife. Alistair had married seventeen-year-old Nicolette Harrison the previous year. She was the blonde daughter of the Latvian baroness Maria Koskull, who presided over a bohemian salon at Argyll House on the King's Road. Alistair and Nicolette were hailed as exemplars of a new unstuffy aristocracy.

One of the guests that night was the writer Sacheverell Sitwell, then in his sixties. He wrote to John a couple of days later, describing his recital as 'an astonishing affair'.

There is obviously nothing, or very little, that you cannot do, and one feels proud to think that you are an Englishman, and not least a Lancastrian! I would not be so presumptuous as to give advice to a musician of undoubted genius, but I hope for two things, that you will get on with writing *your own* music, and you will from time to time play small, simple pieces to melt one's heart, for music is surely an affair of mind and heart [. . .] It was a great pleasure meeting you – also your fiancée, whom we all thought very good looking. This letter brings you all good wishes, and begs you to take every care of yourself and your health and wellbeing, as you are in your own way one in a thousand, and have therefore responsibilities towards yourself, and towards the world, which you must fulfil.

5

TYING THE KNOT

John wasn't obviously interested in Brenda, or in any girls at all. I certainly never saw him being interested in one. John was a fat boy, a clumsy boy, who couldn't tie his shoe laces. He was only interested in playing the piano and eating.

Alexander Goehr

After the professional and social glories of his Wigmore Hall recital, John returned to the tiny house at 77 Bury New Road, Manchester, where he lived with his ailing parents. For several years both Howard and Dorothy had been suffering from heart problems – angina, thrombosis, leaky valves, the whole panoply. Although he was now over sixty and in poor health, Howard refused to retire. He was determined to finish the new English course he was compiling for the school, and Dorothy's letters express a slightly despairing resignation over the matter. Neither she nor Howard liked where they were living but had remained for the sake of John. Now he was engaged to be married and would soon be moving out.

In an article on John that appeared in the *Manchester Evening News* in January 1960, entitled 'This Brilliant Young Man of Music', the journalist gives a picture of the Ogdons' front room, once designated for dining but now commandeered by John for music. His Bechstein grand piano, which had a broken string and had long since been pummelled out of tune, took up most of the space. Piled high on the window sill and the floor surrounding the piano were stacks of sheet music that glissaded to the floor as Six-Pie put the keys through their paces. The remaining floor space was colonized by the columns of dog-eared novels that he and Howard had worked their way through. On the wall behind the piano stool were three pin-ups: a framed autographed portrait of Egon Petri, a line drawing of Busoni torn from an old music programme and a photograph of a young Manchester pianist by the name of Brenda Lucas.

Brenda, a native of Hyde in Greater Manchester, was the daughter of John (Jack) and Martha Lucas. Martha was the headmistress of Hyde Chapel Primary School. As the dominant parent she made the decisions in the house and was particularly strict with Brenda, the elder of her two children, hitting her for misdemeanours and sometimes simply in sheer irritation at her presence. 'Go and play tennis or something!' she'd snap, or 'Go and visit a friend!' – anything to get her out of the house. Martha was on edge most of the time – particularly during the war, when money was scarce and nights were spent down in the cellar for fear of air raids. She did, however, seem more lenient and at ease with Brenda's younger sister, Janet. According to Brenda, her mother was an arch-manipulator, a talent she derived from reading the complete novels of Agatha Christie. Brenda's father, Jack, worked for the local authority, and was in charge of evacuees from London during the war. He was in the Home Guard and wore a tin hat. Brenda remembers him as a fun-loving man who enjoyed his cricket and exercised a calming influence in the home. His way of coping was to make a joke of everything. For all that, it was a cold house.

Brenda was born in November 1935 and as a small girl attended her mother's school. From there she went to a prep school, Miss Barlow's, but had to leave because the family couldn't afford it. She didn't do well at state school, where she was intimidated by all the beating that went on. Too frightened to learn, she failed her high-school entry exams and was sent to a convent school instead. There she redeemed herself through her passion for the piano. Her mother had taught her the notes when she was five or six then sent her to a local teacher, but it was under the sympathetic guidance of Sister Mary Angela that her playing first took wing. She read Eileen Joyce's life story – how Joyce had gone from an impoverished childhood in Tasmania to being a glamorous concert pianist of world renown – and her course was set.

Brenda's parents had been expecting a boy and had picked out the name Rodney for her: so from the start she was something of a disappointment. The piano was not only her rehabilitation but also an escape from the pressure of her mother's vexatiousness and the wretchedness of school life. She started winning prizes at local festivals and in 1949, not yet fourteen, achieved the highest marks in the country for her Grade 8 exams and was offered places at both the Royal Academy and the Royal College in London. Her mother felt she was too young to take advantage of these offers, but three years later, in 1952, she entered the Royal Manchester College of Music at the age of sixteen. She studied with Iso Elinson, John's former teacher, who was known to chase his prettier female students round the piano. To begin with she found the freedom and lack of discipline at the college unsettling. Pupils were expected to find their own way and little effort was made to channel their talents in a particular direction.

Her fellow students remember Brenda as a poor girl who used to wander about the college in a pair of sandals. She was not thin in those days and her thick brown hair, which she wore quite short, framed a full face that dimpled when she smiled. Hers was a broad, radiant smile, full of a winning naivety, which lit up her whole countenance and eclipsed the cold, unwavering look that could inhabit her dark eyes. (The Danish Radio Symphony Orchestra dubbed her 'the lady with the icicles in her eyes'.) She had a message for men, no doubt about that, and was an object of desire among the male students of the RMCM, but for the most part held herself aloof and earned a reputation as *la belle dame sans merci*. Ambitious and self-disciplined, she focused entirely on the piano and was encouraged in this single-mindedness by her mother, who absolved her from cooking and household chores. When she did finally consent to a boyfriend, it was to a handsome rugby player named Patrick from Manchester University: a non-musician with whom she played tennis, swam and went for long walks. She also dated a number of fellow students at the RMCM, including Harrison Birtwistle, who she said proposed to her, and David Wilde.

John arrived the year after Brenda, but it wasn't until he'd been there eighteen months that she first encountered him. Given the real buzz about John at the college from the moment he arrived, it says something of Brenda's rather narrow routine that it took so long for her to become aware of him. Her first glimpse was a rather disturbing one. She had just finished a practice session of her own and was rushing off to accompany a student in his violin lesson when she heard a violent torrent of notes from the concert hall, just up from the main lobby, which stopped her in her tracks. Someone was playing a virtuoso piece of terrific intensity that she'd never heard before. At first she thought it might be a recording – of Horowitz perhaps – but realized otherwise once she'd caught her breath and stopped to listen. Impelled to see who was playing, she crept down the stairs at the side of the stage. She was astonished by what she saw and heard. The hall was empty but for a handful of students; and there, crouched over the Steinway grand beneath a tousled mop of glistening black hair, was John's bear-like form. The way he hunched over the keyboard, like Narcissus peering at his reflection in the pool, suggested an unusual intimacy with the instrument that seemed almost unnatural. There was an animal intentness to his posture that made you feel he might at any moment tear open the keyboard. The playing was unbridled, demonic, disquieting, with a seething, furious quality that seemed to warn her away. The piece was Liszt's *Après Une Lecture de Dante*, also known as the *Dante* Sonata, which begins with the notorious tritone (or *diabolus in musica*) – used in this case to evoke the wailing of the tormented souls in Hell. Liszt was not the concert staple in the 1950s that he is today, but John Ogdon had been unearthing and exploring his scores since he was a boy. When he played one of Liszt's more Mephistophelean pieces, some very dark forces could be unleashed. It is little wonder that Brenda was shaken by her first experience of hearing him perform. There was, she later admitted, something uncomfortably raw about his playing. Almost thirty years on, in 1984, John played the *Dante* Sonata as an encore at the Queen Elizabeth

Hall. Louise Taylor, the daughter of pianist Harold Taylor, was so terrified by his performance that she had to cling to the arm of a friend
after the concert.

When she was introduced to John in the student canteen a few days
later, Brenda was struck by the contrast between the pianist and the
man. The pianist had impressed her with the blazing power of his
playing and authoritative demeanour, yet here was a shy, bulky, inar-
ticulate man with a slightly confused, apologetic air and the wettest of
handshakes. Nor did the grubby shirt and unshaven visage of this
nodding mooncalf raise him in the estimation of the meticulous
Brenda. She heard him play again in one of the open practices at the
college, and this time his 'tender and lyrical voice' was more in evidence. She was in no doubt after this second hearing that John Ogdon
was a true artist and the most naturally gifted pianist at the RMCM.
Beyond that, she didn't give him another thought. She had her own
career to think about and she and John weren't friends. Then, one
evening, as she walked down the Oxford Road to catch her bus
home, she heard someone puffing and panting behind her and turned
to see John homing in on her. 'Brenda ...' he gasped, trying hard to
catch his breath, 'I was wondering if you'd go to the cinema with me?'
'When? You don't mean now?' she blurted. 'Any time,' he replied.
'There are some good films on this week.' He looked at her amiably
and smiled. She studied him briefly, taking in the perplexed look
behind his thick spectacles and the general air of self-neglect, and said,
'Thank you, John, but no.' Then, for good measure, she added, 'I
already have a boyfriend.'

Her practice at college the following morning was interrupted by
John stumbling uninvited into the room clutching the score of a
Mahler symphony. Before she could object he had taken a chair and
a flow of arresting musical insights was issuing from his reticent lips.
Brenda was captivated in spite of herself and soon made room for him
on the piano stool as he began to illustrate a point about Mahler's
approach to composition, propping up the hefty score and leaning forward to peer through his scratched lenses. He sight-read through a
whole movement. Brenda couldn't believe what she was witnessing: it
wasn't just his technical ability or intellectual grasp that impressed

her, though these were remarkable in themselves; it was the imagination that allowed him to project himself into the music with such flair and conviction. It was as if he had the key to the composer's soul – at least, he spoke and played with the authority of one who had.

In the spate of John's oddly unrestrained eloquence Brenda's practice was quickly forgotten; nor did the deficit of his appearance and manners seem to matter quite so much anymore. She found herself listening and learning. When he talked about his feeling for Liszt or his desire to resurrect neglected composers like Busoni and Alkan, he gilded them with a peculiar light of his own that made them stand out in new ways. John soon became a regular visitor to Brenda's practice room; but, instead of giving his musical enthusiasms full rein, as he had on that first occasion, he would often stand gloomily saying nothing – a source of mounting irritation to the young lady at whom he had set his cap. 'What do you want?' she'd bark at him. 'Oh sorry, Brenda,' he'd reply meekly. 'Am I disturbing you?' Conversely, when his attempts to broaden her musical horizons met with resistance he could suddenly show a menacing flash of temper. When Brenda refused his invitation to attend one of the NMM concerts, and ordered him to leave, he gave her a sudden, murderous look before stalking out and slamming the door. Something in his eyes frightened her and she made a mental note to be more circumspect in future. The visits resumed, however, as did the shuffling twilit pursuits down the Oxford Road.

John had insinuated himself, albeit a little clumsily, into Brenda's life, and as she began to include him more she was surprised to discover that he had a considerable appetite for parties. It was true that he often sat there scowling or lost in thought, and showed more interest in his hosts' bookshelves than in his fellow guests; and if he broke his silence it would be to startle his neighbour by asking, 'What do you think of the novels of Zane Grey?' or 'Who do you prefer, Charlotte or Emily Brontë?' Yet, despite his lack of drawing-room graces, he wouldn't have missed out on being there. At other times, especially after a few drinks or if there was a piano, he would become more actively convivial. Another thing Brenda noticed was his susceptibility to feminine charms: his head was easily turned by a pretty figure. As for the women, their maternal instincts were invariably aroused.

Brenda herself claims not to have felt this mothering urge towards John. Rather she felt challenged to draw closer to him musically, to make their friendship less one-sided. Convent-educated as she was, and with a strict and restrictive home life, Brenda felt herself to be a complete greenhorn when it came to literature and history – in both of which John was deeply read. Even on the subject of music she felt tongue-tied in the face of his superior knowledge.

John had a habit of wandering into other people's houses, rummaging in their larders and destroying their pianos. He began to turn up at Brenda's house, drawn by the baby grand her aunt had given her. He would invariably arrive in his long black oilskin, his music case bursting at the seams, and would be taken through to the back room which served as Brenda's studio. At first he went easy on the piano but after several visits began to give it a real workout. When he got bored he would drift into the larder and help himself to anything he fancied, much to the displeasure of the puritanical Mrs Lucas. But, as always happened with John, his innocent blundering eventually endeared him to his victims. Before long he was accepted as an errant satellite of the Lucas household. His persistent phone calls to Brenda were like a recurrent comedy sketch. Half the time he had nothing to say and remained stubbornly silent in the face of her frustrated cries of 'Why are you calling?' and 'What do you want?' It was, in effect, a kind of benign stalking.

Bit by bit, Brenda found herself bossing John around and carping about his appearance and vagueness. The absentmindedness drove her to distraction and she soon wondered whether there wasn't an admixture of guile to it. On one occasion, for instance, he had stayed the weekend at the house of a mutual friend, Margaret Saxon, and had ended up virtually undressing her on the sofa. Being an ardent admirer of John's, Miss Saxon was at least as flattered as she was affronted. Yet a few days later John stood her up for tea, again at her house, and she called Brenda in a state of tearful indignation. John himself called not long after, imploring Brenda to save him from Margaret's amorous overtures! He had inadvertently uncovered a passionate soul. When Brenda challenged him about not turning up for tea John feigned innocence. 'Oh, tea! I forgot all about it; really I did.'

Though she resented being manoeuvred into the role of domestic dragon, Brenda was smart enough to see that John would be a big star. Shy and maladroit he may have been, and with little gift for intimacy, but as Peter Maxwell Davies has said, 'When he sat at the piano this wonderful, super-aware being took over.' Max said he felt very privileged to have been near that because it was tremendously exciting. According to David Wilde, Brenda was determined to have one of the top pianists at the college – and John was the pinnacle. But did she realize how fragile he was emotionally? He seemed to be on the edge most of the time and desperately vulnerable. When he wasn't at the piano he was immersed in a kind of musical lake. Oddly enough, John didn't talk about Brenda to his fellow students; nor do his letters to them mention her. Naturally, they were stunned when they learned of the engagement. 'John wasn't obviously interested in Brenda, or in any girls at all,' says Alexander Goehr. 'He was only interested in playing the piano and eating.'

Brenda wasn't interested in much beyond the piano herself at this stage and was intent on carving out a career as a soloist. In the summer of 1955 she had gone to study with Heinz Scholz at the Mozarteum in Salzburg, where she played the Beethoven Fourth Piano Concerto. While she was away John came second in a local competition to a very pretty girl called Grace Wilkinson, who was on the festival circuit in the northwest. The dent to his pride was all but unendurable and he wrote to Brenda expressing his utter disbelief at the result. She wrote back telling him it didn't matter in the least: he would be a great pianist one day while Grace Wilkinson would amount to nothing. Though he gave the opposite impression, John was extremely competitive and was still smarting from the defeat when Brenda returned from Salzburg.

In May 1956, John and Brenda flew out to Brussels together for the Queen Elisabeth competition, into which they were both entered. Brenda had to make the travel arrangements for John and ensure that his application was in on time, as he seemed awfully hazy about it all and this was his first time abroad. She was wracked with nerves at the prospect of performing at such a prestigious venue with the likes of Emil Gilels, Alexander Brailowsky and Artur Rubinstein on the jury, but John took it all in his stride. For the first time in their year-old friendship, it was she who was leaning on him for support. John had organized his own accommodations through a contact at the RMCM but it was clear that he really wanted to be staying with Brenda, who was lodging with a large Belgian family in a fashionable part of the city. Indeed, before long he was turning up at their house and inviting himself to meals. Though the Janssens at first could hardly contain their surprise at his presence, they soon resigned themselves to having an extra guest at their table. One lunchtime Brenda opened a letter from Patrick back in Manchester, and as she read could sense John glowering moodily from across the table. After lunch Mrs Janssens took her aside. 'That John, he's jealous,' she said. When Brenda shook her head, she spelled it out: 'Brenda, John is in love with you. Can't you see?'

Brenda, like John, was eliminated after the first round of the competition and in her case the strain proved too much. After performing her final pieces she suffered a nervous collapse and took to her bed. Consequently she missed hearing John play. Later on, however, she did join him in listening to the contestants who'd made it through to the second round. It dawned on both of them that the pianists they were hearing – especially those from the Eastern Bloc and Russia – were not only supremely talented but also superbly trained. What the RMCM had to offer was amateur and unfocused in comparison, and they had been offered no proper preparation for the contest. In Brenda this was cause for dejection and on their return to England she was plagued by doubts about her ability to reach the top of the profession. John, on the other hand, possessed a deep faith in his own talent and with it a steely determination to succeed that often went unrecognized by those who didn't see beyond his mild exterior.

Shortly after their return Brenda heard John play the Brahms D-minor concerto with the college orchestra under Sir John Barbirolli. It was a commanding and profoundly communicated performance, and to Brenda a revelation. 'It was like watching the young Beethoven,' she said. She had already witnessed him as an artist of formidable power and imagination, but now he appeared before her as a consummate professional under a world-renowned conductor. He had that innate ability, possessed by all great performers, to rise to the big occasion. It is clear from Brenda's account of the concert that she was beginning not only to take pride in John's success but also to identify with it. So much that she aspired to was embodied in the incongruous form of John Ogdon.

Her doubts about a relationship with John were amplified by her visits to his home. She had never seen such a chaotic place before, barricaded to the rafters as it was with books and music. Dorothy, like the eye of the storm, appeared calm (unnaturally calm, some would say) amid the creative cyclones of the Ogdon household. Howard would be in the back room hurtling across the North Yorkshire moors after Cathy and Heathcliff to the accompaniment of *The Flying Dutchman*, while John worked his way through stacks of scores in the front room. John's siblings had all left home but Paul and Ruth were occasional visitors, both having stayed in the northwest. They were not welcoming to Brenda and still called their younger brother 'baby Johnty', much to her disgust. Howard, when he ventured from his back-room sanctuary, proved a gregarious recluse and was charming in that over-elaborate manner common to the egomaniac. He hadn't been told that Brenda was a pianist, so when he heard her play at their house he overflowed with compliments. He warned her about John's savage temper, of which she'd already had a glimpse, and said that when he was in one of his fits nothing was safe. While Brenda was still perceived as a musical friend of John's and no more, Dorothy was hospitable and maintained a friendly outside. Brenda could see that Dorothy had made an unspoken bargain with John: you cultivate your genius to the full and I will take care of your needs. Consequently John never learned the basics of looking after himself: he couldn't make a cup of tea or put on a sweater without getting marooned in the arms; he left his clothes scattered over the bedroom floor and his dirty bath water in the bath; he even left his cheques lying around for his mother to bank. Whatever he neglected to do, Dorothy was there to take up the slack.

Brenda observed that John's relationship with his father was formal and distant. John respected his father's intellect, and was proud of his book, but there was no intimacy or camaraderie between them. He would sometimes rush back from college to count the words in one of Howard's essays or perform some other humdrum service. It was not a relationship of equals. The difference in their physiques was almost comical: side by side they looked like Laurel and Hardy. In countenance John was soft-featured and resembled his mother and Cornish grandfather, whose mild manners he shared. While Howard's intellectual pride was very much in evidence, and had all the grandiose hallmarks of what the psychologists call 'inflation', it was John's humility that was remarked on by those who met him. Nevertheless, as Brenda found out, John too was very conscious of the greatness that he carried. She has never forgotten the day when as a nineteen-year-old student he turned to her and confided that he was one of the great musicians of all time, in the line of Beethoven, Brahms and Busoni. 'He said it quietly, simply, and with total conviction.' John, one feels, wasn't above using his genius as a fan of peacock feathers to entice the suggestible Brenda.

Brenda and John were virtually the only two of their contemporaries left at college in 1957, and both returned after graduation to continue their studies privately and to teach. Like John, Brenda was beginning to get quite a few engagements in the northwest, mainly on the music-club circuit; but, whereas his reviews heralded a startlingly original talent, hers were on the whole no more than politely encouraging. In both cases the fees barely covered expenses. To help pay her mother for her board and lodging Brenda also taught a couple of days a week at a girls' high school. What time she had to herself she used for piano practice, sometimes up to five or six hours a day. This left almost no time for socializing, though she did still see Patrick – whose presence, though less frequent, continued to be a thorn in John's side. He provided a welcome release from her professional life in a way that John, who lived and breathed music, could not. Brenda characterized her relationship with John at this time as 'an intense musical friendship'. Moreover there was a competitive edge to the relationship that magnified this intensity. Where John was supreme in Brenda's affections was in the attentive ear he lent to her professional concerns and in the advice and sympathy he offered – not to mention his ability to solve all technical and interpretive problems at the piano. His nodding, shyly smiling face became a source of comfort to her.

Like John, Brenda spent time in Liverpool as she too was taking lessons from Gordon Green. She and John would sometimes attend Green's Friday-evening musical soirées on Hope Street. In March 1959 Brenda had something of a breakthrough when she was engaged to play the Grieg Concerto with the Liverpool Philharmonic under John Pritchard. There would be three concerts, the third in Liverpool itself. She was overjoyed. Her first impulse was to call John, and she fairly shouted her news down the phone. She waited expectantly for his congratulations but was met with a lengthy silence. 'John?' She wondered if he was still there. 'Good,' finally came the response, and with it a swift change of subject. Even with Brenda John felt a keen professional rivalry. He never did congratulate her and any support he gave in the ensuing weeks was qualified by a rather patronizing attitude, as if the Grieg was not worthy of serious study. He seemed amused that she could spend months chipping away at a piece that he could master in a couple of days.

Having pocketed any lingering resentments, John did condescend to attend the Liverpool performance – and got more than he bargained for. Patrick (whom John thought routed) turned up with a bouquet of red roses while John came empty-handed. The two men tiptoed around each other with clubfooted formality, while Brenda, buoyed by the support, put in a critically acclaimed performance. The *Liverpool Post* wrote: 'Brenda Lucas played Grieg's Piano Concerto with independent ideas of her own, a free and natural sense of *rubato* and a confident command of tonal variety that stamp her as a pianist with a big future.'

Having made a considerable name for himself with his concerts in the north, John started to land quite a few broadcasts on the BBC Home Service. He already had twenty concerti in his active repertoire – including both the Liszt concertos and *Totentanz*; Rachmaninoff's Nos. 2 and 3; the Busoni Concerto and *Indian Fantasy*; and the Ravel G major – and was tirelessly expanding his solo repertoire. His first Wigmore Hall recital was only a matter of months away. Now, if ever, surely, Brenda would accept him as her husband. One night after a spaghetti dinner at the Midland, one of the grand hotels in the centre of Manchester, Brenda offered to drive John back home. John became amorous and the car seemed suddenly very full. But Brenda stiffened, rebuffing his advances with prim-faced decorum. He leaned away to get a better look at her, his specs glinting in the street lamps – then plunged. 'Will you marry me?' he asked. Brenda hadn't seen it coming and stared back in amazement. 'Please,' he added. 'No,' she replied after a long pause. John looked hurt. Fearing she'd been too abrupt, Brenda put her hand on his arm and said, 'Thank you, John, but really we're just good friends.' He told her he was in love with her, but she said she didn't feel the same about him. He sat back in his seat and let out a sigh. 'Think about it,' he said, and off they drove in silence.

Brenda's mother was pleased with the news of the proposal and urged her daughter to accept, reminding her that she was the only one among her friends who was still unmarried. Brenda couldn't make up her mind. John was a great pianist but she wasn't in love with him. To make matters worse, John was the epitome of airy insouciance when she saw him. There was nothing weighing on *his* mind. After a couple of weeks they were back at the Midland Hotel for another spaghetti dinner and Brenda had decided to give him her final answer: a categorical 'no'. But, as she mulled over the reasons for her refusal, John's sloven-liness and his desire for a surrogate mother being uppermost, images of his brilliance, his modesty and his kindness suddenly took precedence – he was after all an inspiration to her in the only thing that truly mattered in her life: music – and before she knew it there were tears in her eyes and she was saying 'yes'. 'Yes what?' asked Six-Pie, startled out of his reverie. 'Yes, dammit!' she barked. 'Yes, I'll marry you!'

John's engagement to Brenda, occurring as it did in July 1959, coincided with the formal appearance in his life of another powerful woman, Emmie Tillett of Ibbs & Tillett, who would direct his career for the next twenty years. Or rather, she and Brenda, like Scylla and Charybdis, would rigorously control his professional life, leaving him little room to manoeuvre his lonely bark between their watchful straits. At this early stage, however, John felt no restriction. His energy and appetite for all that the musical life offered were inexhaustible. He drove himself far harder than either Brenda or Mrs Tillett could and, besides, his engagements were still at a workable level. If he had misgivings about the relationship with Brenda his growing success seems to have put them out of his mind. In his letters to friends his engagement is mentioned in brief and without reference to Brenda. To Alistair Londonderry he wrote a PS: 'Have just got engaged'. To Ronald Stevenson: 'I must tell you of another great event in my life – I have just become engaged (my fiancée is also a pianist!).' The very next sentence he writes: 'How is your piano sonata progressing?' John had had no previous girlfriends and no sexual experience and had spent his life under the thumb of his mother. It's almost as if he didn't see Brenda as a separate person.

In retrospect, John was probably suffering from bipolar disorder in his late teens – though it would have been masked by his artistic lifestyle and the monomania of his genius. He kept antisocial hours, and when he wasn't plunged in reflective silence was usually muttering under his breath about Alexander Goehr and others whom he thought were doing him down. Yet he craved the stimulation of parties and there were the sudden scintillating monologues on music, literature and history that his long silences had incubated. His addiction to *Moby-Dick* should have been a red flag. For John the book was a kind of *ad hoc* psychotherapeutic manual that told his inner story with uncanny prescience. In the opening chapter, ominously entitled 'Loomings', Ishmael goes to sea on a whaling expedition in order to shake off feelings of depression and thoughts of suicide. Music was John's ocean, and it was to music that he escaped to ward off intolerable thoughts. Music soothed his soul, as the ceaseless motion of the sea lulls the sailor, but it also concealed the figure of Moby Dick, which symbolized the demands and compulsions of the blood, not to mention the violent thoughts attendant upon their repression. Ishmael goes to sea with the all-male crew of the *Pequod*, and John launched out on the ocean of his musical life with his mates from New Music Manchester. Once out at sea the figure of Ishmael is dwarfed by the ship's morose and obsessive captain, Ahab, who pursues the prodigious white whale. Further and further out to sea the pursuer goes, seeking his destroyer, while blind to his own motives. Moby Dick, though nominally masculine, is a primal feminine force, like Ti'amat the phallic sea goddess of ancient Babylonia. Psychologically this is the sort of omnipotence that John experienced in his mother. He was in her power and with that sort of submission came ferocious buried rage. The fact that John travelled everywhere with his father's book, as if it were a talisman to parry his own madness (or an augury of the same), should also have rung warning bells in those closest to him.

In a 1961 essay comparing Sorabji to his literary hero Herman Melville, Ogdon quoted from D. H. Lawrence's analysis of *Moby-Dick*: 'In his "human" self, Melville is almost dead. That is, he hardly reacts to human contacts any more; or only ideally [. . .] he is more spell-bound by the strange slidings and collidings of Matter than by the things men do.' Writing of Sorabji the following year, Ronald Stevenson described the same spirit in talking of the composer's 'peculiar lunar aloofness'. Both men were describing an almost schizoid detachment from ordinary human relationships.

In the same essay Ogdon compared the opening 'clarion call' of *Opus Clavicembalisticum* with Melville's first sentence in *Moby-Dick*: 'Call me Ishmael.' For Ogdon the point of the comparison lay in the Lucifer-like pride of the music's 'swift descent', a quality he felt was shared by Melville's unmediated assertion of identity. But it's hard to see a real connection between Sorabji's dramatic beginning, which is indeed like the fall of Lucifer from Heaven, and the rather conversational, matter-of-fact opening of *Moby-Dick*. The fact that Ogdon consistently yoked the two works together, even at places where they wouldn't be joined, shows how deeply they were wedded in his imagination. Even more striking in a twenty-four-year-old was his obvious empathy with two artists who had retreated from the world to wander the abstract spaces of their own inwardness.

The engagement did not alter John and Brenda's everyday lives. They continued to live with their parents and follow their musical paths. It did, however, change Dorothy Ogdon's attitude to Brenda: she became openly hostile and never missed an opportunity to remind her that she would need to spend her life cooking and cleaning for John and starching his shirts before concerts. Pursuing her own career was out of the question; John would expect her to wait on him at all times. There were rows between the two, with John hovering on the sidelines, subservient to both women yet somehow in control. Joan Parton, a friend of John's who was reading English at Manchester University at the time, remembers seeing Brenda walking down one of the main streets in Manchester with John tripping along several paces behind carrying her handbag! It was, she says, like something out of *Monsieur Hulot's Holiday*. Whenever John went over to Joan's house for a meal he would be terribly anxious about his fiancée. 'Do you mind if I go and phone Brenda?' he'd say. 'I really ought to phone her.' She was always on his mind. Joan married Harold Taylor and John frequently went to their house after college to eat high tea and listen to records. His favourite pianist at the time was Egon Petri; his favourite meal pork chops.

If John's Wigmore Hall recital in September 1959 was a revelation to Brenda, the reception afterwards at Alistair Londonderry's Belgravia home was a defining occasion of even greater moment. This was her first time of meeting the Londonderrys and their social set and she was enthralled by the glamour, opulence and sophistication of it all. She was particularly taken by Nico, the Marchioness of Londonderry of whom John had previously spoken in awestruck tones. Indeed, according to Brenda, John was soon demanding that she look as glamorous and elegant as Nico. 'He ordered me to imitate her,' said Brenda, though it seems she needed little prompting. In her book, *Virtuoso*, Brenda describes her feelings as she travelled back to Manchester alone that night:

I lay on the bed in the sleeping-car wide awake, listening to the clatter of the wheels on the track. It had been a very special evening – one I knew I would never forget all my life long. And it had prompted me to two vital decisions.

The first was that I would become, to the best of my ability, like those women at the party – the women John had so blatantly admired. I would study to make myself as elegant and glamorous as they were – and I would lose my northern accent if it killed me, and learn to speak just as they did.

And my second decision was that I would refuse to enter this privileged world as an appendage to John's apron strings. His mother was right, I was ambitious; I wanted to succeed on my own. I would, I decided, break off our engagement.

If Brenda *did* decide to break off the engagement that late-September night she didn't carry out her intention until more than three months afterwards, in January 1960. It seems very unlikely that the Belgravia supper party was the catalyst for the split. On the contrary, Brenda would have realized that John was her entrée to the gilded halls of the great and the good – a world she was now bent on entering. Her vision of herself changed profoundly that night: from concert pianist in her own right to the glamorous wife of a celebrated artist. It may just have been a glance in the mirror, an image she didn't allow into her conscious thoughts, but a transfer of energy had taken place and from that moment on she would pour her efforts into recreating herself in the likeness of Lady Londonderry. From being a well-padded brunette with a Lancashire accent she would become a fashionably thin blonde-haired society hostess with softly spoken London vowels.

Six weeks after his Wigmore Hall triumph John wrote to Peter Maxwell Davies asking 'in some trepidation' if he would consent to be his best man. The wedding was set for March 1960, and Max accepted. In the letter John mentioned Golding's new novel, *Free Fall*, which he'd just been reading. The book, which is about a man who breaks down under pressure of confinement and the threat of torture, 'thrilled [him] to bits'. He particularly praised the author's rare sense of style – rare, that is, for a contemporary novelist. He also praised Gerard Hoffnung's *Acoustics*, a very different work that had just been published, and alludes to Hoffnung's sudden death that year, aged thirty-four, adding, 'A warning to yours truly.' Finally, as a postscript, he tells Max he's just read a third book – also hot off the press – Mervyn Peake's *Titus Alone*, a hallucinatory meditation on madness that signalled the breakdown of its author.

Brenda most likely broke off the engagement to bring John to heel and assert her control, for he was showing an irritating nonchalance towards the affianced state. His inclination was to continue living the life he and Brenda had lived as students. His priorities remained the pursuit and exploration of music and the cultivation of his friendships with fellow composers. Shortly after he wrote to Max, John performed a typically eclectic programme at the Manchester University Arts Festival comprising works by Goehr, Ogdon, Scriabin, Maurice Emmanuel (Messiaen's teacher) and Stevenson. Championing the music of his contemporaries was often a thankless task but was a duty that John nonetheless took to heart. In late January 1960 he wrote to Ronald Stevenson to give him the news that the reading panel for the Cheltenham Festival had rejected his sonata-length piece *A 20th-Century Music Diary* (1953–59). John considered the work a masterpiece and was determined to premiere it either at Hastings or at the Bishopsgate Institute in London. (In the event he played it that summer at Park Lane House for the Related Arts Centre, adding works by Dennis Todd, Constant Lambert and Busoni.) He reaffirms his faith in Stevenson's work and urges him not to be deflected. Towards the end of his letter John writes,

> I have yet another item of sad news: at the moment my engagement with Brenda has been broken off, a great blow to me, and it seems as if our eventual marriage is very doubtful.
>   Please forgive the inexcusable delay in sending you my Preludes: things have been very difficult here and I fear I have not yet completed them (in a neat copy, that is). I feel their creative content is so slight that I hardly like to thrust them upon you [...]

In her book Brenda writes that John appeared unperturbed by the break-off of their engagement and accepted the return of his Victorian cluster ring without obvious dismay ('Oh, alright,' he said as he took it). Dorothy Ogdon, having done her bit to scare Brenda off, welcomed the news; but John was not swayed by her victory dance. His daily rounds, including regular phone calls and visits to Brenda, continued as normal. The difficulty at home to which John refers in his letter was most likely the poor health of his parents. That spring Dorothy was admitted to hospital for severe angina and suspected thrombosis and Howard was home from school with atrial fibrillation (irregular heartbeat). John had some seventy engagements through Ibbs & Tillett that year, including another two Wigmore Hall recitals, as Emmie T. kept him yo-yoing up and down the country to satisfy her beloved music clubs – of which there were about 800 in the UK at that time. One typical sequence of concerts in June took him from the north to Bournemouth to Manchester to Torquay in rapid succession. John was attracting the big dates as well, even at this early stage of his career. On 11 March 1960 he played Rachmaninoff's 3rd Piano Concerto at the Royal Festival Hall with the London Symphony Orchestra under Pierino Gamba. He tackled the bigger, original cadenza in the first movement, which was, according to the *Times*, proof of his spirit. As so often in his approach to the big romantic concerti that drew blood, sweat and tears from other pianists, Ogdon's musical emphasis was empathy. He sought the lyrical nerve centre of the piece, and all for a mere twenty guineas.

Ultimately John won Brenda over by force of will – at least, that is how she remembers it. He simply wore her down by ignoring the disengagement. It was during a session in her music studio at home in April 1960, a month after the wedding had been due to take place, that she suddenly turned to him and said, 'OK, John, you can give me back the ring whenever you want.' A little smile of triumph crept over his face and he sealed their re-forged union with a kiss. There are other accounts of their re-engagement, however. Many years later John told his close friends the Schurmanns that it was when Brenda got wind of his courting another girl that she turned up one day and demanded: 'Where's my ring?' And before he could say 'Half a dozen pork pies, please' she had grabbed it back and announced the wedding date.

John and Brenda were at a table at the 23 Club in Liverpool when he said, suddenly and apropos of nothing, 'Brenda, I think I ought to grow a beard.' She gazed at the full moon of his face and the two perfect spheres of his spectacles in orbit about it, and thought that a beard might provide some length and generally mitigate the unremitting rotundity of his countenance. 'Yes,' she replied, 'that might be a good idea. Only keep it long.' John placed his hand across his chest. 'You mean down to here?' 'No, no, not that long!' she remonstrated,

raising his hand for him. The next day John began growing the signature goatee that would remain rooted to his chin through thick and
thin. Once it had flourished it immediately seemed characteristic of
the man – even if it did look vaguely false!

John had a remarkable range of friendly acquaintances in the musical world, and they were always putting him up. He also enjoyed many
a convivial sojourn at Alistair Londonderry's County Durham estate,
Wynyard, especially in the early days of his career. The two friends would
sit up all night watching old films.

At the end of April 1960, after a concert in Eastbourne, John went
to stay with Harold and Joan Taylor (née Parton) in nearby Hastings.
Harold motored him over to Rye, where he saw the birthplace of the
playwright John Fletcher and the house where Henry James had lived.
He wrote to Ronald Stevenson the same day and in his description of
James one detects a slight autobiographical touch:

> I thought there was something of James's spiritual quality still pres-
> ent there – it was easy to imagine him ruminating and pontificating
> his majestic way around the narrow cobbled streets. A subtle and
> strange spirit, I think.

As a coda he wrote, 'Brenda sends you her best wishes – we have
now fixed our wedding date for July 23rd, and crises of the past have
been safely overcome.'

Both John and Brenda were very busy musically in the run-up to
the wedding. Just two weeks before the big day John was invited
to play at the prestigious Festival of Two Worlds in Spoleto, Italy –
quite an honour for one so young. On his return to England he
performed the Sunday piano recital at the Cheltenham Festival,
which was given each year to a promising young British artist. He
played Beethoven's Op. 111 Sonata; Brahms's Paganini Variations; the
Constant Lambert Sonata; a group of Busoni elegies; and his own
Variations and Fugue, Op. 4. Colin Mason of the *Guardian* described
him as belonging to 'that type of superhumanly equipped and almost
crankily erudite musician-pianist that can play, and knows, all music.'
Thrilling though it was to hear his mammoth programme with its

hair-raising technical difficulties, Mason wished that Ogdon would consider abandoning such tours de force for 'conventional recitals of more familiar and rewarding music'. As for Ogdon's own piece, Mason considered it wondrously proficient, but melodically indistinctive and lacking in harmonic originality. His style, he added, was vague and indeterminate. 'As Ogdon is still only 23,' he concluded, 'this need not mean that he is not a real composer.' Felix Aprahamian had no such reservations, hailing Ogdon enthusiastically in the *Sunday Times* as 'a young English Busoni'. John sent Sorabji a ticket for his Cheltenham recital but received a reply saying that if there was one thing 'ON THIS EARTH' that he would arrange 'NOT' to be at it would be a 'festival (!!!???)' of British contemporary music. Brenda herself was frantically preparing for her first London recital for the Park Lane Group, which was to take place only days before the wedding.

John was an ardent Hitchcock fan and took Brenda to see the newly released *Psycho* for their final pre-wedding date. The score for the film was written by the composer Bernard Herrmann, who was much admired by John and would one day be a good friend. As with Henry James and William Golding, so with Hitchcock, it was the man's profound psychology and technical mastery that won John's admiration. The cinema had not been quite as important in his life since leaving the RMCM; not only were there more demands on his time but he was also no longer in daily contact with fellow film buffs Harrison Birtwistle and Peter Maxwell Davies. In fact now, with marriage looming, he sensed perhaps that he was being cut loose from many of his student friendships and there was a clash over the wedding list. John wanted to invite all his chums from New Music Manchester, and other student friends, but Mrs Lucas said no. She had her budget and she was going to stick to it. Only hours before the wedding John tried unsuccessfully to make contact with Ronald Stevenson. He wrote to him on returning from his honeymoon:

At 12.30 – 1.00 a.m. on the morning of July 23rd I tried to phone you. Terribly late, but I know you share my penchant for late hours, and some of the most memorable and rewarding late hours of my life have been spent in your dear company. Alas, I was unsuccessful! Three times I tried, and three times I failed. I wished to crown my life as a single person by a conversation with you which would I think have proved memorable.

Ronald Stevenson didn't have a telephone in his house, so John used to call the telephone box across the road. Making contact was a hit-and-miss affair at the best of times.

The wedding did go ahead without hitches, though John turned up at the church without a buttonhole and Brenda's cousin David had to be dispatched to the local florist in Hyde to get him a carnation. Howard didn't have one either and his flies were undone, but his large white handkerchief was a passable substitute for a white flower and matched his whitish wild hair. The service took place at the Holy Trinity Church, Gee Cross, near Hyde, and Brenda's sister, Janet, and cousin Judy were bridesmaids. Their choice of music for the service conjured an unlikely trio: Wagner, Brahms and Sibelius. Peter Maxwell Davies was the sole representative of New Music Manchester and gave an erudite best-man speech that pleased John and Howard but flew over other heads. The reception for about thirty-five people was at the West Towers Country Club near Marple. John and Brenda look like gleeful children who have pulled off an unlikely coup, and of their four parents only Dorothy's smile shows any signs of strain. She had written to Marjory Wood the previous December saying, 'We shall feel very lost when John marries', and expressing the hope that he would continue to live in Manchester.

Brenda wanted a proper honeymoon, so when she learned that John was scheduled to play the Grieg Concerto with the Hallé in Buxton four days after the wedding she asked him if he could get out of it. Dorothy Ogdon put her foot down: 'Under no circumstances will John cancel anything!' she told her. She was deaf to Brenda's pleas, and John rather sheepishly kept his peace. So, as they headed off towards the Peak District from the wedding in their red Mini-Minor, Brenda at the wheel, the accompanying storm was more than meteorological. It rained throughout their Buxton sojourn, with slate-grey clouds settling like a roof over the Derbyshire spa town, home of St Ann's Well. There was a putting game in the grounds of the hotel for when the downpours let up; besides that the newlyweds were immured in their room or the lobby. Brenda's tears of frustration added to the torrents and she scolded herself for having allowed her family – particularly her mother – to push her into the marriage. 'I just did as I was told,' she said later. Any note of romance was dispelled by the atmosphere of brooding resentment. John retreated into one of his ominous silences and both ended up counting the hours until his appearance at the Pavilion Gardens concert hall. After that they were able to leave the whole unconsummated mess behind them. Had John really wanted a honeymoon he wouldn't have gone to Buxton to play the concerto. 'What I expected from him didn't happen,' Brenda later remarked. 'It was bad, hopeless.' The spirit of St Ann (or maybe St Dorothy) prevailed.

Any resentments were soon forgotten when they set up home in their new house, The Maisonette, 17 Didsbury Park, a rented place in East Didsbury, to the south of Manchester. John's Bechstein filled the living room, while Brenda's Brinsmead baby grand was hoisted upstairs into the attic together with the Hansen upright. There they practised beneath the gaze of an ascetic-looking Liszt. The place had no carpets, just bare boards, so the resounding noise of the piano played for hours on end was more than enough to drive their landlord, who lived next door, out of his wits. John was away a good deal on engagements but when he was at home he practised up to six hours a day. There was a barrage of banging on the wall if they played after 6.30 p.m. and a steady war of attrition ensued. But they were happy in the simple business of their lives and the landlord's animosity served to draw them closer. At the end of August John and Brenda went up to Edinburgh, where they gave their first two-piano recital at an event organized by the pianist and conductor John Minchinton – one-time amanuensis to Michael Tippett. He had set up the British Piano Society in an effort to promote piano playing at a time when it was neglected in schools, and for this particular event he brought together seven or eight young British pianists, including John and Brenda. It was a hardworking week with two solo/duet concerts in addition to the two-piano recital. For the latter they played Chopin's Rondo in C, Op. 73; Milhaud's *Scaramouche*; Britten's *Mazurka Elegiaca* and Introduction and Rondo alla Burlesca; and some Schumann Studies. It was the start of a partnership that would endure – even when everything else had collapsed – for the next three decades. They even got to enjoy a proper honeymoon at the beginning of September when they travelled to Bolzano in the South Tyrol, where John was taking part in the Twelfth International Busoni Competition for Pianists. No first prize was awarded that year but second prize went to the Texan James Mathis, a pupil of Van Cliburn's teacher, Rosina Lhevinne. John was awarded fifth prize, for which he was paid the equivalent of £57, which meant that he and Brenda could spend extra time soaking up the sights and sunshine of northern Italy after the competition finished. John had entered without much preparation, so fifth prize was by no means a disgrace. Alfred Brendel had won fourth prize at the inaugural competition in 1949.

John met Sorabji in London that winter, but sadly no account of the meeting survives except a brief mention by Sorabji that John had wanted to lend him the score of Stevenson's Prelude, Fugue and Fantasy on *Doktor Faust*. Knowing that it was the only copy, Sorabji had refused. Sorabji seems to have been very suspicious of people who could play his music; it was connected no doubt to his hypersensitivity to criticism, a fetish that had led him to place what was in effect a ban on public performance of his works. In a letter to Stevenson some months later Ogdon refers to the meeting when he writes:

> Sorabji hardly seemed a pessimistic man: he has maintained a volatility both in writing and speech which hardly seems compatible with 'nursing his griefs [*sic*]'. He has *answered* slights, and that right valiantly!

In 1960 John signed an exclusive recording contract with EMI and just before Christmas began making his first record for them, which consisted of works by Liszt and Busoni. The two recording sessions took place at the Abbey Road studios under the supervision of Peter Andry. Two further sessions were scheduled for March 1961 and the record came out in the summer of that year to excellent reviews. Edward Greenfield of the *Musical Times* wrote that

> In everything Ogdon conveys a rare sense of enjoyment. Even in the heaviest writing there is a shining clarity, not a finger out of place [...] few virtuosi are as successful as this in their first recording.

He did add, however, that John's was 'a dangerously recherché choice of works'.

Around the time that he was making this first record something else quickened in the Ogdon household. Brenda became pregnant and both she and John were deliriously happy at the news. (Brenda has described the early years of their marriage as 'passionately physical'.) Alistair Londonderry, whose daughter Sophia had been born the previous year, wrote to John with details of a new Liszt competition (for British entrants only) that was to take place in January 1961 in London to celebrate the 150th anniversary of the composer's birth. It was being organized under the auspices of the Liszt Society and with a PR link to the new film about Liszt starring Dirk Bogarde, *Song Without End*. The venue for the finals of the competition was to be the opulent surroundings of Londonderry House on Park Lane, the London mansion of the Marquesses of Londonderry since 1822. Though not lived in by the family at the time of the competition, it remained in their possession until its demolishment in 1965 to make way for the Hilton Hotel. The distinguished jury was presided over by the eminent Lisztian Louis Kentner and included conductor Charles Mackerras and composer and Liszt expert Humphrey Searle. Sir Adrian Boult was in the glittering invited audience. The pianist Cyril Smith, who had five pupils in the finals, including Eileen Broster, was also present. John's no-demons-barred performance of the *Dante* Sonata harrowed the judges; by contrast his thoughtful and poetic rendition of the B-minor sonata gave voice to another side of his genius, the contemplative. His eccentric tempi – for instance, he slowed down the great octave passage before the ending – appeared wholly natural in the context of his deeply felt reading. He was unanimously awarded the first prize of £150 and a record deal with Pye (which he couldn't take up because of his EMI contract); second place was tied between his old college friend David Wilde and Benjamin Kaplan, while fourth place went to Hamish Milne, another grand-pupil of Busoni.

John's victory in London is nearly always misreported as first prize in the Liszt-Bartók Competition in Budapest, which was won later that year by David Wilde (John did not enter). Wilde himself laments that his second prize in London meant that from that time on, despite his first prize in Budapest, he was always perceived as 'number two to John Ogdon'. It was a label he found hard to shake. There had been television coverage of the finals so John was very much in the lime-light. In 1961 he undertook 120 engagements, twenty-two of which were in October alone, and that year saw him working with some of the finest conductors in the world. Apart from another trip to the Spoleto Festival in July and a concert tour in Ireland, all his concerts were in the UK. In February he played the Bartók Concerto No. 2 with the London Symphony Orchestra under Georg Solti at the Royal Festival Hall. Neville Cardus described it as the 'best, most musically integrated' performance he had heard for a long time. For a pianist so young John was, he said, 'already unusually powerful and masculine'. He predicted that

> Mr. Ogdon might well find himself, before he is much older, involved in a musical revival of romantic values and implications. He will be wise to get ready for this revival. But already he has given clinching evidence of rare gifts. His technical command over the keyboard is rather staggering, and he is clearly a musician. His future as a complete artist possibly depends on his power to resist the pull of fashion, contemporary or other.

That same month, at a reception of the Classics Club at the Arts Council in St James's Square, John was presented with a cheque for £200 by the Patrons of Music fund as a promising young artist. It was here that he first met the philanthropist Sir Robert Mayer, a notable sponsor of young musicians. In July he played at the first night of the

Proms in Franck's Symphonic Variations and Shostakovich's Piano Concerto No. 2 in F major with Sir Malcolm Sargent conducting. In an amusing piece in the *Sunday Times* entitled 'Sir Malcolm and the Birds', the reviewer, who had attended the rehearsal, observed the contrast between the two protagonists:

> Sir Malcolm radiant in mohair, conducting the orchestra, while the bear-like figure of John Ogdon crouched at the piano, hair on end, beard and shirt buttons in dangerous proximity, glaring at the keyboard through pebble lenses. Ogdon is the youngest (twenty-four) and brightest of this year's Promenade debutants: rather shy, he admitted that he read books and ate food, but wasn't prepared to go further.

Despite John's obvious successes at the keyboard cautionary voices at the BBC continued to express anxiety about his future. Paul Huband, now head of Music for the North of England, had put in one or two adverse reports and wrote to Eric Warr, the assistant head of Music Programmes in London, saying that only a real concern about Ogdon's future had prompted his criticism. 'I am sure you will also be interested to know,' he added, 'that his last professor (at the moment he has no guidance), the very able Gordon Green, is as concerned as I am about various trends which show in his playing.' Huband also felt that John was being overused; withholding his recommendation was perhaps a way of spreading him less thinly. In another memo to Eric Warr entitled 'JOHN OGDON UBIQUE', he pointed out that John had ten broadcasts in the second half of 1961, with the probability of further engagements materializing for that period. 'Is it usual or desirable for us to plug an artist to this extent?' he asked.

John had by now found a new ally at the BBC in composer Robert Simpson. Between them they hatched a plot to broadcast Sorabji's *Opus Clavicembalisticum* but, despite John writing a 'long and persuasive' letter to the composer seeking his permission for the project, Sorabji remained obdurate on the question of public performance. John's letters at this time evince a deep admiration for the work of Bruckner and Sibelius – in particular the latter, whose symphonies and tone poems were, to him, creations of 'sublime genius'. He wrote to Simpson asking if he could broadcast Ferdinand Löwe's 'magnificent' piano transcription of Bruckner's Ninth Symphony and also enquiring about the transcription of Sibelius's Fifth, which he had studied as a boy. John assimilated new music not only in the scores he read but also in listening to records and radio broadcasts and through visits to the Hallé when his busy schedule allowed. In alluding to Ronald Stevenson's compositions in a letter to the composer, John wrote:

> These two aspects of your creation, the one monumental, the other gentler, more intimate, remind me forcibly of Sibelius, in whom I know similar apparently contradictory faces (Janus-like?) co-exist. Last night I heard Beecham's record of *Oceanides*. I wonder if any greater music has been written in the 20th century. It is a very moving and elevating fusion of his two faces.

That July he joked to Stevenson that his new residence, housing as it did copies of the Busoni Piano Concerto and *Opus Clavicembalisticum*, could now no longer be called 'The Maisonette', and with that he omitted it from the address. The same month he completed an essay entitled 'Kaikhosru Sorabji and Herman Melville' for a symposium on Sorabji being compiled by Hugh MacDiarmid. One senses Ogdon's poignant identification with both these artists when in his final paragraph he writes of Sorabji as 'very much alone, and on his own' in the world of contemporary music, even as Melville, creator of Bartleby, the loneliest character in all literature, was 'a creature set apart' in nineteenth-century letters.

When John and Brenda visited Spoleto for the festival that summer Brenda was six and a half months pregnant. She noted with pleasure that John was an audience favourite, but was less enamoured of the personal attention he received from beautiful females. One very hot night they attended a party in the garden of a large villa above the town and Brenda watched helplessly as John was surrounded by a phalanx of worshipping women who gradually elbowed her out of the way. Shy, nodding John appeared curiously in his element, like the god

Dionysus before his Bacchic women, and was oblivious of Brenda's distress. When she could take it no more she hotfooted it through the villa and out into the night, taking flight down the steep hillside. Before she had gone far a rough arm reached out of the darkness and grabbed her; after a struggle she managed to break free and started back up the hill. Her pregnant state and the oppressively humid air slowed her down, however, and her attacker was upon her again in no time. Just then a car appeared and she began yelling and waving; it screeched to a halt and an army officer jumped out. The ruffian vanished, and she was driven back to the party in a state of shock. John had not even noticed her absence, but when he saw her, pale and shaking, he was sufficiently alarmed to give his Maenads the slip and take her back to their lodgings.

John was in Norwich giving a concert when Brenda went into labour on 30 September. His train home on the Sunday got stranded outside Lincoln so he was unaware of the birth until he got back to Manchester and was met at the station by relatives of his wife, who told him he was the father of a baby girl. She had been born on 1 October at St Mary's Hospital, where Brenda's sister, Janet, was a pupil midwife. John was overjoyed at the news and rushed over there post-haste. He and Brenda named their daughter Annabel after Alistair Londonderry's sister, Lady Annabel Vane-Tempest-Stewart (for whom her husband, Mark Birley, would also name the famous London nightclub). John didn't have much time to enjoy the new arrival: he was back on tour the following day, for concerts in Scarborough, Keighley, York and Elland followed by a tour of Ireland. October and November between them accounted for fully forty engagements. Little wonder that John lamented in a newspaper article of the time that he didn't see his daughter as much as he would like.

In another article J.W.M. Thompson, who had been to visit John in his maisonette, wrote:

A serious pianist leads an iceberg life – only the tip, the actual performance, is visible; the bulk of it, the work and study in solitude, is hidden. Ogdon takes comfortably to this stern regime. He is rather shy and doesn't mind being locked up with only a piano for company. He has lost touch with all the boys he was at school with only a few years ago, although they are flourishing all around him in the Manchester ambience. Musicians, spread around the continent, are his friends now.

6

A LION IN MOSCOW

Ogdon's tempi, his trills and octaves, the ease with which any technical difficulties were overcome [. . .] his unique range of piano-colour – all this literally stunned Moscow's sophisticated public. Everybody seemed to agree that such technique had not been 'imported' from abroad since the times of Busoni himself.

Soviet Music magazine, 1962

In May 1958 a largely unknown American pianist by the name of Van Cliburn won the inaugural Tchaikovsky International Piano Competition in Moscow. It was the height of the Cold War; only months previously the Soviets had shocked the West by launching Sputnik, the first man-made satellite to orbit the earth. The Tchaikovsky Competition was intended to showcase Soviet cultural superiority on the world stage. To that end television cameras followed every last detail of the five-week event. Soviet pianists took second, third and fourth prizes; Van Cliburn's victory was totally unscripted. The jury, headed by Emil Gilels, had shown every inclination of following the party line and ignoring the elephant in the room, until Sviatoslav Richter turned the tables by giving Van Cliburn 100 marks out of twenty-five and all the other finalists zero. When asked to explain his conduct, he said, 'People either make music, or they don't.' It was to be his last jury appearance, but his protest had the desired effect. Gilels approached the minister of culture, Ekaterina Furtseva, and together they went directly to Premier Khrushchev. 'Well, what are the professionals saying?' the Soviet leader asked. 'Is Cliburn the best?' When they answered in the affirmative he replied without hesitation: 'In that case, give him the prize!'

Khrushchev had introduced a period of destalinization and had lifted many of the more repressive and paranoid policies of his predecessor. Russia, a land traumatized by the brutal imposition of Soviet ideology, had always revered its artists as prophets and deliverers. Now a political and cultural thaw had been set in motion of which the Tchaikovsky Competition was an important part. The Soviets had unwittingly created an American cultural icon in the person of Van Cliburn, who was accorded a ticker-tape parade in New York on his return to the States – becoming the only musician ever to have received that singular honour. The ice was still thawing when the Second Tchaikovsky Competition came round four years later, in April 1962, and the contest was described with anticipation as 'Moscow's musical spring'. Nevertheless this was still very much the Cold War. The Berlin Wall had gone up the previous year and 1962 saw both the Cuban missile crisis and the publication of Solzhenitsyn's novel exposing the Soviet labour-camp system, *One Day in the Life of Ivan Denisovich*.

John described himself as having been enthused with Russian music from an early age, as his father had been, and it was this affinity that made him feel he ought to enter the competition. It meant cancelling a number of scheduled concerts in Britain, however, and for that reason Mrs Tillett tried to dissuade him from going. He would also have to raise funds for his air ticket and accommodations. 'I think I'll just have to take the gamble,' John told Brenda. 'Fine,' she said. 'Go and have a jolly good bash.' At the root of it all, though, John knew (and Brenda knew) that he had to win a major competition in order to become an international name.

In January that year John had made his first orchestral record, for EMI, playing Rachmaninoff's Piano Concerto No. 2 with the

Philharmonia Orchestra under John Pritchard. It was released in the summer and proved an instant success with the public. Mrs Tillett didn't understand the recording industry (and didn't think it had a future!) so she didn't bother to fight the artist's corner with the recording companies. John was paid a flat fee of £200, with no royalties, a disastrous deal for what became such an enduringly high-selling record. Rachmaninoff wrote his second concerto after a period of deep depression and dedicated it to his hypnotherapist, Dr Nikolai Dahl. The piece is in a sense an awakening and the opening chords of the piano part, which precede the orchestral entry, are reminiscent of the mournful slow tolling of Russian church bells. The mounting tension of the chords, like rising flood waters, is released in a sudden majestic surge as the orchestra introduces the main theme. The piano can either struggle against this tremendous spate of energy and ideas or surrender to it. Most pianists approach the concerto from a heroic standpoint (as does Richter, for example), but Ogdon surrenders – and by doing so releases the work's more dreamlike and introspective qualities. Edward Greenfield in the *Guardian* wrote of Ogdon's 'expansive and thoughtful view of the work', while Bryce Morrison described his interpretation as 'wonderfully poetic and understated'.

Unusually for a virtuoso, John was always acutely sensitive to the movement of the entire concerto – not just the piano part – and ready to submit to the orchestra for the greater good of the music. He probably learned this approach from the Busoni Concerto, which he'd known since he was a boy: for this, according to Busoni biographer Edward Dent, 'the soloist is required to have the will to put himself deliberately into the background when necessary, however difficult his technical task may be, and to have the musical intelligence to see the concerto as a whole.' This came very naturally to John, who throughout his life cultivated the art of fading into the background.

From February onwards John tried to squeeze in as much preparation for the competition as possible, but his concert and broadcasting engagements in the UK and Ireland – fifteen in February and another fifteen in March – left little enough time. He began taking lessons in London with the Hungarian pianist Ilona Kabos. A grand-pupil of Liszt and winner of the 1915 Liszt Prize, Kabos had been married to

Louis Kentner, the pianist John heard at his very first recital in Nottingham. As a young woman she had played for Busoni, who was so impressed that he played for her. Known for her profound attention to each nuance in the score, Kabos was an electrifying interpreter not only of Liszt but also of that other great Hungarian composer Bartók – whom she had also met. In order to make John feel Bartók's rhythms she would dance round the piano while he was playing, exhorting him to 'listen, listen, listen' until he could feel the rhythms with his whole body. Brenda, too, studied with Ilona Kabos while she was preparing for her first Wigmore Hall recital that April, which included works by Liszt and Bartók, and she and John together studied Bartók's Sonata for two pianos and percussion with her.

At the end of March there was another interruption of John's preparations. He had been playing in Norwich when his daughter Annabel was born and he was playing there again when he received news that his father had died of heart failure at Bury General Hospital in Manchester. Howard had been failing for some time but would not admit that he was ill. He had intended to retire from teaching that July and had been looking at plans for a bungalow for himself and Dorothy; he had already bought some new furniture in preparation for the move. He had gone into hospital for tests on his liver and passed away while he was there. He was sixty-two. Dorothy Ogdon was also in very poor health, having had a stroke that January which paralysed her right side. John's brother Paul, who lived on the same road as his parents, was with their father when he died. Paul had been suffering recurring health problems himself from an infection he had developed after having a tooth removed, and was something of an invalid at this time. John was able to attend the funeral as he had a concert up in Manchester that evening. The service and interment took place at All Saints, Stand, the church used by the school where Howard taught. An appreciation appeared in the *Standian*:

> We at School knew him as a tremendous worker with a keen
> analytical brain. In the last few years only those who knew him well
> realized the will-power which kept him going when lesser men

would have given in to ill-health. His great regret was that he would not finish his new English Course. We have lost a most loyal and conscientious colleague.

The notice ends by mentioning his youngest son's success and what a source of pride and satisfaction this had been to Howard. According to Brenda, John's response to his father's death was muted and he remained fully focused on his preparations for Moscow.

The official opening ceremony of the competition had taken place on 1 April in the Palace of Congresses at the Kremlin. The Minister of Culture gave the welcoming words; then followed a speech from the Chairman of the Organizing Committee, Dmitri Shostakovich, who had joined the Communist party in 1960. He began:

Dear Comrades, Friends, Colleagues: today we musicians have a big occasion for celebration. We are opening the Second International Tchaikovsky Competition. Tomorrow morning in the two finest concert halls in Moscow performers will begin a contest which in its scope and standard is one of the most outstanding in the world.

The violin and cello competitions got underway first; the piano competition wouldn't commence until 14 April. Having been given the funds to travel by Sir Robert Mayer, whom he'd met at the Arts Council the previous year, John set off for Moscow on the twelfth. As it happened he flew out on the same flight as Laurens van der Post, who was going to Moscow to begin his odyssey across the Soviet Union from the Ukraine to Siberia. In his account of his travels, *Journey into Russia*, van der Post gives an amusing portrait of John, of whom he had no knowledge at the time. There were only ten passengers in all, seven East Germans, one African, van der Post himself and John, who is described as 'a plump, untidy man who by his looks could easily have been a confirmed beachcomber from any intellectual foreshore of the Western world'. 'He earned my respect,' continues van der Post, 'not only for a superb display of one-upmanship by coolly ordering a second éclair when even the perspiring East

Germans had been forced to retire, but also by reading a large album of piano music throughout the journey as most people would read a thriller.'

The 'album of piano music' was probably Busoni's Piano Concerto, as John had written to the BBC just five days before his departure for Moscow urgently requesting both the orchestral parts and the piano score. He was no doubt planning to play it in the final round of the competition, in which case he would have been disappointed. The organizing committee wouldn't accommodate a male-voice choir – nor for that matter could they allow one of the competitors to hold the stage for seventy minutes when the average length of a concerto was between twenty-five and thirty.

John was met at the airport by his interpreter who, as his guide and minder for the next three weeks, was deputed to keep a close eye on his activities. He was driven to the Hotel Ukraina, which was picturesquely situated on a bend of the Moscow River – a short drive from the Moscow Conservatory, where the competition was being held. The following day John was able to go into the conservatory, where Tchaikovsky himself had taught for twelve years. Here he had a day to practise and meet some of the other competitors before the first round of the piano competition kicked off the following day. There were fifty-six entrants in all, from twenty-four countries, with the Soviets fielding a dozen scrupulously winnowed candidates. The USA had sent nine, as had France. Others came from all corners of the globe, including India, Mexico, Japan, Australia, Cuba, Cyprus and the Philippines. Contestants had to be between the ages of seventeen and thirty-two. John was one of two British entrants in the piano competition (the other, Arthur Thompson, was eliminated in the first round) and tended to stick with the other English speakers, especially the Americans. Contact with the Soviet competitors was generally limited. The jury, headed once again by Gilels, consisted of nineteen members, seven of them Soviet – including Lev Oborin and the composer Dmitri Kabalevsky – and five others from Eastern Bloc or Communist countries. Five jurors came from Western Europe, with Sir Thomas Armstrong, principal of the Royal Academy of Music, representing Britain, and Guido Agosti, a pupil of Busoni, representing Italy. The American and Brazilian pianists Eugene List and Magda Tagliaferro rounded off the panel, which comprised at least five composers.

John was an unknown quantity in Moscow, though two of the jury members, Gilels and Agosti, had heard him as a nineteen-year-old in the first round of the Brussels Competition. One Soviet entrant, however, already had a reputation as a world-class pianist. He had been the winner of that competition in Brussels at the precocious age of eighteen, and at twenty-one had made an acclaimed tour of America. Universally acknowledged as a rising star in the musical firmament, his name was Vladimir Ashkenazy. Ashkenazy had no need to enter the Tchaikovsky Competition and absolutely no desire to. Had he wished to enter, he would surely have done so in 1958. But this was the Soviet Union and the Ministry of Culture was desperate to erase the humiliation of Van Cliburn's victory by carrying off the first prize. Ashkenazy was the obvious choice to spearhead that effort. The selection process began in 1959, fully three years before the competition. Despite his best efforts to avoid being picked, it was made clear to Ashkenazy that he was expected to take part – and to win. When he told Ministry officials that Tchaikovsky wasn't really his thing, and that his hands weren't suited to all those big chords, they were incredulous. 'How can you say that about our great Russian composer?' they demanded. Subtly, and not so subtly, they let him know that his career would be over if he didn't take part; he could forget any idea of performing outside the Soviet Union again. It was an uncomfortable arrangement for both parties. Ashkenazy, a Jew with an Icelandic wife, was already seen as disloyal to the Party and a potential troublemaker. After his 1958 US tour he had been ordered to stay at home for a few years and play to workers and peasants, and his wife had been forced to become a Soviet citizen. So, with everything to lose, Ashkenazy duly entered the competition.

The first round was very much in the minor keys, at least for John. All contestants had to play the Bach Prelude and Fugue in C-sharp minor, a sonata by Mozart (John chose the A-minor sonata, K. 310), Tchaikovsky's Dumka (*Scenes from a Russian Village*) in C minor, and études by Chopin, Liszt, Scriabin and Rachmaninoff.

John chose Liszt's *La Campanella* (in the lesser-known Busoni arrangement); Scriabin's Etude in C-sharp minor, Op. 42, No. 5; and Rachmaninoff's Etude-Tableau in E-flat minor, Op. 39, No. 5. His only foray into the major keys was with the Chopin Etude, Op. 10, No. 1. John was reasonably pleased by his performances, though the Mozart left him a bit nervous. An English student at the conservatory at the time, Allan Schiller, met up with John at the start of the first round and they played to each other in one of the practice rooms. John played the Mozart sonata and Allan remembers being worried for him, as it didn't have a classical feel to it. He seemed to find the rhythms in Mozart quite tricky. He didn't really care for the Dumka sonata, a piece dear to the Russian heart, and it was felt that he had played it rather carelessly. He received the first of many ovations, however, for his Bach, and his rendering of *La Campanella* caused a storm of approval from jury and audience alike. The Russians loved the improvised quality of his Rachmaninoff but he failed to touch them with his Chopin and Scriabin études: both were felt to be somewhat impersonal. The Moscow audiences were large and discerning and, for the most part, generous. They included many world-famous artists and teachers as well as a large number of professional musicians and students. Even the ordinary Muscovites knew their music and were sophisticated about performance standards, although they could be quite crude in expressing their disapproval. Quick to make known their delight with ovations and waves of slowly accelerating handclaps, they were equally forthcoming with snorts and discontented murmurs when they were unhappy with a performance. A memory lapse might even be greeted by guffaws of laughter. All rounds of the contest were open to the public, and tickets were inexpensive and fiercely sought after. There was a tremendous buzz about the competition throughout the city and a special trolleybus stop was created to take people to the concert hall. Everyone was up to speed with the latest news, from the Moscow Conservatory cleaning ladies to the local taxi drivers. John was placed eighth after the first round, a decision that surprised and pained him, but it was more than enough to get him through to the second round together with twenty-three other contestants.

The distinguished Russian critic Tamara Grum-Grzhimailo, who wrote extensively about the competition, was in no doubt that the discovery of Ogdon – 'this lion of the keyboard' – happened right in the first round; though 'the vast audience in the Grand Hall did not immediately spot its new darling in this burly, bearded musician who is so unlike the Van Cliburn ideal of the artist.' He was, she admitted, 'a total surprise'. In poetic language that reflects the profound impact John's playing made on her, she wrote:

> He walks onto the stage with a rather sluggish gait, his spectacles glinting, his round pink-cheeked face bent forward, framed by a small goatee beard. He sits down at the piano and bends close to the keyboard, as if looking into its depths. His hands begin to knead the keys with gentle enveloping movements, the hands of a silent musical sculptor bringing to life a solid block of sound material. It's as if the creation of music were an organic part of his physical existence, the embodiment of the eternal human need 'to create the world according to the laws of beauty.'

Grum-Grzhimailo went on to describe in glowing terms the 'composerly' sound he drew from the keyboard. She praised his passionate intellectual power and stylistic precision, his beautiful timbres and 'unique "calligraphic" signature sound' (including the depth and solidity of his chords), while noting the wilful fluctuations in tempi. His playing was 'full of sharp contrasts (sounds, tempos, states), wild passages that broke the piano speed-barrier and pauses whose silence was somehow fiercely obstinate'. Equally striking was 'the sense of complete creative freedom' that Ogdon evinced and his 'special feeling for improvisation, which only manifests in those of the very highest interpretive skill'. He was, she declared, a pianist of 'inexhaustible imagination'. His unusual appearance certainly impressed the Russians – the Ogdon goatee, said Yakov Flier, gave him the look of an experienced skipper – and they were amused by his habit of pushing his glasses up on his nose during the most breathtakingly difficult passages, as if he possessed a third hand specially for the purpose. English musicians were not well known in Russia, and the general perception was that 'English' and 'virtuoso' were mutually exclusive terms. There was something altogether improbable and mysterious about Ogdon that appealed to the Slav temperament.

When he was not busy practising at the conservatory John was scouting the Moscow music stores for scores and records unavailable in the West or music by young Soviet composers. He also picked the brains of the *Daily Worker* correspondent, who shared his interest in the latest classical music being composed in Russia. Writing to Ronald Stevenson, John confided that his impressions of Moscow were 'tumultuous and not easily explicable or reducible to words on paper'. He did his best not to listen to his rivals, but to focus on his own playing. He did, however, hear Ashkenazy's haunting rendition of the Chopin Etude Op. 10, No. 1, and made a note of the way he kept the right hand very quiet. The two met and complimented each other's playing. Ashkenazy later said of John, 'He had wonderful hands and a very interesting mind. He was a very unusual pianist.' Various events had been laid on by the Organizing Committee of the competition, including a visit to Tchaikovsky's country home in Klin. Many of the competitors preferred to stay back and practise; this included John, though he did go at the end of the competition. There was also a reception at the Kremlin one evening for the English-speaking contestants across all three disciplines (piano, cello, violin), which John attended. The young American pianist Susan Starr remembers standing out on the street afterwards with John beside her. Being curious to break through his wall of reserve, she asked him something just for the sake of asking and received a mumbled response that couldn't really be classified as speech. Half amused, half exasperated, she said, 'John, can you speak?' He looked down at his feet with the shadow of a smile, then suddenly said with a laugh, 'Yes, I can really!' After that she found him quite charming and amusing. Roy Bogas, another American competitor, confessed to finding John 'very private and perhaps more than a little strange on some level'.

After the first round, the twenty-four remaining competitors had the weekend to recuperate and prepare for the more challenging second round, which was to begin on Monday 23 April. John, however, neither rested nor practised but did something outwardly insane: he flew back to London to keep an engagement with the London Philharmonic under John Pritchard at the Royal Festival Hall. To do this he had to get permission from the competition's Organizing Committee, and they were not happy at all. There was quite a flap and it took some behind-the-scenes negotiations before he was allowed to leave the country. He was due to play the Tchaikovsky First Concerto in London, which was also the mandatory piece in the competition finals; so it was thought that this extra concert experience might give him an advantage if he got through that far. John was on tip-top form and Brenda, who travelled down from Manchester to see him, thought he radiated confidence. Donald Mitchell of the *Telegraph* gave his unconditional approval of the performance:

> Once in a while an artist plays a well-known work as if he and his audience were hearing it for the first time. John Ogdon, the soloist in last night's concert [. . .] did just this with the Tchaikovsky piano concerto in B-flat minor. Interrupting his stay in Moscow for the Tchaikovsky Piano Competition, Mr. Ogdon gave one of the finest performances of his legendary career, and if any part of this work is included in the competition one would hope his success to be a foregone conclusion. He is a player who has tremendous reserves of tone and every note in the concerto was significant [. . .] Not for years had I felt so deeply the drama and romance of this work.

He jetted back that same night, but before he left for the airport he told Brenda he didn't think he stood a realistic chance of winning in Moscow. Still, the whole London caper was yet another testament to John's remarkable stamina. Moscow was pretty rough in those days, in terms of board and lodging, and many of the Americans fell sick from food poisoning or the water, or simply felt depressed by the murky grey climate; others had their nerves strained to breaking point by the thinness of hotel walls. John, on the other hand, had the constitution of an ox and ploughed on with enthusiasm and determination. On the Sunday that he was away Emil Gilels was awarded the prestigious Lenin Prize. The timing of the award was certainly felicitous from the

Ministry of Culture's point of view. If Gilels had been tempted to stray from the notion of a Soviet winner, this would surely rein him in to more acceptable ways of thinking.

Now everyone's focus turned to the second round. For this the set pieces were Shostakovich's Prelude and Fugue in C; Balakirev's fiendishly difficult *Islamey: An Oriental Fantasy*; Tchaikovsky's Grand Sonata in G, Op. 37; and a piece specially composed for the competition by Alexander Pirumov, Prelude and Toccata. In addition to these each contestant had to choose repertoire lasting fifty-five minutes. This time, for John at least, it was all a case of major keys. He chose the first movement of Beethoven's *Hammerklavier* Sonata, Liszt's Transcendental Etude No. 5 (*Feux Follets*) and Mephisto Waltz No. 1; Ravel's *Ondine* and *Scarbo*; Scriabin's Sonata No. 5; and one of his own preludes, entitled *In Modo Napolitano*, which he'd composed while still at college.

The Tchaikovsky Sonata is a rambling, rather ponderous piece that is even now rarely heard outside Russia and John's performance was considered too fast and perfunctory, with one critic referring to the 'breathless helter-skelter' of his playing. Tchaikovsky, the presiding spirit of the competition, had proved a stumbling stone once again. His Balakirev was attacked by certain critics for the same headlong approach, yet it caused a sensation among the jury and the other competitors. Even if they didn't like it, they couldn't ignore the scintillating ease with which he had just tossed off one of the most punishing pieces in the repertoire. Ogdon's *Hammerklavier*, on the other hand, was acknowledged as one of the peaks of the competition. Bryce Morrison described it as 'profound and speculative', while one Moscow critic made do with the single word 'staggering'. For Tamara Grum-Grzhimailo it was proof that Ogdon was a mature and original musical thinker with an astonishing sense of form, a philosopher of the piano who improvised not moods but thoughts. His was a world of 'tense, passionate, and at times harsh reflection', but no one could deny his almost telepathic gift for communing with the soul of the composer. His Liszt and Ravel were also hailed as triumphs of interpretive skill and imagination, with special emphasis placed on the searching originality and modernity of Ogdon's readings, his fusion of passion and intellect. After his Ravel – for Yakov Flier the artistic climax of the proceedings – John was called back for an encore.

As for his own piece, a kind of modern tarantella, this was a bold statement of identity that was not lost on the jury. Black-and-white TV footage shows the distinguished composer Dmitri Kabalevsky leaning forward at the jurors' table, listening intently to this latter-day pianist-composer. Grum-Grzhimailo talked of Ogdon conjuring the profoundest associations in his audience. In him several centuries of the history of pianism seemed to come alive and one could see clearly the lineage of Western European piano playing, stretching in a line from Bach to Beethoven to Liszt to Busoni. 'This line has not been lost,' she declared,

> and the twenty-five-year-old English musician, whose piano voice has a wonderful, rather severe baritone timbre, is its new heir and successor. His playing contains the layers of past musical eras, laid down like the rings in the trunk of a mighty oak tree, and we have heard him!

Needless to say John's playing was the subject of heated discussion in the corridors of the conservatory and the cafes of Moscow. Although it was felt that he had lost ground in the second round because he hadn't played the Russian pieces in the Russian manner, his modern, unromantic approach to the piano struck a chord with a culture eager to open the doors to Western influence.

The critics agreed that the general level of playing at the 1962 Tchaikovsky Competition was even higher than it had been in 1958. There were many luminaries to watch out for besides Ogdon and Ashkenazy. There was the young American Susan Starr, who had studied under Rudolph Serkin at the Curtis Institute and was the youngest person ever to appear with a major orchestra (she played with the Philadelphia aged five); her compatriot Joseph Banowetz, a grand-pupil of Clara Schumann and already an experienced concert artist; the young Frenchman Jean-Bernard Pommier who had won the Young Musicians' International Competition in Berlin in 1960; the

twenty-year-old Chinese pianist Yin Chen Tsun, a student at the
Leningrad Conservatoire and widely admired for his fresh, neo-
Romantic approach to the Viennese classics; Georgian pianist Marina
Mdivani, who had studied at the Moscow Conservatory under Jacob
Milstein and the previous year won first prize at the prestigious
Concours International Marguerite Long–Jacques Thibaud in Paris;
and Soviet prodigy Alexei Nasedkin, the favourite pupil of legendary
pedagogue Heinrich Neuhaus, who impressed the judges with the
purity of his playing. It was in fact one of the stiffest piano competitions ever held. After the first two rounds, Ashkenazy and Yin Chen
Tsun stood first equal, with a score of twenty-four points out of
twenty-five. It is not known exactly where John stood, but he comfortably made it through to the finals with eleven others: six from the
USSR, two from the USA, two from France and one from China.
Out of the twelve, four were women. The Soviets went into the final
round with a very good chance of picking up first prize. Add to the
mix Yin Chen Tsun, who was a member of the Communist Youth
League in his native China, and a Soviet-school win seemed almost
assured.

In the third and final round each competitor had to play one of the
three Tchaikovsky piano concertos (all chose the first) and another
concerto of his or her choice. Each concerto was rehearsed with the
orchestra the morning of the performance. All those who commented
on the competition were agreed that John came into his own in this
final round. Somehow he managed to summon all his powers for one
last assault on the citadel. Critics had talked of the way Ogdon made
crushing advances towards a target in his playing; now he did the
same, only his goal was the victor's wreath. He had always had the
knack of rising to the big occasion. The final round began on 1 May
and ran for six days, with two competitors playing each evening. The
final competitors would play on Sunday 6 May and the results would
be announced that night. Ashkenazy played on the Friday evening,
giving a sprightly and mercurial performance of the Tchaikovsky
Concerto; but, as he was the first to admit, this mammoth piece
didn't sit well under his small hands. Nevertheless his interpretation
was very well received by the audience, as was his performance of the

formidably difficult Second Concerto of Prokofiev, a tortuously irate elegy written for a fellow student who committed suicide. For this Ashkenazy received a prolonged and vociferous ovation.

John played the next day, on the Saturday evening. Rehearsals with the Moscow Philharmonic under Kirill Kondrashin had taken place that morning and, though rehearsals were closed to the public, crowds of fans laid siege in the hope of picking up some crumbs of news. The packed Great Hall of the Moscow Conservatory had a festive air that night. Its ochre and cream walls, with their wreathed oval portraits of the great composers, high windows and sweeping horseshoe gallery, were humming with anticipation. In front of the mammoth organ that ranged the full length of the stage hung an outsized banner of Tchaikovsky looking out over the proceedings. The two curtained State boxes were occupied: one by Mr and Mrs Khrushchev, the minister of culture and various party officials; the other by Queen Elisabeth of the Belgians and her entourage. A special section of the gallery had been set aside for contestants and their spouses, should they wish to attend, and tonight this was full. John needed to perform superbly to win and many people were worried that his weak performance of the Tchaikovsky Grand Sonata in round two might portend an overall lack of sympathy for the Russian composer. All the foreign contestants so far, with the possible exception of Susan Starr, had come unstuck on the Tchaikovsky Concerto. But, as one Russian critic wrote, 'Борода не подведёт!' – 'The beard doesn't fail!'

John had had great success with the Liszt E-flat concerto in Britain, and its combination of stylistic intricacy and sudden demonic eruptions suited his temperament perfectly. He may have chosen it as a tribute to his recently deceased father, bearing in mind that the very first performance of the concerto in Weimar in 1855 had been conducted by Howard's musical hero Hector Berlioz with Liszt himself at the keyboard. From the defiant opening-octave passages the piano is engaged in a restless struggle with the orchestra, engendering a tension that permeates even the most harmonious sections. There is a wonderfully improvised quality to the piano part, as if Liszt had made it up on the spur of the moment that winter's night on the River Ilm. Though formally divided into four movements it is really a single-movement work that showcases Liszt's bravura compositional technique known as 'the metamorphosis of themes'. No one 'did' impetuosity at the piano better than John Ogdon; and in the right hands the Liszt is an impassioned and wonderfully impetuous piece, with moments of ironic reflection. That night, inspired perhaps by his encyclopaedic reading of Gothic literature, he turned it into a macabre joust between Faust and the Devil and had the audience on the edge of their seats. Its headlong ending, like a wild moonlit steeplechase, was followed by a tremendous five-minute standing ovation. A dazed-looking John, nodding, sweating, grinning, was called back again and again. The audience thronged the foot of the stage and threw bouquets of flowers. Just after the performance ended Susan Starr entered the competitors' box and found everyone in it going crazy and shouting themselves hoarse. Even though he had yet to play his Tchaikovsky, there were chants of 'Ogdon for first prize!' and 'Ogdon must win!' from the body of the audience. Mrs Khrushchev was heard to turn to her husband and say, 'Why does Ogdon wear that beard? Who does he think he is, Tchaikovsky himself?'

Tamara Grum-Grzhimailo wrote that Ogdon's performance of the Liszt was an unforgettable musical achievement and the absolute high point of the competition:

> The playing was somehow titanic, a mutiny of all the forces of the indomitable human spirit, a dance above the abyss. It was a Herculean struggle, now bubbling with colossal energy, now falling back in wild exhaustion, writhing in despairing and somehow Mephistophelean, violent trills [...] it was the creation of the music of victory.

If John had wanted to choreograph his own triumph, then the Liszt was an inspired choice of concerto. His strong, surging style had brought him to the forefront at just the right moment. As one Soviet critic put it, he 'broke through to the finish like a true conqueror'. The husband of French finalist Christiane Billaud exclaimed after the Liszt, 'It was like a concert, not a competition!' Roy Bogas, one of the American finalists, agreed:

Ogdon's stunning performance of the Liszt Concerto was great fun and he tossed it off with aplomb. I think it was the latter factor that accounted for the spontaneous response of the audience, including the other contestants who attended. Whereas we others (with the possible exception of Ashkenazy) struggled to refine our own repertoire and maintain our accuracy, John simply dazzled us with his perfection, speed and apparent lack of concern about how he might measure up to the jury's standards. It was a brilliant show, but it was also a clever choice of concerto, as the Liszt lends itself to that kind of playing.

It was as if he had been competing not for a prize but for the hearts of his audience. Susan Starr felt that throughout the competition Ogdon had been 'very wise in the ways of keeping his audience listening at all times by doing rather amazing things – colour contrasts you didn't expect, for instance – and he took incredibly fast tempi and could play every single note.' The jury too was swept up in the euphoria, and no one was more excited than Gilels himself.

After an interval John returned to the platform for his final performance of the competition, the Tchaikovsky Concerto. Here he would be under even greater scrutiny: this was in effect the Russian national concerto and everyone in the audience knew it inside out. Yet it held no fears for John. He seized the piece by the scruff of the neck and breathed new life into it with a spontaneous and creative performance that matched power with poetry – and greatly pleased the Russians. The editor of the *Moscow Press Bulletin* wrote: 'Ogdon's flights of fancy, his strength, his boundless virtuosity, all these captivated the audience. The ovations were long and ardent.' The art critic Professor L. A. Barenboim rejoiced in Ogdon's ability to make a work his own while remaining true to the score. 'I am not afraid to repeat words which in the past were applied to the most outstanding artists,' he declared. 'In playing a work, Ogdon seems to compose it anew.' The cheering went on and on while seemingly endless bouquets were conjured from the air and piled on stage. It was perhaps the naturalness and originality of his playing that had made the biggest impression. Susan Starr said that his Tchaikovsky was 'very wonderful'; while

Ashkenazy admitted that John could play the concerto 'like nothing'. John's marvellous recording of the concerto later that year with Sir John Barbirolli and the Philharmonia captures some of that Moscow magic. As for the audience, it was galvanized into new demonstrations of Ogdonomania. Indeed, as the jury filed back into the hall to hear the next finalist, Alexei Nasedkin, a powerful male voice shouted out from the gallery in Russian, 'First prize to Ogdon! Ogdon must win!' and the chant was once again taken up by the rest of the audience, with a chorus of 'Ogdon! Ogdon! Ogdon!' This noisy show of support continued through the final day of the competition. Each time the conductor raised his baton to begin the next concerto, someone from the audience would shout out, 'Ogdon for first prize' and pandemonium would ensue. John was very popular with the Muscovites. The English juror, Sir Thomas Armstrong, was concerned that these demonstrations would influence the jury negatively, though they could quite easily have had the opposite effect (one thinks of Van Cliburn). John's playing in the finals had created such excitement that people remained gathered outside the conservatory long after the evening's proceedings had finished, passionately discussing the finer points of his performances and debating the merits of the other contestants.

The final performance of the competition came from Soviet pianist Eliso Virsaladze the following night, after which the jury retired to make its decision. Gilels had instructed them before the round began that the point system of the previous two rounds would be replaced by discussion. 'After all,' he said, 'we are musicians, not mathematicians.' While it was clear to everyone that the finals had belonged to Ogdon, with other front runners such as Yin Chen Tsun playing well below their best, the judges had to consider all three rounds. The finalists paced nervously elsewhere in the building as the hours ticked by. John, who was in suit trousers, an orange shirt and a mammoth woolly brown jumper, appeared smiling and relaxed. Three hours passed, an unprecedentedly long time for such deliberations, and yet the jurors remained shut up in council. Sunday passed into the wee hours of Monday and still the competitors were kept waiting. Finally, sometime before 1 a.m., they were ushered into the conservatory's Little Hall to hear the judgements. There had been protracted argument among the jury because the Soviet and Eastern Bloc contingent was adamant that first prize should go to Ashkenazy, while the others were as vociferous in their support of Ogdon. Gilels was well aware of the Soviet prejudice in favour of Ashkenazy but was equally impressed by the two favourites and found it hard to ignore the voice of the people – which was of course raised loudly for Ogdon. To award the top prize to someone other than Ogdon would cause outrage both in Russia and internationally. The competition would have been considered fixed. So, in the end, Gilels suggested that they award two individual first prizes, with gold medals and the full prize money going to both Ashkenazy and Ogdon. The whole jury was satisfied with this diplomatic solution, which, most importantly, recognized the superlative and equal merits of both winners. John felt elated and stunned by the news. The result was greeted with a roar of approbation by the audience, who felt that justice had been served. The second prize, in contrast to the first, was split between Susan Starr of America and Yin Chen Tsun of China. Third prize was awarded to Eliso Virsaladze (USSR), fourth to Marina Mdivani (USSR) and fifth to Valery Kamyshov (USSR). In his autobiography, *Beyond Frontiers*, Ashkenazy wrote:

> When the first prize was eventually divided between John Ogdon and me, there were many people in Moscow who thought that he should have had it all by himself. His natural gift for the piano as well as the brilliance of his performances made a great impact on the public; in addition he cut a rather exotic figure and there tended to be a tremendous admiration for and fascination with foreigners, who performed with a type of charisma that we were not used to.

Ogdon did end up having it all to himself in the Russian mind because the very next year Ashkenazy became a non-person by leaving the Soviet Union and settling in London. As a result his name was dropped from accounts of the competition written in Soviet Russia. A book on the competition by the famous musicologist Alexander Medvedev had to be abandoned for this reason. Even so, Russians naturally tended to compare Ogdon not with Ashkenazy but with the 1958 laureate Van Cliburn. Van Cliburn, they said, was the poet of the piano, John the philosopher. As for perception in the West, tying with Ashkenazy probably gave John more prestige than would have been afforded by an outright win: his name was from that moment forth yoked with that of his brilliant and successful contemporary.

In the journalistic crush after the announcement of the prizes, Tamara Grum-Grzhimailo managed to snatch a few words with John. Their brief dialogue went as follows:

Grum-Grzhimailo: 'Success spoils and fame poisons.' What do you say to that?
Ogdon: For Brahms that was irrelevant.
Grum-Grzhimailo: What are your plans for the future?
Ogdon: To extend my repertoire and play better.

Note the trademark impersonality in John's first reply. The interviewer was nonetheless impressed: 'These answers are Ogdon all over,' she enthused. 'A young musician who puts high demands on himself and is selflessly dedicated to his art.' In many ways Tamara had read John better than any Western critic would ever do. Her insight that his playing was imbued with 'profound subjective feeling, which is so far from being egotistical that it appears purely objective' goes to the heart of the Ogdon genius, and some would say the Ogdon psychosis. She also sounded a warning: 'Ogdon's gift could develop in very contradictory ways and is unlikely to settle down happily any time soon. He has ahead of him many difficulties, setbacks, perhaps painful rifts with audiences, agonizing searches for new paths. But we shall not try to guess. Talent, work and time will decide.'

The following day the prizegiving took place at the Great Hall of the Moscow Conservatory, with the prizes handed out by Shostakovich. It was also the closing ceremony of the competition and there was a raft of speeches. As at the school prizegivings at Manchester's Free Trade Hall all those years before, John appeared relaxed and confident as he went up to shake hands with the great composer. The prizegiving was followed by the Prize Winners' Concert, at which John played the first movement of the Tchaikovsky Concerto and Ashkenazy the final two movements. After this there was a dazzling reception at the Kremlin with toasts and more speeches, hosted by the Khrushchevs and attended by Queen Elisabeth of the Belgians. There is footage of Khrushchev raising a glass to the whole room as he stands behind a long banqueting table groaning with crystal and fruit. 'Music can accomplish anything,' he declares; 'music can make you laugh or cry, music leads men into battle with head held high, music is a great force.' Extending his heartfelt good wishes to the youthful musicians who took part in the competition, he expresses the hope that they will perfect their talent for the sake of goodwill and peace, to the glory of all men. Standing behind him were Brezhnev, Mikoyan, Furtseva and other members of the Party Central Committee and Politburo.

When John was presented to the Soviet premier, Khrushchev threw up his arms and with a raucous laugh said, 'Ah, my bearded young friend, how glad I am to see you. I love you.' Then, putting his arm on John's shoulder, he said in a more confidential voice, 'I should like to pull your beard to see whether it is real, but this would create an international incident for British beards must on no account be pulled by Russian politicians!' More old footage shows John bobbing up and down at the end of Khrushchev's arm, desperate to break away from the prolonged handshake. Khrushchev's peasant humour and general horseplay were covers for a very shrewd political mind. He knew the value of such genial capering on the international stage. The winners had eulogies sung to them in high-flown language and were promised triumphal tours of the Soviet Union.

John had tried to call Brenda in the early hours of Monday morning to tell her of his victory but she had not heard the phone, so he called her mother instead. It was in fact via a journalist from the *Daily Mail* that Brenda first learned of John's success, and that evening her family came round to celebrate with bottles of champagne. John did finally get through that night on a very crackly line from Moscow. Brenda could just make out the words, 'Darling, I did it for you.' When she heard them she sobbed with elation. She was not the only one to feel stirred by John's victory. Sir Thomas Armstrong, who had sat on the jury, wrote:

I myself was very proud, and many people were deeply moved by [Ogdon's] humility and humanity – two qualities which, unless I am mistaken, largely account, with his splendid creative musicianship, for the warmth of feeling that he evoked among the Russian public as a whole.

On the Tuesday John was taken to Tchaikovsky's country home in Klin, a village eighty-five kilometres northwest of Moscow. It was the composer's retreat from the bustle and strain of Moscow life, which was, he had come to realize, breaking his health. Although he spent only a year at the Klin house before he died, it was his dream home: uncluttered, a large garden with woods, wonderful views of the Russian countryside, and the calm and quiet to work. John saw the simple Karelian birch-wood table where Tchaikovsky composed his Symphony No. 6 and the final piano concerto, and was invited to play the composer's Jacob Becker grand. This was a ritual now for the winner of the piano competition; Van Cliburn had played on it four years earlier. A group of smiling students stood around the instrument and watched as John began to play. This idyllic rural retreat would live in John's mind as a vision of the sort of place he would like to inhabit, surrounded by books and music and with the peace to compose.

The following evening, after almost a month in Moscow, it was time for John to bid farewell to all the friends he had made there. There were more flowers, both in the limousine and at the airport, and a group of well-wishers to wave him off at the steps of the aircraft. The flight was a gift from the Russian government, as John had used his return ticket to fly back to London for the Festival Hall concert. In addition to his gold medal, which featured a piano on one side and Tchaikovsky's head on the other, he took with him £250 in cash; the remaining £750 of his prize money was kept in an account in his name at the Workers' State Savings Bank, to be used on future tours of the Soviet Union. Brenda was waiting at London Airport that night to greet John, as were a handful of journalists with flashing cameras. According to one British newspaper, there was no red carpet, no reception committee, no welcoming crowds, no bands, no flags, just a delay through Customs. Russian Embassy officials at the airport thought it was disgraceful treatment. 'Why are they holding up a man of such importance?' asked one. 'He should be a national hero. Why don't the British people make him one?' Peter Chambers in the *Daily Express* was more acerbic. 'The return of our conquering keyboard hero stirred up about as much noise and excitement as a pebble dropped down a 50ft well [...] We not only failed Ogdon. We gave the impression that when the British hear the word "culture" we yawn and reach for the knob on our TV sets.'

John did a three-minute interview at the airport with writer Wilfred De'ath for the BBC *Today* programme but he couldn't stop for more because he and Brenda were flying up to Glasgow, where he was booked to play the Bartók First Piano Concerto with the Scottish National Orchestra under Alexander Gibson. The day after that he was playing Rachmaninoff with the Hallé at the Free Trade Hall in Manchester and two days later, on the Sunday, he was back in London playing the Tchaikovsky again, this time at the Albert Hall. Dorothy Ogdon had a ticket for the Hallé concert, where her son was given a rousing reception, but she was not present. Instead, she was having an emergency operation for a strangulated hernia. John spent much of the Saturday, his only free day, at her bedside. He was able to show her the special gift presented to him by the RMCM in honour of his Moscow victory. It was an autographed letter from Tchaikovsky to Adolph Brodsky, former principal of the college, in which the composer asks, 'How definite is your visit to Moscow? Are you going to play there?' A breathless Dorothy, bathed in reflected glory, wrote to Marjory Wood telling her how the nurses would bring daily cuttings from the papers. 'I always thought John would reach the stars,' she wrote, 'and I believe that you felt that he would too.' The following week John breezed through Felixstowe, Cambridge, Bromsgrove, Manchester and Totnes. At the Bromsgrove Festival he premiered his own Suite for piano, a work in six compact interlinked movements, as well as pieces by Messiaen, Goehr and Szymanowski. John Manduell of the BBC was there and was swayed by John's piece, which owed much to Ravel and Messiaen in its preoccupation with chordal patterns. 'It is music which is both valid in itself,' wrote Manduell, 'and couched in terms of exciting pianistic exploration. Needless to say, in Ogdon's own hands the work makes a fine impression.'

John became an instant celebrity in the music world and according to Brenda coped with the extra attention 'to the manner born'. He considered it his due and seemed very happy both publicly and privately, though he still found it hard to project himself through the spoken word. As Brenda remarked to a journalist, 'He leaves the talking to me and gets on with thinking about music.' He also seemed to enjoy the travelling, especially as much of it was now abroad. He had been quickly signed by the American impresario Sol Hurok, and a tour of the States was being mooted for the following year. His fee before Moscow was £60; after Moscow it was raised to £75, though the large leather-bound ledgers from Ibbs & Tillett reveal that he was often paid substantially less – because Emmie Tillett couldn't bear the thought of her precious music clubs going without tip-top artists at basement prices. Later in the summer, owing to pressure from Brenda, John's fee was put up to £100 per recital.

Shortly after John's return from Moscow he and Brenda moved from Manchester down to Spring Grove in Isleworth, London, in order to be close to the musical life of the capital and in easy reach of the Continent. With an advance on earnings from Ibbs & Tillett they bought a three-bedroom semi-detached house with a small garden. The three pianos made the trip wrapped in hessian quilts and John – who was solicitous for their health and had travelled in much less comfort himself strapped into the back of Brenda's Mini-Minor – inspected them carefully on arrival. 'They'll need tuning,' he said. 'Journeys always upset them.' As it turned out they were soon selling the two boudoir grands, as John was presented with a brand-new full-size British-made grand by the Society for the Piano to commemorate his Tchaikovsky prize. The presentation was made at Harrods by the minister for education, Sir David Eccles, in the presence of the Soviet cultural attaché. They just managed to squeeze the piano into their new lounge, but decided to take a studio flat in nearby Richmond where they could practise works for two pianos or rehearse with other musicians. Brenda had bought a new carpet with part of the prize money to soak up the sound of the piano, but confessed to a journalist that what she really wanted was a fast sports car. She couldn't abide housework and soon found a cleaner and a nanny. When John Beverley Nichols came to interview John for *Woman's Own* magazine he pretended he hadn't heard the result of the Tchaikovsky Competition. 'How did you come out?' he asked. John blushed like a schoolboy. 'Well,' he stammered, 'I seemed ... Well, I mean ... When it was all over I seemed to have come out on top.'

It was a time of severing old ties: the move away from Manchester (and with it the dismantling of his vision of himself as a provincial Busoni), leaving his mother behind, the deaths of his father and of Egon Petri, who died shortly after the competition – all these flashed past in the rush to learn the next work and arrive at the next platform. Petri's obituary in the *Times* had identified John as the remaining heir of that 'leonine style' of playing that descended from Busoni. In June 1962 in her letter to Marjory Wood, Dorothy Ogdon expressed her concern about the pace of his life:

> From now on John will be busier than ever, and I shall see very little of him – that is the penalty I willingly pay although I have never stopped missing him – he was such an important part of my life for such a long time. The house has seemed empty since he went. Already he has tours lined up for America, Sweden, and Italy. I hope he will guard his health – it involves a lot of strain.

John was back in Russia at the time she wrote the letter, barely three weeks after the end of the competition. He had been invited to give a three-week tour – seventeen concerts in nineteen days – covering Moscow, Leningrad, Kiev, Tallinn, Kishinev, Odessa, Sochi and Yalta. He was rapturously received, especially in Moscow. At the Great Hall of the conservatory, the scene of his recent triumph, he gave six encores and was almost buried in bouquets as the audience crowded round the stage at the end of the recital. He told a reporter that he found the enthusiasm of Soviet audiences 'most inspiring'. After the concert he appeared on a Youth Café TV programme playing one of his own preludes. John lost his bank book but he and Brenda were

issued with another and spent the rest of his prize money on a holiday in Yalta after the tour, as well as buying gifts to take home. Russia
was the cradle of John's fame and recognition, and the Russian public
the godmother of his success. The tour confirmed his reputation as an
international artist of striking originality.

On his return to England, John could not help but be struck by the
difference between the way artists were treated in the two countries.
He was back on the Tillett wheel, notching up 150 engagements for
1962 alone. It was a pretty harsh, commercial world, with agents and
recording companies to satisfy and little room for musical exploration.
As he would write in darker times, 'One day our artists will be looked
after as they are looked after in Russia. By friends, not enemies.' Yet
the headlong career of the post-Moscow bandwagon was more than
matched by John's boundless energy, and the exhilaration of the
moment appeared to carry all before it.

In the year of his death John was interviewed by Sue Lawley on
BBC TV's *Wogan*. When asked what he considered to be his greatest
achievement he said without hesitation, 'Winning the prize in
Moscow.' In a sense, he had reached the zenith of his career as a
soloist. The agonizing search for new paths had now begun.

7

SLOGGER OGGER

John Ogdon was famous for playing the Tchaikovsky Concerto too many times.

Harrison Birtwistle

At the Cheltenham Festival in July 1962 John gave a memorable performance of Messiaen's recital-long *Vingt Regards sur L'Enfant-Jésus*, using a dynamic range that seemed to exceed the limits of the keyboard – 'from an enormous sound to a nothing sound', as Rodney Friend described it. As he came off stage at the end he said, 'That piano won't forget me in a hurry.' Chatting after the concert, Alexander Goehr asked John what it had been like to meet Khrushchev: it seemed an extraordinary thing for one of his friends to have done. 'It was alright, I suppose,' replied John. For Goehr this exemplified John's approach to life. What mattered was the music; the class and size of audience, the prestige of the venue – these were of no concern to him. Nor did success alter his character: he was the same modest, self-effacing individual that his friends had always known.

John was not a professional concert pianist in the way that Ashkenazy or Barenboim were; the career was incidental to him and his playing had always lacked consistency, with a spectrum that ran from magnificent all the way to appalling. He was first and foremost a musician who used the piano as a medium for exploring music. Overnight, however, he had become the most famous classical musician in Britain and everyone wanted a piece of him. For a deeply private man this was unsettling enough. Add it to the fact that he was attempting to cram three careers into one – the international concert pianist with his large classical repertoire; the avant-garde pianist championing new music; and the aspiring composer – and the strain was immense.

Ibbs & Tillett were aware of the stresses that John's schedule was placing on him, but neither he nor Brenda appeared to realize the dangers. John, in particular, seemed blinkered. He was often approached about dates directly by other musicians, rather than through the agency. In January 1963 the conductor Norman del Mar asked John if he would record Michael Tippett's Piano Concerto for the BBC in Glasgow. John said yes, but his assent drew a concerned letter from Audrey Hurst of Ibbs & Tillett to del Mar:

> We learned with some dismay that John Ogdon has agreed to play the Tippett in Glasgow on April 18th next. Mrs. Tillett feels very strongly that he should not have done so, and if you could see his schedule at the present time, you would, I know, agree! He has nearly forty engagements between now and then, including a tour of Sweden, and we cannot imagine when he would find time to learn a new work! [...] For some months we have been refusing any further engagements for him during the next few months in an endeavour to prevent him overworking.

Norman del Mar was not taking no for an answer, however, and immediately fired back with the following:

> I am a little distressed about the situation as I understand very well the points you raise. On the other hand, John is a very unusual artist with great facility for learning new music and, indeed, when speaking to him when we met, I raised this very point as to whether indeed the pressure of work would make the preparation of so difficult a piece as Michael Tippett's Concerto a hardship. He

expressed himself as extremely happy and eager to do it with me at this time and, on the strength of this, I have already invited Michael Tippett who, as far as I believe at present, has every intention of coming to Glasgow specially for the occasion.

Audrey Hurst wrote back saying that in view of del Mar's persuasive letter Mrs Tillett had agreed 'quite against her better judgement' to allow John to accept the engagement. In December of that year John recorded the Tippett Concerto with the Philharmonia Orchestra under Colin Davis, coupled with Sonatas Nos. 1 and 2. Stephen Hough bought the record several years later, when he was still a boy; it was an important and inspirational moment for him, offering as it did an introduction to a certain kind of British music that later influenced his choice of repertoire.

John's ability to learn new and complex scores in double-quick time sometimes got him into hot water and made him vulnerable to exploitation by orchestras, recording companies and the BBC. He became the stand-in man *par excellence*. When a major pianist cancelled, the cry was always 'Send for Ogdon!' Those who called upon him knew that they wouldn't have to change the programme, whatever the repertoire, because if John didn't know the piece he would happily sight-read it. He saved Peter Andry's bacon at EMI on many occasions. He once even stood in at the last moment for the soprano Victoria de los Ángeles at the Royal Festival Hall (fortunately for everyone he didn't attempt to sing), in response to which the *Times* was full of praise:

> The warm reception accorded Madame de los Ángeles's gallant 'deputy,' Mr. John Ogdon, after his display of *diablerie* in Liszt's E-flat piano concerto, made it clear that none of the large audience felt the evening to be in vain. Furthermore Mr. Ogdon's sleight-of-hand in his two 'operatic' solos almost succeeded in passing off Busoni (of *Turandot* and *Carmen*) as an equal of Liszt.

His extraordinary stamina at the crease earned him the nickname 'Slogger Ogger'.

Being perpetually on the road, John spent very little time at the house in Isleworth. At this stage of his career Brenda accompanied him on the most important foreign tours, which sometimes involved two-piano recitals. On the whole, though, it was a tough and solitary routine of travel, interviews, rehearsals and performance. Busoni wrote of his depression when faced with the 'provincial round' of the travelling virtuoso's life, and even confessed to taking little or no trouble over his playing on such dreary tours. John knew of Busoni's attitude from Dent's biography, which was a kind of bible to him. Anton Rubinstein, whose cast-iron constitution Ogdon shared, had also expressed his dismay at the life of the concert pianist. Here he is on his American tour of 1873:

> May Heaven preserve us from such slavery! Under these conditions there is no chance for art – one simply grows into an automaton, performing mechanical work; no dignity remains to the artist; he is lost [. . .] During the time I remained in America we travelled through as far as New Orleans, and I appeared before an audience 215 times. The receipts and the success were invariably gratifying, but it was all so tedious that I began to despise myself and my art. So profound was my dissatisfaction that when several years later I was asked to repeat my American tour, I refused pointblank.

For the modern pianist the constant merry-go-round of airports, hotels, green rooms and concert halls leaves little room for enchantment. It is a lonely, lopsided life that, according to pianist Philip Fowke, requires the heart of a poet and the hide of a rhinoceros – an impossible combination, one would have thought. Eric Fenby in his memoir of Delius avers that 'Music as an art is a glorious thing, but music as a profession is an anathema.' One way or another, all professional musicians have to live out the contradiction these words so starkly lay down. There are new cities, cultures, time zones and languages to adapt to, new pianos and new acoustics. The latter can be a real challenge, and practice sessions before a recital are essential in order for the pianist to tune in to the instrument and the way the hall distributes the sound. John would most often relax before a concert by lying on his hotel bed reading novels, usually mysteries or detective stories. Raymond Chandler, Dashiell Hammett, Rex Stout (creator of Nero Wolfe), Michael Innes, Agatha Christie, Conan Doyle – he loved all the classics of the genre, and was an exceptionally fast reader. P. G. Wodehouse, whom John savoured as a superb stylist, was another favourite. As the concert got closer he would pace up and down, going through the music in his head – and this would continue backstage. After the concert there was the whole social dimension to deal with: a succession of strangers wanting contact and an autograph. John would stand there nodding in embarrassment as he was lauded to his face, not quite knowing where to put his heavily perspiring body. The after-concert parties helped him release the adrenalin that had built up during the performance, and despite the perplexity of ordinary social interaction he did enjoy having people around. The cycle ended with the following morning's newspapers: the ritual of reviews. His self-belief notwithstanding, John was acutely sensitive to criticism. There was little time to brood, however, as it was quickly on to the next city, the next hotel room, the next hall, the next green room, the next reception.

Evgeny Kissin, one of the pianistic superstars of today, makes fewer than fifty appearances a year and talks openly of the stress of performing. During a concert he gives of himself to the last ounce, and the adrenalin boils to such a pitch that it takes him a long time to cool down afterwards. He finds it hard to sleep on the night of a concert and the following days are used for recharging himself. Kissin is in control of his professional life and sets his own rhythm. Conversely, Ogdon's rhythm was determined by those around him, and this has led to the charge of exploitation. Alexander Goehr sees Ogdon as 'the victim of a system that takes exceptional talent and drives it into the ground'. He adds: 'The music profession can be particularly callous in that regard.'

John had never shaken off the mantle of the tongue-tied prodigy and was ill-equipped for the clockwork world he was entering. He was, as Rodney Friend said, 'one of the freaks', and so utterly unsophisticated that irony in a non-literary context confused him. Here, if ever, was an artist that needed handling with kid gloves. That's not to say that the circuit wasn't at times tremendously exciting and enjoyable,

especially to begin with. Brenda, who tended to see the more glamorous side of the life, described it as huge fun. They were, she said, on
a cloud of concerts, parties and recording sessions. 'We seemed sus-
pended on a wave of continually mounting success, which carried us
onwards, exhilarating, dizzying, moving faster and faster.'

In fact John had a fourth career, and that was his piano duo with
Brenda. In 1962 they were invited by Lord Harewood to play the
Bartók Sonata for two pianos and percussion at the Edinburgh
Festival. Brenda was determined to impress and came out in a gold
Lurex dress that shimmered beneath the stage lights. She had an elaborate hairdo held together by silver pins, which was no match for the
frenzy of Bartók. They had not gone far into the piece before the pins
began flying out, making it a sonata for two pianos, percussion and
hairpins. In the early years their musical partnership seems to have
been a source of pleasure to John, despite the extra work it entailed,
because he knew it pleased Brenda. He also enjoyed exploring and
mastering the two-piano repertoire, which is not extensive, and before
long composers such as Alan Rawsthorne and Malcolm Williamson
were writing works especially for him and Brenda. They made a
number of recordings, including the Rachmaninoff Suites for two
pianos and Messiaen's *Visions de l'Amen*.

It is probably true to say that even in John's day a pianist could not
claim a truly international reputation until he had successfully toured
the United States. Even Sviatoslav Richter, the great Russian pianist
who was notoriously contemptuous of sophisticated publics, eventually made his way across the Atlantic, at the age of forty-five, and
scored a stunning success. He didn't like America and returned as
infrequently as possible, abandoning it completely in 1970, but even
as a Soviet citizen and winner of the Stalin Prize he felt he had to go.
Besides its home-grown Modernist movement (Morton Feldman,
John Cage, Milton Babbitt, Philip Glass et al.), America was home to
some of the finest composers and musicians who had fled Europe and
Russia during the Second World War, including Igor Stravinsky.

John's agent in the States, Sol Hurok, was a Russian émigré who
had arrived in New York from an obscure Ukrainian village at the age
of eighteen. Now a seventy-five-year-old entertainment mogul who

wielded the same (if not a greater) degree of power in the US music business that Emmie Tillett did in Britain, Hurok made it his business to turn top-class musicians into celebrities. Chaliapin, Nureyev, Artur Rubinstein – all had benefited from his pugnacious promotion. The great man was something of a prima donna himself and with his trademark fedora and cigar was an instantly recognizable figure in Manhattan. He bullied to get what he wanted and was notoriously swift and dogmatic in his opinions. John and Brenda set off for the States at the beginning of January 1964 for a tour that would see him play at thirty venues across the North American continent. They were still very much on that cloud of concerts and parties that Brenda had spoken of, and had little doubt that John would conquer America just as he had conquered Russia.

Dorothy Ogdon's health had continued very poorly since John had left Manchester and she had not been down to London to see their new home. When in November 1963 she wrote to Marjory Wood for the last time it was John who occupied her mind:

Well the time is drawing near to John's visit to the States – he leaves on January 5th. You will think I'm fussing, but knowing how casual he is about clothes I wondered if you could tell him what he will need to bring (without telling him I'd asked you). He doesn't wear a hat, and I believe they can get frost-bitten ears if they don't protect them – also I suppose it is necessary to wear fur-lined boots; he seems to go gaily along in thin shoes in any weather. If I am being unduly anxious just ignore this, but I think he often catches cold through not wrapping up after concerts, when he has been perspiring heavily.

At present he is in Portugal, where he went from Italy, where he did a fortnight's tour. He has been to Russia again, Germany, Norway, Sweden, Vienna, Holland etc., so is a very busy man. On top of which he has made (I think) six records. Four actually out and two to come, some in Russia too. I don't know how he copes with it all, concerts with Brenda, festivals and things – little wonder that I've not seen him since April! So I play his records and try to imagine him in the next room.

John and Brenda flew directly to New York, where they were
taken to meet Hurok. Unsettled by his aggressive charm, they came
away with the impression that John needed to perform at his very best
to secure the wholehearted cooperation of the gruff ringmaster. They
flew from New York to a frozen Midwest, where John was due to
begin his tour. At his first concert on American soil, in Cincinnati, he
played Chopin's Concerto in F minor, probably the first Romantic
concerto ever written. John was warmly received by the Ohioans but
he and Brenda were taken aback by the noisy forwardness of the
people at the post-concert reception. John of course had no social
repertoire beyond a nod, a smile and a grunt and was their opposite in
almost everything. He was soft and formless, cocooned in myriad
threads of musical thought. Despite his lumbering dimensions, he
seemed to hover rather than stand – as if he hadn't quite fully incar-
nated. His experiences were related to the lives of the composers he
revered: those were his coordinates, the guys that kept him fixed to
earth. As he helped himself to another drink he might think of Wilkie
Collins' speaking tour of the States ninety years earlier, in 1874, and
his drug addiction at the time, and be comforted by the thought that
Busoni loved the novels of Collins and was presented with the collected edition of his works by Chatto & Windus in 1923, the year
before he died. 'Hmm, yes,' he'd murmur, half to himself, 'I suppose
one can see the retrieval of the moonstone as a metaphor for what
Busoni was trying to accomplish through his new aesthetic of music.
Yes, yes . . .' He was also a master of the inconsequential or out-of-the-
blue, and might suddenly say apropos of nothing, 'Henry Litolff, the
Belgian composer, dyed his beard orange in April 1850. At least I
think it was April. Liszt dedicated the E-flat concerto to him.' His
mental excursions aside, he was lionized to within an inch of his life
and came away feeling thoroughly mauled. The parties were terribly
important, however, as they provided an opportunity for the dragons
who funded the symphony orchestras to meet their prey. Ignoring the
parties was not an option for an artist who wanted to be hired again.
So when John was asked by his flushed hosts for 'a toon' he dutifully
returned to the piano to play a few informal encores.

The snow continued throughout their trip to Cincinnati, and when the time came to fly up to Columbus, Ohio, the airport was closed and they had to make do with a Greyhound bus. Brenda was missing two-year-old Annabel – who was back at home with her nanny – and moaned that she wanted to go home; John sat stony-faced against the swirling snow, grimly determined to fulfil his engagements. After his final concert in Ohio they flew back to an ice-bound New York for the biggest recital of all – his Carnegie Hall debut. He and Brenda were well entertained by staff from the Hurok office and were taken to the Russian Tea Room, next to Carnegie Hall, where they were seated on the right-hand side of the restaurant, traditionally reserved for celebrities. There was also a dazzling party in a mansion apartment overlooking Central Park. Beneath the steely charm Brenda sensed a reserve, as if the cognoscenti were holding back from embracing John until he'd proved himself. In their eyes he already had three things working against him: his Englishness, his lack of personality and the fact that he had appeared from nowhere. John could expect an urbane and sceptical audience who would not take gladly to the sight of a half-eaten pork pie poking out from his coat-tail pocket. This was no club recital in Heckmondwike. Because John had succeeded Van Cliburn as Tchaikovsky laureate, there was a particular (not to say pointed) interest in him. The New York critics – indeed American critics generally – were known for their blunt assessments. Puncturing balloons was one of the perks of the job – and John was a big balloon. A few well-aimed thrusts and his career in America would be in tatters. John was ashen-faced when they arrived backstage before the concert and his nerves were in no way settled by the news that there was a bevy of leading musicians in the audience.

His chosen programme could not have given a better musical self-portrait. It lent scope to his lyric and imaginative gifts, his intellect and his sudden iconoclastic furies. He opened with the Prelude and Fugue in C-sharp minor from Book 2 of *The Well-Tempered Clavier,* followed by Beethoven's Op. 109 sonata. Ross Parmenter in the *New York Times* was immediately taken with the 'beauty of Ogdon's quiet tone' in the Bach as well as the composure that enabled him 'to play so slowly and with such inwardness'. Alan Rich in the *Herald Tribune* praised his remarkable control of tone and instinctive feel for structure,

bringing out as he did the rise and fall of the musical line in each section of the Bach, producing 'a graceful curving of the music into an
organic whole'. John had been drawn to the final three Beethoven
sonatas in his student days, as had Liszt, and Op. 109 was the one he
played most frequently, relishing no doubt its more improvisatory
approach to the traditional sonata form. It was the work's lyrical,
almost Schubertian qualities that he stressed on this occasion, and the
'quiet understatement' of his account was much praised. He sent his
audience to the intermission with both books of the Brahms Paganini
Variations, one of the most technically and artistically treacherous of
all virtuoso piano works – and, as with the Beethoven, a real staple of
John's concert repertoire. The Variations, originally published as a set
of studies, were written for Liszt's greatest pupil, Carl Tausig, whose
technique was considered to be without flaw. Clara Schumann called
them the 'Witch's Variations'; certainly it takes a measure of wizardry
to reconcile the warring styles of Brahms and Paganini. John erred on
the side of Paganini and was taken to task by Parmenter, who criticized
him for playing too fast and compromising his articulation. Alan Rich
could not have disagreed more:

> The Brahms Paganini Variations were something else again. Here
> this 27-year-old Britisher unleashed the whirlwind. It was a stun-
> ning revelation of piano sonority, of technique and control, and of
> a lot more besides. It was that 'lot more' that provided the real fas-
> cination in Mr. Ogdon's concert. Here, finally, is a young pianist
> with the ability to overwhelm, not merely with his stunning pianis-
> tic facility, but with his power to think about music and to project
> it into his playing.

Once again, as in Russia, critics were picking up on John's imaginative approach to the keyboard and his ability to get behind the
notes.

Rich and Parmenter also disagreed about John's Variations and
Fugue, Op. 4, with which he opened the second half of the recital.
Parmenter dismissed it as a pastiche of 'fine pianistic effects', while
Rich found it a substantial work 'full of intensely original musical

creation'. It was no coincidence that John placed Busoni's Sonatina Seconda next to his own piece, as a tribute to his pianistic idol. It's a weird work, almost like a ghost story, with markings such as *lento occulto* emphasizing its richly esoteric character. Searching and unstable, it is drawn from the same source as Busoni's opera *Doktor Faust*, and there is much in it that portends a kind of transcendence or crossing over between musical worlds. It was Ogdon territory *par excellence*. Even the tetchy Parmenter was won over by the 'mystery and odd colours' John was able to conjure up and the 'individuality of intelligence' that he displayed. But he felt he rather ruined the effect by following up with two Liszt warhorses, *La Campanella* (in the Busoni version) and the Mephisto Waltz No. 1, which, he wrote, 'our American whirlwinds can do better'. Alan Rich, who entitled his piece 'John Ogdon's Huge Talent', summed up his impressions with this concluding tribute:

> John Ogdon proved on his first visit to New York that he stands apart. He is a towering, deep, original and compelling musical personality, and his horizons should be without limit.

The dean of New York critics, Harold Schonberg, thought that John was a keyboard artist who had 'very much to say'.

A long line formed backstage after the concert. One middle-aged lady approached John, her head bowed and handed him a photograph face down so he could sign the back. As he was writing she said, 'Hello, John' – and the familiar voice sent him hurtling back far from the glitz of New York to Mansfield Woodhouse and the war years. It was Marjory Wood – or 'Mith Wood', as he used to call her. When they embraced she noticed that he was drenched in sweat from his performance and that the frames of his glasses were held together by a gold safety pin. Despite the long line behind her she took his hand to stretch his span, as she had always done when he was a boy. Then she told him to turn over the photograph: there was John's mother, Dorothy, smiling up at him. Marjory had brought her to the concert, so that she too could witness her son's triumph. They both laughed at the ingenious ploy. There was another surprise in store for John. Peter

Maxwell Davies, who was studying with Roger Sessions at Princetown, also came backstage. He remembers Brenda looking down her nose at him and saying, 'What are *you* doing here?'

In a rather sadistic rite of passage John and Brenda were handed the early-morning edition of the papers at the reception after the concert, and were expected to open them in front of the other guests. Cavils in the *New York Times* notwithstanding, they were in the event relieved to see that John had been as warmly received by the critics as he had been by his audience. When they finally got to bed, just before dawn, it was with a grateful feeling that John had made it in America. The next day they arrived at Hurok Concerts in high spirits and were ushered into the office of Walter Prude, a tall, immaculate, dry-witted man. 'Great recital, John,' he said, echoing his comments of the night before. His words etched themselves on the air. 'Very impressive.' John smiled. Then the viper struck. 'Pity about the reviews,' he continued. 'I can't do anything with them, I'm afraid. They're simply not good enough.' Evidently someone high up in the office, maybe Hurok himself, had not liked the concert and had decided that their money would be wasted on a nationwide promotion campaign. If John needed reminding, here was further evidence of how arbitrary and cut-throat the world of professional music could be.

Now the tour began in earnest, from coast to coast, beginning in Boston and ending in California. John played in Philadelphia, Pittsburgh, Chicago, Toronto, Montreal, Los Angeles and dozens of smaller towns in between. When he played with orchestras the big Romantic concerti were the order of the day – especially the Tchaikovsky, which he played with the Montreal Symphony under Zubin Mehta. The weather on the East Coast, in Canada and the Midwest remained sub-zero, which meant further travel delays. Brenda found the whole experience gruelling and after about ten days of non-stop touring decided that she must return home to England; she was feeling so worn down herself that she could offer John little support. They were in Pennsylvania and within days of Brenda's decision John received a call in their Pittsburgh hotel room from his brother Paul to say that their mother Dorothy had died in hospital on 29 January from a heart attack. She was sixty-one and had survived Howard by less than two years. It was the only time Brenda saw John weep, but he quickly put it out of his mind and refocused on the tour. He did not return to England for the funeral.

Brenda flew back from Detroit – much to the dismay of the Ladies' Committee of the Detroit Symphony Orchestra, which had counted on her presence at the post-concert reception. She was bluntly informed that her attitude would do her husband no good. John meanwhile headed west to the wide open spaces. He attracted American composers who had heard of his interest in modern music, such as the pianist-composer Leonard Klein, who had studied with Petri. Benjamin Lees, Henri Lazarof, Richard Yardumian, Ray Luke, Richard Wilson, Michael Baker, John Powell, Paul Creston and English-born Peter Racine Fricker are some of the contemporary US composers whose works John played. He was interested to see how little known Busoni's music was in the States, and he wrote to the BBC from his hotel in Oklahoma City asking if they would send a copy of the recording of his January 1963 performance of the concerto with the Philharmonia Orchestra to the head of the Festival Foundation in New York. He asked this favour not for himself but in order to 'materially assist the cause of promoting Busoni's music in the USA'.

He was enthusiastically received by audiences wherever he went in America. They warmed to his modesty and obvious integrity, and were fascinated to be invited to join him at a very deep level. In the town of Provo, Utah, the Joseph Smith auditorium was packed to its capacity of 1,300 for John's recital. Salt Lake City journalist Harold Lundstrom praised John's 'expression of intimacy with Bach's thought' and went on to describe his reading of Beethoven as more of a séance than an interpretation. High praise indeed, but also movingly apt given the recent death of his mother. Though Lundstrom moaned about the quality of the piano provided that night, he ended by comparing John to one of the all-time wizards of the keyboard:

Not since the hey-day of Horowitz have I seen such dazzling exhibitions of technique, and never, I'm sure, have I heard more beautiful or accomplished trills (which alone were worth the price of the drive to Provo).

Reviews like these changed Hurok's opinion of John and he was soon letting it be known that he wanted another Ogdon tour the following year. There could have been no clearer signal of John's success in America: he had triumphed after all.

John scarcely had time to draw breath after America before he was off on a one-month Scandinavian tour that also took in Holland. John probably appeared more times in Sweden than in any other country over the course of his career, thanks largely to his excellent Swedish agent, Henrik Lodding, and the unfailing enthusiasm of the audiences there. On his return, at the end of April, he was lauded for a recital he gave at the Wigmore Hall for the Institute of Contemporary Arts. Alongside pieces by early twentieth-century keyboard explorers Busoni, Nielsen, Grainger and Szymanowski, this included works by four young contemporaries: Birtwistle, Goehr, Maxwell Davies and Bo Nilsson. The *Times* reviewer spoke of Ogdon's 'conquest of a terrifying succession of obstacles', his only misgiving being a certain lack of finesse. The following week John played Cyril Scott's Piano Sonata No. 3 at the Royal Academy of Music in the presence of the spry, velvet-coated composer, whose dreamland he was affectionately adept at evoking. Far from dreamy was the blistering account of the Liszt Sonata that John made for EMI at the end of April that year. It is one of the truly great works of the piano literature and, in many ways, the spiritual autobiography of its quixotic author. This is Liszt at his most searching, honest and un-self-forgiving, embracing the Devil with as much fervour as the Almighty yet somehow maintaining his sanity. The piece was dedicated to Robert Schumann, who had (unknown to Liszt) just lost his and was in the asylum at Endenich having thrown himself in the Rhine. John once astonished Ronald Stevenson by telling him he thought there were only five piano pieces worth playing – this from the man who played everything! – and that one of them was the Liszt Sonata. The work gives the impression of a man who is searching for the root of silence but runs away terrified whenever he gets too close. John plays it with a pinpoint zeal and tautness of structure that is altogether electrifying and bears comparison with Horowitz's high-voltage recording of 1932, also with EMI. If one wanted to make a case that John was angry at his mother's death, his recording of the Liszt Sonata could certainly be adduced as evidence.

At the beginning of May John and Brenda began the long journey out to Sydney for the start of a four-month tour of Australia and New Zealand. The tour was organized by the Australian Broadcasting Commission (ABC), who flew them out first-class and saw to it that they were well looked after throughout their stay. Little Annabel and her New Zealand nanny travelled with them; with fourteen pieces of luggage it was more royal progress than concert tour. John played with all the orchestras run by the ABC in all six states with a raft of different conductors, and gave recitals in the town halls of all the major cities. He also performed in Tasmania. He played quite a wide solo repertoire, including some of his own works, while his concerti ranged from Beethoven to Bliss. In Sydney he gave the first performance of a work written specially for him, Malcolm Williamson's Piano Concerto No. 3, conducted by Joseph Post. Other composers, such as Larry Sitsky and Don Banks, were keen to meet him. Brenda gave six concerts on her own and two with John, travelling separately for some of her engagements. In Perth they met William Walton, a composer John admired very much, and a friendship ensued. He was on tour conducting his own music and they shared not only platforms but also many a convivial meal. He had travelled the 2,500 miles from Sydney to Perth by train, which took more than a week, and his witty, ironic account of his misadventures had the Ogdons in stitches.

In early June, while John and Brenda were in Brisbane, the Beatles arrived in Sydney for their first and only tour of Australia. The Ogdons reached Melbourne in July, two months into John's own tour, and for John this visit was undoubtedly the highlight of his Antipodean odyssey. His brother Karl, whom he hadn't seen for twelve years – since he was a boy of fifteen – was living in the East Brunswick suburb of Melbourne with his young wife, Gwen. When Karl first arrived in Australia, in 1952, he had stayed with his sister Pippa up in Darwin, but soon adopted a nomadic lifestyle. He travelled around collecting Australian folk songs with the poet John

Manifold and then continued on his own, covering some 10,000 miles in the wilds of the Northern Territory and northern Queensland. He supported himself by singing his repertoire of three songs in country pubs and eventually amassed quite a treasury of folk ballads and Aboriginal songs. When he moved to Melbourne, where his maternal aunt Wynn lived, he became the resident musician of a bohemian tavern called The Swanston Family. He lived in a garret above the pub, just about eking out an existence composing for and playing piano and guitar, but in truth he had no money. He also wrote poetry and was part of a group of folk artists who met and performed at the pub.

In 1961, when he was thirty, Karl met eighteen-year-old clerk Gwen Anderson in the city magistrate's court, whom he married the following year. He found a job at the State Library in Melbourne and he and Gwen bought a house in the suburb of Canterbury with money inherited from Howard. In addition to his job at the library Karl taught piano and classical guitar from home and was a much-loved and respected teacher. His home also became a resort for other artists, mainly connected to the Melbourne folk revival, and on weekends he loved nothing better than to be surrounded by his musician, poet and painter friends. He continued to compose and in the year of John's visit a volume of his music was published, entitled *Selected Works, 1956–1964*. He sometimes played at the Emerald Hill theatre on Sunday afternoons, sharing a platform with folk singers as well as classical and flamenco guitarists. One of his guitar students, Gary Kinnane of the University of Melbourne, recalled one such occasion:

> When Karl came on I was rather afraid for him, sitting there small, black-bearded, very shy, fearing his lack of volume would make him hard to hear in that packed auditorium. I shouldn't have worried. He played a substantial and beautiful sonata he'd composed, got through it faultlessly – you could have heard a pin drop – and the audience gave him a huge, enthusiastic reception at the end. It was an absolute triumph, which Karl took in his characteristic modest, serious-faced way.

He and Gwen had been saving up to visit England, but Karl spent all the money on lottery tickets because he was hoping to help out a friend in Sydney who was short of money. He was, according to Gwen, unworldly and 'irresponsibly generous', and always succumbed to a hard-luck story. Though he never made much money, Karl did manage to provide for his family.

Despite making a life for himself at the other end of the world, and making space for his creativity, Karl was still the nervous, unstable young man who had fled England all those years ago. Friends described him as bookish, deeply sensitive and attractively offbeat. Though his severe stammer did improve after his marriage, he was still subject to sudden fears and depressive episodes and, like his father before him, would lock himself in his study, barely coming out to eat or attend to the everyday rituals of life. When he was holed up there he would read voraciously – mainly history but literature as well – and his pipe, stuffed with his favourite Erinmore tobacco, hardly left his lips from dawn to dusk. As he smoked he consumed gallons of thick black tea – again shades of Howard, who wrote to him right up to the bitter end telling him to *leave the music to John*! Karl tended to see the world as a dark place and was convinced that Australia was going to be taken over by hostile forces. The beginning of some very strange behaviour was marked by a trip he made with two or three friends to look for land up a mountain, where they could be safe from attack. Gwen urged him to seek psychological counselling but her pleas were always resisted.

Karl was immensely proud of John and very protective towards him, and Dorothy's letters had kept him up to date with his career. He often told Gwen how unworldly his brother was and how the life he was pursuing was not suited to him. Gary Kinnane clearly recalls Karl telling him about John's forthcoming visit, referring to him as his kid brother. 'I don't think I ever before or since saw the particular look of glowing pride in his eyes as on that day,' he says. The Melbourne press made much of the reunion of the two brothers, and they were pictured raising a glass to each other in Tattersall's pub, where members of the so-called Push drank. Karl had written a piano sonata for John, which he presented to him for the cameras. 'I hope to play my brother's sonata when I return to England,' John was reported as saying. One journalist, Barrie Watts, noted that getting John to talk was very difficult until Karl arrived – and then the two of them were off, chatting away happily to each other. It was, he wrote, 'for all practical purposes the end of the interview'. Fortunately John and Brenda were both giving concerts in Melbourne so they were there for two weeks in all, which included Karl's thirty-fourth birthday on 14 July. They took trips as a family, and one day Karl and Gwen drove John and Brenda out to the bush to meet an old artist friend of theirs who had built his own house. John was delighted with it all and very talkative but Brenda, who seemed detached from Karl and Gwen's interests and way of life, refused to sit down as she couldn't bear the thought of marking her butter-coloured suede suit.

John of course was allowed into the inner sanctum, Karl's study, where they would play and discuss music. It was fortunate too that they were seeing each other so soon after Dorothy's death and could chew the cud together, though both were naturally reserved when it came to matters of the heart. Whether prompted by Karl's example or not, John took to tobacco around this time and from thenceforth to his death twenty-five years later could be seen only through a thick shroud of cigarette smoke. The year of his mother's death, 1964, seemed to signal the beginning of a retreat into himself, a kind of self-veiling, though as yet the veil was sketchy and penetrable and his movement away from those around him largely imperceptible.

A newspaper article entitled 'Black for Bach' appeared about Brenda, describing the various evening dresses she had brought for her concerts and quoting her reasons for choosing a black taffeta gown for her upcoming performance of Bach's D-minor Concerto. This sartorial choice proved ominous when her performance was savaged by German-Australian composer Felix Werder, who as music critic for the *Age* described her technique as 'student-like'. The sense of public humiliation she felt at his words goaded her into a far-reaching decision: from now on she would put her family before her solo career. The black dress was packed away along with all the other concert gowns. Melbourne was the last stop of their Australian tour. Little did John know when he said goodbye to Karl that he would never see him again.

After Australia they went on to New Zealand, Fiji and finally Singapore. It was by now mid-August and they had been away from home for fourteen weeks. Brenda felt utterly drained and decided that instead of flying back to England they should take a three-week holiday in Greece. They went to the resort of Lagonisi, southeast of Athens. While Brenda was able to relax on the beach, happy in the knowledge that she was pregnant with their second child, John seemed unable to let up. He took out his composition paper and started writing again, thought ahead eagerly to the next round of concerts and how he might better champion the work of his contemporaries – and even began to talk about founding a festival of modern music. In a postcard to Ronald Stevenson, now a professor at the University of Cape Town, he mentioned that he was reading volume one of Robert Graves's *Greek Myths* and Ezra Pound's *ABC of Reading*, and that these texts were enhancing his enjoyment of his surroundings. He had found the lack of interest in Percy Grainger's music in Australia disappointing. Observing John far from the madding crowd, and sensing how driven he was and unable to unwind, Brenda felt the first muted pangs of dread. Nothing but music and literature seemed real to him.

Touring resumed straight away on their return, with a trip to Romania and Russia with the LPO. In Romania John met Basil Horsfield, the partner of conductor John Pritchard. Horsfield ran his own management agency in London and was quite well connected in the music world through his close association with Pritchard. He could see that John was dissatisfied with his current arrangement at Ibbs & Tillett, whereby the constant round of music clubs left little or no time for composing, and the two men got to talking. Back home John discussed this meeting with Brenda; when she then spoke with Basil he told her he could get them many more two-piano dates (something Mrs Tillett hadn't wanted to do). By December John was writing to the BBC informing them that all matters relating to his engagements and professional life would henceforth be dealt with by

Basil Horsfield Management. Emmie Tillett felt stunned and betrayed because she considered John her protégé, having taken him under her wing before his career had begun. Now she put the screws on him and closed doors everywhere: in the UK Emmie had influence in, if not a monopoly of, 80 per cent of the market. For instance, Gerald MacDonald, manager of the Liverpool Philharmonic, was planning to engage John for 1966 but received a letter from Emmie effectively forbidding him to do so – if he hired John, he would never get Jacqueline du Pré, Janet Baker, Shura Cherkassky or any of Emmie's other gold-star artists. Letters of this ilk were sent out far and wide and the usual deluge of dates began to dry up. Basil simply did not have the contacts to compete with Emmie. (Hurok in America operated in the same way as Emmie; all sorts of wheeling and dealing went on. His way of getting dates for lesser-known artists was to say to concert organizers, 'We'll send you Artur Rubinstein but you have to take so-and-so as well . . .') That said, John had plenty of dates already booked through Ibbs & Tillett for 1965 and 1966, and his recording contract with EMI was not affected at all, so there was certainly no shortage of work. This included two tours of America. The first was under the auspices of Hurok, but then quite suddenly and unaccountably the old man dropped John from his books – no doubt under pressure from Emmie. There was no love lost between Brenda and Emmie. In her diary for 18 May 1965 Emmie recalled bumping into the Ogdons at the Festival Hall that night. Her terse entry speaks volumes: 'John Ogdon and Brenda appeared in artists' room. Shook hands with him, ignored her.' For her part, Brenda described Emmie as 'a horrible old lesbian'.

Not long after John left Ibbs & Tillett he and Brenda moved to a larger, fully detached house, this time in Golders Green, and within weeks their second child – a son, Richard – was born. He was given the middle name Peregrine, possibly as a reminder of his father's endless travels. John wrote to his friend and collaborator Alun Hoddinott at the end of May: 'Richard (the new baby) is 5½ weeks and in great form – gurgles and so forth! Annabel has taken very well to him.' John had just returned from Frankfurt when Richard was born and the very next day flew out first-class to New York for the start of a North American tour with the BBC Symphony Orchestra. Antal Dorati and Pierre Boulez were the conductors and Jacqueline du Pré the other soloist. John had been engaged to play concerti by Beethoven, Bartók and Tippett. The same musicians teamed up again for a groundbreaking tour of Eastern Europe and Russia in January 1967, with Sir John Barbirolli replacing Antal Dorati. BBC footage shows John on the night train to Warsaw practising the Bartók Second Concerto on his silent keyboard and knocking back shots of vodka with members of the orchestra. Pierre Boulez, who had been denounced by the Soviet press as a threat to Russian music, was given a ten-minute standing ovation in Moscow for his novel piece, *Éclat*.

Golders Green was something of a Jewish ghetto in the 1960s, so it was hard for John and Brenda to feel part of the community. John of course loved pork, especially pork pies and pork chops, and Brenda cooked heaps of bacon for him. The smell of bacon fat wafted from their open windows out into the streets of Golders Green. 'We were incredibly naive in those days,' says Brenda. 'Like children.' Ashkenazy lived in nearby Hendon and he and his wife were invited to dinner. It was a modest home, he recalls, and the Ogdons themselves were friendly, modest and warm. It was a pleasant dinner. John said very little but as they were leaving he thrust a large book into Ashkenazy's hands and mumbled something about what a wonderful work it was. It was John Fowles' *The Magus*, which had just that year been published. The book is a rather chilling exploration of the power over human consciousness of illusion, equated throughout the novel with art. Perhaps, like its hero, Nicholas Urfe, John had begun to feel that he was an actor in someone else's charade.

As intended, John finally had more time to compose. He sent Ronald Stevenson a postcard from Chicago in March 1965 saying that he was reading René Leibowitz's *Thinking for Orchestra*, which although 'rather mechanical in its practicality' was, he thought, useful for him. In New York earlier on the same trip he met the pianist, conductor, eccentric and Busoni enthusiast Daniell Revenaugh. A native of Louisville, Kentucky, Revenaugh had studied piano with Egon Petri and composition with Darius Milhaud at Mills College in California; in 1960 he had gone to Zakopane in Poland to rescue Petri's collection of Busoniana, which the pianist had abandoned

when he fled Europe in 1939. Now Revenaugh was organizing
various events for the Busoni centenary in 1966 and wanted to discuss
the possibility of recording the Busoni Concerto with the Danish-
born pianist-composer Gunnar Johansen. Revenaugh had already
contacted a number of recording companies but no one would touch
it. Busoni was in those days still considered a specialist composer; if
he was known at all it was for his Bach transcriptions – and even they
were denigrated by the purists. John in his innocent way picked up
the phone in his hotel room and called Peter Andry of EMI to ask
if he would be interested. Andry agreed to do it but with John, not
Johansen, as the pianist. Revenaugh also set up the Busoni Society
with Johansen and Rudolph Ganz (whose niece John had stayed with
in Basel) and John, together with Alistair Londonderry, was invited to
join the Board of Advisors.

The peripatetic Revenaugh shuttled back and forth between
Florida, London, California and Switzerland. There were many
obstacles in the way of the recording and it was only through Alistair
Londonderry's intercession that it finally came about. Revenaugh was
kept as conductor of the Royal Philharmonic Orchestra (and the Men's
Voices of the John Alldis Choir), though Peter Andry had wanted
Charles Groves. The concerto took up three sides of two LPs. Brenda
suggested that the fourth side be given over to her and John playing
two pianos – a cost-effective option – but Revenaugh preferred
Busoni's Sarabande and Cortège, Op. 51, composed as studies for the
opera *Doktor Faust*. This was discussed at a meeting at EMI's offices
in Manchester Square. Alistair Londonderry shared Revenaugh's doubt
about the two-piano suggestion and asked how much it would cost to
record the orchestral pieces. Ultimately he was happy to pay the £1,800
to make it happen.

Daniell Revenaugh could be quite overpowering when he was
seized with an idea. He swept into the Ogdon home and virtually
took it over with his plans for the Busoni Concerto. He was frequently
over there to run through something or other on two pianos, no
matter what the hour. Brenda felt their lives were turned upside
down and she was sometimes forced to insist that John and Daniell
abandon the pianos because the children were trying to get to sleep.

By this time John had become a heavy social drinker – a fact that people other than Brenda were beginning to notice. Certainly William Walton expressed his concerns to Brenda in the summer of 1966, but when she raised the matter with John she received a chilling look and the words, 'Mind your own business.' His favourite tipple was Martini and he was getting through about one and a half bottles a day. Brenda felt uneasy at the way he would stay up half the night with his musician friends, craving constant stimulation, his energy levels flagging little if at all.

In the centenary year itself John played Busoni's *Indian* Fantasy for piano and orchestra at the Proms with Jascha Horenstein conducting the LSO. The recording of the concerto happened the following year, in June 1967, at No. 1 Studio, Abbey Road, under the direction of John's old friend and recording partner Suvi Raj Grubb. Despite the vast scale of the piece, it became the least-edited major recording ever made at EMI (all the edits were on a single 3"x 5" card). Alistair Londonderry attended the recording sessions and left an amusing description of John 'informally packed into his tight-fitting beach-shirt and flannel trousers, puffing away desperately at an endless succession of uninhaled cigarettes and managing to play superbly at the same time'. Indeed, photographs show an ashtray on a stand beside the piano crammed full of stubs. Grubb paid tribute to John's stamina saying, 'I know of no one else who could have played the Busoni Concerto through twice in one day with no sign of fatigue or loss of concentration.' John likened the Busoni Concerto, with its very long phrases and gradual build-up, to a Bruckner symphony. 'It has the same sort of emotional impact,' he said, 'and becomes cohesive as it goes along. On the first page you can't exactly tell where it's going, but later on everything ties up.' After the final session Revenaugh bought beer for the entire orchestra.

It was the 'Summer of Love' and one of the Busoni sessions had to be cancelled when George Martin engaged Studio 1, as well as the leader and several members of the RPO, for the broadcast of 'All You Need Is Love' for *Our World* – the first live, worldwide satellite production. The previous year an article about John entitled 'Concert Pianist "Digs" Beatles' had appeared in the Montreal *Gazette*. He was reported as saying that he found their music 'fresh and spontaneous' – and when he was the castaway on *Desert Island Discs* in September 1967 'Lucy in the Sky with Diamonds' was among his eight chosen discs.

Revenaugh returned to Florida after the editing sessions, having bought a London taxi as a souvenir. One day he got a call from John, who'd just received the final pressings of the record prior to release. 'Danny,' he said, 'I think they've left a bit out.' And sure enough they had: some twenty bars from the fourth movement! With Revenaugh in London again it was back to the editing room to find the missing bars. How fortunate that John took the trouble to listen to it right through before its release. This recording of the Busoni Concerto later won the Montreux Prize and the Deutscher Schallplattenpreis and was nominated for a Grammy. It has now been in the EMI catalogue for more than forty-five years and remains the benchmark performance.

In October 1964 John had premiered another piece dedicated to him, George Lloyd's Piano Concerto No. 1 (entitled *Scapegoat*). Of it John wrote, 'The piece is a torso, a Hercules: it is unforgettable.' The work was unpublished, as were all Lloyd's works at that time, and it says much for John's influence with orchestras and conductors that this fine piece received its premiere with the Liverpool Philharmonic under Charles Groves. Lloyd, like John's grandfather, was a Cornishman. He had been badly shell-shocked in the Second World War and as a result of the trauma had lost his concentration and given up composition for many years. John greatly admired Lloyd for having pulled through his serious wartime illness. *Scapegoat* is about war and man's inhumanity to man. From man's inability to take responsibility for his own transgressions emerges the habit of scapegoating, painting others with his own sins and then turning his fury against them. For Lloyd all war is a form of scapegoating. Some twenty-four years John's senior, Lloyd became a compositional mentor to the younger man as well as a good friend. When John began his own piano concerto while on tour in Japan in 1966 he turned to Lloyd for help and advice on orchestration, and the two men met many times for what Lloyd himself described as 'composition lessons'. These were by no means all one-way; for his part, John provided Lloyd with insights into writing for the keyboard. Throughout his concert career he performed many of Lloyd's shorter pieces, such as 'African Shrine' and 'The Road to Samarkand', and was a dogged champion of his friend's unfashionably tonal and melodic music.

John's compositions were influenced by literature and film and in this respect his friend Bernard Herrmann made a strong impact. Herrmann, who was renowned for his scores for the Hitchcock films *Psycho*, *Vertigo* and *North by Northwest*, had studied with Percy Grainger at New York University. Thus Herrmann, as with so many of John's musical friends, had a connection with Busoni. (He'd even written a cantata on themes from *Moby-Dick*.) John's piano concerto is a terrifically energetic piece, fantastic, multifaceted, laced with Faustian bravado – not unlike a supercharged musical version of a Charles Williams novel. The piece is twenty-seven minutes long and wears its influences on its sleeve; a range of musical signatures – of Berlioz, Bartók, Ravel, Prokofiev, Shostakovich and Walton – construct a vivid kaleidoscope of sound. If anything there are too many influences at work, which has the effect of drowning Ogdon's own voice unless one is prepared to accept him as an unabashed musical chameleon. For all that, it is a curiously compelling piece that evokes the restless soulscape of its author. John Roseberry of the BBC visited John's house in November 1967 to hear him play the final draft of the work and subsequently wrote a memo to the head of the Orchestral Department:

I would recommend that we broadcast this interesting work with the composer as soloist. (John may well yet turn out to be some Liszt or Busoni born out of his time!)

Style: 'Free' tonality (harmonically nothing like as complex as Schoenberg)
Expression: Post-romantic
Difficulty of Solo Part: Enormous
Orchestration: Carefully considered, though certain string passages *may* prove tricky and/or ineffective. Triple woodwind, four horns, five trumpets, tuba. Timps, percussion, harp, strings.

Scheme: Three movements. 1. Is big and climactic – convincing
except for a boring *fugato* build-up in one place. Official
cadenza. 2. 3/8 *moderato* – intimate – some nice harmonic
things. 3. Very brilliant toccata in 2/4.
Rignold, I understand, is to be the conductor.

John premiered his concerto at the opening concert of the second
Cardiff Festival of Twentieth-Century Music in April 1968. He was
partnered by the City of Birmingham Symphony Orchestra (CBSO)
under Norman del Mar (not Rignold), and the performance was
recorded for Radio 3. It was, according to John's music publisher, 'the
first considerable work by an internationally famous British pianist'.
Kenneth Loveland of the *Times* thought that the piano part was
scintillating but 'as a vehicle for Mr Ogdon's own splendid accom-
plishments, the concerto achieved a success which was probably in
excess of its actual musical value'. He praised the string harmonies of
the slow movement as well as the rhythmic buoyancy of the work in
general, though the latter perhaps served to compensate for 'the medi-
ocrity of some of the thematic ideas on which the concerto leans'.
The composer Robert Simpson felt it was brilliantly played and much
the best concerto that had been written for John; however, he was
scathing about the string section of the CBSO and wanted to hear it
played by a first-class orchestra at a Prom.

The Cardiff Festival of Twentieth-Century Music had been founded
in March 1967 by John and Welsh composer Alun Hoddinott, the genial
professor-elect of music at Cardiff University. They had known each
other since 1962 and John was a committed exponent of Hoddinott's
piano works, which he found 'very impressive in their improvisatory poetry and unusual use of the bass sonorities of the piano
as a sort of syntax per se'. The idea for the festival had been
John's. A few days before it opened he wrote an article for the *Western
Mail*, entitled 'Modern Composition on Divergent Paths', which
began:

The lapis lazuli waters of the Mediterranean are of a world far
removed from the essentially occidental relationships of modern

art, and yet the idea of starting a Festival of 20th Century Music first came to me in August 1964, while I was on holiday in Greece.

Later on he states the purpose of the festival:

I think our ambition in the festival has been both to present 20th century music in the historical perspective of the recent past, and to show the divergent paths of the present. A conspectus of the earlier 20th century is already possible; but at the present time music of Steinbeckian passion is being created by composers of totally opposed aesthetic orientations, and I think it is our duty to show these polarities of thought clearly and without prejudice.

One of the festival's most successful elements was a rehearsal orchestra under John Carewe – conductor of the BBC Welsh Orchestra – that gave young composers a chance to hear their own music. The emphasis of the joint artistic directors was on new commissions as well as first performances of works already in manuscript or print, and they managed to promote a number of Welsh composers, including David Wynne, William Mathias and Grace Williams. At the inaugural five-day festival John performed prodigies of stamina and pianistic resourcefulness. On the opening night, 16 March, he played Hoddinott's Piano Concerto No. 2 and the Liszt E-flat concerto with the CBSO under Hugo Rignold. The next day he gave a lecture recital, playing Scriabin's Fifth Sonata, Busoni's Sonatina Seconda and Szymanowski's *Masques*. On 18 March he gave a duo recital with Brenda that included the premiere of his own Dance Suite, a piece that drew its inspiration from ritual dances associated with the spring; on the nineteenth he gave another performance of the Hoddinott concerto, this time pairing it with the Rachmaninoff Second. Finally, on 20 March, in what the composer John McCabe described as 'one of the most astonishing feats of sheer physical strength I have ever witnessed from a musician', John gave a lecture recital in the afternoon (which included Messiaen's *Cantéyodjayâ*; Goehr's Three Pieces; and Boulez's fiendishly difficult Sonata No. 2), and then in the evening gave the final concert of the festival, comprising Hoddinott's Sonata

No. 3; five studies by Debussy; Alan Rawsthorne's Ballade – especially commissioned for the festival and dedicated to John – and Ravel's *Jeux d'eau*, Sonatine and *Gaspard de la Nuit*! It was at this first festival that John and Brenda met John Dankworth and Cleo Laine, who opened proceedings with a performance of Walton's *Façade*.

After John's performance of his Dance Suite Alun Hoddinott was quoted as saying, 'He's going to be the Liszt of the twentieth century, better than Rachmaninoff. I have never heard such piano playing.' In his subsequent piece in the *Guardian*, 'Following Liszt's footsteps', Gerald Larner quoted John as saying that he was very interested in composing and wished that he had more time for it. There followed a very revealing passage:

> I wondered whether, having at the age of 30 achieved the status as a performer that anyone else would hope to achieve in twice the time, he now had more ambition as a composer than as a performer. He said that as a student it had been his ambition to be a composer but that piano playing was now his first concern. He is 'very interested in contemporary music' (particularly Messiaen) and he wants to expand his repertory to the earlier classics (particularly Haydn).
>
> 'Besides, I don't feel I have mastered the art of playing the piano yet.' So he wasn't thinking of retiring from the concert circuit within a few years' time to devote himself to composing? 'And send me out to work, I suppose,' interpolated his wife and gifted partner in two-piano music. Which seemed to be the last word on that subject.

Liszt himself happily abandoned the life of the concert pianist aged thirty-five, comparing it to that of 'a man walking across country, tearing off and throwing into the air seeds, flowers, fruits, and tree-branches, yet neither sowing nor ploughing nor grafting'.

John had been a participant in the Cheltenham Festival of Contemporary Music for many years, and his contacts there proved useful in establishing the festival at Cardiff. The previous year at Cheltenham Ashkenazy had performed a piece he'd commissioned from John. Ogdon's Theme and Variations is a curious set of ten variations on an original theme, lasting about seven minutes, which could be entitled 'Robert Schumann from the bed of the Rhine – greetings'. Everyone agreed that it could not have received a better first performance from Ashkenazy, who had rehearsed the piece under John's direction at Golders Green. It was played again at the 1967 festival, this time by the brilliant young Spanish pianist Rafael Orozco, who had won the Leeds Competition the previous year. John was very much a Cheltenham stalwart – or 'hero', as Gerald Larner called him – and gave no less than three premieres at the 1966 festival: Alun Hoddinott's Piano Concerto No. 3, which was written for him, Czech composer Petr Eben's Piano Concerto (English premiere) and Ronald Stevenson's hugely demanding *Passacaglia on D.S.C.H.* The following year he was premiering Robert Simpson's Piano Concerto, also dedicated to him, and Richard Arnell's work for piano and orchestra entitled *Sections*. He premiered David Wynne's Sonata No. 3 and gave performances of works by Grainger, Tippett, Rawsthorne, Birtwistle, Maxwell Davies, Thomas Wilson, Sebastian Forbes, John Joubert, Boris Tishchenko and a host of other lesser-known composers. Whatever was being written for the piano, John wanted to play it. As William Mann wrote in the *Times* after hearing his performance of the Simpson Concerto:

> It must be intensely heartening for composers to know that they have John Ogdon to play their piano works. He introduces a great quantity of new music for piano year by year, and performs it not only with astounding virtuosity and power but gives every impression of enjoying the task.

John had often been called the Champion of Lost Pianistic Causes. His zeal in this regard can probably be traced back to his relationship with his father, who had always presented himself as a neglected genius and probably required placating and championing within the family circle. So whenever an obscure or under-appreciated artist came along, John buckled on his armour and rode into battle.

*

Unhappy with the way John's performing career was contracting under Basil Horsfield, Brenda made a big effort at a rapprochement with Emmie Tillett. In February 1967, after various softening manoeuvres, she made an appointment to see Emmie at her office, and admitted that she and John had made a serious misjudgement in changing agents. Emmie wrote about it in her diary:

6 Feb 1967: Told office of my interview with Brenda Ogdon on Saturday morning. She was evidently very distressed. Admitted to them making ghastly mistake and would I take John back!! Told her she had courage to admit; would not say no.
9 Feb 1967: Spoke to John Ogdon on phone from New York. Sounded just the same as if nothing had happened.

The move back was officially made on 1 April 1967. Terry Harrison, who took care of John's international bookings when he returned to Ibbs & Tillett, had the feeling that at thirty John had missed his chance to have a really huge career – partly because he spent too much time on out-of-the-way repertoire, and partly because his primary ambition was to become a composer. Composition was always in the back of his mind. Consequently in the music business he was never quite seen as a mainstream international virtuoso pianist. There was always something slightly off-centre about him. And, though he had become a sort of national talisman in the British classical-music world, and played a good deal in the Commonwealth and America, as well as in Russia, Japan and Scandinavia, in Central Europe there wasn't as much quality work as he merited. The British artist tended to be patronized in Middle Europe; and John never played with the Berlin or Vienna Philharmonic, nor was he invited to the Salzburg Festival.

John was an occluded personality, whom people found hard to read. One of the negative effects of this was that he rarely if ever built strong relationships with conductors and orchestras. An international partnership with a leading conductor, who could have nurtured him and indulged his enthusiasms, would have paid enormous dividends for both his concert and his recording career and helped to keep him on an even keel. Terry Harrison, a fellow northerner, felt a strong

affinity for John and understood his fragility. He saw that his professional life was unstructured and chaotic, and that in terms of repertoire
he was all over the place. He appeared to lack discrimination and readily agreed to whatever was put in front of him. 'Oh yes, I'll do that,'
was the common refrain. 'It's a lovely piece.' He seemed afraid to say
no – and pressure at home may have contributed to this fear. Harrison
was doing his best to shape a career for John that would suit his
unusual gifts and temperament and at the same time place him in an
international league. This meant filtering out the unimportant elements, diminishing the supply (so that he wasn't overexposed) and
structuring the season so that there was plenty of time for him to learn
new repertoire, to rest in between concerts, to practise and to compose. But anything that he put in place with John's agreement was
swept away by Brenda, who would challenge him if John wasn't giving
concerts or making records every day. He once put aside a whole
month for John to compose but Brenda was soon on the phone, voicing her unhappiness. As a result he felt John was overplaying and
didn't have time to prepare new repertoire; his performances suffered
and he became more remote.

The Polish pianist Andrzej Czajkowski, whom John had heard and
admired at the 1956 Brussels Competition, provides an illuminating
comparison. He was hugely talented, but fundamentally unbalanced.
Having been in the Warsaw ghetto as a child, where he narrowly
escaped death, he settled in England and became a British citizen. Like
John, he was a composer, but unlike John he gave only about forty
concerts a year – which provided a perfectly decent income – and
focused his remaining energies on composition. John was so impressed
when he heard a broadcast of Czajkowski's *Inventions for Piano*, Op. 2,
that he arranged for them to be published.

For all his success, John was curiously isolated. He frequently wrote
of the loneliness he felt when he travelled. He was essentially a sociable creature; even if he said nothing in company, he enjoyed the
presence and conversation of others. And where music was concerned
he throve on the spirit of the hive, delighting in the exchange of
insights and creative ideas. If you isolate the honey bee she will expire
in a few days – not from cold or hunger but from loneliness. As

Maeterlinck so beautifully puts it, 'Her whole life is an entire sacrifice to the manifold, everlasting being whereof she forms part.' John understood this sociability as an essential element of music. He was a member of the musical hive. On the other hand, he felt marked out by fate to perform some extraordinary role and that of itself heralded a certain kind of loneliness. The picture Brenda paints of him in Ischia in the summer of 1968 speaks to this latter vision: pacing darkly up and down the music room all day, shoulders hunched, a frown of concentration on his face, while everyone else was enjoying the sea and sunshine.

In March 1968 John went on a tour of New Zealand that again took in Fiji, but this time he went alone. When he got back home he was very distant with Brenda and refused to embrace her. When she tried to coax from him what the matter was he was silent, but then let out a terrible roar and hurled a porcelain figure against the wall.

> The impact was such that it exploded, the pieces scattering over the floor. John swung back to face me: his fists were clenched threateningly, his face was flushed and distorted, and the violence that blazed in his eyes is something I shall never forget. I stood rooted to the spot in sheer panic [...] the demon that sometimes took possession of his playing had at last appeared in our everyday life.

Brenda found out only years later that he had fallen in love with a girl while in New Zealand. She was a social worker but he wouldn't say more. According to the Schurmanns, this New Zealand relationship was almost wholly a figment of John's mind. It had clearly opened a door, though, because he admitted to Gerard that he would leave 'B', as he called Brenda, if this girl (or one like her) were to walk into his life. 'I would love to go to New Zealand again,' he'd muse. Shona, the girl in question, was both flattered and bemused by John's interest in her. He left her a curious gift at his hotel in Christchurch – a pair of handmade sterling silver coffee spoons with greenstone handles – and after his return to England continued to write and telephone for a year or so. When one of the two spoons snapped along the handle, Shona felt a strange foreboding.

John could perhaps sense the drawbridge being pulled up on his professional life, and was desperately searching for ways over the moat. It is no coincidence that the New Zealand amour and the first performance of his piano concerto should have come so soon before he and Brenda made their fateful move from Golders Green to 13 Chester Terrace, a five-storey, cream-coloured, Corinthian-columned Nash mansion overlooking Regent's Park (the Lebanese ambassador lived at No. 3). The house, which they bought for £40,000, boasted a 42-feet-long drawing room, a service flat, an elevator and access to the private Crown Estate gardens. It had belonged to Princess Margaret's friend Lady Glenconner, whose husband bought the Caribbean island of Mustique. The Regency of course was notorious for gambling, aristocratic excess and an almost pathological pursuit of pleasure, all of which happened under the batting eye of a mad king. According to Brenda, she and John took a childlike delight in their new and opulent surroundings and were blissfully unaware of the social dimension of their move. They just wanted somewhere to house their two grand pianos!

While their new house was being completely redecorated and refurbished the Ogdons stayed at the Savoy Hotel. With a secretary to type his letters John wrote from there to thank Alun Hoddinott for his hospitality during the Cardiff Festival and his gift of a painting by Thomas Jones, as well as to say how much he had enjoyed premiering his Fifth Sonata.

John had rather lost touch with Peter Maxwell Davies and Harrison Birtwistle since they'd set up the Pierrot Players and latterly, in 1967, had taken joint direction of the Fires of London, a contemporary music ensemble that scored many scandalous successes. The year after John moved to Chester Terrace they put on Maxwell Davies's monodrama, *Eight Songs for a Mad King*, based on the words of King George III. It was scored for baritone and six players, who took up their stations on stage in large ornamental birdcages. John attended the premiere, but it is not known whether the glaring ironies of the piece hit home as the door shut on his own ornamental pen.

8

GILDED CAGE

The supreme vice is shallowness.

Oscar Wilde, 'De Profundis'

The life of a touring concert pianist is full of mishap and surprise. Fortunately John was never a prima donna of the Michelangeli school, where strange pre-concert rituals (such as being served a rare brand of coffee twenty-one minutes before lights up) become contractual demands and even the smallest missed detail can mean sudden cancellation or at least a nasty tantrum. John just rolled up his sleeves and got on with things. In many ways he had quite a workaday attitude to the piano, which was, after all, his workplace. He made the best of whatever instrument was placed before him (unlike Horowitz, who had his own piano flown from New York to wherever he was playing, be it Houston or Moscow), and was remarkably adept at coping with surprises.

At a performance of the Rachmaninoff Third Piano Concerto at the Queen Elizabeth Theatre in Vancouver in 1967 one of the wedges securing the piano's wheels came adrift and the instrument began to lurch from side to side. John managed to follow it around on his stool, much to the amusement of one reviewer who cited this as the reason why 'Ogdon was not as infallibly accurate as usual'. Nevertheless, he concluded, 'the concerto came off brilliantly'. On another occasion, at a midday concert being broadcast by the BBC from Manchester's St Peter's Square, John had just reached the final three of the Chopin Op. 25 studies (*Octave, Winter Wind* and *Ocean*) when the pedal lyre came unstuck. Left with no pedals at all most pianists would stop playing, because they provide the body of the sound – without them you simply can't get the sonority when you want it. Not John. He carried on playing with extraordinary power and unnerving commitment, as if the pedals were mere toys.

Sometimes his sense of humour was sorely tested, as when he walked out on stage at the Freiburg concert hall during an LPO tour of Europe to find that the piano was locked. After bowing to the audience he turned to the offending lid. He made to lift it – first gently, then with more force – but it remained securely shut. Finally he bent his knees like a weightlifter and heaved up on it. The conductor peered down at him, the orchestra looked at their shoes and the capacity audience began to titter. John stared furiously into the wings but no one came to his assistance. Realizing that he had become the protagonist in a farce, he stormed off. Eventually an ancient man with a bunch of keys at his waist was found napping in the basement and was rewarded with an ovation as he hobbled on stage and unlocked the lid. When John returned there was thunder in his looks and his opening chords well-nigh splintered the instrument. It wasn't the most satisfying tour for him, there being no relief from the Tchaikovsky Concerto from start to finish – grist to Alexander Goehr's tart observation that winning in Moscow had turned John into a 'Tchaikovsky merchant'.

On another occasion the joke was deliberate and directed at John, but he managed to turn the tables on his tormentor. He was in Jerusalem to play the Liszt E-flat concerto with Georg Solti and the Israel Philharmonic. On the morning of the concert a formal-looking note appeared under his hotel-room door: 'By order of the Chief Rabbi, all beards are to be shaved on this most holy of days.' Aghast at this sudden assault upon his trusty disguise, John grabbed the phone and was about to call Reception when he remembered the date – 1 April. He had no doubt as to the author of the prank and it didn't

take him long to settle on an appropriate riposte. At the concert that
night, when the time came for the first-movement cadenza, John
launched into the cadenza from the Tchaikovsky B-flat minor concerto instead. In a trice Solti swung round on the podium to stare
white-faced at John, who gave a cunning little smile before returning
with seamless aplomb to the Liszt. Solti later took the whole thing in
good sort, though he was mortified to see that John still had his
beard.

In the late 1960s the name John Ogdon was as famous in the world
of British classical music as the Beatles were in the realm of popular
music. Aspiring composers and musicians beat a path to his door,
eager for the endorsement of the Ogdon name. John had amassed a
large library of scores and texts on music, as well as other volumes that
reflected his roving literary interests, but his prodigality in giving away
scores, even autographed first editions, was legendary. He once gave
away a leather-bound two-piano version of Busoni's Piano Concerto,
for instance – originally a gift from Ronald Stevenson. Those who
borrowed from him knew that he wouldn't ask for anything back, so
the parasites had a field day. It is true that some of those who flocked
to Chester Terrace to have their work sanctioned were talented bona
fide young composers or musicians but others were there to satisfy
their vanity. John himself appeared incapable of turning anyone away,
so Brenda had to steel herself against the growing legions of hangers-
on. More to John's liking, but still an irritant to Brenda, were the older
generation of composers who patronized him. Bernard Herrmann, for
example, found a London refuge at the Ogdons' home (according to
John, it was the only place in London where he and his wife Norma
were invited). As well as Herrmann, men such as Robert Sherlaw
Johnson, Alan Rawsthorne, Richard Yardumian, Peter Mennin, Cyril
Scott, Robert Simpson, Larry Adler and George Lloyd were frequent
visitors. One or more of them might turn up in the afternoon to
discuss what they were writing and John would inevitably insist that
they stayed for dinner; dinner would be followed by more wine and
more discussion, and so it would go on. John sat at the centre of these
gatherings like a great electrical exchange box, puffing, nodding,
taking everything in, and at the same time silently processing a mass of

complex ideas and musical-philosophical 'problems'. A constant haze of smoke acted as a benign exclusion zone, keeping him safely aloft his musical cloud. His ruminations seemed constant and he often appeared to be listening to something in the distance that no one else could hear, his silences punctuated by a meditative refrain of 'Yes, yes'. Sometimes he'd get up to illustrate a point on one of the two Steinway grands that adorned the great first-floor drawing room. It was said that John drove EMI's producers crazy by insisting that he be allowed to record works by Yardumian and other living composers whose commercial value was negligible. Brenda thought that Yardumian was just one more hanger-on and she resented having to spend so much time with him and his family at their large colonial home in Bryn Athyn, Pennsylvania or at Oyster Bay on Cape Cod. John, on the other hand, loved being part of a bustling, artistic family and spent many a happy hour in the well-stocked music library at Bryn Athyn, with its records and books and unusual paintings by the Dutch Swedenborgian artist Felipe Smith. Richard and Ruth Yardumian had thirteen children and belonged to a splinter group of the Swedenborgian Church, the Lord's New Church Which Is Nova Hierosolyma. The leader of the church, the Rev. Theodore Pitcairn, funded Yardumian's music, much of which was religious in content. John was already fascinated by Swedenborg's theology from reading Sheridan Le Fanu and knew Henry James's father's book on the subject, the latter having become interested in Swedenborg following his nervous breakdown in 1841. John did give generously of his time to Yardumian, but in this case he was the recipient of a great deal in return, both in hospitality and musical inspiration.

Another American who came to Chester Terrace was the composer-pianist Raymond Lewenthal, who was largely responsible for the revival of interest in Alkan's works in the 1950s and 1960s. When in New York, John used to visit Lewenthal's apartment for breakfast and spent some considerable time poring over Alkan's Grande Sonate, Op. 33, with him. John much admired Lewenthal's Schirmer edition of the piece, as well as his own compositions, such as his fantasias on Glière's *The Red Poppy* and *Ilya Mourometz*, praising the way he treated the extreme registers of the piano 'with Busonian élan'. John was also friendly with Benny Goodman, whom he valued for his straight-forward, extrovert personality. They too had met in New York.

Composers saw in John a golden ticket because he could play their works brilliantly without having to learn them. His name was their passport to recognition. For the most part, however, it was a two-way street: he enjoyed their company and was interested in their ideas. Where he ran into trouble was with mediocre people who flattered themselves that they were worth his time. Even here, though, their opportunism may have coincided with a need in John himself to fill the house with guests as a way of shielding himself from the taxing intimacies of family life. There were lavish parties arranged by Brenda, too, though – pre- or post-concert receptions for up to fifty with stand-up buffet, or dinner parties for ten or more guests. In retrospect she was much criticized for forcing these events upon a reluctant and indifferent John, who could usually be found smoking in a corner, apparently oblivious to what was going on around him. The busi-nessmen and politicians and their wives, the aristocracy – these weren't really John's bag, and to them he was a weirdly self-absorbed artist. In order to spread her net, Brenda encouraged her guests to bring another couple with them, and so a social circle was created with its obligatory round of parties. John's frequent tours at least excused him from attending all the functions to which he and Brenda were invited. Brenda was away a good deal too. 'It's a lovely house,' she said of 13 Chester Terrace in an interview with ABC's Ellis Blain. 'We don't see very much of it – that's the only thing.' Then she turned to John, 'It's a lovely house, isn't it?'

They had a substantial staff, comprising at various times a Portuguese couple who kept house, a nanny for the children, a secretary and a part-time chef and chauffeur. Until they were sent off to board the children were usually taken to school and collected by one of the staff. Their nanny, who was in her late sixties, had 'practically brought up the chil-dren', according to Brenda. 'It's rather a treat for me to see my children,' she said. It is easy to believe that John – like Brenda – took a childlike delight in his luxurious surroundings, but status symbols meant little to him beyond the enjoyment of the moment. This is where husband and wife diverged. John was blind to social distinctions and as far from being a snob as one could possibly imagine. But Brenda made no secret of her joy at moving up in the world and now she had the perfect platform for her ascent. Unfortunately, she had as little sense of money as John; but, for five-and-a-half giddy years, relying on John's insane work rate to keep the glory ship afloat, Brenda stepped into the limelight. John was desperate to please her but was all the while undergoing an inner eclipse that he was powerless to articulate.

In 1968 John was voted one of three Outstanding Young Men of the Year by the British Junior Chambers of Commerce; two years later he was named Instrumentalist of the Year by the Composers' Guild of Great Britain 'for his manifold performances and recordings of the music of fellow-composers'. He continued to go out on a musical limb, playing works such as the Malcolm Lipkin Piano Concerto and Benjamin Lees' *Odyssey I & II* (written for him) and commissioning new works, for instance Alexander Goehr's *Nonomiya* for the 1969 Macclesfield Arts Festival. In January 1968 he devoted an entire Wigmore Hall recital to the works of South African composer Arnold van Wyk. He remained a stalwart of the Society for the Promotion of New Music, through which he met many composers – among them Francis Chagrin, Graham Whettam and Richard Arnell, whose works he played. He also did much to rehabilitate neglected works from earlier generations. His performance of the Schoenberg Piano Concerto with the BBC Symphony Orchestra under Pierre Boulez was the finest that the chief music critic of the *Times*, William Mann, had heard. If one looks at the really great recordings John made in the five years from 1969 to 1973 they include Messiaen's *Vingt Regards* (Decca, 1969), *The Piano Music of Carl Nielsen* (RCA, 1969), his own Piano Concerto (EMI, 1970), the Complete Sonatas of Scriabin (EMI, 1972) and Alkan's Concerto for Solo Piano (RCA, 1973), surely one of the finest recordings of all time.

Many have commented on John's essential sweetness, but it was a curiously passive quality in him – an absence of malice rather than an active good. In fact there was an absence of almost everything except music – and even that, one felt, was done *through* him rather than *by* him. His daughter Annabel's childhood label for him, Teddy Bear Father, seems hauntingly apt. With this passivity, however, came a freshness of vision and a certain whimsy that could be very attractive. Who else could have written this postcard to the Hoddinotts in September 1968?

> Dear Alun & Rhiannon,
>   Just a line to send greetings from Bulawayo. Lovely weather – saw some white rhinos today, which made me feel obscurely imperatorial.
>   Love from,
>   John

Obscurely imperatorial! One imagines the great pianist sitting on an elephant in a pair of empire-builders, surveying his thick-skinned vassals. At the time of the Busoni Concerto sessions EMI's Suvi Raj Grubb would telephone Daniell Revenaugh and announce himself with the single word 'Grubb'. One day Revenaugh turned to Ogdon and said, 'John, what do I say when I hear that?' John replied, 'You could say "Butterfly".' The other side to the sweet-passivity coin was a terrible sense of isolation. As Brian Masters puts it, 'You wanted to bring him into the human fold; to say, "Come and join us, John."'

At the Chester Terrace revels John smoked away amiably at the head of the table, puffing between mouthfuls, juggling cutlery, glasses and burning cigarettes. Brenda would be at the other end with a little silver bell to ring for the next course. The parties were quite glamorous and Brenda enjoyed formality, so black-tie dinners were not uncommon. The food was specially prepared by the chef or ordered in from Harrods and the flower arrangements were by Moyses Stevens. At larger receptions flunkeys stood at the door to announce the guests. (Denis Matthews and his wife once had Brenda running to the door when they gave their names as Sir John and Lady Something.) John Peyton, the minister of transport in the Heath government, was a frequent guest, as were Alistair Londonderry and his new wife, Doreen Wells, the Hon. Simon and Sheelin Eccles, Richard Croucher, Ben Worthington and his wife and so on – all pukka types. Representatives from John's professional life included Peter Andry of EMI and Wilfred Stiff of Ibbs & Tillett, who kept a watchful eye on proceedings. On the artistic side the composer Gerard Schurmann and his wife Carolyn were often invited, as were the Russian émigré composer Alexander Tcherepnin and his Chinese wife, Ming, Andrzej and Camilla Panufnik, the writer Brian Masters, John Dankworth and Cleo Laine, and the photographer Clive Barda and his wife. André Previn and Mia Farrow were regular guests. John described Mia Farrow as 'looking like a Dresden shepherdess' as she sat cross-legged on their Chinese carpet. John was a fan of the BBC series *André Previn's Music Night*, which was first broadcast in 1971 and presented classical music to a vast new audience. To his mind, it 'brought back the *espièglerie* of the Edwardian era in all its flamboyance'. When John played the Liszt Second Piano Concerto with Colin Davis at the Last Night of the Proms his dinner guests were conveyed to the Albert Hall in a white Rolls-Royce. Sometimes the post-concert celebration would be dinner for eight or ten at Tiberio's in Mayfair, where the party would last into the wee hours. The Ogdons were extremely generous hosts.

John's old friends from Manchester were disconcerted by his new surroundings and found him barely recognizable as the genial, probing fellow they had known at college. They felt he was living out of context, in an artificial world that conflicted with who he was. Peter Maxwell Davies found it hard to talk to John because Brenda kept interposing herself. Harrison Birtwistle's one and only visit was an alienating experience. He felt as though he'd never really known John, and found it irksome to be called 'Henry' by so many unfamiliar people. 'It was tasteless, pretentious, horrible,' he says, 'and there was poor John in the middle of it. He looked as if he was on the moon.' Rodney Friend, also a guest that night, seemed to agree:

> John was overplaying, Brenda overspending. It was deeply unhealthy. John was basically a peasant boy, who should have been allowed to function in a world he knew – a world of music and weird musicians. They were his real family, particularly the composers.

At the end of the night John stood at the door to say goodbye as his guests filed out. When Harry reached the front of the queue he thanked John for a nice evening and wished him well. John, who was nodding and smiling in all directions at once, didn't seem to register his departure and was already shaking hands with someone else. Several minutes later, as he was talking to yet another guest, he suddenly turned to the door and shouted, 'Bye, Harry!' But Harry was long gone. It was in fact the last time he would see him.

On occasion John would emerge from his 'foggy fortifications', as his friend Keith Cole called them, and take the floor before his assembled guests – not as a pianist but as an orator. Pacing up and down, looking for all the world like a second Chesterton, this usually tongue-tied soul would expound with marvellous fluency on a theme from music, literature or history that had been gathering and organizing itself in his intricate mind. Such disquisitions were as unexpected as they were compelling and no one seemed more surprised than John. As at the piano, it was as if he had been possessed by another spirit. His effusiveness spent, he would retire to the margins once more and sink into his accustomed mulling. It was in the smaller gatherings that he participated more; some of these could be quite boisterous, especially when music was involved and a number of guests fell to playing duets or pieces for six hands. After one particularly wild evening, during which everyone got very drunk, John ended up on the floor under the same blanket as Cleo Laine. Brenda was fond of taking everyone off to Annabel's, the private nightclub on Berkeley Square. Daniell Revenaugh and his then girlfriend went there with John, Brenda and Larry Adler: it was, he said, one of the most excruciatingly awkward evenings he'd ever spent.

According to Brenda, John needed the parties as a way of releasing adrenalin and unwinding. 'Brenda,' he'd say, 'I want a party!' and that was that – a party he would have. Many of his friends have found this picture of John's assertiveness hard to believe. It's true that he didn't know how to make decisions in the sense of mapping out a personal life for himself – he left all that to Brenda – but he could be suddenly demanding. In this their relationship was similar to those of many other brilliant musicians and their spouses wherein the women are perceived to have run their partner's life (one thinks of Yehudi and Diana Menuhin – who signed themselves 'Yehudiana' – or Vladimir

Howard and Dorothy Ogdon with their five children: Ruth, Philippa and Paul (standing), Karl and John (sitting), Prestwich, c.1950.

John with the Scouts while at Manchester Grammar School.

Left, John aged two, Leigh-on-Sea, Essex, 1939; right, aged eight, scholar elect of the RMCM.

John Ogdon, Marjory Kasen (née Wood), daughter Elaine and Dorothy Ogdon, summer 1952.

John with his first piano teacher, Nellie Houseley, 1962.

John with his early mentor Ronald Stevenson at Stevenson's home, West Linton, 1959.

The New Music Manchester group in 1955. John is seated in the centre; round him from left to right are Alexander Goehr, Harrison Birtwistle, Elgar Howarth, Peter Maxwell Davies, John Dow and Audrey Baker (Goehr's girlfriend).

Caricature of John during his college days drawn by Rodney Friend. The note reads, 'P.S. John stayed at the house for a few days – this is how I remember him at our little upright.'

Kaikhosru Shapurji Sorabji (1892–1988).

John's musical hero, Ferruccio Busoni (1866–1924).

Brenda Lucas in 1956, the year she entered the Queen Elisabeth International Competition in Brussels.

John and Brenda at their home in Golders Green, 1966.

John and Brenda's wedding reception, West Towers Country Club, near Marple, Cheshire, 23 July 1960.

Annabel and Richard Ogdon, *c.*1970.

John and Brenda
at Abbey Road
while recording
Rachmaninoff's
Suites for Two Pianos,
November 1972.

John gives his Model-D Steinway
a helping hand, 13 Chester Terrace,
November 1972. Brenda looks on
from the doorway.

John recording the Busoni Concerto
at No. 1 Studio, Abbey Road, with
Daniell Revenaugh conducting the
RPO, June 1967.

The first page of Act 2, Scene 1 of John's comic opera, *The King of Alsander*, based on the novel by James Elroy Flecker. The score is peppered with telephone numbers, train times and notes to self, such as 'I encourage this – say that you're sorry'.

John at the Palace of Congresses in the Kremlin after his victory in the Tchaikovsky Competition, May 1962. On his right are Soviet premier Nikita Khrushchev and fellow winner Vladimir Ashkenazy.

John recording the Tchaikovsky Concerto with Sir John Barbirolli, Abbey Road studios, London, 1962.

John sight-reading during a recording session with Chris Rice at St Silas Church, Chalk Farm, 1986.

John working on Gerard Schurmann's Piano Concerto with the composer, Chester Terrace, 1973.

John backstage at the Queen Elizabeth Hall before his 270-minute recital of Sorabji's *Opus Clavicembalisticum*, July 1988. With him, from left to right, are Paul Rapoport, Alistair Hinton, Ronald Stevenson and Alastair Chisholm.

John on a No. 41 bus in Manchester, December 1984.

and Wanda Horowitz, for example). And yet the great power and influence of these women didn't override their husbands' sudden tyrannical outbursts and commandeering of authority. Making decisions and laying down the law are two different things. John could not assert himself calmly and reasonably: alternating between helplessness and tyranny, he either submitted or erupted.

John brought a huge amount to the Cardiff Festival, and not only as an indefatigable performer of new works. His influence and contacts were instrumental in attracting top-class musicians and composers – such as Peter Maxwell Davies and his Pierrot Players in 1968 and John McCabe, whose Canto for Guitar was commissioned for the same year. He also secured Sir Arthur Bliss and Sir William Walton as patrons. Walton was by now a good friend and John had got to know Bliss when he played his Piano Concerto at his 75th Birthday Concert at the Royal Albert Hall in 1966 with the composer conducting. As for his role as composer, premieres of Dance Suite in 1967 and the Piano Concerto in 1968 were followed in 1969 by his String Quartet. After the 1969 festival, however, John was worked out of the committee entirely and dropped as artistic director. According to Gerard Schurmann, now that the festival was established John was 'cheated' out of his share by Hoddinott and the Welsh side. They had used his name then dumped him; and in the programme for 1970 there was no mention of him whatsoever. In an article in the *Western Mail* to mark the fifth festival, in 1971, Ogdon was referred to simply as one of the past performers, while the festival was described as 'the brainchild of Alun Hoddinott'. John was deeply upset and indignant but incapable of confronting those who had abused him. He would simply shake his head and say, 'It's not right, Gerard.' John had tried to alter the Welsh bias of the festival and give it a broader base, which included jazz and even pop. He had also suggested a more professional scale of remuneration and planned to commission works from Birtwistle and other members of the Manchester group, whose aesthetic ran counter to Hoddinott's. Ironically, he had written to Hoddinott not long before his ousting suggesting that 'as artistic directors it might be valid to consider "backing into the limelight", so to speak, as I think Britten does at Aldeburgh'.

In addition to his performing, composing, recording and festival work, John took one or two pupils at Chester Terrace. Charles Hopkins, himself a polymath who shared many of Ogdon's recherché musical interests, was nervous when he approached the imposing façade of the house, but was soon put at his ease by John's warm welcome and his absolute attention to the matter in hand. For the first lesson they worked on the Brahms Second Concerto; Hopkins found himself paying more attention to what John was doing in the orchestral part, which he embellished with a wealth of detail absent in the piano reduction, than to his own solo part. Alistair Londonderry, who sat in on one of these lessons, recalls John singing the orchestral part. Hopkins noted John's ingenious approach to fingering, his stillness at the keyboard and the illusion he managed to create that his hands weren't moving – and this in spite of the phenomenal speed of his finger-work. Conspicuous also was his undogmatic approach to technical and interpretive matters. Hopkins had heard of John's sight-reading exploits but was unprepared for the day that he brought in an autograph copy of Luciano Berio's unpublished Sequenza IV, whose UK premiere he was due to give. It was, Hopkins said, a truly humbling experience to watch John 'unravel the complexities of Berio's hieroglyphs so comprehensively at one attempt', especially considering how long it had taken him. John was prodigal with his time, with lessons often running to three or four hours, while his grateful pupil would leave laden with scores from the Ogdon library, many of them first editions. As for payment, post-dated cheques were the order of the day.

Hopkins had studied with Gordon Green, as had his friend and fellow Chester Terrace pupil Gordon Fergus-Thompson. John talked a lot to Fergus-Thompson about orchestral colour, how to play cantabile and how to reflect for instance the sound and character of an oboe on the piano. He helped to diversify the latter's sound palette, which, at the time, was rather monochrome, especially in the lower registers. Technically, however, John was probably not the best of teachers: everything came so easily and naturally to him that he didn't have to think about questions of technique. This prodigality, encompassing as it did a vast repertoire, meant that he rarely refined or perfected anything. Where he came into his own was with his deep insights into a composer's intent. It was wonderful, says Fergus-Thompson, to go to someone who was so liberated. He didn't make you feel that there was a hierarchy of things that should be learned. He believed that an artist should follow his temperament and bring a high level of understanding to the music.

Musically nothing fazed him. At the end of one lesson Fergus-Thompson said to John, 'Looking forward to hearing your Brahms D minor on the radio tomorrow.' John, who was to give a live-broadcast performance in Glasgow the following evening, looked blank. 'Oh,' he said, looking in his diary. 'Oh yes, I have got to play it.' He knew the piece and his interpretation would be shaped by the moment. This was very much the case when in October 1969 he gave two performances of the Brahms D minor with the eighty-seven-year-old conductor Leopold Stokowski and the American Symphony Orchestra in Carnegie Hall. It was thrilling music-making, as the tapes of the rehearsals reveal, with Stokowski's white fire every bit as intense as Ogdon's greener flame. The two artists, fifty-five years apart in age, enjoyed the experience of working together so well that they planned to make a record of the Brahms, but their commitment to separate recording companies got in the way.

Brian Masters, a close friend of Alistair Londonderry, used to go to Chester Terrace quite regularly for lunches at which he, Brenda and John spoke only French. Brian himself was fluent in the language, while John spoke good accurate French in an accent that was laughably English in its diffidence. He seemed to enjoy hiding behind another tongue and was less inhibited at these lunches because it was as if it wasn't he who was speaking, but a French voice. Such 'subterfuges' assuaged a personality disorder that was becoming more pronounced as the 1960s gave way to the 1970s.

A number of unrelated incidents began to form a picture that gave cause for concern. The first time that Brenda was made aware of any problems was following John's 1969 tour with the Allegri Quartet. One of the violinists, Hugh Maguire, approached Brenda backstage at an orchestral concert and said, 'You know, John gave us a lot of trouble; we were worried about him.' He didn't go into detail – and

Brenda didn't ask – but she thinks that John disliked the ensemble work because he found the rehearsals repetitive. He probably just wandered off. He had also thrown a cup of coffee at a secretary at the BBC – a sudden outburst that took everyone by surprise. There were reports from Harold Shaw, John's new agent in the States, that he was becoming erratic and wasn't playing as well as usual. He was behaving strangely and people were beginning to notice. In 1972 John injured himself in his New York hotel room and subsequently became disoriented; his London agent, Martin Campbell-White, had to cover for him. In fact instances of disorientation became more frequent. On tour in Finland John would call his Scandinavian agent, Henrik Lodding, and say, 'I need to talk to someone. I'm lonely.' According to Lodding, John was drinking quite heavily at the time and was known to go to bed in his tails after post-concert parties.

At EMI John was now working with David Mottley and turning out some wonderful recordings, including the complete Etudes-Tableaux of Rachmaninoff and the Sonatas of French composers Paul Dukas and Henri Dutilleux. Yet here too there were sudden onslaughts of desolation. In the middle of one recording session Mottley looked through the glass to see John sitting at the piano with his head in his arms. 'Are you alright?' he asked. 'I don't think so,' replied John. 'I want to go home now.' 'Would you like some coffee?' asked Mottley, hoping he might be persuaded to stay. 'I don't know,' came the forlorn reply. At home, too, he seemed more withdrawn and Brenda would often find him reading his father's book. Nevertheless, side by side with this dogged reserve was an increasingly high-handed and dictatorial attitude to Brenda and the children and a desperate impatience with any obstacles he found in his way. On one occasion he insisted that Brenda accompany him on a three-week tour of South Africa, Namibia and Kenya – and not just her but the children as well. She was to book first-class flights. Brenda objected – the children were at school – but he simply ordered her to take them out. Any defiance on her part, however mild, was met with threatening looks and clenched fists. Annabel remembers a number of 'very scary' outbursts during the Chester Terrace days. If he was running low on cigarettes, for example, he would become intensely anxious: the thought of running out altogether sent him into a terrible tailspin. Sometimes she was frightened enough to cry, but her tears only made John angrier and he would shout at Brenda as though she was to blame. One minute you'd be talking to him and everything would be fine; the next minute he'd be extremely agitated, as if he was about to explode. (In the back of the car once he suddenly became very angry at something Brenda said and tried to get out while it was moving.) Gradually, his whole personality changed. It was as if he had been seized by an overwhelming desire to escape from his reality.

He would always apologize after an incident, and for the most part Annabel found him gentle, warm and approachable and true to his nickname of 'Teddy Bear Father'. He'd even make bear noises sometimes. He was very thoughtful and always brought back toys or dolls from abroad; for Richard it would be a car or a ship. He was generally an indulgent father, not at all strict, and wrote regularly to them when they were away at boarding school. Music was of course a constant presence in the home, with both parents practising a great deal and a steady stream of visiting musicians. John didn't push his children towards the piano, though both took it up at school; he then proved a source of encouragement, taking the time to listen and offer advice. Annabel reached Grade 8 and remembers playing *La Cathédrale Engloutie* by Debussy. Richard was given a tape recorder when he was five or six, and would record John's playing at rehearsals.

John's physical health also began to give him problems. In 1970 he suffered from repeated attacks of gout, which marked the beginning of a running saga with his feet. In April 1971, when he went up to Liverpool to play with the Liverpool Philharmonic, he was met off the train by Gordon and Dorothy Green. He staggered out of the carriage saying, 'I have to get to a doctor; there's something wrong with my foot.' The Greens rushed him to the matron of the local hospital, who was a friend of theirs. When she removed his shoe they were all knocked back against the wall by the stench: his foot was septic. The following year he had a hiatus hernia, brought on by weight gain, stress and smoking. Ironically one of John's heroes, Sorabji himself, had raged about Ogdon's lifestyle as early as 1966 in a letter to Ronald Stevenson:

I find a certain deterioration in Ogdon's playing recently. His style has coarsened and thickened – like his figure it seems. He is doing FAR FAR too much don't you think AND if he is going to be such a silly ass as to smoke cigarettes, i.e. turn himself into a human blast furnace for the consumption of vegetable refuse, that's his look out [. . .] But he is asking for trouble if at HIS age he goes on putting on bulk like that.

In March 1970 he gave his first recital for the Allmusic Plan at the Stables, Wavendon, of which he was a director – an event that has lived brightly in the memory of those who turned up. John Dankworth had driven to London under leaden skies to collect John and Brenda from Chester Terrace in his Rolls-Royce Silver Shadow. Not long after they set off for Buckinghamshire it began to snow and by the time they approached Wavendon they were driving through swirling shrouds of white. The storm knocked out the electricity supply as well as the phone lines and when the snow eventually stopped the ground began to freeze. Many doughty souls had braved the elements, blankets in hand, to reach the hall, but was it fair to ask the pianist to perform in an unheated, unlit, half-empty auditorium with sub-zero temperatures outside? Dankworth was taken aback by John's resolve: people had made the effort to get there, he said, so the least he could do was perform. And perform he did! In the freezing cold, with an old woolly cardigan over his tails, the keys dimly lit by a couple of candles from the local church, John held his audience spellbound with performances of Bach's Chromatic Fantasy and Fugue; Beethoven's *Appassionata* Sonata; Ravel's *Gaspard de la Nuit*; and the Mephisto Waltz No. 1 and *La Campanella* by Liszt.

In August of the same year John toured Japan with the New Philharmonia Orchestra as part of Britain's cultural contribution to Expo 70, the World's Fair that opened in Osaka. There was a brief holiday in Spain after Japan but, that aside, from August 1970 well into 1971 John worked at an insane rate. (Martin Campbell-White wrote to the BBC on 27 July 1970 wondering whether any producers would care to take advantage of the fact that John's only free dates between then and the end of March 1971 were 12–16 October!) Japan was followed by a four-week tour of South Africa, and so the whirligig spun ever faster, with John – like the middle-aged Liszt before him – on a jittery diet of tobacco and black coffee. And, also as with Liszt, his nerves became horribly irritated under so much stimulation and his habitual mask (which in the case of both men was an exaggerated humility) would drop, revealing the festering resentments underneath. These would break forth in flashes of dyspeptic wrath, principally towards Brenda. Liszt had been on John's mind through much of 1969, for he had been writing a long and masterly chapter on the late piano music for a volume edited by Alan Walker entitled *Franz Liszt: The Man & His Music*. In his introduction John wrote movingly of Liszt's emotional exhaustion in 1860 after the 'enormous energy which he [had] poured out of his life for over twenty years in the service of others'. He compared Liszt to Herman Melville in as much as both men underwent a marked personality change in later life, which John describes as 'a withdrawal into complete introversion', and quotes Liszt's melancholy statement to Dr Franz Brendel: 'It seems to me, now, high time that I should be somewhat forgotten.' One can't help noticing the personal touches in what John chose to emphasize, as when he wrote,

It is hardly surprising, then, that [Liszt's] old enthusiasms alternate more with a mood of reticent despair in the last years, and that he writes to Lina Ramann: 'I am deeply mourning in my heart, and the mourning must burst forth in music here and there.'

It may be that this 'reticent despair' describes John's own feelings at the dawn of the new decade. It seems that no one realized just how close to despair he was when he began his American tour at the end of January 1971. Yet barely a week later he was on his way home again after a deeply disturbing incident. He had gone to San Antonio, Texas, to play the Yardumian Concerto, and on arrival at his hotel began to hallucinate. Wherever he looked he saw crosses – not just small crucifixes but huge luminous crosses hanging in the sky. His hallucinations were aural too: when he reached his sixteenth-floor room he heard voices summoning him to the ledge outside his window, which he duly obeyed. He was immediately noticed from the street and the police were called. John ended up in a psychiatric ward; his doctor there contacted his agent Harold Shaw, who arranged for him to be flown back to London via New York.

John had been brooding over his father's book and certain passages clearly acted upon his mind as powerful suggestions – specifically those recounting Howard's own obsession with crosses, whereby this symbol 'achieved a steep penetration into the depth of his mind, and served him adversely for years'.

> Religious crosses seemed scarcely to be involved [...] but in any other context the cross-symbol had a very depressing effect. I saw them everywhere [...] crosses in text-books, 'plus' signs, crosses painted on roads, crosses in window frames, brick walls, which were simply masses of interlaced crosses, I picked them out, fasci-nated ... anywhere and everywhere [...] I think that this cross-inhibition was of the same family as the Yattara, based on a principle of squares, and used to kill one of the Kings of Burma.

What happened to John on his return is not known, but it's likely that his agent covered for him, citing illness if concerts had to be cancelled. Not long after the incident, which was kept out of the newspapers but probably did the rounds of the musical grapevine, John was featured in *Time* magazine. The article, entitled 'Unromantic Romantic', made much of his ambition as a com-poser, noting that he was 'bidding hard to join a select though all but vanished company of virtuoso pianist-composers'. Fellow pianist Stephen Bishop-Kovacevich was quoted as saying, 'Ogdon has absolutely volcanic energy. I mean, the piano actually moves some-times.' This was, the feature writer stated, contrasted starkly with John's personal manner: 'His handshake is a boneless fadeaway. His response to a lengthy conversational thrust of a close friend is likely to range from a non-committal "Mmmmmmm", to a rare "Very interesting".'

*

John received a shattering blow at the beginning of September that year when he took a call from his brother Paul in Manchester telling him that Karl had died in Melbourne. He was just forty-one. Karl's life had changed quite drastically in the seven years since he last saw John. In 1964 he had been childless; at the time of his death he was the father of three small children, two daughters and a son, but he and Gwen were no longer together. Psychologically Karl had been disintegrating and in addition to smoking heavily had come to rely increasingly on alcohol. His hair and beard turned grey in his thirties and he brooded about his mental health, fearing that he might succumb to the same fate as his father. He ordered books from America and learned self-hypnosis. He gave up his job at the State Library and attempted once again to earn his living entirely through music. He gave lessons in piano and guitar and sold some of the pieces he composed. He was also the Victoria agent for the Perth guitar-maker Andries De Jager and always had a couple of De Jagers at home, which he would play before selling on. He did somehow manage to provide for his family and was, according to Gwen, a patient and indulgent father. The children didn't witness his explosive temper, yet it was one such eruption that caused his separation from Gwen. She had confronted him about one of his female students and he had become violent, going into an icy rage that scared her. She was rescued by friends, who took her and the children back to their home. They would not allow her to return unless Karl convinced them that he would seek counselling for his psychological problems. This he refused to do, and the split became permanent. That was in 1970.

After the separation Karl became ill and depressed. He suffered a heart attack and had several spells in hospital. His doctor, who was an old friend, visited Gwen and urged her to return to her husband: he felt that if she didn't something terrible would happen. Gwen did go to speak to Karl, and found him wandering around in his dressing gown. He told her that he missed the children – and informed her, almost as an aside, that he had burned all the letters he'd ever received from his family. Once again he refused to see a therapist about his strange despairs. From then on Gwen visited him with the children from time to time, when she would take him food and collect some furniture for her new home. One weekend at the end of August she called on him to say that they were going down to the peninsula a couple of hours away to get some sea air. Although she didn't know it at the time, by the time they got there he had had another heart attack and died.

John was devastated by Karl's death – it was an absolute crisis for him – but he kept his feelings bottled up. His misery may have been compounded by a missed opportunity the previous year, when for the second time he gave an ABC tour of Australia (from April to June). Gwen certainly didn't see John on that trip; she didn't even know about it, which makes it doubtful that Karl knew. If he had, he would surely have mentioned it to Gwen and made sure that John met their children. Perhaps John tried to get in touch but Karl was in hospital or going through a bleak patch barricaded in his study. John's feelings of self-reproach when Karl died must have been acute, especially as his brother had died alone and in financial hardship and John had missed the funeral.

John was in his gilded cage but Karl had been an untamed spirit who had broken free from his parents and family. In this he showed the spirit of his mother, who had run away from her Methodist father to marry a penniless writer. He had wandered through the outback collecting indigenous music, had busked for food and shelter and composed to his heart's content. John deeply admired Karl for his vagrant, creative lifestyle and told friends that he had been very brave to do what he did. For all his success John had not lived his life according to the dictates of the spirit, which bloweth where it listeth. He had remained the child prodigy in the adult's body, doing ever more prodigious things to impress his long-dead parents but unable to stake out his own path. Karl's lonely death was a mirror in which John perhaps saw himself for the first time as the victim of his father.

John had a low tolerance for pecuniary strain and, while the life that Brenda had created for him at Chester Terrace was one of ostentatious wealth, there were underlying financial stresses at work. Both John and Brenda were utterly unsophisticated. Coming from Manchester, neither had a clue about London life and how much it would cost to maintain a five-storey house in Regent's Park, to say nothing of the social circus they had set in motion. Like children building a house of cards, they couldn't resist going higher and higher. There was an innocence to it all. Brenda in particular took a gleeful pleasure in their new powers and possessions and she tended to assume that John shared her elation. When they bought a smart white Audi Brenda would take guests to the second-floor window to look down at it in the street. All talk was of the Audi and no opportunity was missed to take people down the road in it. If Brenda saw all the luxury as a reflection of John's talent, his brilliance as an artist, then perhaps there was a sense in which she wanted to live up to his celebrity and provide it with what she considered a suitable setting. In that regard the luxurious home could be seen as a measure of her respect for his gift.

John and Brenda had so enjoyed their sojourns at La Mortella, the Waltons' villa on the volcanic island of Ischia, that they contemplated building a home of their own somewhere on the Mediterranean. In the autumn of 1971 Brenda saw a notice in the *Sunday Times* advertising plots of land. The site in question was on a mountain surrounded by pine and cork forests overlooking the Costa del Sol a few miles from Marbella. She persuaded John to go out there with her when they had a few days to spare and take a look at El Madronal, as it was called. Despite John's unease, he and Brenda agreed to buy Plot 32 while they were standing on it in the Spanish sunshine – though they would have to raise the money against the value of Chester Terrace. They hired both English and Spanish architects to design a villa in the style of an old Spanish farmhouse, and contracted a local builder. By March 1972 the land was wholly theirs but the building of the villa didn't begin until the autumn of 1973, by which time the construction costs had risen dramatically to an estimated £2,000 a month (£21,000 in today's money). Assailed by doubt at last Brenda sought the advice of friends, all of whom counselled her to take out an injunction to have the work halted. But it was John who now insisted that things must go ahead. When Brenda raised the matter at a dinner for close friends at Chester Terrace, John was adamant that all the concerts he had booked would pay for it and refused to be drawn into a discussion. Brenda's tears served only to provoke his ire. 'Stop crying, Brenda,' he shot at her. 'There are thousands of people in this world who are very much worse off than you.' Her relationship with John deteriorated rapidly after the purchase of Plot 32.

Shortly after they acquired the land in Spain Brenda began an affair with an aristocratic Spaniard. John was naturally disturbed when eventually he found out, though whether he made this known to Brenda is uncertain. He did complain about it to Gerard Schurmann – who has said that Brenda was active in her pursuit of men during the Chester Terrace days. Once, while she and Gerard danced at a party at Chester Terrace, she was quite open with him about her frustrations. He was advising her to be discreet, so as not to hurt John, when out of the blue she said, 'What about you, Gerard?' 'I'm afraid that's out of the question, Brenda,' he replied, laughing, 'because Carolyn is so terribly jealous. If she sensed anything in that direction it would be the end of me!' Brenda's conduct may have been her way of dealing with the stress and tension of living beyond her means; it certainly appeared to have a nervous root.

But what of the effect on John? It seems he did brood on these infidelities; indeed many of his outbursts may have been the result of an intense build-up of jealousy. He was devoted to Brenda in his way, and not unromantically, though his attempts at affection were never less than contrived, as when he turned to Gerard Schurmann at dinner one evening and said loudly, 'Do you like Brenda's new blouse?' The affection displayed by Brenda to John, at least in public, was equally self-conscious and formulaic, as if her adoration was for the talent, not the man. The only thing John had ever had to do to satisfy his mother was play the piano brilliantly. It now appeared that his growing desire to compose was in direct conflict with his wife's ambitions for him.

There was a widening gulf between Brenda's slender sophistication (her expensive clothes, dainty thin physique, Mayfair hairdos, crocodile-skin handbags and soft, ironed-out voice) and John's obese and shabby state. It became increasingly obvious that the one was the shadow of the other. Theirs was a curious mismatch that brings to mind the marriage of Vulcan and Venus. Vulcan was a lame god, clumsy and unprepossessing, with weak legs and massive upper-body strength. Yet he was wondrously skilled and capable of the most delicate and ingenious artistry. Venus, on the other hand, the goddess of love, was beautiful, seductive and inconstant; and her infidelities were a perpetual torment to her awkward husband, who loved and admired her nonetheless. The two could not be parted, because their union had been ordained by Juno. Despite the Venusian persona there was quite a puritanical streak to Brenda. Her neatness was severely challenged by John, who left a trail of ash wherever he went. She must have known he wasn't going to change his slovenly habits, but she kept on at him all the same.

John spent a good deal of time with Gerard Schurmann in the early 1970s – especially in 1972, when Schurmann was commissioned to write a piano concerto by the Bournemouth Symphony Orchestra and decided to write it for John. Schurmann, who was a friend and student of Alan Rawsthorne, describes the idiom of the concerto as 'thorny and modern', though it has its roots in the great virtuoso concerti of the nineteenth century and was written to challenge the Ogdon technique. Schurmann, who worked closely with John as he composed the piece, shares Liszt's transformational technique when it comes to varying themes – so that the material is being constantly reworked beneath the surface. The piece is in two movements of thirteen and fifteen minutes respectively, the first movement opening with a lengthy cadenza that sets a rather sinister tone. When the first movement was completed John was so enthusiastic that he clamoured to perform it on its own. 'It's got to be heard!' he told Gerard. Two performances were arranged for January 1973 in Ireland, one at the Gaiety Theatre in Dublin, at which John also played Liszt's *Totentanz* (or *Dance of Death*) – in many ways the perfect companion to Schurmann's macabre masterpiece – and one in Cork. The Movement for piano and orchestra, as it was called, which John played from memory, was very well received.

In between finishing the first movement of the concerto and starting the second, Schurmann wrote a fifteen-minute solo piece, *Contrasts*, which John had commissioned for his series *Virtuoso Piano Music*, published by Novello. John premiered *Contrasts* for the Redcliffe Concerts of British Music series at the Queen Elizabeth Hall in May 1973, a concert that included works by Tippett, Rawsthorne, Maxwell Davies, Lennox Berkeley and Andrzej Panufnik, whose *Reflections*

John was also premiering. There were only forty people in the audience, but the *Times* critic William Mann voiced his appreciation:

> What a selfless pianist John Ogdon is! By now he could spend the whole year touring the world with his interpretation of favourite classic and romantic masterpieces, as so many renowned virtuosos do. Instead he regularly devotes a good part of his energy to the study and championship of contemporary piano music, particularly by British composers, although he must have realized that after weeks of preparation he will seldom be asked to repeat any of these works. He persists, of course, because he is a composer himself and the music of our time is among his major interests. Those of us who share that interest are grateful to him ... and wish that his example may persuade other young virtuosos to follow his lead.

Gerard Schurmann, a pianist himself, made his *Contrasts* incredibly difficult and John was up late working out fingerings but on the night he played it superbly and without difficulty. Indeed, according to Schurmann, it was so fast you could hardly hear it. In contemporary pieces he hadn't heard others play, John he felt gave too free a rein to his leonine instincts and failed to bring all the requisite feeling to the music. In this regard his enthusiasm could be self-defeating. He relished the technical side of the piece: almost as if he was devouring something he would scoop it up and take it down in one. Yet speed was his Achilles heel. Not only would the piece be barely recognizable sometimes, so fast did it shoot by, but if there was a pause between movements he wouldn't want to stop. Even so, composers hardly ever criticized his playing, being wary of alienating one of their few champions.

Only twenty-five people attended another recital of contemporary works at the New York Cultural Center in December 1972, at which John gave the first performance of George Lloyd's *The Aggressive Fishes.* The crowds did turn up at the Festival Hall, however, to hear him play Benjamin Britten's little-heard *Diversions* for piano and orchestra. The piano part is for the left hand only: Britten wrote the piece for Paul

Wittgenstein, who lost his right arm in the First World War. 'Now Mr. Ogdon,' wrote the admiring *Times* reviewer, 'to whose interpretative mill the entire piano literature is evidently grist, has learned the *Diversions* and filled an unnecessary gap in the concert repertory.' John also championed Robert Sherlaw Johnson's very difficult Second Sonata, during which he had to dive inside the piano to pluck the strings, bang them with drumsticks and run the back of his fingers over them. As long as it involved the piano, John was oddly athletic.

John didn't talk to Gerard about his own compositions, but he did work on transcribing Schurmann's Six Studies of Francis Bacon for piano. John also shared with the Schurmanns his dream of having a little cottage in the country, where he could compose and write programme notes and essays and limit the dates of performance. Gerard and Carolyn imagined him in this cottage surrounded by books and scores. It was the vision that had entered John's soul when he visited Tchaikovsky's 'cottage' at Klin and saw the composer's writing desk looking out over the meadows and birch forests.

For EMI in 1972 John recorded the complete sonatas of the visionary Russian pianist-composer Alexander Scriabin to mark the centenary of his birth. In April that year he gave an extraordinary all-Scriabin recital at the Théâtre des Champs-Elysées in Paris in the presence of surviving members of the Scriabin family. This was the same theatre that had hosted the premiere of Stravinsky's *Rite of Spring* in 1913. In the programme the recital was billed as '*un concert du style de notre folle époque*' ('a concert in the style of our crazy era'). In the first half John played Sonatas 1, 9 and 10 as well as *Vers La Flamme* ('Poème en forme d'une sonate'), which was intended by Scriabin to be his Eleventh Sonata. The second half was devoted to Sonatas 3, 4, and 5. Even for John, to play seven Scriabin sonatas in a single recital, all from memory, was a tremendous accomplishment.

John had always been sharply attuned to the peculiar tensions in Scriabin's music, its swings of mood and morbid raptures. It is a unique sound world, full of arcane colours. The tolling of bells, strumming of harps and endless trills all create a rich atmosphere somewhere between fairy tale and nightmare. Like Wagner, Scriabin saw music as a means of transcending art, of passing through the veil.

He used trills to create what he called 'luminosity', and the Tenth
Sonata, with its incessant trills, is meant to create radiant vibrations in
the atmosphere such as might be felt at the moment of ecstasy. The
Tenth, which Scriabin had difficulty playing, was also described by
him as a 'sonata of insects' – for insects to his mind were little 'kisses'
of light, born of the sun. Strangely enough, he found insects erotic
and uplifting. The Ninth Sonata, on the other hand, is called *The
Black Mass* and Scriabin said that he was 'practising sorcery' when he
played it. At the time of his death Scriabin was planning an apocalyptic concert at the foot of the Himalayas in India that would
collapse the manifested world. He called it the *Mysterium* and had
bought a white suit and sun helmet for the purpose of conducting it.
When John was in South Africa the following year he gave a lecture
in Durban on Scriabin and Busoni and their influence on modern
music.

In June 1972 John and Brenda returned to Japan. This time the
Japanese critics were baffled and frustrated by John and their customary politeness seemed a little frayed. Listening to him, said one, was
like looking through a clouded window. 'A stoop man with thick-
framed glasses sat in front of us, looking uncomfortably large on a
small piano stool,' wrote another. His grasp of structure was praised
and his restraint in dazzling technical passages, but he didn't touch
their hearts. His objectivity in trying to 'logically compose the music
so that it was clear and understandable' left his audiences unsatisfied.
One perceptive critic, writing in the *Yomiuri Evening News*, pierced
deeper in a passage that has ominous undercurrents:

> As if he was trying to get rid of otherworldly thoughts to concen-
> trate on the music, there was a sense of despair in the way Ogdon
> faced the piano. However, what this gesture gave out was a feeling
> of instability, as if he was trying to find exits in a blind alley.

Maybe John was making an extra-special effort to keep his emo-
tions at bay at this time, although his Busonian approach to the
keyboard had always called for a lofty attitude to what we commonly

call emotion. In a radio interview in the early 1960s he had this to say about emotion in music:

> One doesn't try and put emotion into the music; one tries to express the very considerable emotion that is already there in the music. The emotion is a spontaneous thing and is generated by the piece in playing it – by the harmony the composer uses it automatically comes out that way. I feel that the composers of some very emotional music, like Rachmaninoff, often played their music with terrific regard for the structure of the piece, with almost a feeling of coldness, which seems somehow to counteract the incredible warmth of the music and made his playing so marvellous.

When John looked at his diary for 1973 he would have seen tours and concerts in Ireland, the USA, Switzerland, Austria, Germany (twice), Scandinavia (twice), Spain, Monte Carlo, South Africa, Namibia, Kenya, Canada, Holland, Belgium, Italy, the Canary Islands and Northern Ireland – this on top of all his domestic concerts and recording and broadcast engagements for EMI and the BBC. He would be giving around 200 concerts that year and earning on average £450 per engagement, which was far too little for an artist of his stature and proven reputation. All in all, his crazy work rate meant that, allowing for royalties, he would be earning roughly £100,000 per annum (more than a million pounds in today's money). Ashkenazy, by contrast, had been earning £450 per recital back in 1967 and by 1973 was up to at least £750 (more likely £1,000). By rights Ogdon should have been on the same fee scale as Ashkenazy; this would have allowed him to cut the number of concerts per annum by between 70 and 100 with no diminution of income. It is insane that an international artist of John's calibre was being kept on the Southend Pier/Music Club circuit. One can be sure that Ashkenazy wasn't playing on Southend Pier or with tin-can orchestras like the Cleethorpes Sinfonia. Among other Ibbs & Tillett artists Clifford Curzon and Janet Baker were earning £500 per concert, John Lill £600, Paul Tortelier £1,000 and Dietrich Fischer-Dieskau £1,350. When Terry Harrison and Jasper Parrott broke away from Ibbs &

Tillett in 1969 they set up their own agency, Harrison Parrott, and took Ashkenazy and others with them. Emmie Tillett's failure to move with the times led to a general haemorrhaging of staff and artists at Ibbs & Tillett. John had of course already left the agency once; having returned cap in hand in 1967 he now felt duty bound to stay despite the obvious drawbacks. His bridges had been burned. John's agent Martin Campbell-White left Ibbs & Tillett in July 1972 to join Harold Holt, leaving the newly joined company director Wilfred Stiff to take over John's bookings. Stiff, who eventually took control of the entire company from Emmie, would be John's agent for the rest of his time there. Had John joined Harrison Parrott in 1969 he would have found their approach much more sympathetic. Employing a new concept of management, they developed the artist's career holistically – allowing him to grow in accordance with his particular character and sensibilities.

As 1973 dawned, Brenda noticed John's behaviour take another strange turn. He would appear in the kitchen at Chester Terrace looking agitated and say, 'Brenda, I want to talk.' She'd ask what he wanted to talk about and he'd come out with a stream-of-consciousness that sounded like rubbish. She would try to stop him because he wasn't making sense and she had other worries. What he was saying appeared to have no relevance to their lives. With hindsight, she believes he must have been losing his mind even then. Had she known and faced what was happening, the severity of his breakdown twelve months later may well have been mitigated. Again, other musicians noticed the change in John. When he went out to Houston to give the American premiere of his piano concerto, his conductor friend Lawrence Foster remarked on how withdrawn and uncommunicative he had become. There was barely anyone at home.

In the summer of that year, at the invitation of J. J. Johannesen, John gave masterclasses at the Shawnigan Lake Summer School on Vancouver Island. It wasn't a happy experience. He, Brenda and the children were billeted on the shore of the lake in a cabin that Brenda describes as primitive. Everything else was first class, however, including membership of the country club and opportunities for swimming, sailing and water-skiing. The food laid on for the faculty was also excellent. But John was going through a phase of exaggerated self-belief and superiority. He adopted a highhanded attitude to his family and drove himself remorselessly in his work. The proximity of his wife and children clearly needled him and there were sudden accesses of rage accompanied by expressions of wild hatred towards Brenda, usually when she tried to entice him away from his work. John's 'primeval hunger for notes' kept him maniacally focused, but the more he fed himself with notes the hungrier he became. One is reminded of Ivan Dmitrich in Chekhov's harrowing tale of madness, 'Ward No. 6', who possessed this same craving for texts:

> From his face one could see that he was not reading, but devouring the pages without giving himself time to digest what he read. It must be supposed that reading was one of his morbid habits, as he fell upon anything that came into his hands with equal avidity, even last year's newspapers and calendars.

Twice in the previous two years John had been contacted by Wilfred Bain, dean of the music school at Indiana University in Bloomington, about joining the faculty, but hadn't given it a second thought. Now, at Shawnigan Lake, he performed a concert with the violinist Ruggiero Ricci, a professor at Bloomington who recommended the life there as a good way of combining a performing career with a salaried post.

Meanwhile John and Brenda's two-piano engagements had been stepped up both at home and abroad. (A letter had gone out from Ibbs & Tillett in December 1970 to the BBC saying that Brenda Ogdon would no longer be available for solo recitals but would still accept two-piano engagements with John.) For John this meant a considerably augmented workload – especially given the endless run-throughs that Brenda insisted upon. During dinner one evening at Chester Terrace with one of Brenda's wealthy friends, Richard Croucher, an inebriated John launched into a vicious attack on Brenda's playing and the whole notion of their two-piano partnership, implying that she must be deluded to think she was worthy to share a platform with someone of his genius. The whole thing was clearly a farce, and only she couldn't see it. Richard Croucher cracked a joke about it that was funny and cruel, and John began to laugh. Brenda burst into tears but composed herself sufficiently to get up from the table, fetch Croucher's coat from the hall and ask him to leave.

Throughout 1973 John's behaviour towards Brenda became progressively mean and belligerent and there were occasions when he did his best to outrage her. In October, for instance, after a poorly attended recital at Bolton's Victoria Hall, John told Brenda that he had enjoyed a post-concert orgy with three Bolton hookers!

In November that year, the day before John was due to premiere the Gerard Schurmann Piano Concerto, he and Brenda were joined by André Previn and the LSO to play Mozart's Concerto for Three Pianos, K. 242, at the St Cecilia's Day concert at the Royal Festival Hall in the presence of the Queen and Duke of Edinburgh. After the concert John and Brenda were taken upstairs to a big reception room where they joined a line of people waiting to meet the royal couple. Peter Andry of EMI, who had arranged the concert, was standing on the near side of the Queen. André Previn and Mia Farrow were ahead of John and Brenda, and the line alternated: man, woman, man, woman. Brenda suddenly realized that she was out of sequence, being ahead of John and next to Mia Farrow, so she gestured to John to go ahead of her. 'No, no,' he said, 'it doesn't matter.' And so the line progressed until Brenda reached Peter Andry. Then, as she chatted and readied herself to curtsey to the Queen, John suddenly grabbed hold of her, shoved her to one side and shook hands with the startled monarch himself.

9

DISINTEGRATION

I was obsessed with the thought of going mad.

Robert Schumann

That November, not long before their appearance before the Queen, Brenda had found John one day in front of an open window at the top of 13 Chester Terrace gazing out over the park. Despite the bracing November air he complained of breathlessness, but rejected Brenda's suggestion that he see a doctor. His sense of suffocation was internal; it was as if his soul was gasping for oxygen. Several days later, however, John himself reverted to the subject of doctors over breakfast – though he wanted to see not a physician but a psychiatrist. When Brenda asked him why, he confessed that the texts of books and scores were being subtly altered to put him off balance. At least, he found them changed; and the changes contained some quite disturbing messages. Brenda duly phoned around and made an appointment for him with a leading psychiatrist, Dr Dorrell – though there would be quite a wait. In the meantime John threw himself with redoubled intensity into learning the Schurmann Concerto, which he was scheduled to premiere at the Portsmouth Guildhall on 21 November 1973. There were to be three concerts on consecutive days, all with Paavo Berglund and the Bournemouth Symphony

Orchestra – Portsmouth being followed by Bournemouth and the Royal Festival Hall. John's increasingly disturbed mental state made concentrated effort painful. He seemed to feel the added pressure of all the publicity the new concerto was receiving, and took his responsibility towards the work and its composer very seriously. He was afraid of letting Gerard down. Though his performing and recording schedule meant that he had to snatch whatever moments he could to come to grips with this extremely difficult work, it was nonetheless ordained that he should play it without the score.

Had the Schurmann Concerto been written as programme music it would surely have told the story of Edgar Allan Poe's *The Fall of the House of Usher*, a macabre tale of psychic disintegration that takes us to the very root of manic depression: repressed libido. The living entombment suffered by Madeline Usher might be evoked in the opening piano sequence of descending bass notes. The sense of foreboding these create reverberates through the following bars and on through sudden fiery eruptions of trapped energy: the suspense is unremitting. The piano's conflict with the orchestra might reflect Usher's struggle for liberation, which is won but as the briefest of reprieves. The sheer effort of freeing herself from the sepulchre robs her of her remaining vitality. The piece did more than test the Ogdon technique; it shook him heart and soul.

The day after the St Cecilia's Day concert John and Brenda headed down for the premiere at the Portsmouth Guildhall. It was a nervy time for Gerard. A few days earlier John had announced that he couldn't possibly play the concerto because the omens were against it. He had read a review of *Cosi Fan Tutte* in the *Times* that predicted disastrous consequences if the concert went ahead. 'It's a warning to us, Gerard,' he confided. 'I think we'd be better off not doing this.' Brenda helped Gerard to coax him through the crisis, but for a day or so it looked as though they might have to yield to the obstinacy of his delusion. In the end John played magnificently, with sensitivity and characteristic stamina, and there were approving reviews for both him and the new concerto, which was paired with Rachmaninoff's Rhapsody on a Theme of Paganini. After the concert the Lord Mayor and Lady Mayoress of Portsmouth presented both John and Gerard with a framed print of HMS *Victory*. The Finnish conductor Paavo Berglund surely deserved one as well: he had had to conduct from a chair, having been badly injured in a car accident the previous summer. It was a stroke of genius on his part to choose Sibelius's Sixth Symphony as the concluding work of the evening, with its narrative of dissolution. 'When shadows lengthen' was the motto that the composer himself chose for the piece.

The next evening's performance, in Bournemouth, was to be recorded by the BBC. John's state of mind had not improved, despite his Portsmouth success, and his inhibitions about performing Gerard's piece reasserted themselves. Then, with the hour of the concert drawing near, he vanished. Gerard, Carolyn and Brenda paced up and down the Winter Gardens wondering where he could be. He had already missed the sound test for the recording; now the audience was seated and it looked as if they might have to cancel. Gerard was tearing his hair out in frustration. Just as they were giving up hope a dishevelled John was spotted heaving himself up the stairs. As one they ran down and grabbed him, took him backstage, pushed, pulled and tugged him into his tails, then propelled him onto the platform. The recording may have proved unusable (the balance was wrong), but once again the piano acted as an earthing board for John. The keys beneath his fingers quelled all interior storms and he performed with his customary assurance.

In Bournemouth the Schurmanns and the Ogdons stayed in the same hotel. As Gerard and Carolyn were preparing for bed that night there came a rapping at their door. It was a sobbing Brenda complaining that John had hit her. 'Gerard, I want you to sleep with John!' she cried. 'No!' came the indignant reply, though Brenda did at least prevail upon him to go and talk to John. All three of them – Gerard, Carolyn and Brenda – trooped back to John and Brenda's room, where John was sitting up in bed reading. Gerard asked him what had happened but as he began to explain how he had turned the light on because he'd wanted to finish the chapter Brenda got worked up again and accused him of clonking her one. 'I don't think I hit you, Brenda,' John countered rather unconvincingly. 'I just wanted to read.' They managed to reassure her and she got back into bed. Gerard and

Carolyn sat in chairs at the end of the bed and remained there half the
night with Gerard telling funny stories. They were all laughing by the
end of it. It was quite comical, recalls Carolyn, to see John and Brenda
sitting up in bed listening to Gerard's stories. The final performance of
the concerto – at the Royal Festival Hall the following night, in the
presence of the Finnish Ambassador – passed without incident.
William Mann of the *Times* wrote that Ogdon 'deserved all the
applause in the world for his supercharged reading'.

A few days later John and Brenda went to dinner at the Kensington
home of Brian Masters. John was on edge the whole evening and
drank heavily. He asked Brian quite openly at dinner if he had any
dope in the house: he wanted to get stoned. After dinner Brenda kept
Brian company in the kitchen while he did the washing up. When
they re-joined the others in the drawing room John appeared riled. He
was nodding his head, shuffling his feet and avoiding Brian's gaze. By
the time they said goodbye he seemed his usual diffident and appreciative self, mumbling what a marvellous evening it had been; inside,
though, he was seething. When they got home he slammed the front
door behind him and turned to face Brenda with a look of burning
hatred. She had no sooner asked him what the matter was than John
came roaring at her. She jumped to one side and a large wall mirror
took the impact, showering the carpet with shards of glass. 'This charade has got to stop!' he shouted, fixing Brenda with a wild look. She
managed to dodge past him, fling open the front door and make a dash
for the car. John chased after her and lunged for the passenger door just
as she was pulling away from the kerb. She drove straight back to
Brian's, arriving around 1.30 a.m. About an hour later John called
asking to speak to her. Brian told him that she was OK and would be
spending the night there, but that she didn't want to talk. 'Oh well,'
said John, sounding resigned, 'if that's the way she feels.'

Allowing time for the housekeeper to be up and the daily to arrive,
Brenda returned to the house the following morning to find that the
storm had blown over. It was a contrite John who came to the door
and apologized for having drunk too much the previous evening.
Indeed he was so gentle and keen to make up that she was tempted to
forget everything he'd said.

That afternoon John flew to Belfast to play the Liszt E-flat concerto in Larne, County Antrim, with the Ulster Orchestra under its principal conductor, Edgar Cosma. His performance of the work was predictably brilliant. The next night he played it again at the Ulster Hall in Belfast, but this time his rather hesitant and perfunctory reading baffled the critics. Most astonishing of all – given that he knew the piece like the back of his hand – was the fact that he played from the score. Clearly there had been some sort of crisis earlier in the day. When John got back to his hotel that night he entered into a shattering conflict with his father. No one knows the exact details of what transpired, but he carved crosses on his temples and cut his hands. He later told his psychiatrist that the crosses represented the wounds that his father had inflicted on him during their fight. The ritual cutting perhaps reflected John's growing sense that he was destined to bear the cross of his father's madness. Melville wrote of his protagonist in *Moby-Dick*: 'Moody stricken Ahab stood before them with a crucifixion in his face; in all the nameless regal overbearing dignity of some mighty woe.'

When John got back to Chester Terrace the following morning Brenda was in the hall to greet him. 'Get me a psychiatrist,' he said, hurrying past her and up the stairs. Brenda was weak-kneed at the sight of her tormented, bleeding husband, whom she could hear pacing up and down in the drawing room above her. She collapsed into a chair and it was several minutes before she regained sufficient composure to make the necessary calls. She phoned Dr Dorrell, whom John was due to see the following week, and Brian Masters too. Both arrived within the hour.

An almost debonair John came downstairs to greet them. He seemed unaware of the bleeding crosses on his temples, and when Brian asked him what he'd done to his face he said, 'What do you mean?' – then said he must have cut himself shaving. He was a shocking sight. Dr Dorrell went upstairs with John, leaving Brian below with Brenda. When he returned downstairs the doctor said that John was suffering from paranoid delusions and aural hallucinations and that his thought processes were flawed. He was seriously ill and needed to be in hospital: the sooner the better. He then phoned the

psychiatric unit affiliated to the Middlesex Hospital and arranged
for John's admittance. When Brian went up to see John he stared at
the palms of his hands and said, 'Look, they have gone red. I wish I
knew why.' He said too that he must have 'flunked something', but
he didn't know what. He seemed unable to rid himself of a strong
sense of guilt.

After Dr Dorrell left, John had lunch upstairs on a tray. When
Brenda went up to pack his overnight bag she found that he had
covered his face with white powder and was wearing lipstick. Not
wanting to provoke him, she ignored his grotesque appearance and
tried to coax him down to the car. John was no longer so willing to
go to hospital and wandered from room to room downstairs – anywhere to avoid the front door. Finally, with Brian's help, Brenda got
him outside and into the back of the car. It was quite an odyssey
through unfamiliar parts of North London, such as Stamford Hill and
Seven Sisters. There was a lot of traffic and John was in the back
taking his clothes off; whenever the car stopped at the lights he would
try to get out. Brian managed to distract him by talking about the
novels of the spiritualist and amateur pianist Marie Corelli, thinking all
the while, 'What the hell am I in? This is surrealistic.'

John's disquiet increased when they got to the hospital. He walked
round and round in circles until some nurses led him off to a bare
room with a bed. While they waited for the doctor John began
undressing himself, like Lear unbuttoning on the heath, as if to strip
away a false self. As he took off his clothes he told Brian that in 666
years the old people would murder all the babies to give themselves an
extra piece of life. There appeared to be no mediating ego whatsoever;
he was completely open to the symbolic fantasies of the unconscious.
When John eventually calmed down and stopped pacing he spoke
with childish wonder of the wetness of water, the greenness of grass
and the softness of women's hair before eventually falling asleep.
Brenda and Brian left after they'd seen the doctor. They were both
exhausted when they arrived back at Chester Terrace, and Brian
departed immediately for his Kensington home.

Brenda hadn't been back long when the phone rang. It was John,
sounding normal and insisting that he was coming home right away.

'I know my rights,' he said before hanging up. Around supper time a taxi drew up outside the house and Brenda saw John disembarking. His suitcase was unstrapped, with clothes hanging out, and he himself was heavily tranquillized. Brenda made another call to Dr Dorrell, who said he would be over the next morning. She didn't feel safe with just herself and the maid in the house, so once again called on Brian – who loyally showed up to listen to another round of John's paranoid disquisitions.

The following morning Dr Dorrell insisted that John return to the Middlesex Hospital, this time to a more secure ward. It was lunchtime when they arrived there and for some reason they were taken to the women's acute ward. The doctor took one look at John and said, 'This man has got to be taken into care.' Brian and Brenda, nervous witnesses of what looked like bedlam, with women leering and howling at John, were adamant that they should first talk to someone in authority; so while John was led off to the refectory they were taken to the doctor's office. The doctor reiterated his original assessment: John was in a fragile and dangerous state and could not be left alone for fear of suicide. He needed to be in hospital, under close observation. In the refectory to collect John, they found him with a plate of food on his head, courtesy of one of the harpies. While he was being cleaned up Brian said to Brenda, 'We can't leave him here, this is a madhouse!' And to himself he thought, 'This is one of the world's great pianists. How can we possibly abandon him to a fate like this? No, no: we've got to find something more professional.' As John had not been formally committed they were at liberty to take him home, which they did. He was by now extremely withdrawn; and, with Brenda too drained to act, Brian took it upon himself to phone around. It was settled, finally, that John would be admitted to the Priory, Roehampton, in Southwest London, as a private patient. While all this was going on John shuffled about smoking as if it was nothing to do with him.

The Priory was built as a private house in 1811 in the Gothic-revival style and still sits in its own grounds adjacent to Richmond Park. It became a psychiatric hospital in 1872; although it has since become the favoured retreat of celebrities with addictions, in 1973 it was more an old-fashioned mental hospital – with elegant public rooms (including one with a grand piano) and comfortable private quarters for the patients. There were no bars on the windows or padlocks on the doors, as there had been at the North London madhouse; instead an attendant was posted outside John's door twenty-four hours a day. For his part John was drugged on arrival and pronounced 'temporarily insane'.

When she and Brian visited John the next day Brenda was advised by the Priory's medical director, Dr Flood, that John's condition was even more serious than initially suspected and that electroconvulsive therapy (ECT) was his only hope of improvement. Although ECT was most commonly used to treat severe depression or mania, the paranoid-schizoaffective psychosis with which John had been diagnosed shares many traits with manic depression – including paranoid and grandiose thoughts. John would suffer some memory loss, but Brenda was assured that this would not be permanent. Aware that her decision might have far-reaching consequences for the rest of John's career, she asked for time to consult with friends.

Brenda had forty-eight hours in which to make her choice. Gerard Schurmann was intransigent in his opposition to ECT for John; he thought it could be a catastrophic error. Brian shared Gerard's concerns. For him, John's genius was rooted in the way his brain was organized; if you disorganized the brain you could interfere with the genius. There was, therefore, a straight choice: either you had a world-famous pianist on the edge of insanity or you had a less-famous pianist who was safe. Wilfred Stiff prevaricated, as did others in John's professional sphere. If the treatment was refused, however, John would be sent home from the Priory in danger of killing either Brenda or himself. Everyone knew the risks involved with the treatment but it seemed the lesser of two evils. Besides, they were out of their depth and trusting the professionals seemed the sanest course of action. So on Wednesday 5 December, with a heavy heart, Brenda gave her permission and the treatment went ahead.

Though John had been sedated and bedbound on admittance, Brian was able to chat with him when he visited a few days later. John was standing at the window, his back to Brian, looking out over the parkland.

'You know, Brian,' he said, 'there are only three people who have understood it.'

'Understood what, John?'

'The meaning – the meaning of it all.'

'Tell me.'

'One was Jesus, one was Hitler, and the third is me.'

John went on to talk about a world conspiracy involving his father, Hitler and the Moors Murderers. It was based on a new vision of the universe that couldn't be expressed in words.

John had been given a revelation – quite natural in terms of the psychology of the prodigy, who is the chosen vessel of a special gift. Indeed there was always a sense in which John was the servant of his genius and therefore receptive to higher realms of inspiration. (For this reason he loved writers like Emily Brontë, who wrote not about people but about the spiritual forces that work through them.) According to Alistair Londonderry, another regular visitor to the Priory, John surfed the astral plane and had many conversations with the likes of Genghis Khan and Hitler. He also said nasty things about Brenda, but when Alistair asked him why he didn't leave her he lapsed into silence. Tragic though this all was, Alistair couldn't help seeing the funny side. When told by Dr Flood that John had not yet played on the asylum piano Alistair remarked, 'Well if he does I can tell you what he'll play: "I hear singing and there's no one there".'

John was in the Priory for just three weeks, being discharged on 22 December – just in time for Christmas. He was spaced out on phe-nothiazines (antipsychotic drugs such as Largactil) and was little more than a muted onlooker of the seasonal festivities. He was apathetic and flat and showed no interest in the piano. He later confessed that he felt as if the life had gone out of him. His children, Annabel and Richard, accepted their father in his new state and treated him as they had always done: as a giant teddy bear. According to Annabel, she and Richard were sealed off in their own world at the top of the house and had little idea of the breakdown happening below. Richard had just begun at prep school in Oxford that September and, like John, was heavily overweight. Both children, however, were remarkably genial and well balanced.

There were many identifiable catalysts for John's breakdown, including overwork, bereavement, guilt and a stressful marriage; being unable to devote proper time to his creative work could have been an additional factor. (There was also a bruising relationship with a fellow musician, of which more later.) But what of the likely *causes*? One has to go back to John's early relationship with his parents and the lack of real intimacy there. His father was remote, self-obsessed and emotionally absent, while his mother worshipped him as a prodigy (but not as her child). One could suppose that out of the fires of Dorothy's adoration sprang up a false self that identified root and branch with the phantom of genius. This prodigious self was the one John tried to strip away during his breakdown, for it had suffocated something vital in him: the life of flesh and blood. When he cut himself he was defacing the doll that his mother had created for her worship. As a child he had done everything in his power to be his mother's idol, but all the while the human John was living unnourished in the shadows. That human John was an exquisitely gentle and sensitive spirit who dared to break cover only in the delicacy (the *morbidezza*) of his pianissimo playing or the agile poise and unselfconscious beauty of his literary style. The white powder and lipstick he wore at the time of collapse might be seen as a bolder statement of this essentially feminine aspect of his nature.

John had over-identified with his father prior to his breakdown, but then in Belfast came the mythic struggle with Howard in which he tried to separate himself from the man who represented his false self. But he ended up defeated and bearing the marks of a crucifixion. He also became a channel for messages from the astral plane: a chosen vessel, one of a handful of souls to whom a new world order was confided. This new world order can be interpreted as the new order trying to be born in John's soul, for each breakdown is an attempt by the self to reorganize the psyche. In John's case the energy that sought admittance was the raw libido for which music had always been a substitute or sublimation. Unfortunately the natural movement of his soul towards a solution of childhood inhibitions was frozen by the heavy barrage of drugs and electricity that the doctors prescribed. The libido cannot be fought or rejected – as Ahab, who dies attempting to kill the white whale Moby Dick, finds to his cost.

Howard Ogdon was more Ahab than John, as his obsessive pursuit of his own madness attests. Like Ahab declaring war on the white whale, Howard in *Kingdom of the Lost* declares war on the Unconscious because he sees it as a disintegrating force. The book is an account of his struggle to bring this great leviathan under the control of his will. Nietzsche warned against fighting dragons as the assailant tends to morph into the very thing he battles. In many ways John became his nemesis, the white whale, and lived submerged in the waters of the unconscious, lost to the world of everyday contact. On the other hand, he lived in terror of it. The piano, the equivalent of Ahab's false ivory limb, was his fortification against the white whale that symbolized his neglected instinctual nature. With his goatee and mischievous grin John was like a strange centaur that had limped out of the pages of Greek mythology, except that in place of the animal or lower half of his body was something crafted and man-made. From the time he first read *Moby-Dick* as a teenager he must have sensed that a confrontation with the god that had been sacrificed to give his genius ascendancy was inevitable.

The dozen or so concerts that John had lined up for December, including engagements in Italy and Spain, had of course been cancelled. Then in January 1974, barely a month after his breakdown, John began to touch the piano again. To begin with he could only manage half an hour's practice a day, but after little more than a week he was back on the concert platform for a couple of two-piano recitals with Brenda. His first major engagement followed on 16 January, at the Royal Festival Hall, where he played the Delius Concerto with the RPO under Sir Charles Groves. He played from the score but it came off effortlessly, with one reviewer describing the performance as 'absorbing in a narcotic kind of way'. Though the familiar fire was missing, it was a minor miracle that he was playing at all. Three days later he gave a Wigmore Hall recital of his own compositions. It was a taxing programme and he acquitted himself well. Max Harrison of the *Times* thought John's pieces were 'of unfailing pianistic effectiveness' but pointed to a lack of personal character. He felt that the biggest piece, John's Sonata of 1972, was rather one-dimensional, 'with adventurous keyboard writing spoilt by a too-easy resort to rhetoric'. Any reservations he had were qualified by real appreciation for John's sterling contribution to contemporary music, however. 'John Ogdon has done so much for other people's music,' he wrote, 'that he is entitled occasionally to indulge himself with an evening like this.'

Had these first tentative recitals been a disaster John's career could have suffered a severe blow. His breakdown had been kept a secret – only a few close friends knew about it – but the façade of normality would be hard to keep up should he give a string of sub-standard performances. Concerts were henceforth cancelled when it was clear that John was too ill to play and there was more caution about accepting everything that was offered. Many of the engagements he did keep in the aftermath of the breakdown were two-piano recitals with Brenda. In a letter of 15 February 1974 from Ibbs & Tillett, Robert Ponsonby, controller of Music at the BBC, was told that John did not want to play the Hoddinott Piano Concerto No. 3 at the Proms in August because to do so would mean travelling down from Edinburgh that day. 'He realizes,' reads the letter, 'that in the past he has tried to work to too tight a schedule, and now knows that he cannot keep this up.'

Nevertheless there was a steady flow of concerts in January and February and John appeared more engaged. His doctor gave the green light for his US tour at the end of February and off he went, accompanied by Brenda. He toured with the Denver Symphony Orchestra under Brian Priestman in Colorado and in New York – where they were joined by Richard Rodney Bennett, whose Concerto for orchestra was receiving its American premiere. Also in New York John made what would be his last appearance at Carnegie Hall, playing the Shostakovich Second Concerto. The tour finished in California, from where John and Brenda flew home. A few days after their return John hit another reef and fell into a mood of blank dejection. Brenda, who had persuaded herself that he was over the worst, took it very hard. It was dawning on her that John might never fully recover and the implications for their life together scared her. Concerned he wasn't making a proper effort to shake off his brooding lethargy, she tried to goad him into action. But it was no good; people can't be shaken out of a depression. The anxiety of the Ogdons' precarious financial situation, what with the spiralling costs of the house in Spain and a 15 per cent interest rate on their Chester Terrace mortgage, was causing Brenda to lose weight quite dramatically.

John gave a Queen Elizabeth Hall recital towards the end of April, Bryce Morrison's review of which began: 'John Ogdon used to be famous as a leonine virtuoso'. He was puzzled by John's muted demons. In the *Appassionata* Sonata he charged him with 'domesticating Beethoven's passions to an almost eccentric degree', while in the Liszt Sonata he again noted that John was 'happier in introspection than bravura'. In summary he wrote that Ogdon 'carried self-effacement and modesty too far, almost as if he equated passion with a form of vulgarity'. The following month, when John played a Mozart concerto with the London Philharmonic at the Festival Hall, he was reunited with his old college chum Rodney Friend, who was then leader of the orchestra. In the interval Rodney drew Brenda aside and said, 'John is strange, *very* strange.' He felt that the playing was unhinged, and it scared him. What he was telling her, he later explained, was that John shouldn't have been there, under such pressures, not even knowing what day of the week it was.

At the end of June 1974, for the second year running, John was invited by Daniell Revenaugh to give a recital and masterclasses at his Institut de Hautes Etudes Musicales at Crans-Montana in Switzerland, though this time his torpid state precluded any heroics. The year before, however, having been the centenary of the birth of German composer Max Reger, Revenaugh had had the idea of performing Reger's Piano Concerto with the student orchestra. It's a large neo-classical work (forty-five minutes in length) with monstrous chords, complex counterpoint and arabesque ornamental passages, but Reger was one of John's musical heroes and, although he'd never performed it in public, he knew the score and was soon up to speed. Revenaugh got on the phone to Berlin and ended up hiring the Philharmonie and chartering a plane. It turned out to be one of the great musical experiences of Revenaugh's life. They performed on consecutive nights (1 and 2 July), and Radio Free Berlin recorded the concerto on 15" tapes. Rudolf Serkin, who had made the only other recording of the work, heard the tapes and pronounced Ogdon's version superior. As in the Busoni Concerto, there was an instinctive rapport between Revenaugh and Ogdon. They did, however, disagree on one thing. The second movement starts out with a piano solo, which John insisted on playing so slowly that it was almost impossible for the orchestra to come in effectively. Daniell had a serious word with him about speeding it up and in the end they did manage to rehearse the passage successfully. Then at the concert John reverted to his original tempo! For all that, says Revenaugh, the Reger Concerto was the greatest playing he had ever heard from John.

Revenaugh's Institute was supported by the Italian-American Pier Francesco Talenti, who was close to Nixon. Talenti was getting his money into Switzerland via the Institute and told Revenaugh to keep the books in pencil. Revenaugh, who was concerned that John was giving concerts anywhere and everywhere in a wholly indiscriminate fashion, suggested to Talenti that they keep Ogdon in Switzerland, find a chalet for him, put a piano in it and pay him an annual stipend of £40,000 to play and record whatever he wanted. 'He would have done insane things like record the complete works of Alkan,' says Revenaugh, 'but they would have been fantastic things.' It never happened, but John greatly enjoyed his visits to the Institute. There were lots of attractive girls there and his beady eyes would follow their every move. One in particular caught his eye, a pianist called Eleanor from New York, and John would hold hands with her in the back of the car.

Once back from Switzerland Brenda rented a villa in Spain for two months and had John's Steinway grand shipped out so that he could practise while they were out there. The house had a large garden, a croquet lawn and a swimming pool, which suited the children, and Brenda brought her house help over from London, who proved invaluable in putting on the sort of dinner parties that were by now a staple of her social life. Indeed, according to Brenda, her dinners became the talk of the Costa del Sol. But all her efforts to provide a comfortable and congenial setting for John were wasted. However beautiful a depressive's surroundings, they can only ever be a reflection of his inner hell. John sat through everything, including meals, in hollow-seeming introversion, not even replying when he was spoken to – and to cap it all he never touched the piano that had been imported for him at such expense. His only activity was smoking, and this he did for the most part lying on his bed. In the end Brenda gave up hounding him and left him to suck, bear-like, on the sullen paws of his gloom.

Finally came the time for John to fly back to the UK for a concert in Glasgow. He was met at the airport by Gerard Schurmann, whose concerto he was playing with the Scottish Symphony Orchestra under Alun Francis. It was to be broadcast by the BBC and Brenda had requested that Gerard be there to keep an eye on him. John had an upset stomach when he arrived and was disoriented after his flight from Malaga. He gave a horrible performance. After the concert Gerard and John went to a fine restaurant near the City Hall. While Gerard combed his way diligently through the substantial menu, John sat staring at the tablecloth. 'Can I just have an ice cream, Gerard?' he asked. 'No, you can't!' came the reply. 'Oh, alright then,' said John meekly, 'I'll have a spaghetti first.' Gerard had to travel on to Edinburgh that night, while John was due to fly down to London the next day. There was something of a panic at Ibbs & Tillett when he didn't turn up; but after several calls they found that John was still at the hotel because of his stomach complaint. He remained there for three whole days.

On the morning of 25 August, a Sunday, the Schurmanns arrived at Chester Terrace to take John to the Phyllis Court Club at Henley-on-Thames, where Gerard was a member. John had been looking forward to the day out and they expected to find him ready to go. They rang the bell and pounded on the door, but there was no sign of life from inside the house and no John to let them in. They had confirmed arrangements with him the day before so knew he must be in there. They tried calling him from a phone box but still to no avail. Feeling increasingly anxious, Gerard decided to call the police, who wasted no time in smashing one of the basement windows to get in. John had taken an Ogdon-sized overdose of barbiturates and they found him lying upstairs in a coma. (It turned out he had rowed with Brenda on the phone the day before about their escalating debt crisis.) He was taken by ambulance to University College Hospital, just round the corner, where his stomach was pumped and he lay unconscious for two days. Carolyn Schurmann called Brenda, who flew back as soon as she was able – leaving the children in the care of her housekeeper.

John was booked to play the Brahms Second Concerto at the Proms on the day after he overdosed, with the performance broadcast on Radio 3. His place was taken by his friend from student days David Wilde, who played from the score. A notice appeared in the *Guardian* saying that John was 'comfortable' at UCH, where he had been admitted for observation. The press had caught wind of the story, as they usually do when the police are involved, and reporters gathered outside the hospital, but some expert handling by Wilfred Stiff of Ibbs & Tillett ensured that nothing of substance found its way into the papers. When John was transferred to the Priory on 27 August the *Guardian* simply reported that he had been discharged from hospital: the implication being that he was now back at home. The façade may have been crumbling, but for now it remained in place.

By the time Brenda reached the UK John was in the Priory and had regained consciousness. The immediate danger was over and she found her smiling husband sitting up in bed chatting affably with the nurses. Her concern quickly turned to anger and she berated him for putting everyone through such torment. John immediately switched to his default setting (apologetic) while Brenda hastened back to Spain to shut up the house and collect the children. John was kept at the Priory for five days, and on being discharged went to stay with the Schurmanns in Finchley.

There had been a severe storm while Chester Terrace had lain empty and the first-floor balcony at the front of the house had collapsed. When John returned home he was completely helpless and unable to concern himself with the mundane problems that consumed Brenda. Once again he was physically there but incommunicado, a huge, frustrating wreck of a man who could not be scolded into life. Their relationship had all but broken down. Each was unconsciously punishing the other; and while Brenda became practically skeletal John ballooned with all the drugs. Gerard and Carolyn Schurmann were happy to have John at their house, so he returned to Finchley in what was a trial separation from Brenda – though no one called it that. Gerard stopped composing for nine months – refusing all commissions – and gave up his conducting career in the hope that he could bring lasting change to John's life. He certainly felt strongly that John needed to be removed from the pressure cooker of his marriage so that he could gain a fresh perspective on things.

John didn't take a lot of looking after at Finchley and adapted immediately and without awkwardness to life with the Schurmanns. He tended to do what he was told and would defer to Gerard in almost everything. 'What do *you* think, Gerard?' was a question constantly on his lips. John spent a lot of time in Gerard's studio at the bottom of the garden, where he practised hard for a forthcoming tour of South America that he and Gerard were scheduled to undertake in mid-September. He seemed happy, industrious and motivated. 'Can we go to the studio now, Gerard?' he'd ask. The three of them went on picnics and enjoyed strolls or bouts of gardening, and John and Gerard even played football together. They went to Henley and had a couple of get-togethers with musician friends, which John always enjoyed. As the days passed he began to speak openly to them about his marriage and they urged him to consider the possibility of leaving Brenda and setting up on his own. He told them that Brenda had destroyed his confidence and that he no longer felt able to make advances to other women. Nor could he conceive of finding another woman who could hold her own against Brenda. 'She's damaged me, Gerard,' he'd say forlornly.

One Sunday, a couple of days before John and Gerard were due to set off for Buenos Aires, Brenda called the Schurmanns' house asking to speak to John. There was a phone extension in the studio, where John was practising, and though he wasn't keen to speak to her he took the call at Gerard's prompting. Gerard and Carolyn – feeling *in loco parentis* and responsible for John's wellbeing – listened in on the house line. In a call she now regrets Brenda charged him with selfishness and lack of interest in her; she also raised the spectre of financial ruin. According to the Schurmanns John kept crying out to her, 'You don't know how much you've damaged me, Brenda.' When he told her that he was enjoying being at the Schurmanns the call took a dramatic turn.

'In that case,' said Brenda, 'you'd better make arrangements to have your piano moved to the Schurmanns', and I'll contact a solicitor about a divorce. That's what you want, John, isn't it?'

'No I don't, Brenda,' he insisted tearfully.

'Well, your behaviour suggests that you do, and I think it's best for you if we get a divorce.'

John kept denying that he wanted a divorce. He was sobbing, and saying that he was helpless to do anything. When the call was over Gerard rushed down to the studio and brought John back to the house to try to comfort him. By now, though, he had withdrawn into his shell and was very hard to reach. To distract him from his misery Gerard talked about the forthcoming tour, John's first visit to South America. Eventually John admitted that he couldn't cope with Brenda; there were times when he loathed her like the devil. In tandem with these darker feelings, however, was a deep dependency. 'What am I going to do, Gerard?' he asked. Gerard told him to put it all out of his mind and focus on the tour, which was only a few days away. It was as if Brenda had been trying to provoke John into react-ing, perhaps because she felt that he was unsympathetic to her plight (their shared plight) and was slipping beyond her control. She was ter-rified of what the future might hold.

The Schurmanns put John to bed and he seemed resigned about what had happened. But during the night he swallowed a couple of bottles of Tryptizol and Melarill, which he'd hidden in his luggage. Gerard and Carolyn had been in charge of his pills and had no idea he'd got a separate stash. In the morning when Carolyn went in to wake him he was sitting up in bed with his glasses on, as if awake, but completely motionless. She phoned the doctor, who told her to call 999 immediately. He was taken to Barnet General Hospital, where once again he had his stomach pumped. It was astonishing that he survived this second massive assault on his body. When Gerard went to visit him he was lying in bed running his fingers up and down his pyjamas. 'Am I playing all the notes, Gerard?' he asked.

On the advice of her sister, Janet, a nurse, Brenda decided that John should be spared a further stint at the Priory and sent instead to the Maudsley, which was the cutting-edge research hospital for mental disorders and the first mental hospital to open for voluntary patients. John was taken directly there from Barnet General and was admitted to a locked ward, Ward No. 1, where he was put under the care of Dr Steiner. The Maudsley was not so heavily invested in drug regimes. There were group-therapy sessions and a number of activities for patients, including cooking and painting. To an outsider it might have looked rather like a hippy commune. John was taken off drugs to clear his system and encouraged to talk about what was troubling him. He said he was now afraid of sex, and mentioned that Brenda was on the verge of divorcing him. His main complaint was one of emotional dullness. He experienced the world as drab and felt that something was missing, though he didn't know what it was. The diagnosis remained one of paranoid schizophrenia and his condition on discharge was given as 'unchanged'. John was there for only seventeen days and left because he wanted to pick up the threads of his life (as he put it) and return to his concert schedule. An appointment was made for him to see Dr Steiner to discuss the possibility of marital therapy as an outpatient. No medication was prescribed. The prognosis was stark:

> The likelihood of a recurrence of his acute psychosis is unknown. There seems little prospect of him regaining the spark of life and creativity he feels he has lost. This could have grave consequences for his career as an international concert pianist.

Remarkably, on leaving the Maudsley John gave sixteen concerts in four weeks, including a tour of Italy during which he played the Busoni Concerto three times – once in Empoli, the composer's birthplace. November was patchier: several concerts were cancelled, including trips to Germany and the States, though he gave two notable and well-reviewed performances of his friend Alexander Tcherepnin's Sixth Piano Concerto with the Hallé Orchestra under Iwaki Hiroyuki. Come December John had once more deteriorated and his defences were breached. He was sleeping badly, had poor appetite and was wracked by delusional fears. He felt he was fading away and open to attack by animals and that people were trying to murder him. This persecution mania extended to sexual assaults.

On 9 December there was a gala event at the Royal Festival Hall to raise money for the International Piano Library. Fourteen pianists were involved (among them Jorge Bolet, Shura Cherkassky, Tamas Vasary and Radu Lupu) and the master of ceremonies was Victor Borge. John was playing Tilo Medek's *Battaglia alla Turca* for two pianos with John Lill. He wandered out on stage under his wavy crop of whitening hair looking extremely unhappy and confused – forsaken, even – and desperately ill. Fortunately the piece was short and John acquitted himself more than adequately. However awful he was feeling he nearly always managed to wind himself up, make his way to the piano and connect with the right notes. A recital in Bologna the following day was cancelled, but the day after that he was back in action at the Albert Hall to play the Tchaikovsky Concerto with the Young Musicians Symphony Orchestra under James Blair. During the afternoon rehearsal his playing was half-hearted, almost *sotto voce*, and Blair could only imagine that he was saving himself for the evening, rather like a singer. Nevertheless he was very concerned, there having been no communication at all between him and his soloist. The performance, alas, was no different, and proved a nerve-wracking experience. John struck the notes apathetically and without feeling. 'It was like listening to the Tchaikovsky Concerto through a veil,' said Blair. 'It's the weirdest thing I've ever dealt with.' The audience perhaps sensed that there was something wrong and received the performance politely, while the critics kept their pens in their pockets. By any measure it had been a disastrous concert – technically correct, but simply not music.

John was in such a dreadful state afterwards that Brenda and Wilfred Stiff drove him straight back to the Maudsley, where he was admitted via the emergency centre under certification. In his psychiatric examination John was described as 'obese, dishevelled, sad, distressed and prematurely grey' with bowed head and tears in his eyes: a picture of severe depression. Several times he asked to go home. In addition to the thoughts of persecution he had feelings of guilt and low self-esteem and felt he deserved to be punished for committing some sort of 'spiritual crime'. He had seen headlines in the papers that drew attention to his cowardice in becoming ill the previous year. He also reiterated his belief that he was suffering from schizophrenia. He was put on chlorpromazine (an antipsychotic used to treat schizophrenia), Valium, Mogadon, and at night sodium amytal. In addition to his mental distress he was suffering from an accelerated heartbeat and shortness of breath, as well as a festering ulcer on his left heel. When he demanded to leave after a week he was sectioned because of the perceived risk of suicide.

This time John was placed on the Villa Ward under the supervision of Professor Michael Shepherd, a leading diagnostician and academic. He made good use of group and individual psychotherapy sessions and his condition rapidly stabilized. He was visited by his children at Christmas and to them seemed more withdrawn, more wreathed in smoke. Shepherd told Brenda that John should stay inside for a minimum of six months, possibly an entire year. Brenda's response was to insist that John discharge himself immediately and this triggered a relapse. Though it was a long haul from Finchley to Denmark Hill the Schurmanns were regular visitors. They felt obliged to look out for John, as Brenda was busy disentangling the Spanish situation and wasn't much on the scene. One day Carolyn baked John a large cheesecake, which they took to the Maudsley assuming it would last him a good while. John was very grateful and Gerard cautioned him to go easy with it – it was quite rich. John was whisked off to a family wedding in Manchester with Brenda the following day, so the Schurmanns next saw him a couple of days later. Gerard asked him where the cheesecake was. 'Oh, I ate it all,' he said, sounding surprised. 'But when?' asked Gerard. 'The same day you brought it,' he replied. 'It was very good cheesecake, Gerard.'

After only five-and-a-half weeks at the Maudsley John was discharged home on 21 January 1975 and instructed to attend the hospital as a day patient. His prognosis read: 'Good if not subjected to too many pressures immediately, e.g. domestic, financial, professional, marital.

However, wife seems unable to allow her husband to resume his responsibilities slowly, and this may well precipitate a relapse.' Once again John returned to the stage astonishingly quickly. On 30 January he was back at the Festival Hall for a tribute concert for Sir Michael Tippett's seventieth birthday, at which he played the *Emperor* Concerto with the LPO under John Pritchard. Stephen Walsh of the *Times* described his playing as 'impetuous but often extremely beautiful'. This was followed by a two-week tour of the Soviet Union during which he gave ten concerts, in Moscow, Leningrad and the Georgian capital, Tbilisi. As always in Russia, he lifted the level of his playing and was rapturously received. His relationship with America, where he headed next, was more ambivalent, and this tour had to be cut short because of his health. Brenda felt that the daggers were out for her in the music world, with the common perception being that she was pushing John to give concerts when he should have been in hospital. She began to wonder whether she shouldn't have listened to the Maudsley's recommendation that he take a prolonged break. Even with John still earning they were forced to put Chester Terrace on the market.

As 1974 and 1975 proved, it was impossible to use the quality of John's playing as an index of his mental health. In the middle of April 1975 he went on a tour of Holland and Scandinavia with Gerard Schurmann. According to Gerard, John was not only switched on but also in fine spirits and very solicitous for the wellbeing of others. He would get Gerard up in the morning and make sure he got to rehearsals punctually. They had a convivial time together, staying up all hours of the night talking and drinking. In Malmo, Sweden, John played Gerard's concerto (under the baton of the composer) and it was the best performance that Gerard had heard him give. They were feted by an admiring public. At the end of the month John was back on the Continent: this time in Belgium, where he played the Brahms 2nd Concerto with Sir Charles Groves. While in Brussels, however, he fell to brooding over an argument he'd had with an opera singer and had alarming thoughts of torture and destruction.

When he returned home John spent most of the time lying in his dressing room smoking and took his meals alone. On 30 April he was

scheduled to travel to Oakengates in Shropshire for a concert but said
he didn't want to do it and refused to get out of bed. Brenda remonstrated with him and when she couldn't move him insisted that he at
least call Ibbs & Tillett himself to cancel. 'You do it,' was the surly
reply. She repeated her request, then went downstairs to her office in
the basement. There she decided to call the agency after all, as they
would need time to find a replacement. While she was on the phone
she heard the lift coming down from upstairs. John walked quietly into
the room and sat down by her desk. The next minute she was dialling
999. John had cut his throat with such savagery that he had severed his
left external jugular vein, left facial artery and left submandibular
gland. White tendrils were protruding from his neck and blood was
running down his chest. Had he fainted upstairs, or simply not come
down, he would have died very quickly. As it was, the ambulance
from University College Hospital was there in minutes and, after a
massive blood transfusion, John survived his third suicide attempt in
eight months. He had narrowly missed severing the trachea, which
would have been instantly fatal. His place at Oakengates was taken by
the Chinese pianist Fou Ts'ong.

John spent eight days in UCH, where doctors gave him a stern
talking to about the severity of what he'd done. Then he was transferred to the Maudsley. He was reluctant to leave the Villa after just
five days, but Brenda had arranged for him to be cared for by Dr
Flood at the Priory. The Maudsley notes describe him as being 'at
great pains to comply with his wife's wishes, to whom he is markedly
subservient'. The Maudsley had recommended another course of
ECT but this time Brenda stood firm against it. The Panufniks visited
John at the Priory and found him in a padded room. 'How are you?
How are you feeling?' asked Camilla. 'Very well, thank you,' he
replied, and the conversation petered to a close. John left the Priory
and returned home after eighteen days. It was four weeks since he
had cut his throat. Somehow he then travelled to Finland with
Brenda to give a course of masterclasses at the Jyväskylä Arts Festival.
So parched were his mouth and lips from the antidepressants and
antipsychotics he was taking that he developed a passion for ice-
cream; except cigarettes, he craved nothing else. His smoking, if

anything, had become more seamless; the stage would be littered with butts after his classes. There in the white nights he bathed himself in smoke and ice, and still the flat, joyless, life-sapping air clung to him.

With forthcoming trips to America and Australia Brenda hired a woman to chaperone John. After a disastrous recital at the University of Maryland for the International Piano Festival, John fared much better musically on his six-week tour of Australia – though it must have cost him dear to return to Melbourne. He phoned Karl's widow and they met for tea at his hotel, but John didn't ask about Karl's death. When he was out in Perth for the International Festival of the Arts the ABC provided him with a local guide, who picked him up at the airport. In the car he seemed agitated; all he'd say was, 'I have to get to a telephone.' The guide asked the driver to stop, and stood there while he made his call.

'Brenda, John here. Where am I?'

'You're in Australia.'

'Oh, Australia. Why am I here? Have I got a concert?'

John played concertos by Beethoven, Tippett, Shostakovich and Tchaikovsky. He also played his own piano concerto again (he'd played it on his 1970 tour), but it was less well received this time. Maria Prerauer gave the most measured and intelligent review, entitled 'Ogdon beset by Ogdon'. She felt that the worst enemy of Ogdon the composer was Ogdon the phenomenal pianist:

> If pianist Ogdon were not so brilliant, his gifts so prolific – digital dexterity, profound knowledge, extensive repertoire – composer Ogdon would have had less of a musical encyclopaedia to fall back on for his Concerto No. 1. Willy-nilly, it seems, he can hardly avoid sometimes composing from memory. And there seems to be insufficient creative imperative behind it to transfigure that memory.

All the other reviews for his concerto and solo performances were full of praise for Ogdon's growth as an artist and his uncanny ability to dive down into the music and unmanacle the very forces that had inspired it. His Liszt B-minor sonata was described as 'almost terrifying in its satanic proportions' and 'enough to make some of our more vigilant clergy send for the exorcist'. Unaware of his recent breakdowns and mental agonies, the critics greeted his many peculiarities as the reckless flourishes of a thoroughly eccentric Englishman. His personal appearance was a source of insatiable fascination.

> He shambles on to the stage, a stooped bulky figure with a mop of white curls and his trousers wrinkling alarmingly around his ankles, a cross between contemporary portraits of Beethoven, Schubert and maybe Billy Bunter. A tiny forked beard at the very tip of his chin adds the finishing touch.

So Beethoven, Bunter and Beelzebub. Others thought he had a touch of the exiled prophet about him.

Brenda took advantage of John's absence to take a small villa in Spain so that she could give the children a holiday and oversee the sale of Plot 32. Both Ogdon houses were now on the market and they had nothing in reserve. They began to reconsider the offer of a professorship from the School of Music at Indiana University, which seemed the only solution to the chaos engulfing their lives. It would mean a regular salary for John, plus medical insurance and the supportive framework of a college campus with fellow musicians of world-class stature. Rumours of John's breakdown and suicide attempts were now beginning to leak out into the music world, and the American post could provide a welcome refuge from possible tabloid assaults. So when John's next US tour came round, only a week after his return from Australia, he and Brenda took the opportunity of visiting the Bloomington campus and meeting the new Dean of the Music School, Charles Webb. A lunch was put on for them with other members of the faculty. Menahem Pressler, a professor of piano there since 1955, noticed that it was Brenda who answered whenever John was asked a question. Pressler's wife sensed that John was mentally unwell and told her husband as much, to which he replied: 'You are ridiculous to say this. Here is a man who has learned all the Scriabin sonatas and plays them by heart. If he's not mentally well, then who is?' Both John and Brenda liked the relaxed atmosphere of the campus, and the very high standards of musical education offered, and all but made up their minds to take up the offer.

Back in England, November saw Chester Terrace sold on a poor market for a comparatively modest £97,500, much of which was swallowed up by the Ogdon overdraft. The never-occupied house in Spain followed months later. With their furniture in store they went back to live at the service apartment at the Savoy Hotel, where the children joined them for the school Christmas holidays. A measure of John's feelings over their recent losses can perhaps be gauged from a performance he gave at the Festival Hall that December, where he played the Tchaikovsky First Concerto with the New Philharmonia Orchestra under Michael Tilson Thomas. Joan Chissell of the *Times* – who was apparently unaware of John's recent tribulations – headlined her review 'Back from Banishment':

The second half of the programme could have been entitled the return of the native, for it brought John Ogdon back to this plat-form after extensive global travel. His approach to the B-flat minor concerto seemed designed to support the tag that if you scratch a Russian you find a Tartar below, so aggressive was the strength and drive. Fiery octaves, like many a finger-flight, were exciting in their way. But lack of romantic mellowness and grace even verged on the unstylish and insensitive at times [...] It was to the credit of the conductor and orchestra that at least they tried to turn them-selves into Tartars too.

John's approach to the concerto had not changed when he played it again in January with the LSO and Walter Weller, also at the Festival Hall. But this time the orchestra could not cope with 'Mr Ogdon's full-blooded, foot-stamping vitality, vodka glasses thrown over the shoulder, admittedly not without the occasional breakage'. Smetana's *Macbeth and the Witches*, which was due to precede the concerto, was replaced by Dvořák's *Noonday Witch*, a tone poem based on the Slavic tale of a mother who, in trying to protect her child from the Noon Witch, accidentally smothers him. Keith Horner, who reviewed the evening, felt that something of the curse of Smetana's usurped witches hung over the concert.

The Ogdons had by now formally accepted the offer from Indiana University, but John wouldn't be starting there until August 1976. It came as a great relief to Brenda, therefore, when her cousin Helen called to say she had found them a house not far from Sevenoaks in Kent. It was a rustic place with low ceilings and beams of black oak, called aptly enough 'Four Wents', meaning 'crossroads'. It was a bitterly cold February when they moved in, with John still in the jaws of the maelstrom. Whatever drugs he was taking, he also fell back on the booze; Brenda had to lock up the vodka. A little room at the top of the house was used by John as a study; sometimes he also took his meals there. On little hooks on the walls were dozens of hotel-room keys from around the world which John had forgotten to hand in when he checked out.

On 5 February John gave a recital at the Queen Elizabeth Hall, which included the first English performance of Gerard Schurmann's *Leotaurus*, a set of variations on a theme from his piano concerto. He hadn't brought any music to the rehearsal that morning (to which he had urged Gerard to come) and seemed at sixes and sevens. Gerard asked him if he intended to play the new piece from memory. 'Not if you have the music, Gerard,' John replied. When Gerard enquired what else he was playing, John said he didn't know – and asked him if he could go outside and take a look at the poster! Seeing the state John was in, Gerard asked Wilfred Stiff if they could drop his piece from the programme. Stiff was having none of it. 'For heaven's sake,' he expostulated, 'he's bad enough as it is; if you do that to him, he'll collapse altogether.' So they all did their best to lift John's spirits and get him on stage in a positive frame of mind. The concert was terrible, and even the sympathetic Joan Chissell thought that the music had lost its magic for John. In the Chopin Op. 25 studies he played very fast and never once lifted his foot from the sustaining pedal. David Murray of the *Financial Times* spoke of Ogdon's 'devoted sympathy' and rich tonal palette in *Leotaurus*, but then suggested that his own stars were in extraordinary disarray: 'Having chosen a programme as leonine as could be imagined, he set about it with the impersonal destructiveness of the proverbial bull in a china shop. He did it without apparent malice; indeed he gave no sign of any feelings about the music at all.' Meanwhile the *Telegraph* spoke of 'the seemingly obsessive denial of musical meaning' and concluded that 'Ogdon the poet had gone on strike'.

After the concert the Ogdons returned to the Savoy accompanied by the Schurmanns and John's young minder of the time, Charles. Brenda and John had separate rooms and everyone else ended up in John's while Brenda went to bed next door. They ordered champagne and sandwiches and had a fine old time. John was greatly enjoying himself and they were all roaring with laughter. Gerard had never seen him looking so cheerful – abandoned, almost – telling jokes, laughing and offering himself up as the butt of their mimicry. After about an hour-and-a-half of this merrymaking (it was well past midnight) Brenda began banging on the door. Then she stormed into the room and said, 'Gerard, Carolyn, Charles, I want you to go. Or shall I call security?' Rather than play Sir Toby to her Malvolio, they decided to call it a night.

In mid-February John gave a recital at the Herkulessaal in Munich, again offering a large virtuoso programme of Beethoven, Schumann, Liszt and Ravel. The *Munich Evening News* described his Liszt B-minor sonata as 'a trapeze act without a net', while the *Munich Mercury* branded him 'a flagrant extremist' whose extravagant pianism recalled 'the great days of the slightly mad lions of the keyboard'. Joachim Kaiser, the czar of German music critics, wrote a review entitled 'A pianist is changing' in which he red-flagged what he saw as Ogdon's artistic crisis and drew attention to his suffering technique. In his view far too much that he heard was neither interpretation nor virtuosity, but 'the pronouncements of a composer, who is explaining something'. He also referred a little cryptically to 'an overall failure due to nerves'. His criticisms, he said, were offered with the same respect and concern that were expressed seventy years earlier towards Eugen d'Albert, a pupil of Liszt, who was the world's leading player of Beethoven and whose pianistic technique deteriorated markedly. D'Albert was known as 'the little Giant', and it is significant that Kaiser should have drawn this parallel with Ogdon, for it was of d'Albert that the conductor Bruno Walter wrote, 'In his intimate contact with his instrument he appeared to me like a new centaur, half piano, half man.' Ogdon was, without doubt, a latter-day piano centaur. He couldn't really be called a pianist – one who plays the piano – because there was no division between him and the instrument.

With the black wing of depression still shadowing him, John returned to the Priory for a week at the end of February so that his condition could be reassessed and more colours added to his rainbow of drugs. When he came out he was off to Vienna to play the Busoni Concerto with the ORF Symphonieorchester under Leif Segerstam, after which he and Brenda flew to the States for more concerts and a house-hunting session in Bloomington. They found a roomy ranch-style place in the Marlin Hills a few miles outside town, light and spacious with large plate-glass windows overlooking a wooded valley at the back. The basement had sliding glass doors that gave out onto a swimming pool cut into a split-level timber deck perched on the hillside. They put down a deposit instantly and took the first steps towards arranging a mortgage. Very soon they were the proud owners of 312 Lookout Lane.

At the end of March two BBC recording sessions of music by Medtner, Shostakovich and Schurmann had to be rescheduled and eventually aborted because John was unfit to play to the required standard for broadcast. The years 1974 to 1976 were frightfully lean for John in the recording business. Apart from some two-piano works with Brenda in January, he managed only a single record in 1974: the Cyril Scott piano concertos with Bernard Herrmann and the LPO (for the Lyrita label). In 1975 a compilation of recordings from 1972 was released under the title *Pianistic Philosophies*. It included works by Dukas, Dutilleux, Schmitt, Messiaen, Britten, Lloyd, Yardumian and Ogdon himself. In his capriciously eloquent introduction John wrote of the Swedenborgian inspiration of Yardumian's music and in so doing made it clear that he construed *Moby-Dick* as a profoundly symbolic work:

The Swedenborgian religion has been described as a doctrine of parallels, in which events in the actual world reflect spiritual events and are simultaneously reflected in the human mind. The building of Noah's Ark is (a) probably factual and (b) represents man building his powers of reasoning. The archetypal Swedenborgian novel should thus be *Moby-Dick*.

He ends with a mischievous flourish: 'Most theologies admit the existence of the Devil, who is not absent from the Finale of my Sonata.' In January 1976 John recorded the little heard Glazunov Piano Concerto No. 1 in F minor, as well as Yardumian's *Passacaglia, Recitative and Fugue*, both with Paavo Berglund and the Bournemouth Symphony – but that was it for 1976, and it turned out to be his last recording for EMI. There was nothing after this until 1984, an astonishing reversal and decade of famine for an artist who had turned out a cornucopia of dazzling recordings in the 1960s and early 1970s. Having played at the Proms eighteen times between 1959 and 1972, he drew a complete blank there too between 1973 and 1983. Thirteen Wigmore Hall recitals between 1959 and 1974 were followed by a duck during the next seven years.

It was without doubt incredible that John was playing at all in the mid-1970s, given the neuromuscular and other side-effects of the drugs he was taking. Cramping, muscle stiffness, tremors, poor coordination, parched mouth, constipation and that enervating combination of lethargy and restlessness that is so marked a feature of depression were just some of the devils he had to cope with. He did perk up unaccountably sometime in June, not long before he set off with Brenda on his first tour of South America, where he played in Brazil, Argentina, Colombia and Chile. His spirits were high throughout the tour, and without the overlay of grandiosity that had marred them in the lead-up to his breakdown. He did make one *ex cathedra* pronouncement shortly after the South American trip: he insisted that the children stay in England for their education instead of moving out with them to the States. Annabel, who was almost fifteen, was at Benenden in Kent, and eleven-year-old Richard was at Summer Fields in Oxford. In early August Annabel accompanied John to Yugoslavia, where he was playing at the Dubrovnik Festival, and proved herself a caring and responsible companion. She was highly personable, mature for her age and shared John's quality of inwardness minus the moroseness. The two of them possessed a deep, unspoken bond.

Back at Four Wents Brenda was firing off letters to Charles Webb at Bloomington, raising matters to do with work visas, temporary accommodation, medical insurance and John's forthcoming absences on tour. She was successful in obtaining references for John from a stellar quartet comprising Benjamin Britten, Sir William Walton, Sir Georg Solti and André Previn. It's unlikely that anyone had ever laid such distinguished siege to the ivory towers of Bloomington.

In the middle of August, his new note of enthusiasm undiminished, John flew out to Indiana to take up his professorship. Work was still being done on the house at Lookout Lane, so he was lodged at the Memorial Union on campus. Brenda stayed behind in England to see the children back to school. She now had no qualms about John being on his own and was even allowing herself to believe that he had turned over a new leaf.

Interlude

RED HERRINGS

Denies any abnormal experiences, however is worried about Raymond Herrick [sic] talking about him. Features of the depression were an obsession about an opera singer insulting him [. . .] Ruminated over an argument with a singer and had thoughts of torture.

Case notes on John Ogdon from the
Maudsley Hospital

In late October 1963, with the Tchaikovsky prize firmly under his belt and a towering reputation in his native land, John had a chance meeting that was to have profound repercussions for the rest of his life. At a concert in Ealing arranged by the soprano Victoria Sladen he found himself in the green room with a tall, imposing, dark-featured baritone of Flemish ancestry called Raimund Herincx who excelled in performing operatic characters of a sinister and ruthless bent. If he had a signature role at the time it was probably Baron Scarpia in Puccini's *Tosca*, though Mephistopheles ran the Chief of Police a close second. He would later be celebrated for Faber in Tippett's *Knot Garden* and the inquisitorial White Abbot in Maxwell Davies's *Taverner*. At thirty-six Herincx was ten years older than John and the complete antithesis of the shy, self-effacing northerner.

We don't know what passed between the two men that night (they were performing in separate halves of the programme), but one can be fairly certain that Herincx was at his most charming and condescending towards the younger artist, whose talent and renown seemed to fascinate him. For his part, John was probably subdued by Herincx's bombastic charisma – one can picture him nodding shyly at the older man's blandishments and appreciating his insights into music. Both artists were on the Ibbs & Tillett books, and Herincx had heard tales of John's exploits from the staff at 124 Wigmore Street. At the time, both were also living near Richmond, in southwest London.

John met many different musicians on his travels and it is possible that he thought little of this encounter. A few months later, though, in the spring of 1964, the phone rang at the house in Isleworth and with Brenda out it was John who took the call. Herincx had been given the Ogdons' number by someone at Ibbs & Tillett. He wanted to know whether John would be willing to give a charity concert in aid of the Thames Valley Grammar School, where the singer had been a pupil during the war. Herincx was probably hoping that John would give the concert gratis but asked anyway what sort of fee he would charge. John was thrown by the question – he never handled his own bookings and had little sense of money. Tentatively he suggested half fee, which at that time was 70 guineas or £75. The next thing he knew, the phone had been slammed down on him. It's impossible to discern what real effect this first call had on John, though it later became apparent that it did prey on his mind; either way the concert never took place because (according to Herincx) John had been booked to play elsewhere by Ibbs & Tillett.

Eight years later, in 1972, John was approached at a party by a crony of Herincx's, the music critic Denby Richards, who reminded him of what had happened in 1964 and gently berated him for having asked a fee for a charity concert. Stung by this unwarranted rebuke, John told Richards that if Herincx had wanted him to play for nothing he should have asked him directly. John being John, however, he then proffered his services once more. Not long after this exchange Brenda answered the phone to Herincx: he and his wife, Astra Blair, were to hold a concert series at their Bedfordshire home to raise money for handicapped youngsters; would John be willing to give a recital? Brenda agreed that he would. She waived the fee but insisted on £50 travel expenses. When Herincx raised no objection she instructed Ibbs & Tillett to send him written confirmation of the arrangements.

Nevertheless Herincx was clearly not content. When he called again a few days later John picked up the phone. According to John, Herincx proceeded to take him to task about the proposed expenses, telling him roundly that a man who lived so high on the hog should be ashamed of himself for claiming travel costs for a charity concert. John, he said, was 'getting above himself'. He also said that the £50 expenses meant that John could not be presented with a photograph of the child he was to sponsor. It was a venomous thrust.

The concert went ahead in October the following year. John gave more than 200 concerts in 1973 and was already close to breaking point when he arrived in Bedfordshire. There was a very nice little concert hall attached to Quinville House, Herincx's home, where monthly concerts were given with considerable panache. That after-noon Herincx attended John's rehearsal. John was playing a lesser-known Beethoven sonata when he suddenly stopped and gasped, 'Wrong turning!' There followed a brief dialogue:

Herincx: No, John, that's not a wrong turning.
Ogdon: Wrong composer!
Herincx: Wrong Beethoven?
Ogdon: Og-don.

John had inadvertently moved from Beethoven into one of his own pieces. Just before the concert John presented Herincx with a copy of his father's book. It was a poignant gesture and at the moment he handed it over he felt something go 'snap' in his brain. The recital itself was a success; though John felt that Herincx's even delivery in his post-concert address was ruffled by his lingering resentment over the business of travel costs. For Herincx at least this had detracted from the purity of the event.

It is unlikely that John ever saw Herincx again after this concert: only six weeks later, in December 1973, he suffered his breakdown.

However, his relationship with Herincx lived on, certainly in John's mind, and he kept up a flow of letters and postcards until at least the mid-1980s. Herincx once received six letters in one day from Tokyo, some of them inordinately long. On other occasions correspondences were brief, although John took delight in sketching fishes in the margins and on the envelopes and punning on Herincx and herrings. One missive was simply a picture of a fish with the words, 'You may have won a major advantage at Brighton but, my dear Raimund, you're nothing but a great big fish!' According to Astra Blair the letters were 'unpleasantly worded, but not abusive', though Herincx himself told a friend that they were frequently vicious. He says he never replied to a single one but this had no effect on John's hypergraphia.

Herincx claims to have destroyed all the letters after John's death. There does exist, however, a curious document written in John's hand on Japanese hotel notepaper. It is undated but clearly comes from the time of his disastrous tour of Japan in February 1979, when he was staying at the Hotel Grand Palace in Tokyo. It probably gives a good flavour of the sort of thing he was writing to Herincx. Apart from a series of opening statements, in which John refers to himself in the third person, the diatribe – if it can be called that – proceeds in the form of a dialogue between three of John's musician friends, Robert Simpson, Gerard Schurmann and Daniell Revenaugh. Even when putting pen to paper in the privacy of his hotel room John was unable to ascribe an ego to himself by using the first person singular – no doubt because he had some cutting and trenchant things to say about his fellow musicians and the musical establishment. (Herincx himself is characterized as a second-rate opera singer, a malingerer and a dangerous pig, while a well-known conductor is described as a shit.) He felt unable to abandon the self-effacing persona for which he was universally loved and patronized so he applied the 'does he take sugar?' sanction to himself, appointing others to talk for him. One is reminded of Robert Schumann's habit of writing in the third person in his music reviews, often splitting himself into the characters of his imaginary aesthetic circle, the *Davidsbündler* or 'League of David'. Simpson, Schurmann and Revenaugh exercise the same function as

Florestan, Eusebius and Meister Raro. Both Schumann and Ogdon, it seems, loved masks.

Many of John's customary inhibitions, including his excessive modesty and courtesy, are swept aside. The text begins in block capitals:

THE MOST NATURALLY GIFTED PIANIST WAS
GETTING ABOVE HIMSELF.
WHAT WAS THE TROUBLE?
HE WASN'T DOING ENOUGH FOR RAIMUND
HERINCX!
BUT HE DIDN'T KNOW RAIMUND HERINCX!
EXACTLY.

Throughout the piece Ogdon expresses a commanding sense of his own brilliance, comparing himself with Richter and Horowitz, and even claiming that his 'machine-gun precision' at the piano was unique, his gifts truly irreplaceable. At one point he has Gerard Schurmann say of him, 'But when we have an artist who can deliver the answers, we mustn't abuse him.' By the same token Herincx's ignorance of 'the delicate balance of the artist' is lamented. Herincx is incapable of understanding Ogdon, whose personality was 'one of Mozartian equilibrium with contrasting thoughts held in perilous centrifuge'. John – or rather his mouthpieces – emphasize Herincx's jealousy of him, and his mind turns obsessively on the two phone calls eight years apart – in particular Herincx's alleged slamming down of the phone in 1964 and his accusation in 1972 that John was getting above himself. 'I gather the flow of invective actually stopped when Ogdon went mad,' he observes through Revenaugh. His other friends voice the view that artists in England are looked after by enemies, not friends, and are 'up against the old boy network'.

In many ways Ogdon's tirade serves to confuse the picture, as he states quite clearly that the first concert Herincx asked him to give was at a secondary-modern school in Wood Green and not the Thames Valley Grammar School. John writes that he was glad to be out of this first concert because he 'didn't much care for these solemn people', meaning Herincx and his cronies. Later on John has Gerard

Schurmann say, 'It's fantastic that the concert in Wood Green didn't materialize after John had agreed to play.' Herincx, says Revenaugh, exaggerated beyond all reason John's 'sin' in asking for a fee, while at the same time walking away from the consequences of his words.

After receiving the sextet of letters from Tokyo Herincx threatened to sue. He and his wife felt harassed by the continual barrage of angry letters, which accused him of plotting to ruin John's career. Herincx contacted Wilfred Stiff of Ibbs & Tillett, who advised Brenda of the situation and wrote a formal letter to John asking him to desist. On the advice of Lord Londonderry, John responded by going on the attack. Less than three months later, in May 1979, he wrote to his solicitors seeking advice about bringing a suit against Herincx, whom he blamed for the emotional and financial hardship he had suffered since his breakdown, not to mention the fatal blow to his reputation.

> I feel strongly that my breakdown need never have happened, but was precipitated by various encounters with an opera singer, who verbally attacked me. His attack included the words: 'Have you ever felt mentally disturbed?' He also attacked my musical achieve-ments, my career, and my high standard of living. I can go into more detail when I come to London in June.

Much of the Ogdon-Herincx relationship remains puzzling, partly because so little record of it survives and partly because John was as secretive in his dealings with others as he was in his creative work. This secrecy extended to Brenda, who was often the last to know what he was up to. However, the unsent Tokyo-hotel denunciation does seem to suggest that the two men shared little or no contact during the eight years between their phone calls of 1964 and 1972.

When Ogdon was committed to the Priory in December 1973 there was no denying his obsession with Herincx, whom he perceived as an omniscient, all-controlling figure. He talked of him without let to those who visited, neurotically rehearsing the key episodes in the saga and expressing his guilt and resentment over what had happened. Charity was a persistent theme, and he began to fear words that began with the letter C (just as his father had before him). John determined that it was Herincx who had been altering his texts and scores as a way of sending messages to him, as well as using the radio and television to transmit instructions. He had even started sending electrical impulses directly into John's body that caused tingling in his skin. Moreover, it was Herincx alone who fully understood the new world order that Hitler, Howard Ogdon and the Moors Murderers were putting in place. He was its arch-coordinator. Bearing in mind Howard Ogdon's crazed 'empire-building' when he was in the Nottingham County Asylum, it is difficult to resist the conclusion that John went mad by the book – his father's book.

Herincx has never written on the subject of his relationship with John but graciously agreed to be interviewed for this book. Now in his eighties, he remains a striking figure: tall, bearded and powerfully built, with a bass-baritone voice of formidable penetration. Herincx is a Falstaffian raconteur, prone to comic exaggeration. For instance, he told several times of having to compete with a bank of roaring tubas when he sang Wotan in Wagner's *Die Walküre*; each time the number of tubas increased (like the number of Falstaff's assailants). 'Now when those five Wagner tubas turned round to me . . .'

It is hard to draw out a consistent and entirely coherent account of his relationship with Ogdon: Herincx speaks in a sort of stream of consciousness, a florid top-hat soliloquizing rich with melodrama and sudden deviation. Nothing quite follows from what went before and contradictions jostle each other. Yet there is no doubting his profound insights into his subject. If Ogdon was of the thinking type, Herincx is an intuitive who wins you over with the force of his personality. It's not hard to see how simultaneously alluring and threatening the reticent pianist would have found him.

Herincx's version of the story is quite different to John's. He says that he and John never fell out – and that John in fact did two other concerts for him between 1964 and 1972, both in Bedford. In advance of the first of these, at the Dame Alice Harpur School, Herincx gave a recital with Denis Matthews to help raise £13,000 to buy a new Steinway grand for John to play on. At the second, in Mander College, it was so cold that Herincx had to warm John's hands in his own before he went on. On both occasions John was paid £250 in cash at his request. 'He wanted cash in his pocket, as that was something Emmie Tillet didn't allow,' says Herincx. Before one recital Herincx took John to the County Hotel in Bedford for a steak because he felt he frightened the children ('[They] didn't like this great weird man with bulging eyes and great shoulders!'); before the other his wife prepared scrambled eggs in the kitchen. Also on both occasions John was put on the last train back to London with his cash in a brown envelope plus (also as requested) forty Senior Service cigarettes and several bars of chocolate. He was always profuse in his thanks to Herincx, nodding and mumbling 'You're so kind to me.'

Herincx believes that John was 'the world's greatest pianist', unrivalled in power and magnificence ('he wasn't a sensitive pianist, he was a magnificent one'), and that he truly came into his own as an exponent of Beethoven. One performance John gave of the *Appassionata* drove Herincx to tears because 'it was too gigantic for any one human being'. His power came, he says, from the shoulders, hence that characteristic hunched-over-the-keyboard stance. He once hit the piano so hard during a recital that Herincx had to call in a tuner during the interval. 'When he put a chord down, by God you knew about it! Ashkenazy couldn't cope with it, nor could any of the others!' cries Herincx, flourishing his arms. John, he says, 'didn't overwhelm you with emotion but with the magnificence of his conception, his intellectual fearlessness. He made you think.'

Herincx also claims that John attended the opera several times to hear him sing. In early 1971, for instance, when the two were 'quite friendly', John went to see him play Faber in the opening run of Michael Tippett's *The Knot Garden* at the Royal Opera House. According to Herincx, John absolutely adored it because he shared Tippett's quirky attitude to modern music and the composer's deep feeling for structure (one that had survived the decimation of the melodic line). After this John told Herincx that he should devote more of his professional life to modern music and started sending him sketches of operas and arias that he'd written. He even wrote a piece about fishes for him and one about John the Baptist. Herincx confirmed that John the Baptist and baptism in general were subjects of great interest to Ogdon – who was born under the astrological sign Aquarius, long associated with John the Baptist.

It was apparently at this time that John confided in Herincx about the madness in his family and sought his advice: he discussed his father's breakdown and his fears for his own sanity, and wondered if he should tell his son, Richard, about it. Herincx felt flattered and confessed himself 'quite fond of the man'. He also says that John told him that Howard had neither been good to him nor valued him. If Herincx's story is true, this would have marked an extraordinary opening-up on John's part – an extremely rare act of trust that would have left a person of his sensitivity acutely vulnerable to any perceived breach of confidence. 'I became a sort of psychiatric adviser to John,' says Herincx, 'and then a scapegoat for his anger.' John, it seems, had a premonition that all was not well with himself and reached out to Herincx, who adopted the role of mentor. Or was it Herincx who spotted John's creeping malaise and forced him to confront it? According to Brenda Ogdon, Herincx turned up insistent to see her at Chester Terrace one day when John was away. This was well before John's breakdown yet Herincx told her he was sorry about what was happening to her husband. Brenda was incredulous and showed him the door. In retrospect, she sensed that he was perhaps feeling guilty. He may simply have wanted to share his insights into John's condition, however: it is Herincx's opinion that John's big breakdown in December 1973 was cumulative, the result of a number of smaller episodes over the years.

Herincx was perhaps one of the very few who knew how to connect with John as a man, rather than a musical prodigy, and consequently won his trust. Yet John played down the relationship, even to the extent of denying it, because it opened doors that scared him. Those observing the relationship were full of misgivings: John's psychology was so fragile that even an experienced psychotherapist would have had to tread very carefully. Emmie Tillett for one was unhappy with their apparent closeness. Howard Greenwood, a friend of Herincx who also knew Ogdon, feels that Herincx was foolish to venture unqualified down certain paths and take up the mantle of guru. Herincx, it seems, went out of his depth.

Herincx recalls that on one occasion, late at night, he drove John back to Chester Terrace, where the front door was opened by a man claiming to be the plumber. John was visibly upset and wouldn't enter the house. Herincx says that subsequently every time he and his wife invited John and Brenda out to dinner Brenda brought along the 'plumber'. Herincx and Astra were invited to only one reception at Chester Terrace, and even then Brenda hardly exchanged a word with Raimund.

Herincx's animus towards Brenda Ogdon is palpable. He is scathing about her musical talent and her book, which he has had removed from the libraries in Bath and Aberdeen 'as being specious and spurious'. He says he wants to set her false record straight and that if she were to 'go too far again' he would assemble 'a phalanx of musicians to finish her off'. According to Herincx, he neither asked nor expected John to do a concert for no fee and never fell out with the man. It was only when John started sending unpleasant letters that Herincx's friendly attitude changed. 'We could have put the boot in because the man was clearly crackers,' he says. 'If we had put the boot in with the support of so many of our instrumental friends – so many – and conductor friends, we could have destroyed his career.'

The final episode in the Herincx saga occurred on 5 November 1975. John and Brenda had flown in from New York to Manchester the previous day for concerts with the Hallé (at the Free Trade Hall and then in Sheffield, on the sixth and seventh respectively). In New York John had been troubled by a boil on his heel brought on by the drugs he'd been taking; he could hardly walk and Brenda was advised by a doctor there to cancel the Hallé dates and take John straight home instead.

On the morning of the fifth John got up in good time and left the hotel at nine thirty, telling Brenda that he was going to the hall to get some practice in before the rehearsal (a rather un-John-like thing to do). He then ambled over to the taxi rank outside. It's not clear whether he actually wanted a taxi but when one of the cabbies called out, 'Where to, gov?' John replied, 'Royal Festival Hall, London, please.' Unbelievably, the driver then hared off down the M1 without

question or down payment. After 100 miles or so John asked him to
divert to Quinville, the Herincx home. When Astra opened the front
door she was flabbergasted to see John standing before her. By the
time she had informed him that Raimund was in America a very irate
taxi driver had joined them at the door: John had smoked non-stop
from Manchester, dropping his cigarette butts all over the back of the
taxi; he had also ripped his musical scores to shreds. Not only had the
driver not yet been paid but his car had been trashed into the bargain.
John stood there mutely, seemingly in no mood to explain his behaviour, so Astra invited them both in while she considered what to do.
It was by now early afternoon.

Astra Blair had her own music agency, principally for singers, and
was well acquainted with the world of professional music and musicians. Once she had served her guests with coffee she phoned Ibbs &
Tillett and was informed that John was scheduled to play in
Manchester the following night, was meant to be at rehearsals that day
and was staying at the Midland Hotel with Brenda. She then phoned
the Hallé's manager, Gerald Temple, who told her that in John's
absence he had already spoken to Brenda and she was unaware of
John's whereabouts. At Temple's suggestion Astra then called Brenda
to let her know that John had been found. Brenda was horrified to
learn what had happened – and was in tears at the thought of the taxi
bill. Eventually it was arranged that the taxi driver would drive John
back to the Midland Hotel, where she would pay the fare. So, after
more than 300 miles and seven hours in a taxi, John was finally
deposited back in Manchester that evening. The following night the
concerto was moved to the second half of the programme but any
precautions proved unnecessary: John acquitted himself more than
adequately – though one observer recalls that he kept looking over his
shoulder during the performance.

What really did happen in the years between 1964 and 1972? It is
hard to know how friendly the two men truly were, or even how
often they met. If meetings did take place it seems strange that Brenda
didn't know about them, even allowing for John's secrecy. It is possible that Ogdon felt insulted and browbeaten by Herincx – and equally
possible that he felt threatened by what some have construed as the

personal nature of Herincx's interest in him. Their relationship certainly meant something to John but exactly what is difficult to ascertain. Nor are its aggressive undercurrents easy to fathom. Why would Herincx slam down the phone on John in 1964 if the two were barely acquainted? This was hardly the way to court a famous artist. More importantly, no one would do that to someone they'd met only once before. Either Ogdon and Herincx were already well known to each other or Herincx had a brusque and perplexing manner. (Indeed, in his Tokyo diatribe John had one of his friends say, 'As I understand it, this man Herincx has a power mania.') We are left with a slew of unanswered questions.

At the time of Herincx's first phone call to John, in early 1964, John had just returned from his inaugural US tour, during which he had received the news of his mother's death but hadn't flown back for the funeral. It was an extremely busy and stressful year for him, with two major tours (two months in America and Canada and four months in Australia and New Zealand) as well as numerous shorter excursions in Europe. He began smoking that year, aged twenty-seven. We can assume that because of his immature personality John was unable to shrug off Herincx's call as irrelevant, just 'one of those things' that happen from time to time. John didn't have the usual emotional filters and Herincx's words possibly hung fire in his mind as a judgement from on high while a poisonous guilt set to work in him. On the surface life may have carried on much as before but deep down things were different and the world a less welcoming place.

John had always been impressionable to senior male figures – Ronald Stevenson, Gerard Schurmann and Alexander Goehr, for example – whose authority and strength of character he seemed unable to resist. Brenda felt nettled by John's submissiveness to these men but perhaps in the case of Herincx she also felt threatened. It is not hard to see in Herincx a substitute father figure who, while at times tactless and invasive, appeared to take a sympathetic interest in the younger man, even adopting a tutorial role. They shared a profound love of music and were both married to women who had initially tried to follow the same career as their husbands. Herincx expressed concern for John's wellbeing at a time when he was not receiving emotional support from his wife. Most tellingly, Herincx apparently managed to penetrate John's walls of reserve to the extent that John opened up about his childhood and his father's insanity – subjects that had been locked away since he was a small boy.

It is significant that John's mother had just died when Herincx made his first call because in a way she had always been the obstacle to a positive relationship between John and his father. She had bound her youngest son to her from infancy, partly to protect him from his father's madness and partly to nurture his musical genius. Now that she was gone, John was free to re-engage with the notion of the father. He may also have felt inclined to release himself somewhat from the all-encompassing power of Brenda and Mrs Tillett.

Several months before Herincx's second call, John's brother Karl had died in poverty in Australia; so Herincx's alleged assertion that John was living in irresponsible luxury may also have struck a nerve and triggered further feelings of guilt. These would no doubt have been exacerbated by the fact that John had failed to visit his brother on his 1970 Australian tour. More than any of his siblings, Karl had borne the brunt of his father's bullying. It is conceivable that Herincx, with his hectoring manner, may have become a scapegoat for John's anger towards his brutal father. With his childlike sensibilities John perhaps drew little distinction between Herincx and the dark characters he played on the operatic stage.

Howard's return home after his confinement and wanderings must have impacted greatly on the seven-year-old John, who in his absence had become the man of the house – a usurper – with Dorothy at his beck and call. He may even have felt responsible, as children commonly do, for Howard's original disappearance. Herincx's reproaches could well have served to revive this dynamic in John's mind, especially if he felt essentially unworthy of his newfound wealth. After all, John didn't break down when he was destitute or the work had dried up; he broke down at the point of greatest success and wealth, when he had reached the summit of his career.

In referring to the 1972 incident John characterized his relationship with Herincx as 'the loosest of professional kinship'. This makes sense of much as reported by John but also forces us to conclude that everything in between is Herincx's fabrication, which is unlikely. It is worth bearing in mind, too, that in conversation with close friends John would sometimes blame Brenda, not Herincx, for what happened. Herincx himself described John as 'patently obviously truthful (the man did not lie!)'. Yet it is surely unwise to say of someone who lost his mind that he always spoke the truth. In February 1983, on the BBC *Nationwide* programme, John told the interviewer that he was composing a song cycle for baritone voice based on his father's long poem, *Clipstone Camp*. 'It's written for a very dear friend of ours, Raimund Herincx, who lives in Bedford,' he enthused. He was about to go on, but was interrupted.

The details of the relationship between these two men may never be resolved. There is no doubt, however, that John came to believe in the existence of a conspiracy to destroy his career – and that at the centre of this supposed collusion stood the daunting figure of Raimund Herincx.

10

AMERICAN PIE

I met a girl who sang the blues
And I asked her for some happy news
But she just smiled and turned away . . .

Don McLean, 'American Pie'

Edgar Allan Poe, to whose work John (and Howard) frequently turned, was concerned in his writing with what D. H. Lawrence described as the 'disintegration-processes' of the psyche. Poe's characters struggle with fears of annihilation and madness, and some of his most powerful stories are those in which he uses natural catastrophe as a metaphor for the soul's transformative upheavals. In 'A Descent into the Maelström' Poe tells the tale of three fishermen whose boat is drawn down into the terrifying vortex of the Moskoestrom in an archipelago in the Norwegian Sea. One of them dies at the very horror of the sight, while another is thrown overboard by the insane force of the storm driving them towards the maelstrom. The third, the narrator, has the courage to look directly and with fixity into the whirlpool. Consequently his terror turns to fascination – and in that fascination are the seeds of the action that will release him. When he looks into the abyss he sees otherworldly beauty and magnificence as well as irresistible destruction. He is, in effect, looking into the heart of the human soul at its point of greatest torment and possibility:

> The rays of the moon seemed to search the very bottom of the profound gulf: but still I could make out nothing distinctly on account of a thick mist in which everything there was enveloped, and over which there hung a magnificent rainbow, like that narrow and tottering bridge which Mussulmans say is the only pathway between Time and Eternity. This mist, or spray, was no doubt occasioned by the clashing of the great walls of the funnel, as they all met together at the bottom – but the yell that went up to the heavens from out of that mist I dare not attempt to describe.

As the bark whirls about the outer circuit of the vortex at a steep angle, the narrator observes the way in which the various swallowed objects travel down its walls, noting what is dragged to oblivion and what resurfaces. Then, having lashed himself to a water-cask, he plunges from the boat into the vortex; there, while the craft is sucked to the bottom he remains buoyed up in one of the higher circles – until suddenly the walls grow less steep, the gyrations less violent, and the slackening whirlpool delivers him to the level seas above.

Looking back on his ordeal he describes how he felt more composed 'in the very jaws' of the whirling gulf than he did when he was approaching it. Once inside, time ceased and his mind became superbly concentrated as a higher intelligence took the helm. What had seemed to be chaos is now perceived as a deeper ordering principle: by plunging into the vortex he surrendered himself to the superior organizing power of the unconscious. If ever there was an evocation of the process and purpose of depression it is here. The brothers who succumb to terror and cannot face what is before them perish. The third has the courage to look and to go deeper – to embrace his doom – and he survives. As Strindberg wrote, 'Not everyone is capable of madness; and of those lucky enough to be capable, not many have the courage for it.'

As a society our tolerance for madness, never mind our courage for it, is low, and our attitude to depression has been slow to improve

since Ogdon's time. Even the *word* 'depression' is depressingly inap-
posite, unless one thinks quite technically of a weather front. William
Styron's 'brainstorm' is nearer the mark, but nothing captures the
whirling heights and depths with such dramatic intensity as Poe's
'maelstrom'. Many of the drug-based therapies still in favour today
work to stabilize but not resolve the condition, effectively keeping the
patient whizzing around on the edge of the whirlpool in a sense of
ever-impending catastrophe. Here, prevented from passing the 'narrow
tottering bridge' to face the transformative depths, he remains rooted
in the soil of the egoic mind with all its chattering fears and taboos.
Yet the core error (many have gradually come to see) in treating the
mentally ill is to see the unconscious as the source of chaos and confusion and the so-called conscious mind as the source of order: it is
in fact the other way round. It is the mind or ego that, in its superfi-
ciality, creates mayhem and disorder. The unconscious, on the other
hand, however disorientating, has its roots in divine order. (Ultimately,
though, the division of mind into conscious and unconscious is a false
dichotomy that closes the door on the reality of a holistic perception.)

John's strong sense of fatedness – that he was destined to follow in
his father's footsteps – gave his own madness a literary or histrionic
flavour. The fearsome Moskoe-strom of Poe's tale, no less than Moby
Dick, was a vivid metaphor of the destructive power of the shadow.
Just as Ahab fought the whale, Howard Ogdon battled the unconscious: because he mistakenly viewed it as his enemy. Because the
unconscious was, for him, a malicious force that imperiled his sanity
he projected his shadow onto his youngest son, and in a sense displaced his madness onto him. John was greatly influenced by his
father's view of the unconscious and he too grew to fear and fight its
unknown depths, instead of allowing himself, like Jonah, to be swallowed and transformed. It was because Jonah had refused the call of
the Lord (i.e., had ignored the unconscious's demand for wholeness)
that a terrible storm was originally unleashed upon him.

John's friendships suffered during the years of his breakdown. Not
many of his friends knew it was happening at the time, so visits were
rare in the mid-seventies. John stopped writing to Ronald Stevenson
in 1973 and their correspondence did not resume until a decade later.

This was not untypical. Many of his friends found it difficult to be in touch with John after 1973 – not only because he was personally less accessible but also because they disliked having to go through Brenda, who could be a forbidding gatekeeper. Now he had moved to Indiana, there was a sense that he might be wandering off into the wilderness.

Although he found it almost impossible to make 'real' friends, being unable to confide in others or discuss anything personal, people were nonetheless drawn to John as a deeply tolerant and non-judgemental soul. This remained true in America, though on campus there was a competitive edge to relations within the faculty. John was already being approached by students the day after his arrival. One was Edna Chun, a doctoral student, who accosted him outside the elevator at the Union after breakfast. He was incredibly polite and enthusiastic and told her to meet him at his studio so that he could hear her play. She played the Beethoven Sonata Op. 109 for him and as he moved and swayed in his chair she was immediately struck by how engrossed in the music he was. The meaning of the music was clearly more important to him than the performer's accuracy, phrasing or general competence. He must have heard the piece hundreds of times, yet it was as if he was hearing it for the first time. Edna noticed the same thing when she sat behind John at concerts in the Musical Arts Center. He moved in his seat and was so intensely involved in the music that he forgot everything around him.

John was tasked with teaching piano majors at both undergraduate and graduate level but ended up with more graduates, who were best able to profit from his unsystematic teaching style. While he said some brilliant – if cryptic – things in class, his pearls were not scattered liberally and his students had to do a certain amount of digging in order to come away with more than smiles and nodding platitudes. The minimum teaching load was eighteen hours or eighteen students per week. Additional responsibilities involved attending faculty meetings, sitting on auditioning committees and the regular assessment and evaluation of students, a process known as 'jury' and 'upper divisional'. There were also group classes in which all John's pianists took part and played for each other. Under other teachers these could be an ordeal, with the sessions conducted as trials of sorts whereby students' performances were brutally dissected by their peers. In John's studio, though, the focus was always on the music and he wouldn't allow students to criticize each other. When someone had finished playing he would say, 'Did you hear that? Isn't it a wonderful piece?' and then invite discussion on aspects of interpretation. He was proud of each of his students and rightly protective of them.

As for faculty recitals, it was up to the individual to decide how often he performed. On average John gave two or three a year. Though his colleagues held him in awe musically, the faculty recitals had something of a gladiatorial vibe to them: the piano professors, always supercritical of their peers, would huddle in the audience like a knot of vultures, listening intently for any slips. (Zadel Skolovsky got so spooked that he refused to play in front of them.) John gave his first recital shortly after he arrived. The next day he was sitting alone at lunch when he was joined by an English professor, Charles Forker, who saw him looking lost. Forker complimented him on his recital but got nowhere. John didn't want to talk about his own playing. Forker fared no better with other topics. All his questions about how John was settling in at IU, for instance, were met with monosyllabic replies. He scored a little better with seventeenth-century literature, however. An expert on John Webster, he realized from chatting that John was familiar with Webster's work and knew the major plays, such as *The Duchess of Malfi*. But even here it was hard to keep the conversation going. Having begun quite brightly, John sank back into silence. Then he suddenly looked up from his plate and said, 'Are you busy this afternoon, or would you like to go to the movies?' Forker said he'd be happy to take John to any of the several movie theatres in the vicinity but needed to find a schedule to see what was playing. 'It doesn't matter what's on; it doesn't make any difference,' said John. Such nonchalance astounded Forker, whose compliance was rewarded with a trashy, utterly unmemorable film that John appeared to enjoy.

The move to Bloomington was potentially perfect for John. He had a salaried job of considerable prestige, health benefits, a pension, a daily routine, less pressure, beautiful countryside and a large musical family on his doorstep – the new start he desperately needed. Brenda assumed that they were moving to America for good, and the Dean of the Music School, Charles Webb, envisaged a long and distinguished teaching career for John with tenure after seven years.

Bloomington was arguably the best music school in the States, better than Oberlin, Juilliard or Curtis, with world-class teaching staff and facilities. It had been Charles Webb's predecessor, Wilfred Bain, who first approached John in the early 1970s on the recommendation of Sidney Foster, Chair of the Piano Department. Bain had been told by the President of IU, Herman B. Wells, to build the finest conservatoire and not to spare the dollars, so was looking for pianists in the superstar category (he even invited Horowitz to join the faculty!). Abbey Simon, a former colleague of Foster's at the Curtis Institute of Music in Philadelphia, also became involved a few years later. Simon had been called by John's US agent, Harold Shaw, asking if he could suggest a professorship in America for John to save him from financial hardship. Simon had little hesitation in recommending Bloomington.

Long before John's arrival Wilfred Bain's wife, Mary, was spreading rumours that he was crazy; this was, she said, why he had been unable to take up her husband's invitation. So in many ways John was walking into a vipers' den. Sidney Foster, who was an ally and admirer, told the faculty to make allowances for John's everyday communication problems and to focus instead on engaging him on a musical plane. One day after a 'hearing', at which a professorial committee would hear a student play from a recital they were giving, Foster turned to the faculty and said, 'Before you all came today I witnessed something phenomenal.' Then he asked John if he would mind showing them something of what he had been doing that morning. John shyly consented and, sitting down at the piano, began to sight-read a Strauss tone poem for full orchestra. It was, according to Henry Upper, monumental. You saw his tremendous musical insights taking shape as he performed, for this was no mere recitation. He had the uncanny ability to sense a piece's entire structure from the first page. Foster was fascinated with John and after the performance asked him to show everyone his hands. One of the professors present that day said they appeared boneless and curved in rather than shaping out. The fourth and fifth fingers, in particular, were super-flexible and there was a large gap between the two digits, which could both be stretched to an unusual degree. They didn't look like human hands.

John's brilliance, allied with his vague and non-committal approach to administrative affairs, caused resentment among certain of his colleagues. His reticence was an additional handicap, and could make him seem offhand and disinterested. The Cuban virtuoso Jorge Bolet took John out to lunch when he first arrived on campus but couldn't get a word out of him. John often missed faculty meetings but when he did turn up he would sit nodding in his habitual garlands of smoke and agree to everything that was proposed. Physically he was the embodiment of chaos. It was like having a great ball of oxygen in the room, with gas escaping in little Teletubby-like sighs, grunts and squeaks. When Sidney Foster died suddenly at the age of fifty-nine in February 1977, John lost a valuable support just six months into his Bloomington career. Foster was succeeded as Chair of the Piano Department by Karen Shaw, a career woman and administrator who felt threatened by John's musicianship. Shaw could be cutting about John behind his back, as could a number of the other professors. He was an innocent in their world of political scheming.

John's frequent absences from campus became a bone of contention. Faculty members were allowed fifteen days each semester (or a total of thirty days per academic year) away from campus on personal business without a deduction of salary. John's absences far exceeded these parameters. A mere two weeks into his first semester and he was off to South Africa for a month's tour; after a few weeks back at Bloomington he followed this up with concerts in England, Scotland, Scandinavia and Hungary. He missed ten out of the sixteen weeks that semester. The following term he was equally booked up and was away most of January and February and half of March, mainly with engagements in the UK, while April saw him fly out to Vancouver and Mexico City for two weeks. There had always been a tension in the faculty between the big names, who toured widely and brought prestige to the University, and the more workaday teachers. Some of the stars had a rather cavalier attitude to their students. When Edna Chun first arrived at Bloomington she applied to Abbey Simon, who told her, 'I'm never here. If you want detailed tuition, go to someone else.' For John, however, the real tensions lay elsewhere. By taking on a heavy touring schedule in addition to his professorial duties, he was submitting to the very pressures that had led to his breakdown. The whole point of going to America – to find a more relaxed and creative lifestyle – had quickly been forgotten.

Even the old financial stresses returned. He and Brenda had bought a large, expensive house and were making considerable refurbishments; then there was the cost of shipping out their chattels from the UK. In a letter to Brenda from South Africa in September 1976, John cautioned her about committing to the shipment. 'The question of whether we would strip ourselves too much at the moment is a delicately-balanced one,' he wrote, having first been careful to praise her extravagantly for all the work she had been putting in on the move. They also joined the Country Club in Bloomington and entertained quite lavishly. When they returned to England for concerts their London base was the Grosvenor House Hotel. On top of everything they had to find the school fees for Richard and Annabel.

John received communications from the dean in March and June of 1977, about reassigning classes when he was away and urging him to give as many extra lessons as he could while on campus. John was now hopping across the Atlantic quite regularly and at the beginning of March he became disoriented at Heathrow while waiting for a flight to Holland. He had checked his luggage in and gone to the departure lounge, but failed to get on the flight. He just sat there until an airport official happened to recognize him. Ibbs & Tillett were contacted and Wilfred Stiff drove out to Heathrow; seeing John's confusion, he had him admitted to the Priory. He was there for only a week, and his visit was kept from the dean, but the price of confinement was a new regimen of drugs.

On the whole John was held in high regard by his pupils, though some of his undergraduates complained that he never said anything or offered guidance. When one of them mentioned this to Menahem Pressler the wise old owl shot back with, 'Well, why don't you ask him?' John was known for his courtesy and kindness to his students and for giving them all As no matter how they played. Though his expectations were high he never put a student down, and seemed to

sense that the greatest gift any teacher can give is confidence. He
also gave them his absolute attention for those sixty minutes of
lesson time. He had a natural love of sharing his knowledge, inherited perhaps from Howard, and cared deeply about his teaching.
When he was on campus he never missed a lesson and was never
late. He was generous with his time and would often give a student
more than one lesson a week, or allow him or her to play for him
whenever they wanted. When students arrived John would invariably be sitting by the window, puffing away in the dark because he
didn't care for the electric light. He would offer them a cigarette;
these were always declined but that didn't stop him repeating the
ritual the very next lesson. Rather than talking about technique
John would make his points by playing. To impose a view was anathema to him, partly because his own view was always changing. He
was responsive to the individual style of his students and let them be
who they were.

For Andrew Axelrod and Clipper Erickson, both graduate students,
one of the thrills of studying with Ogdon was his wide-ranging,
quixotic exploration of out-of-the-way repertoire. He would play
anything they happened to bring in; and if he didn't know it he
sight-read it. His incautious approach was infectious. Axelrod once
brought in the Reger Bach Variations as a deliberate bait because he
hadn't prepared the piece he was meant to be studying and, sure
enough, John squeezed him over on the piano stool, pushed his
spectacles down on his nose and read the whole thing through. They
had visionary conversations together about Scriabin, Sorabji, Reger
et al., and John recalled Sandy Goehr's aphorism from his college
days: 'If you've reached Reger, can't you move one step forward and
accept Schoenberg?' He introduced Clipper Erickson to Busoni,
Szymanowski, Medtner and Messiaen, and would play Nielsen and
Cyril Scott as well as his own works.

Edna Chun felt that John's comments reflected an unusually deep
knowledge and understanding of the music. When she played the
Beethoven Op. 110 for him he turned to her and said 'You know,
Edna, this is *not* a romantic piece' and in a lesson on Debussy's *L'Isle
Joyeuse* he talked knowledgeably about the painting by Watteau that

had inspired the work. If a pupil didn't play a piece well John said nothing; he simply guided them in another direction. What he couldn't abide was for the score of a great piece to be treated with levity. During a lesson on Chopin's F-minor ballade, for example, Edna made a flippant comment about a certain passage sounding like something else and John didn't like that at all.

When a student was learning a concerto John would take the orchestral part on the second piano, which was for some an over-whelming experience. When Clipper Erickson had to make an audition tape of the Grieg Concerto for a competition he had entered John played the orchestral part so loudly and crashingly that Clipper had difficulty in cutting through with the solo. Similarly, when Edna Chun was learning the Prokofiev First Concerto, John tore into the piece, wanting to play it faster and faster and bringing real excitement to the work. Edna, on the other hand, had to slow it down so that she could remain in control when she played it in public.

Sometimes John's students would go over to Lookout Lane for class parties, where they would listen to rare recordings, discuss inter-pretation and enjoy a meal with John and Brenda. On one occasion dinner was well under way when they all noticed that John, at the head of the table, wasn't eating anything. 'John, why aren't you eating?' came the chorus. 'I don't have a fork,' he replied forlornly. When his students gave recitals John would invite them over for tea afterwards, and there would frequently be other guests present. There was an active social life among the professors and their wives and those affiliated to the university. Within the music department the Ogdons were particularly friendly with fellow piano professor James Tocco and his wife Gilan, the Chilean composer Juan Orrego-Salas and his wife Carmen, and William and Nelda Christ. At one house party Professor Alfonso Montecino was impressed with John's knowl-edge of the classical song repertoire. John accompanied his wife, the mezzo-soprano Siri Garson, in three of his favourite Sibelius songs, 'The Tryst', 'Black Roses' and 'Ingalill'.

John's students were bowled over by his faculty recitals and mar-velled at his ability to project a pianissimo to the back of the hall. His performance of the Beethoven Op. 109 was the most spiritual, the most sublime that Clipper Erickson had heard (and he knew the recordings by Schnabel, Brendel and Gieseking). Others remember his *Hammerklavier*, played with Beethoven's original metronome markings, as something wondrously profound and imaginative, breathtaking in its fiery precision. Josef Gingold thought it 'incredible', while it prompted Henry Upper to speak of 'a kind of super-intellect driving the forces of John's creativity'. Certain professors in the piano department had strong reservations, however. Menahem Pressler said that Ogdon played it as if he'd had a lobotomy, because there was no connection between his fingers, the piece and him. Karen Shaw had the same impression. She went backstage beforehand to wish John luck, and to her he seemed programmed to walk on stage, do his business and then go home – almost as if he was an automaton. She felt he lived a very tunnelled existence. Gregory Robbins, who reviewed the performance for the *Herald-Times*, Bloomington's largest newspaper, wrote that 'Ogdon opted for a blindingly brisk tempo in the first movement that might have pleased Carl Czerny, but few others'. John opened another faculty recital with Beethoven's Op. 110 sonata – halfway through which he suddenly took a shortcut. 'I'm going to kill him,' Brenda was heard to say.

The Bloomington campus was a beautiful place to work. Its imposing grey edifices of locally quarried Indiana limestone are rarely oppressive, being set as they are in almost 2,000 acres of green space. At the heart of the old campus are Dunn's Woods, where for centuries the sycamore, black walnut, hickory, ash, yellowwood, red oak, red maple and American beech have flourished. Through them runs a clear, tuneful creek known on campus as the 'Jordan River'. The town itself is full of attractive stores and restaurants, some of them quite quaint, which radiate out from the historical courthouse square. Further out are the usual malls with their cinema complexes and department stores. The music department is enormous and some of its modern buildings are faceless concrete structures. John's studio, however, was in the old music building, Merrill Hall. It was a light, airy room on the ground floor with lemon-yellow walls, two Steinway grands side by side and a desk and swivel chair by the large shuttered

window. Just along the corridor was a small 500-seat recital hall –
though the main performance space was the 1,500 seat auditorium in
the Musical Arts Center, which opened in 1972. It was there that faculty recitals, opera and ballet all took place. During one production of
Aida live elephants were brought on stage, and the university had the
wherewithal to tackle vast operas like *Parsifal*.

John, it seems, often had difficulty finding his studio and would
wander around aimlessly. A lot of the time he didn't appear to know
when the students were out of session, and would come in to teach
when they were on break. He cabbed around a good deal between
Lookout Lane and campus and from campus into town, and was a
familiar sight out on the circle in front of the old music building waiting for his taxi. In the winter he was a particularly conspicuous figure
in the gigantic fur hat with ear flaps he'd bought with his Moscow
winnings in 1962. When he wasn't teaching he would often amble
over to his favourite ale house and eatery, Bear's on East 3rd Street.
This was the first port of call whenever a student was unable to locate
him. Nine times out of ten there would be John, tucking into a pizza
or a burger and fries washed down with mugs of steaming coffee.

Pianistically, John was on excellent form from the middle of 1976
through to the end of 1977. His tour of South Africa in September
1976 was sensationally reported in the press over there. The following
year, in February, he gave a series of concerts in England with the violinist Ruggiero Ricci playing works by Debussy, Busoni, Joachim and
Szymanowski; in April he played the Busoni Concerto in Mexico
City and then in a mammoth programme at the Romantic Festival at
Butler University in Indianapolis he played Alkan's Concerto for solo
piano, Liszt's *Totentanz* (in the solo-piano version) and pieces by
Busoni and Chopin. In June he gave an all-Scriabin recital at the
inaugural Spoleto Festival in Charleston, South Carolina, that drew
forth superlatives from former *New York Times* music critic Robert T.
Jones.

In July, after a fundraising recital at Annabel's school, Benenden,
John, Brenda and the children flew out for a four-week holiday on the
secluded northeast coast of Corfu. Their sizable house, the Villa
Virginia, had views over the Ionian Sea to the mountains of Albania.

Staying nearby was the writer John le Carré (or David Cornwell, as he was known in everyday life) with his wife and son, and they were soon exchanging visits with the Ogdons. John admired le Carré's writing and the two men had long conversations about literature as they sat in the sun drinking the local wine. According to le Carré, John devoured books at huge speed and was 'recklessly erudite'. For him talking to John was a real pleasure because of the speed of the younger man's intelligence. He was very quick to take a point – nothing needed to be signalled – so they were able to co-exist comfortably on a plane of books and ideas. Le Carré was much appealed to by Brenda, who talked about John as a very troubled man. As a result he became 'prisoner's friend' and took John on at a social level. There were times when agreed meetings had to be postponed because John was not well or there was a problem, but by and large he was fairly sociable. In addition to his semi-gregarious forays John was busy composing a new piano sonata and a sonata for solo flute.

Staying a few bays over from the Ogdons and the Cornwells was Humphrey Burton, head of Music and Arts at the BBC, with his wife and family. Also there were the conductor and composer Antal Dorati and his pianist wife, Ilse. The Burtons were lying on the beach one day minding their own business when a large boat hove into view and they could hear greetings shouted from the deck. Humphrey looked up to see a party of people wading ashore – and one person, bulkier than the others, taking much longer to disembark. The Ogdons were soon upon them. There followed a social gathering in one of the local tavernas, after which they went back to the Villa Virginia and up on the roof enjoyed a handsome, elegant meal served by a man wearing Indian robes and a fez! Burton remembers it as extremely luxurious, but also a little awkward because of the element of formality introduced by Brenda. John, whose hair and beard had been dyed chestnut, sat at one end of the table in a suit jacket dreaming away in coils of smoke while Brenda made bright and brittle conversation at the other end. John's habitual reply of 'Yes, yes' to whatever was proposed, even if it was a choice between red or white wine, was of great amusement to the children and soon became the catchphrase of the holiday – at least for the Burton family.

By Brenda's account they spent many days on expensively appointed boats, often courtesy of the Cornwells, sunning themselves and drinking champagne. At the first sign of an upturn in their fortunes, Brenda and John were already throwing money about by the fistful. In her book Brenda admits that they were like 'incorrigible children', living yet again at the limits of their income. John enjoyed their Corfu vacation so well that when the time came to return to Bloomington he presented Brenda with an extraordinary fait accompli. Without consulting anyone he had booked a large yacht for them to live on for an additional two weeks, proving himself in one fell stroke to be a worthier resident of Toad Hall than Brenda. She was having none of it, though: she cancelled his booking on the spot and they flew back to Indiana for the start of the new semester. Annabel and Richard went with them, having several weeks of their summer holidays left.

John's pattern of performing heavily during term time continued and he was away for two months from September to November. In addition to being on the jury of the Van Cliburn competition in Fort Worth, Texas, he had concerts in Canada, Venice, Iran (for the British Cultural Festival) and Czechoslovakia. When he did finally return to campus in the middle of November he had no more concerts booked until the following February. Instead of accepting this as a heaven-sent break, however, Brenda bemoaned the lack of engagements and set in motion a new cycle of worry. When February arrived the dean asked John to cut down on his forthcoming concerts. 'And so John found himself trapped in a strange vicious circle,' writes Brenda, 'on the one hand worrying about too few dates being offered him, and, on the other, feeling unable to accept them if they were, after all, to come his way.'

When the children returned to school after the Christmas holidays, in January 1978, John was more withdrawn and took up his old smoking post on the bed; he was also increasingly irritable and prey to sudden outbursts. The voices in his head returned and he began writing letters to Raimund Herincx again. He didn't share his emotional problems or open up about them in any way. He stalked about the house muttering to himself, and there was a coiled-up violence in his

hunched body. If he began to talk – and there could be a dam-burst
of loquacity – it would be a monologue about music or a certain composer. To Brenda it was fascinating but unhelpful. Mentally he was on
a very high plane; its loftiness was his refuge from the encroaching
flood waters below.

In February 1978 John gave the US premiere of Gerard
Schurmann's concerto at Michigan State University in Lansing. It is
extraordinary how often this piece cropped up like a red flag when
John was descending into a depression, like some uncanny coefficient
of his madness. That same month marked the halfway mark of John's
three-year contract and the dean had written asking him to submit
materials in support of his reappointment for the 1979–80 academic
year. These could include student evaluations and a report of his professional activities on and off campus. John was clearly not up to
writing the report, so Brenda wrote it for him and signed herself
'John Ogdon'. Though she conceded that she didn't have any evaluation sheets to hand, many of John's students wrote letters in support
of his reappointment and the Student Representative Committee,
having interviewed all fourteen of his pupils, provided a ringing
endorsement:

> John Ogdon has something very special and he is communicating it
> to his students. Clearly, the more advanced student, one with strong
> musical ideas, the thinker, is Mr. Ogdon's kind of student. He is
> definitely not for everyone. But clearly, in the minds of his students
> and in the opinion of this committee he is an enormous asset to the
> musical community of Indiana University.

Then comes this extraordinary statement, which suggests that the
students held a more enlightened view than the faculty:

> I would like to end on a philosophical note in reference to ques-
> tions that have never been raised concerning negative aspects of
> John Ogdon other than his teaching style. John Ogdon is unique.
> He does not fit the mould. There is a great tendency to fear and/or
> reject that which is different, unknown and not easily understood.

To reject the acknowledged genius of John Ogdon on the basis of his ability to perform certain administrative tasks is a harsh judgement indeed. It is, in effect, to deny this kind of genius a place in our larger social system because of inadequacies which must ultimately be considered subordinate to the richness and worth of his enormous intellect. If whether or not someone fits the established mould becomes the ultimate criterion for our decision, then we have indeed made a dangerous and sad value judgement.

Peter Sage, who wrote this paragraph, evidently sensed which way the wind was blowing. A number of faculty members wrote in to the dean to express their reservations about John, most crucially Karen Shaw and Henry Upper. Shaw cited John's 'excessive absence from campus', his failure to appear on committees and his 'vague perception of our programs and procedures'. His overall contribution was, she said, 'far below what is expected'. As John began to fall apart during the rest of the year, Shaw's points were increasingly borne out.

At the beginning of the year John had begun work on a comic opera based on James Elroy Flecker's fantasy novel *The King of Alsander*. He wrote the music and libretto together and after three months had almost completed the first act. The music is light and highly melodic and in places reminiscent of the French composer Léo Delibes, whose ballet *Coppélia* John had seen in Nottingham as a boy. In it he quotes from a number of lesser composers whom he admired, such as Chaminade and Ivanovici, reminding us that all his works are essentially tributes to the composers he revered. There is great humility in his compositional stance, which is no doubt why transcriptions appealed to him as keenly as they did. We are in familiar Ogdon territory with *The King of Alsander*, because it is the story of a grocer's boy, Norman Price, a voracious reader and dreamer who is pointed towards a faraway land by a white-haired seer, a priest of Isis, who turns up in his father's shop one day. The land is Alsander and Norman is chosen as its king. His adventures and the means by which he is chosen have the feel of a Masonic initiation rite, and this esoteric strand no doubt appealed to John. Norman's everyday life is swallowed up by a poetic world of myth and symbol, and the novel ends with a magnificent vision of Isis rising from the ocean.

James Tocco, who occupied the studio next door to John's, recalls a conversation in which John unexpectedly engaged him on the question of taxes. He was rather taken aback by the anxious tone of his intervention, having assumed – given his lavish home and healthy roster of concerts – that John was comfortably off. 'John, is money something that you're concerned about?' he asked. 'Yes,' John replied. 'I worry about it all the time.' Towards the end of April 1978 John received a letter from the university's president approving his reappointment as Professor of Music for the academic year 1979–80. Around the same time he received some heavy VAT charges in a letter from England and in a sudden fury let fly at a crystal chandelier in the hall at Lookout Lane, an episode eerily reminiscent of his mirror-smashing antics at Chester Terrace.

John and Brenda were scheduled to leave for Europe (via Mexico) in less than a week but Brenda realized that it was now, for the first time since their move to America, essential to seek professional help. John's GP referred him to a young psychiatrist by the name of Michael Johnson. According to Johnson, when John first turned up in his office that May day he looked like a homeless person. His shirt was stained, his trousers were unzipped and his transactional quality was 'bumbling and vacant'. He was confused, disorganized and apparently oblivious to his condition. Johnson had no idea who he was and supposed he should call a family member to make sure he returned home safely. He was certain of only one thing: this was one of the sickest patients he had ever witnessed on first interview. He almost had him hospitalized.

At this first meeting John wasn't able to articulate his distress and had no sense of the extent to which his illness was affecting him. He was simply in it. He was on the standard antipsychotics of the time – Thorazine, Stelazine and suchlike – which caused cognitive slowing and disrupted fluency of movement. He did manage to convey that he was on the music faculty at IU and was teaching students, but that was about the extent of it. Johnson used the meeting to try to establish a basic measure of trust. He didn't care about John's position or talent, whatever they might be; he was simply responding to him as a man in distress. As an emergency measure he prescribed haloperidol (known by its brand name, Haldol), a powerful antipsychotic, which was considered indispensable in treating urgent psychiatric cases. (It was also used by the Soviet government to break down dissidents.) This was a tough call: John was on the verge of hospitalization, yet about to undertake a two-month concert tour. There wasn't an antipsychotic drug whose psycho-motor effects did not compromise coordination. As it turned out Haldol, as well as giving John a very dry mouth, did cause him loss of motor control. They were already in Mexico when this became evident, but Brenda saved the day by cutting down the dosage before performances, a balancing act that created some scary moments. In Hilversum, Holland, for instance, John was to perform the Schurmann Concerto but Gerard was aghast at his chaotic playing during rehearsals – he simply couldn't synchronize his hands. Brenda's reassurances proved correct, however, and a further cut in the dosage enabled John to give a sterling performance that helped consolidate Gerard's stature in his native land. The following day Gerard's assistant conductor, René Benschop, was consigned to look after the Ogdons and show them round Amsterdam. Brenda, no doubt buoyed by her pill-balancing acrobatics, told him, 'Could you take John to the market please; he wants to buy me a diamond!'

John had a whole raft of concerts in England, including a number of charity events. He gave one such gala recital at St John's Smith Square in the presence of HRH Princess Alice, Duchess of Gloucester, but his biggest test of the tour came at the Queen Elizabeth Hall on 4 June – where he faced an audience bristling with musicians, critics and musical grandees. Brenda was extremely nervous on John's behalf as she glanced round the packed auditorium, yet later described his portly figure hurrying on to the stage as possessing 'an authority that was by now almost Brahmsian'. Never one to bask in applause before a performance, he was already seated and playing before the clapping had died out. And he played superbly, his far-seeing artistry taking his audience captive. Bryce Morrison began his review in the *Telegraph* the next morning with the words, 'A warm

welcome to John Ogdon ...' before hailing him as 'among the most
gifted and original of all young pianists'. (It was surely difficult to associate the word 'young' with the saturnine, stooped figure that
appeared from the wings, his hair all grey or whiting.) Morrison
talked of 'heaven-sent touches scattered liberally through Ogdon's
performances', with Scriabin's Fifth Sonata 'conceived in an astonishing spectrum of colours and dynamics'. In the four Schubert
Impromptus, Op. 90, 'tempi (slow as well as fast) forbidden to lesser
mortals made a deeply poignant experience of numbers one and
three', while 'an occasional rushed fence in Liszt's B-minor ballade
and *Dante* Sonata seemed of passing moment, given performances of
such blazing panache and poetic engagement'. Despite the excellent
reviews it would be almost another three years before John was invited
to play in the capital again. From England he returned to Mexico
City, where he played both Brahms concerti in a single evening with
the Philharmonia Orchestra of La Universidad Nacional Autónoma
de México under Jorge Velasco.

Once John was back in Bloomington for the humid summer
months his condition continued to worsen and he saw Dr Johnson on
a regular basis. Brenda accompanied him on his second consultation
and filled in more of his background and medical history. Seeing the
two of them together brought home to Johnson the extremity of
John's passivity. Brenda acted as the aggressive force in John's life,
while his own passive aggression manifested as sullen obstinacy.
Obedient yet resentful, John was infantile in his dealings with Brenda
and kept secrets from her – such as his creative work – like a child
hiding his favourite toys. At the therapy sessions he always deferred to
her. When asked a question, his reply would invariably be, 'What do
you think, Brenda?'

John could hardly drag himself out of bed in the mornings and
what little energy he had was ploughed into his obsessive deliberations
over Raimund Herincx. The dean was increasingly concerned about
John's absences, as well as his introspective state when he was present,
and there had been more formal complaints from undergraduate students that his lessons were all smoke and no instruction. He asked
John to cancel some of his engagements for the autumn semester,

including a scheduled recording of Liszt's Transcendental Studies with Enigma Records in London. John wandered the campus like a lost soul on welfare. Andrew Axelrod would stay up late practising in one of the studios and once found John shuffling along Bloomington High Street at one thirty in the morning, walking the wrong way from home. He was like a big ghostly teddy bear padding along, though there was no label giving his name and address. Andrew called Brenda and put him in a taxi. Towards the end of the summer John turned up for a crisis meeting with the dean in a pair of skimpy purple shorts.

In the midst of this chaos Brenda enlisted the help of Edna Chun, who already took care of John's mail for him and acted as his eyes and ears on campus. At the beginning of September, when Brenda left for England to see Richard settled for his first term at Eton, Edna moved in to Lookout Lane to care for John. She did household chores, such as cooking, laundry and ironing, drove him to campus every day and took him to doctor's appointments and concert engagements. She noticed that John didn't do anything outside his teaching and performing; dealing with his mental illness was taxing enough. He would often lapse into silence and just sit there smoking. When she asked him what he was thinking about he would say, 'Oh, I really don't know!' Whenever Edna invited friends over for dinner John was the most cordial of hosts. Kind, warm and strangely down-to-earth on such occasions, he would manage to dredge up a smattering of small talk. Despite his struggles with his illness, his moral character never altered. 'He was the most ethical person in this universe,' says Chun, 'and close to a saint.'

On 10 September Edna drove John the 130 miles to Cincinnati for a recital at the Xavier University as part of their annual piano series. She went backstage with him because he seemed unusually nervous that night. He was really quite ill and hadn't rehearsed at all. Before he went on he turned to her and asked if she was ever nervous before she performed. He knew he wasn't ready for the concert and his performance was more than a little ragged. Nancy Malitz of the *Cincinnati Enquirer* took him apart in a review entitled 'Pianist Ogdon, once winner, is out of shape'.

Ogdon wasn't playing like a prizewinning pianist Sunday. He chose prizewinning repertoire [. . .] but he didn't play like a prizewinner. He missed fistfuls of notes, displayed uneven keyboard touch, sloppy pedaling, faulty memory and, what is worse, he seemed to be sitting back and watching these things happen, whether out of carelessness, or apathy, or helplessness one cannot know. But it had the effect of short-circuiting the poetic power of much that he played, of blurring the coloristic and stylistic distinctions among Beethoven and Schubert and Ravel into one surprisingly mediocre muddle.

John had to play to bring in money and sometimes he wasn't well enough to prepare properly. As soon as he got the cheque for the Cincinnati concert he put it in the mail for Richard's school fees. The truth was that he and Brenda were living on the false premise that John was a fully fit earner with a full-time international career.

Brenda had become friendly with James Tocco's wife, Gilan, and was aware that she and James were good friends with the composer Samuel Barber. She called Gilan one morning and told her about the autograph letter from Tchaikovsky to Adolph Brodsky with which John had been presented by the RMCM after his Moscow victory. Then came a startling request: Brenda wanted Gilan to take the letter to Samuel Barber on her next trip to New York, and to ask if he wanted to buy it. Barber lived in a very plush apartment on 5th Avenue; he certainly had money. As soon as the opportunity arose Gilan did as Brenda requested – but the composer wanted nothing to do with the letter. Indeed, the next time he wrote to Gilan he began, 'Dear Gilan, I am typing this letter to you so that you can't sell it!' He never again sent her a handwritten letter.

That October John was scheduled to begin a six-week tour in Europe. On the day of his departure Edna drove him to Indianapolis Airport and put him on an American Airlines flight to Chicago, from where he would catch his connection to Heathrow. At Indianapolis she told the airline staff that John was disabled and needed assistance, but they simply kept asking if he needed a wheelchair. She saw him onto the flight and returned to Lookout Lane. At Chicago's O'Hare Airport

John went to the wrong departure lounge. It so happened that Menahem Pressler was passing through the airport on his way back to Bloomington and saw him sitting there with bowed head. He felt a forlorn feeling just looking at him: John was wearing one black sock and one red one and appeared to be in his own unhappy fog. Pressler asked him if he knew which flight he was catching. 'Yes, yes, I am watching,' replied John, but he had already missed it.

Brenda called Edna the following day to say that John had not arrived in London. Edna called Dr Johnson, who advised her to go up to Chicago to look for John. This she did without delay, and there she found him: sitting in the cocktail lounge, smoking away and apparently unaware that he had missed his flight. He had been there all night and had been robbed of the $400 cash that Brenda had asked him to bring over. Edna eventually put him on a flight to Heathrow, but when he finally arrived he was in a shocking state and his GP, Dr Hudson, sent him straight to the Maudsley. According to the hospital notes he was neglected, dishevelled and disoriented in time. His clothes were dirty, his fingers nicotine-stained and his hair dyed orange. Perplexed and vague, he lacked spontaneity. Eye contact and short-term memory were both poor. He denied any abnormal experiences but was worried about Raimund Herincx talking about him. The doctor's appraisal was wrapped up in the quaint old phrase 'distressed gentleman'. Extraordinarily, John left after just six days to continue his tour in Hungary. His condition on discharge was given as 'unchanged' and the prognosis reaffirmed what had been stated many times in the past: 'continual pressures make recovery unlikely'. He was kept on Haldol and an antidepressant called Imipramine, and given Cogentin to counter muscle spasms, while his nights were laced with Mogadon.

Hungary was a disaster. John played erratically and without control, while his self-care continued to be appalling. His concerts in England were more accomplished but equally wayward. Only in Monte Carlo, where he played the Liszt E-flat Concerto at the opera house, did he recapture his old laurels and even add some fresh leaves. Here he was hailed as 'both virtuoso and poet', one of a dying breed – small consolation perhaps for a tour that had put him back in the shadows.

Wilfred Stiff in London and Harold Shaw in New York were now both urging John to take a year away from the concert platform. The dean of IU was also sensitive to John's failures on the international circuit, which he feared might reflect badly on the university. There had already been a disastrous concert in Dallas earlier that year, when John stopped playing in the middle of the Tchaikovsky G-major concerto and left the stage.

By the time John returned to Bloomington word had already got around that he had spent twenty-four hours at O'Hare Airport. Dean Webb had interviewed Edna Chun about the incident. He was now very concerned about Ogdon's mental state and his inability to interact meaningfully with students. He began attending John's lessons to observe his teaching and found that a student could play for fifteen minutes without John saying anything, and that only the more enterprising students would make the effort to engage him. It was obvious that John's exaggerated reserve was not part of a thought-out pedagogical technique but was a function of his illness. He smoked throughout the lesson, sometimes having two cigarettes on the go at once.

John's obsession with Herincx always seemed to be awakened by failure in his professional life and this juncture was no exception. He endlessly rehearsed past events and conversations, seeking some kind of expiation, and behind all his ruminations was the tyrannical shadow of his father. John could plot revenge in his mind but couldn't reflect on himself; in this he was once again childlike. He was now frequently violent towards Brenda. They could be sitting together having a perfectly normal conversation when he would suddenly lunge at her. Carmen Orrego-Salas saw the bruises and told Brenda, 'You can't go on like this.' It was no longer possible to keep up the façade of normality. Brenda conceded that she was now unable to cope with John on her own and went to see Dean Webb. Dr Johnson, meanwhile, had begun to draw his own conclusions.

Johnson had trained at Washington University in St Louis, where they were using the British nosology to make diagnoses. He was reading texts by Eliot Slater and Martin Roth, both of whom had been at the Maudsley. This nosology, which had a bias toward schizophrenic diagnosis, was the one that those treating Ogdon in the 1970s had inherited. Moreover, when the doctors at the Priory learned of Howard Ogdon's medical history they were swayed into giving John the same diagnosis. The more Johnson learned of John Ogdon's illness, however, the more he believed that the British had misdiagnosed both father and son (though Howard had of course diagnosed himself). Like Howard, John had not become sick until midlife; his was a late-onset condition that was periodic or cyclic in nature. Johnson concluded that John had a bipolar disorder that was paranoid and psychotic in nature. The paranoia and grandiosity that John displayed were classic symptoms of mania. John also had some obsessive-compulsive features to his illness, which periodically fell into abeyance but never left him. His relationship with music was obsessive, as were certain mental patterns of a ritualistic nature, which included his almost totemic relationship with *Moby-Dick* and his tortured friendship with Raimund Herincx. Central to John's psychology, Johnson realized, was his prodigy or genius. This was the whale that swallowed all the other fish. His genius, one could say, was an obsessive-compulsive disorder.

In November 1978 Johnson had John admitted to Bloomington Hospital – because of his recent violence and also because he wanted to keep him under observation while he put him on a new drug, more in line with his fundamental mood disorder. Lithium was still a fairly new treatment; the parameters of its use were still being discovered. It could prove toxic, especially on the kidneys and thyroid glands, so regular blood testing was essential. It could also cause *diabetes insipidus*. Lithium carbonate is a salt that occurs naturally in the blood, while lithium itself is the most widely distributed metallic element in the universe. It has antidepressant properties and helps to regulate the sodium-pump mechanism in the brain cells. If kept within the therapeutic range, its side-effects tend to be mild. However, it can cause tremors and weight gain as well as diminishing energy levels (by giving rise to under-activity of the thyroid) and some patients complain that it makes everything feel grey and flat, neither up nor down. Many creative people dislike it for that reason. On the other hand it eliminates the severe mood swings that cause havoc in the lives of manic depressives. As such, it greatly reduces the risk of suicide. John was given Norpramin as well, a tricyclic antidepressant that helps increase concentrations of serotonin in the brain, but from now on lithium would be the 'background' drug used to depressurize his internal storms.

John remained in Bloomington Hospital for six weeks, leaving now and then to give concerts – for instance a faculty recital he gave with the violinist James Buswell. Other engagements were cancelled or – as in the case of a recital of his own works at the Musical Arts Center – postponed to the following year. Karen Shaw again began writing to Dean Webb, expressing her frustration over John's missed lessons and general 'inaccessibility' and advising that his continuance as a member of the faculty required 'serious examination at the earliest opportunity'. There was further consternation when Brenda stepped in to cover for John while he was in hospital. Shaw, who had not been consulted, was furious and wrote to the dean to condemn the move in the roundest terms. Brenda, she said, was not qualified to teach at IU and 'possessed no credentials which would put her in the same category as a professional and internationally recognized musician'. Besides, Shaw had received no official notice that Mr Ogdon was unable to perform his duties.

John spent Christmas in the hospital but returned home in early January. The effect of the lithium was not instant, and he was still feeling very low and mumbling about Herincx. On 12 January he gave a disastrous performance of the Grieg Concerto with the Edmonton Symphony Orchestra under guest conductor Paul Freeman. '. . . And the music went "clunk"' was the headline John Charles gave his review in the *Edmonton Sunday Sun*. So 'unfortunate' was the performance that Charles sensed that this was more than just an off night. Ogdon's playing was, he said, both harried and perfunctory.

In the second movement Ogdon finished several passages abruptly, catching the conductor off-guard. He began the last movement in staccato fashion which ill suited the music, and punched out the final notes of the last movement's intermezzo section, which should quietly evaporate like morning dew. If Ogdon had been attempting a Lisztian, demonic approach to this warmly lyrical work it might not have worked, but could have been judged on its own terms. But Ogdon didn't seem to be doing anything but trying to get through the evening.

He concluded: 'Grieg's piano concerto never sounded like that before and it is hoped never will again.'

This was too much for Harold Shaw, and John was dropped from his books. He now no longer had a US agent. The fact that he was a full professor at Bloomington probably helped him secure a replacement, but unfortunately he fell into the toils of a profane thirty-three-year-old Italian-American impresario with a Napoleon complex by the name of Joseph Scuro, who had a one-man agency in Manhattan called International Artists. Scuro modelled himself on Sol Hurok, for whom he had once worked, and his principal experience was in the operatic field. He was ill equipped to cater to John's special requirements as an artist and ultimately got him almost no work.

At the end of January 1979 John was scheduled to fly out to Tokyo for a two-week tour of Japan. Michael Johnson was consulted by John's agent and felt unable to say no because he didn't want to 'deprive a destitute man of his income'. So John went, with Brenda, and people walked out of his concerts. There was technical brilliance but his tempi and rhythms were erratic and jarred with the music. Altogether he seemed detached from what he was playing. While in the capital he holed himself up in the Palace Hotel writing wrathful epistles to the singing whale. Towards the end of the tour, however, John's mood showed distinct signs of improvement and his eyes lost their thick, troubled look. From Japan the Ogdons flew to London; Brenda remained there while John went up to Manchester to stay with his sister Ruth, who accompanied him on his concerts in the north and Scotland. When he rejoined Brenda to fly back to Bloomington she was delighted to note that he was almost back to what she remembered as his old, pre-breakdown self. She was daring to believe that lithium was the solution to John's problems after all. In another two months she was convinced that John 'was ready again to reclaim his place on the circuit as one of the world's finest pianists'.

This view of Brenda's encouraged her in another project that had been simmering for a number of years: a biography of John. Now she saw the opportunity of using such a book to jumpstart John's faltering career. She had written a short text of some 20,000 words, a kind of scrapbook with letters, reviews and commentary. While in London she had sent this to Brian Masters, asking for his advice – in particular she wanted to know if he could turn it into a full biography. Masters wrote back declining her request, saying he was 'not musical enough to cope' with such a task. He advised her to find a ghost writer to whom she could talk freely and at length; failing that, she should put the thing into cold storage for a more auspicious time. He wasn't altogether sure that John was 'ready to have himself spread open before the public in this way'. The music world knew that John had been ill but a veil had been drawn over the facts. There was, however, much harmful speculation behind his back, so Brenda's idea of bringing everything out into the open was in many ways valid.

Waiting for John on his return from London was a letter from Dean Webb dated 25 February 1979, in which he wrote 'with deep personal sadness' to inform John that it would not be possible for IU to recommend his continuation as professor of piano beyond his original three-year appointment. In other words, John was being fired. He was permitted to continue teaching through the next academic year, until May 1980, at which point his association with the Indiana University School of Music would officially end. The decision, wrote Webb, was based upon John's 'inability to communicate effectively with his students and to serve in collegial fashion on hearings, committees and juries'. Webb, Upper and Shaw were the three Fates who had pronounced upon John. His dismissal was known to other faculty, but because he otherwise kept it to himself John's students were unaware of the decision and between March and December that year many of them wrote in recommending his reappointment. Even Brenda was kept in the dark for several months. When John did finally show her the letter it came as an almighty shock and she lost all confidence in him. He had always been secretive but this was a breach of trust that struck to the heart of their relationship. As a wife she felt betrayed. Having a high opinion of his own genius, John probably felt deeply insulted by these people giving him the boot. On one level he didn't accept that it had happened and simply put it out of his mind.

John responded well to the lithium and the decline he suffered in 1978 was halted. His moods may not have been subject to the same dramatic swings but the price of his new equilibrium was a subdual. His playing for the rest of 1979 was mixed (there were tours of England, Sweden and Italy) and, although there were moments of great insight and beauty, there was also much that was disconnected and unclear. One of the undoubted highlights was a faculty recital in April composed entirely of his own works (including the sonata for solo flute he had written on Corfu). The concert sparked excited discussion among faculty and students, partly because John through his eccentric presence and devil-may-care brilliance at the keyboard convincingly conjured up for them the lost figure of the virtuoso pianist-composer. There was also a slight whiff of the circus act about John – a giant Telharmonium console in human form – as he squinted through frosted specs at the crowded staves of his own haphazardly annotated scores, most of them written in Biro. This was the scariest page-turning experience of Clipper Erickson's life: John had cut and pasted various sections of the music, so Clipper was required to turn the page at one place for John to play a couple of measures, then turn back two pages for the next section, then forward four pages and so on. John took it all in his stride but Clipper was a nervous wreck by the end. Peter Alexander of the *Herald-Times* was impressed and bewildered in equal measure:

Ogdon's music is difficult to describe. Each piece, each movement is different, and all are filled with a bewildering variety of the most strongly contrasted ideas, mixed together with a whimsical and disconcerting disregard for continuity or apparent logic of organization. One finds the most puzzling contrasts, sudden changes of mood that spring without warning upon the unwary listener.

John was essentially a vertical thinker, hence the 'whimsical and disconcerting regard for continuity'. His non-sequiturs, whether in speech or music, were such only because the scope of his calculations was marvellously instinctive and untrammelled. What appeared chaos to others was a kind of order to him – he could, after all, make complete sense of a Sorabji sonata. Some would say he was too open and receptive for his own good, a result, perhaps, of having remained a part of the preverbal matrix that is usually lost to consciousness when the ego emerges and begins to perceive reality (both ideas and objects) as something exterior. In John's case, remaining an intrinsic part of the matrix – and therefore experiencing reality as essentially interior – may have had something to do with the absence of the father from his earliest years. He remained an unadapted child of the unconscious.

Aware of Brenda's search for a ghost writer, Michel Block, a pianist on the faculty at Bloomington, put her in touch with an English writer by the name of Michael Kerr, who had many friends in the musical world. When they were in London in June 1979 she and John had lunch with Kerr, during which Brenda had explained how she wanted her book to reveal what John had been through as a prelude to declaring that he was better and back to playing at his best. She told him that they'd met 'this marvellous doctor' in the States who had at last found the drug that would keep her husband sane. She pointed at John across the table and said, 'Look at him, he's better. You can see he's better.' John nodded and smiled. He really did seem better. Kerr was generally *au fait* with the lifestyle of the concert pianist and had come face to face with mental illness through the breakdown of a close relative. Nevertheless he wasn't sure he wanted to be involved with this book and asked for time to think about it. Not long afterwards, however, Brenda was on the phone saying, 'Now, about our book. I've arranged a meeting with a publisher ...' His objections sounded feeble and he soon found himself sitting opposite Roger Machell, a senior editor at Hamish Hamilton. Machell asked him to do an outline and things went from there – without really agreeing to it he had been contracted. Brenda would provide the memories and Michael would craft them into a readable text. His own research was kept to a minimum.

When the Schurmanns were in town Brenda took Michael to meet them. It was all very polite but when Brenda left, Gerard and Carolyn told Michael that if he wrote the book from Brenda's perspective he would be the laughing stock of the music world. Despite his initial reservations, Michael thought otherwise. He saw that it was possible to describe the roles – both functional and dysfunctional – that Brenda and John played in each other's lives without demonizing either of them. Moreover, it was his feeling that John wanted the book to be written. At least, he approved of the idea that he was better and wanted to return to playing at the highest level – even if he did seem to be more of a spectator of his life than an active participant.

Michael went out to Bloomington for two weeks that summer and got to observe the Ogdons at close quarters and record hours of interview with Brenda. He also chatted to John but learned little about him in the process. John didn't appear to perceive himself as an individual with a story to tell; his account of his childhood, for instance, never extended beyond a handful of platitudes about how wonderful it had all been. He couldn't volunteer anything for the book but was happy to agree with what was conveyed to him of the emerging story. Michael began to realize that John wasn't as well as Brenda had suggested, and that there was a measure of wishful thinking in her assessment. John was curiously inert and Brenda constantly had to badger him to practise. He would go indoors when ordered to do so but then they would find him lying on his bed smoking or working on his opera. (He was thrilled by contemporary opera during this period in his life, and much inspired by the operatic works of the various composers in the composition department at Bloomington. Among the productions he saw at the Musical Arts Center were John Eaton's *Cry of Clytaemnestra*, Walter Kaufmann's *The Scarlet Letter*, Frederick Fox's *Ambient Shadows* and Bernhard Heiden's *The Darkened City* – all made a 'strongly felt impact' on him.) Michael found Brenda to be a strange mixture of canniness and naiveté, but didn't feel that she was using the book to try to justify herself. Indeed, he was often surprised by what she let him include. She could be brutally honest about herself but was not consistent; her sudden changes of view or angle made it hard for him to orient himself. She didn't place anything substantial off limits, though: it was the small things that caused problems, rather than the broad portrayal of herself. Brenda didn't have good concentration outside music, so Michael had to read the typed-up pages out loud to her. As her ghost he wrote in the first person – and as he read her passages such as, 'I walked out and slammed the door', Brenda would stop him and say, 'No, Michael, I've never slammed a door in my life.'

When sorrows come, they come not single spies. In the autumn of 1979, after twenty years, Ibbs & Tillett dropped John from their books. The company was in considerable turmoil, trying too late to adjust to the new landscape of the classical-music business as shaped by Jasper Parrott, Terry Harrison and others. John, who had once been such a stalwart, was widely perceived as unreliable – even a spent force – and the deep affection he inspired in the British musical establishment was now tempered with wariness and mistrust. If he was being booked in the autumn of 1979 it was at rural venues in Britain and America, with the odd date in Mexico thrown in.

John continued to see Michael Johnson for psychotherapeutic sessions, during which Johnson began to gently excavate what appeared to be the foundations of John's depression: the guilt and buried grief he felt over the death of his mother and his brother Karl. In his therapy Johnson tried to give voice to the non-musical elements of John's life. What was it like to be a father? What was it like to be married? What day-to-day tensions did he have to deal with? By exploring such questions he hoped to unearth the human, as opposed to the prodigal John. He had to put aside his protective and paternal impulses toward John and transform those feelings into something fraternal, so that they related to each other as equals and fellow men in the world. What made it hard was the fact that John always related to Michael from a position of deference and inferiority. Instead of answering his questions John would say, 'What do you think, Michael?' Though he established a measure of trust and connectedness with John, Johnson came to believe that nothing had been resolved during the course of the therapy – which in the end lasted some two years. John was by nature impervious to talk therapy. His inability to reflect on himself, coupled with a monumental passivity, made that kind of healing impossible. It wasn't that he actively resisted it; it was simply alien to his way of being in the world.

As the book on John took shape and prepared to trumpet his recovery to the world, he himself was largely confined to harbour and showed little inclination to practise. He had been bitten by the Szymanowski bug and was eagerly exploring the symbolist music of the Polish composer at the expense of practising the classical repertoire for a forthcoming tour of South Africa. For the first time since he arrived at Bloomington he was on campus for practically the whole semester, but professionally this was too late. With her husband facing unemployment in May and a blank slate of concerts, Brenda made the decision at the beginning of the year to return to England to look for work. One of the first things she did when she arrived in London in March was to consult a divorce lawyer, but the unpleasantness and expense of it all put her off. Nevertheless, she was seriously considering leaving John. John himself didn't express any feelings about her sudden departure, and her perception was that as long as someone was taking care of him he didn't much mind who it was. On the other hand, most people who had observed them together in Bloomington would say that John was lost without Brenda. Andrew Axelrod remembers him as 'a big, fluffy blueberry ball' following Brenda around and doing his best to stay in step. When she stopped, he stopped; when she looked round, he looked round.

Before her departure Brenda had arranged for John to be looked after by a Mormon woman, who did his shopping and cooking, drove him to and from campus – and even tried to convert him to Mormonism! John, however, was not seduced by the Latter Day Saints and was soon relying on students to run errands for him. He was well covered for cigarettes: a small grocery store called Farrer's on the north side of the square in downtown Bloomington would deliver cartons of fags to the Ogstead whenever an emergency call came through. Inevitably John forgot to pay his household bills, so his phone and utilities were cut off. Mortgage payments also went by the way. Michael Johnson made home visits and found John in a sorry state. There was very little furniture in the house and the Tchaikovsky prize was sitting in the middle of the living room floor. John slept on a mattress on the floor of his bedroom, surrounded by overflowing ashtrays. More often than not he'd be lying there, barely able to talk, like a Scandinavian warrior of old lying in the ashes. His teeth, hands, beard and hair were all heavily stained with nicotine. 'Holy smokes!' thought Johnson. 'What am I going to do with this guy?' Eventually he had no option but to hospitalize him. When two of John's students, Michel Kozlovsky and Clipper Erickson, visited him in the ward they found him virtually incoherent. He did, however, ask Michel what he was doing. Kozlovsky, who had been studying the Bartók Second Concerto with John, said that he was diligently practising the piece, whereupon John immediately replied, 'Ooh, one eight four!' (In the second movement there is a semiquaver passage that bears this impossible metronome marking.)

Back at the university John's final semester fizzled out in a haze of illness and confusion. He was more withdrawn and his inner dialogues were interrupting the flow of life, so it was harder than ever for his students to learn from him. Contacts with other faculty members were now minimal and rather awkward, given that he was on his way out and many of them had voted for his departure. Henry Upper and his wife were present at a farewell dinner given by James Buswell of the violin department at a restaurant downtown. They witnessed what Upper describes as 'socially inappropriate' behaviour on John's part, which included eating with his hands and – horror of horrors! – devouring his crayfish tails. John was very keen on vampire movies, and the appearance of Werner Herzog's *Nosferatu the Vampyre* drew him to the cinema several times. To many his interest in the demonic and satanic dimensions of life stood strangely with his own peaceable and gentle nature.

James Tocco received a call from John's estate agent, Hazel Rossi, to say that John was selling his Hamburg Steinway grand – would Tocco be interested in buying it? At Lookout Lane John answered the door in his vest and concert trousers, shirtless and unshod. He was cordial and ushered them into the half-empty living room where the piano stood. Tocco sat down and played a few bars, to get a feel for the instrument, and was struck by how beautiful the tone was. John was asking $6,000: a steal. Tocco would have snapped it up immediately but for the sight of John standing there half-dressed with a forlorn expression on his face. He asked what John would practise on if he sold his Steinway. 'Oh, I don't know,' replied John. Tocco knew there was no way he could buy it – he'd have a guilty conscience for the rest of his life. Within days of his visit the piano had been seized by bailiffs.

Not everything was doom and gloom, however. The university decided to grandfather John's studio so that he could continue to use it for practice and give informal lessons to those of his students still completing their degrees. At the same time a female companion turned up in his life – no one knows from where – and began taking care of him at Lookout Lane. She was a woman of about thirty, very gentle and discreet, with a gift for handling John. Under her influence John resurrected his ever-popular musical soirées. People would drift in, everyone bringing a dish or two so there was a lot to eat, and the house was filled with music and debate once more. There was the odd reminder of just how ill he still was, though. One evening John's former physician, who was in his sixties, turned up with a couple of young Oriental girls. Everyone got to listening to a Chopin Nocturne and when it ended the doctor started criticizing the piece. Suddenly John was out of his chair yelling at the top of his lungs, 'No, no, NO! This is my house! Get out!' The man jumped up, white-faced, looking as if he was about to be shot, and scurried out of the house, followed by his brace of floozies. The explosion had come without warning and many of those present were absolutely terrified. Everyone left very soon afterwards. John's friend Michael Duff was the last to leave. As he was going through the front door, John said, 'A pleasure to have you here, Michael, as always.'

Michael Duff was an amateur musician and composer who had a very successful business making bows for stringed instruments. He and John would get together fairly frequently to play and discuss music. Once he turned the pages for John as he sight-read a set of fiendishly difficult Alkan studies. It actually scared him to see John's eyes on stalks with the sheer effort of concentration, boring into the score like drills. Page after page he played without missing a note, then he'd get up and smoke furiously for five minutes before turning to Michael and saying, 'Shall we do another one?' He loved the thrill and hazard of sight-reading impossible scores: it was the musical equivalent of hotwiring a car. Duff once took a couple of fugues he'd composed to John, who flipped through them for about twenty seconds then sight-read them both. When he was done he looked at Michael and said, 'Was that alright?' Michael was speechless. Tentatively he asked John how he had arrived at his interpretation. 'Oh,' said John. 'In the first one I thought it might be interesting to stress the harmonic changes, and in the other one the cross-rhythms. Have I got them right?' This was way over Michael's head. It had taken John seconds to master complex fugues that meandered their way through a number of different keys.

John was generous to students even after officially leaving the faculty. He invited the composition students of the composer Frederick Fox to his house for dinner, asking them all to bring a piece they'd written. After dinner he sight-read his way through the pile of scores on the piano. Stephen Suber's piece was called *Captain Feckhtenburger of the Space Patrol* and was a reconstruction of music he'd heard in a childhood dream. He was astounded when John played it through note-perfect at about twice the tempo he'd had in mind. To him it was a real honour to hear his music come alive in the hands of such a master.

John had an eventful summer, and for much of it his daughter Annabel, now reading English at the University of California in Santa Barbara, was there to take care of him. He flew to Canada to be on the jury of the Montreal International Competition, which was won by the twenty-one-year-old Ivo Pogorelich, but when he didn't arrive back in Bloomington as scheduled Annabel telephoned Brenda in London. So began the familiar round of calls to the hotel he'd been staying at, the airport he'd been flying out of and the competition administrators – but no one had the least idea where John was. After three or four nervous days Brenda finally received a call from the airport hotel at Montreal. John had been barred from boarding his return flight because his American visa had expired. Consequently, he had holed himself up at the hotel without thinking to let anyone know. He seemed surprised that there had been such a hue and cry over his absence. Instead of taking the necessary steps to renew his visa, however, he flew on to Vancouver, where in typical John fashion he shuffled the burden of repatriation onto his old friend J. J. Johannesen, who ran the Shawnigan Lake Summer School.

John was missing Brenda, and Annabel's presence that summer seemed to sharpen his longing. He was forever trying to contact her in England, though she was often hard to reach. He told her that he was polishing his repertoire in preparation for a full return to the concert platform – not because he was, but because he liked to tell her what he thought she wanted to hear. Now that he was unsalaried the financial strain was particularly acute. Annabel recalls him flying into a rage about a bill he received; there was a dog barking outside and John ran out and began waving his arms and shouting at it. It looked weird to see him flinging his arms about but he was clearly in a good deal of distress. Annabel also observed him writing scores of angry letters to Herincx.

Brenda had found a flat in Cornwall Gardens, off the Gloucester Road, and had put an advertisement for advanced piano pupils in the *Times* under the name 'Mrs John Ogdon'. In addition she resumed her career as a performer, giving solo recitals wherever she could. Her collaboration with Michael Kerr was proceeding apace, though uncertainty over John's recovery and her future with him made it hard to determine the tone and direction of the book. Kerr went grey writing it and at several points was tempted to give up altogether.

John himself had a concert in England in November, and he flew over early, at the end of October, to attend a recital that Brenda was giving in the Brompton Road. No sooner were his feet back on home soil than he announced that he would not be returning to the States. Never mind that all his things were back there: he was fed up of living on his own and could not imagine a future without his wife of twenty years. Brenda, however, was not keen for a reunion. She felt emotionally bruised by the failure of Bloomington, their virtual bankruptcy and John's persistent mental struggles. She no longer wished to live with John Ogdon.

11

HALFWAY HOME

There was another door inside, stranger than the first, but the lacks was gone, and it opened easy.

Sheridan Le Fanu, 'Madame Crowl's Ghost'

John had felt an affinity with the lifestyle in America and its popular culture but he had also missed England. He enjoyed having a local cafe, going to the corner shop to buy his fags, walking to the Odeon to see the latest film and generally living in a close-knit community. There was a certain comfortable familiarity to it all. When he arrived back in England in 1980 things were rather different: he had no money and nowhere to stay. This problem was initially resolved by the mysterious Lady Arthur, a benefactress connected with the Musicians Benevolent Fund, who gave John a room in her house off Kensington High Street. She was very concerned about John's plight and worked hard to get him some cash from the MBF. When the Schurmanns visited John there Lady Arthur took them aside and told them that she'd managed to get £250 for John. Gerard's advice was not to give it to John, because he wouldn't know what to do with it; he suggested that she give the money to Brenda to spend on John's behalf. The next time they met, Lady Arthur told the Schurmanns that she'd done as Gerard recommended – but that Brenda had gone straight out to Harrod's and bought herself a coat. In justification Brenda told Gerard, 'What could I have done with £250, when we owe £30,000?'

After his sojourn at Lady Arthur's, John stayed in a bed and break-fast in SW7 – round the corner from where Brenda was living. He acquired a new agent, Basil Douglas, a well-respected artists' manager of the old school who had run the English Opera Group for Benjamin Britten, though there was no prospect of concert engagements any time soon: these were generally booked up to a year in advance. Douglas had a large house on St George's Terrace in Primrose Hill where he lived with his partner, Martyn C. Webster, and ran his agency with his business associate, Maureen Garnham, who was also resident. Christopher Tennant worked for Basil Douglas Ltd during the Ogdon years and described the house as 'a strange old dogs' home for waifs and strays'. When staff weren't sitting around chatting they performed endless clerical tasks, such as retyping the address book. Those who did have ambitions in the music world soon became impatient with the complete absence of anything business-like.

Basil Douglas himself had known John for a long time – they'd met at the Schurmanns' parties in Finchley. Low-key and quaint, with a gentle, self-deprecating irony to his speech, he had an excellent under-standing of musicians as a breed. In Rob Daniel's fly-on-the-wall documentary about John, *Coming Back*, made in the second half of 1981, there is a charming scene featuring John and Basil in the green room at the Queen Elizabeth Hall. John is preparing to go on stage for a recital in aid of the Mental Health Foundation. We see him dressing himself with improbable agility, pulling his crumpled clothes out of a battered suitcase and negotiating bow tie, cufflinks and even a but-tonhole. Then Basil pops John's balloon by pointing out that the top button of his waistcoat is missing. 'If I was a good agent,' he says, 'I'd have a safety pin, but I don't.' John looks a little confused because he knows he's meant to reassure Basil that he's a good agent, but isn't sure how to do it. 'Oh well,' he mumbles, 'I don't know ... I don't think so. Mmm ... Yes ... Yes.'

Basil Douglas was really the ideal agent for John at this juncture of his life, because he wasn't driven by money and was very sensitive to the fact that John's career needed rebuilding slowly. In an interview with Rob Daniel he said, 'I have to be careful about spacing his engagements because it's important that he should not be subject to undue stress.' Basil encouraged a family atmosphere at St George's Terrace. All the agents worked in the same room together, all had lunch together and all were encouraged to attend concerts given by Basil Douglas artists.

Douglas had quite a varied list. There were a number of harpsi-chordists, including Trevor Pinnock; the harpist Marielle Nordmann; guitarist Julian Bream; violinist Ruggiero Ricci; and the Chilingirian Quartet. He had also cornered the sitarist market, with Ravi Shankar, Vilayat Khan and Nikhil Banerjee – a trio of India's finest – all on his books. He had at one time represented Charles Mackerras and the flautist Jean-Pierre Rampal, and his pianists had included Angus Morrison, Charles Rosen and Yonty Solomon. Nonetheless, by 1980 his list wasn't quite what it had been in his heyday and John found himself a big fish in a small pond.

Douglas's artists often visited the office and sat around talking about the things they wanted to do. John would turn up in a total shambles, his shock of white hair sporting autumnal tints as the dye grew out, looking for all the world like 'an exploding horsehair sofa', as one friendly observer put it. He would ponder aloud about ideas for repertoire, which were largely impractical. 'I think I ought to play Tommy Pitfield's Sonata,' he'd say. 'Such a marvellous composer, and such ... Mmm ... Considered pieces. Yes.' John also visited to prac-tise on Basil's slightly out-of-tune grand piano – though he tended to doodle at the keyboard or go off at tangents rather than getting down to what others considered serious concert repertoire. It was all pretty fitful and distracted, but then so was he: he had large debts in England and America and was virtually homeless.

Though he didn't express it, John was clearly simmering with resentment at having to live in a B&B while Brenda had her own flat just round the corner. Like a faithful old servant or lovesick knight, he was kept at arm's length by la belle dame. They did meet up from time to time – with old friends or with Michael Kerr, who was nearing completion of Brenda's Ogdon biography. On one occasion they met

Michael and his wife at a restaurant in South Kensington near the studio where Brenda had been practising. As the waitress took their order Brenda began querying and criticizing John's choice of food and drink. Suddenly, without warning, he picked up a chair and hurled it across the restaurant, letting out a bull-like roar. This was a truly disturbing incident to witness and the restaurant was immediately cleared of people. It was a reminder of John's inability to negotiate obstacles or deal with conflict: he either obeyed or exploded; there was no middle ground.

For New Year John went up to Manchester to stay with his elder brother Paul, whom he hadn't seen for years. While there he received a call from Brenda requesting a transfer of funds to the States. Following the conversation John was incandescent with rage, shouting obscenities and fulminating against his wife. He was described as being out of control for several hours. Brenda had been in Bloomington to see to the house and put their chattels in storage. While she was out there a faculty lunch was organized for her at the Memorial Union. Both the dean and associate dean were present with their wives, as were James and Gilan Tocco. They all knew that Brenda was writing a memoir and were nervous of the line she might take. Everyone was confining themselves to pleasantries when Gilan Tocco suddenly spoke up: 'Brenda, you're writing a book,' she said. 'You're not going to say naughty things about us here in Bloomington, are you?'

On his return to London John was faced with a bill from his landlady for £300 but had no money to pay. In frustration he smashed one of the windows in his room, lacerating his hand, then phoned his psychiatrist at the Maudsley, David Somekh, and asked to be seen urgently. He called a taxi (for which he also couldn't pay) and was driven to the hospital. On the phone John had told Dr Somekh that he had slipped in his room and hit the window as he fell, but at the Maudsley he confessed that he had broken the glass deliberately. 'I thought it would be a good idea to spend a few days in hospital,' he said. 'I have no money.' John was duly admitted on 20 January and remained there for just over two months. His case notes state that: 'It is the view of his colleagues that he is presently playing well but his earning capacity as a musician is now much less than a few years ago, and he has less motivation to rehearse. His indifference to his appearance has led him now to be viewed as a complete eccentric.'

During his first few days on the ward John was tense and very neglectful of his personal hygiene. He was also abusive and physically threatening to staff and patients if his frequent demands for cigarettes were not met. He denied this behaviour, however, and denied that he had any marital or financial problems. At the end of the month he was presented to Professor Michael Shepherd, who confirmed the manic-depressive diagnosis made by Dr Johnson and added that John was clearly suffering from a personality disorder 'characterized by a dependency on his wife and professional advisers and a refusal to take responsibility for his care, financial affairs or even his appearance'. As the weeks passed John became less withdrawn and less depressed and resumed work on his opera. He also started to play the battered Blüthner piano in the hospital gym. His old friend Keith Cole visited one afternoon; the pair hadn't met for fifteen years and John's first question was, 'Have you written anything lately?' As it happened Cole's rock opera *Ulysses* had just been published and John wanted to know all about it. Then he handed Keith an old manuscript book: the first act of *The King of Alsander*. The score itself was in red, blue and black Biro with the musical notes frequently jostled by memos, phone numbers, shopping lists and train times. John played through a few sections and they got to discussing matters of staging and orchestration. Keith stayed only an hour (apparently because he couldn't stomach any more of John's tar-like coffee) but the men promised to keep in touch. *The King of Alsander* was also read by Luke Rittner of the Association for Business Sponsorship of the Arts and there was a vague plan to have it put on by Kent Opera, though this didn't come to anything. John was tremendously excited by it all, however, comparing the process of shaping the opera to 'swimming out to sea'.

It was as well that John was getting some practice in at the Maudsley, because he had been chosen to replace the German pianist Hans Richter-Haaser in a recital at the Queen Elizabeth Hall on 5 February. It was part of a series of recitals by different pianists of Robert Schumann's major works for solo piano. Suddenly this was being touted as John's official comeback recital. In addition to

Schumann's Symphonic Studies he chose Beethoven's Op. 109 sonata (which he had played at his Wigmore Hall debut in 1959) and a set of three fantasy pieces by Szymanowski, entitled *Masques*. All the pieces John chose are noted for their freedom of form. Of the Symphonic Studies he observed, 'Though they're not the most pianistic pieces in the world, they are very beautiful musically.' There was a good deal of publicity before the concert, which was ramped up when it was discovered that John was living in the Maudsley. The whole thing became quite a circus and it was no surprise that the hall was packed when he eventually stepped out on stage. It was the sort of occasion that only John could conjure up: one in which a huge, confused, wounded, homeless, heavily medicated mess of a man transformed himself into a wondrous flute for the very spirit of music to breathe its magic through. In the Op. 109 Ogdon was commended by William Mann of the *Times* for connecting with Beethoven's serenity and simplicity. Though technical hurdles were rushed, there was no doubting John's complete involvement in the music.

In Schumann's Symphonic Studies, the full-throated passion of romanticism dominated Ogdon's reading, not without attendant hazards. It was indeed a sketchy performance by the standards of this pianist's glorious youthful period, *but powerfully felt and projected*, and with moments of exquisite delicacy [. . .] which reminded us of the brilliant technique and musical imagination that Ogdon has within his power. It is good that he is amongst us again, robust enough to add three encores.

Moura Lympany joined in the standing ovation and afterwards told a newspaper reporter: 'He was absolutely glorious, just as he used to be, and he hasn't lost his wonderful touch.' Still in his tails and clutching a packet of fags, John was interviewed by Jon Snow for BBC2's *Newsnight*. He was euphoric and spoke of how thrilled he was to be playing again. He also mentioned his enthusiasm for Szymanowski ('perhaps the best Polish composer since Chopin') and said he felt that whereas his playing used to be slightly brittle at times he felt he now had command of a fuller sound. His triumph was also reported on

ITN's *News at Ten* and made the front page of the *Guardian*, which John no doubt read over his porridge at the Maudsley the following morning. Was there pause for reflection? One minute he had been in a psychiatric hospital in grey tracksuit bottoms and a grubby sweater, a lost soul among other lost souls, and the next he had been standing in evening dress before London's cultural elite on the stage of the Queen Elizabeth Hall. Then midnight had struck and it was back to a life by the ashes. It would have seemed surreal to most people but John didn't appear to weigh his experiences in a comparative manner. Whatever his life held at that moment seemed natural to him.

Rodney Friend went to see John not long after the concert and found him sitting in a chair among the other broken people. 'Hi, Rod,' he said, as if he'd seen him only yesterday and not seven years before. He was a bit vacant after that and hardly said a word. Rodney felt he had to get John out of there, if only for a couple of hours, so having got the necessary permission he drove him out into the Surrey countryside. When they stopped for tea John ate mountains of strawberry cake but was largely silent; he had lost his ability to switch on that remarkable energy that Rodney remembered so well. Instead Rodney now saw 'this quiet, disconnected person', like a machine that had been unplugged.

While John was in the Maudsley Basil Douglas, together with John's solicitor and psychiatrist, applied to the Court of Protection for an order that would make him a Patient of the Court. This was done with a view to protecting John's finances: knowing the destructive effect of financial worries on John, Basil wanted to relieve him of their burden while at the same time making sure that what money he did earn was put towards providing him with a decent standard of living. He wanted to avoid the sort of reckless squandering that had caused John so many problems in the past. Applications to the Court of Protection are frequently made by family members wishing to protect a mentally ill and financially incompetent relative from exploitation. Like John, the composer Malcolm Arnold suffered from bipolar disorder and was a colossal spendthrift. He was made a Patient of the Court not long before John, following an application made by his daughter (Arnold was unmarried at the time). In John's case the application was not made by his next of kin. Indeed, by the time Brenda learned of it the matter was pretty much rubber-stamped.

The Court order was made on 12 May 1981 and remained in force until John's death. The Official Solicitor was appointed as receiver but the work was done on his behalf by one Graham Preston, a senior case worker at the Court of Protection. Under the order John's signature no longer had legal force; Preston, himself a pianist, now signed all legal and financial documents, including contracts for concerts and other engagements. Monies from John's concerts were paid to Basil Douglas, who would take his commission before forwarding the remainder to the receiver. For monies owed all John's creditors had to apply to the receiver, whose job it was to balance the books and keep John in cigarettes and minicabs. Brenda was naturally unhappy with the arrangement, which deprived her of any say in John's finances and forced her to petition the Court for an allowance out of John's earnings.

Before John was discharged from the Maudsley his old friend Ben Worthington, who was chairman of the trustees of Wimbledon Cheshire Homes, found him a place at one of their halfway houses. With four staff, Gaywood was home to ten or twelve residents recuperating from breakdowns. Most of its residents had been there for years and there was a family atmosphere about the house. John's place at Gaywood was paid for by Ben, and everything was done for him there: his meals were cooked, his laundry was taken care of and, most importantly, he had company − because even if he didn't actively engage with others he still liked to have bustle around him. There were no activities laid on; TV and tea parties were about the extent of the entertainment. The trustees did, however, arrange for a grand piano to be delivered to the junior facility across the road (the front windows had to be removed to get it in), and John would give recitals there for a handful of residents. 'Any requests?' he would ask shyly after giving a no-holds-barred performance of a Scriabin sonata. Just before he arrived at Gaywood he gave a recital at the Wigmore Hall in aid of the Leonard Cheshire Foundation. Alongside the usual fare of Schubert, Grieg, Chopin, Liszt and Scriabin, John took the opportunity to give the first British performance of Stephen Suber's eccentric piece *Captain Feckhtenburger of the Space Patrol*, which he'd first encountered in Bloomington. The performer is required not only to play the keys but also to stamp, blow a whistle and strum the strings! Joan Chissell in the *Times* was full of admiration for John's multitasking. After the concert he stood at the edge of the stage and applauded himself.

It had taken only six years to go from Chester Terrace to Cheshire Home. However, had John not been sent to Gaywood he would most likely have ended up at Cane Hill Asylum in Coulsdon, where Charlie Chaplin's mother once resided and which by the 1980s had become something of a refuge for the abandoned and dispossessed. John, of course, had been using the Maudsley as a halfway house, and would have occasion to do so again. There was much about John in the early 1980s that resembled the middle-aged Brahms, a lifelong bachelor who smoked constantly, wore old patched clothes and observed humble habits. Brahms ate at cheap restaurants and drank litres of coffee at his favourite Vienna tavern, the Red Hedgehog. His lodgings, where he lived and worked surrounded by his precious collection of musical manuscripts, were presided over by his trusty housekeeper, Frau Celestina Truxa. Under different circumstances it is perhaps possible that John could have lived such a life.

John's passion for Szymanowski, the aristocratic novelist and composer who died the year he was born, followed him into the Cheshire Home. In May he sent out letters announcing the formation of a Szymanowski Society and calling an inaugural meeting to be held at Gaywood. In the event only Harold Taylor and Ronald Stevenson turned up (the latter coming all the way from Scotland), so they adjourned to the nearest coffee shop and spent an enjoyable afternoon reminiscing. John seemed quite fired up about the meeting; he would phone Alistair Londonderry in the middle of the night and say, after his customary pause, 'Are you interested in the Szymanowski Society, Alistair?' In June he did a BBC recording of Szymanowski's *Metopes*, Op. 29, and George Enescu's Sonata No. 3. He must have had an 'episode' during the session at Maida Vale because he wrote to his friends Miron and Carola Grindea apologizing for his behaviour. 'I do occasionally get agitated attacks which require some medication,' he told them, 'and I can only hope you were not too upset.' He also said what a good piece he thought the Enescu to be: 'very interesting contrapuntally'.

The media attention John had been getting brought quite a few old friends out of the woodwork – people who hadn't seen him since his original breakdown. Alexander Goehr read that he was in the Maudsley and went to see him there. He found him sitting in a ward. John immediately went off to make a cup of tea but had no sooner put it down than it was taken by a mad woman. The conversation went as it had always done: they talked about composition, and John mentioned that he wanted to get down to the Melville project that had been on his mind since his student days. Goehr felt that John was no crazier than he had been in the flat in Manchester when they rolled him up in a carpet.

John Minchinton, who knew Basil Douglas and had brought John to Edinburgh in 1960, renewed his friendship, too. He and his wife Jessica frequently had John to stay at their house in Dulwich and Minchinton began to accompany John to concerts, doing his best to make sure he practised for them. He would sit with him and talk about the music, lulling him into running things through. Very soon the two were inseparable and attended social events together. They once turned up blind drunk to a tea-party that was being given by the daughter of a very celebrated and very austere piano pedagogue from Eastern Europe and proceeded to roll on the floor together in their paper crowns. They hadn't been invited, but it seems that their hosts were too astonished to evict them. Minchinton's presence as unofficial minder was at least a great boon to Basil Douglas, who had had several nervous moments with John in the early days. John would, say, board a train in London bound for Edinburgh and get off at York and go straight back home, as if he'd suddenly remembered that he'd left the oven on. Once, before a concert in Chichester, a party of dignitaries arranged to meet him at the station but he failed to disembark – Graham Preston set off after the train in his car and managed to catch up with him in Portsmouth. As Basil Douglas admitted in a newspaper interview of the time,

'John can end up at an airport and not be sure where, when or if he is going anywhere. He just sits there reading a book and waiting for a Tannoy announcement.'

In June 1981 came the publication of Brenda's book with Michael Kerr, *Virtuoso*. Large extracts appeared on the front page of the Weekly Review section of the *Sunday Times* under the title 'Madly Gifted', with a picture of John playing the piano at the Maudsley. Reviews were very mixed. Many hailed Brenda's courage and forthrightness in bringing to light the taboo of mental illness; others condemned her for washing her dirty laundry in public. The latter view was taken by the psychiatrist Anthony Storr, who wrote that 'throughout this brutally frank account, there is a preoccupation with money and a tone of self-justification which are bound to make one question Mrs. Ogdon's motives in writing it'. John Robert-Blunn of the *Manchester Evening News* wondered whether John would be able to 'surmount his wife's revelations', adding that 'In my opinion it will take him at least a decade to live this book down'. In a highly coloured review entitled 'The Crucifixion of a Genius' the Irish music critic Fanny Feehan declared that John never really stood a chance of sanity when all the composers he idolized were themselves completely cuckoo. It was surely right for Brenda to be open about John's illness and he himself wrote in the foreword that his duty lay 'in frankness, not concealment' – but the real question, as Storr pointed out, is one of motive: exactly *why* did she write the book?

Clearly it was to tell the world that John had recovered from his breakdown and was back to playing at his best – but there was almost certainly an altruistic slant as well: the wish to share a message of hope with the families of others suffering from mental illness. As she writes in the afterword, 'If John and I could get through, if he could find a way back to health, then there must be hope for almost everyone else.' The most sensitive and probing review was written by Rebecca West in the *Sunday Telegraph*. She felt that many of the Ogdons' problems in London stemmed from the fact that they were innocent northerners, almost characters from one of D. H. Lawrence's early novels, hard-working, set in their ways and with a childlike view of Britain as divided into rich and poor. West felt the Ogdons tried to leap from poor to rich in one go, without taking into account the various gradations in between. Such a move could not possibly be sustained, but additionally the Ogdons never truly felt a part of the world they had conquered. West saw John's breakdown in similar terms, in the sense that it was a wrangle over a charity fee that spurred his mental torments and the question of charity took on a religious significance for him. Music was his currency and he instinctively knew that it was something to be given freely, just as he had been given his talents freely by the Almighty. It was a way of giving love, too, and there had been precious little of that kind of charity in his childhood home. To charge for a charity concert violated the essence of music and the essence of John.

David Wilde, John's friend from his college days and newly appointed professor of piano at the Music Academy in Hanover, was on a plane from Germany back to London when he saw the first instalment of *Virtuoso* in the *Sunday Times*. He was so horrified by what he read that he made up his mind to start a campaign to have it banned. He rang round his musical friends, all of whom agreed to sign his petition – until, that is, he got to Sandy Goehr, who warned him against the demonization of Brenda. 'Could you have coped with John?' he asked. 'I know I couldn't.' That was the end of the petition.

In the summer, while *Virtuoso* was busy dividing opinion in musical London, John flew out to Vancouver with his son Richard, now sixteen, for the Shawnigan Lake Summer School, where he was teaching and performing. John was considered the biggest star there, though the school attracted a decent roster of international artists, including Ruth Laredo and Mitchell Andrews. This was not John's happiest summer. He had no money and very few concerts waiting for him in England, his wife didn't want to see him and he wasn't playing at his best. He was meant to be performing the Brahms Second Concerto but substituted the Rachmaninoff Second at the last moment because he couldn't be bothered to put in the extra effort that the Brahms required. His main preoccupation that summer was plotting a trip down to California to see Annabel, but he didn't have the funds to go. The inner pressures began to build and before long the inability to make the visit had assumed the proportions of a crisis and he exploded. John's eruptions were always very sudden; there were few warning signals – though instead of his usual 'Yes, yes, marvellous' he might say, 'Why do you think that?' On this occasion a taxi didn't turn up on time. John felt thwarted and punched the student who had been assigned to look after him.

Rob Daniel was a student at the National Film School when he read the *Sunday Times* article and had the idea of making a short film about John. He followed him between August 1981 and January 1982, filming him at the Cheshire Home, Basil Douglas's house, the London hotel where Brenda was staying, the flat she subsequently moved to and backstage at various concert venues. Towards the end of August he went to the airport with his small crew to meet John and Richard on their return from Vancouver. When they got back to the Cheshire Home the residents were tucking into a cooked tea. We see John going round the kitchen greeting everyone by name, shaking hands with the men and kissing the women. 'How are you, angel?' he says to a matronly lady who won't let go of his hand. This wasn't done for the cameras; it was John's routine whenever he entered a room. He had clearly been brought up by his mother to observe all the social niceties and rather overdid them in his eagerness to pre-emptively placate everyone. (Eyebrows were raised when he shook hands with every single member of the USSR Symphony Orchestra at a rehearsal in Moscow in 1963.) On this occasion, after doing his rounds, he senses that someone is missing: 'Where's Nicholas?' he suddenly asks, looking puzzled.

Everyone seems delighted to see him. They ask about his trip. 'Oh, it went terribly well,' he says, stirring his tea with a knife. (There is much signalling behind the scenes because of this before someone says, 'Never mind, Ken.') John's shirt is soaked in sweat as he lights a cigarette. With tea cleared away he sits at the empty table smoking and strumming his fingers while a resident called Jim sits by the window playing the guitar and singing 'Trouble in Mind', a blues song by the Jazz pianist Richard Jones. 'Trouble in mind,' he sings. 'I'm so blue, but I won't be blue always . . .' John looks more than mildly peeved that someone else is playing on his film. Later on we see his room upstairs, which is messy and bare bones. He's lying across the unmade bed composing, a pen in one hand and a cigarette burning down in the other. He concentrates intently, wincing strangely with his mouth. There are some copies of *Virtuoso* and a bundle of tapes on the chest of drawers and wedged behind the mirror over the sink is a poster of Brenda, together with some old concert tickets and other scraps of paper.

When Rob Daniel arrived at six thirty one morning he found John outside in apricot pyjama bottoms and a royal-blue dressing gown that was open to the elements. He had waylaid the milkman and was waxing lyrical about Szymanowski's music. 'Yes, yes, that's right,' said the milkman, nodding vigorously and looking a little alarmed. After breakfast that day John was filmed in one of the sitting rooms, smoking and drinking coffee, totally unconscious of the fact that his great Hogarthian belly was hanging out of his dressing gown. Brenda was due to return from the States that morning and he was very tense and wanted to call the airport to page her. She had been conducting a yard sale at Lookout Lane, at which John's fabulous collection of records and scores was sold off together with some beautiful furnishings. The remainder of their chattels were put in storage and the house was sold. Another chapter had closed.

Brenda was now staying at the Durrants Hotel, a smart establishment near Oxford Street. It is painfully clear from the interviews Rob Daniel shot there that John wanted to be living with Brenda again, while she felt that he was better off at the Cheshire Home or the Maudsley, where he could be properly looked after. 'If I attempt to do all that again,' she says, 'I'll be in my grave. I've done it once and lost hundreds of pounds of weight!' John grimaces; in fact both John and Brenda grimace and wince in identical fashion throughout the interview, with sharp intakes of breath. They are like identical twins seen through a distorting mirror, an impression reinforced by the strange claret and white his-and-hers suits they are wearing. The whole thing is wonderfully bizarre. John, it turns out, has a season of forty concerts coming up for 1981–82 and is pleased with all the publicity he seems to be getting. When Brenda asks him if it's true about the forty concerts, he says, 'Yes, I think so. Probably. Lovely. Tremendous.' There's a sudden pause and, as if on cue, they both look up at the walls, which are covered in paintings of nudes. As for the lithium, 'it seems frightfully jolly' as a drug. Brenda tells the interviewer that John has too many gifts for one person and praises his tremendous musical imagination. This releases a volley of squeaks and grunts from nodding-puffing Six-Pie. Perhaps they could live in Hampstead, he ventures, trying to steer Brenda away from the play-grounds of the rich and famous. 'We've never actually found ourselves in Hyde Park, but you never know,' says Brenda in a sudden mad dash for the non-sequitur prize. They both start laughing like children, John's Bunterish guffaws punctuated by Brenda's languid shrieks.

Next up Mr Warts of Burton's Menswear arrives to measure John for a formal concert suit. John sticks his arms out, like a half-hearted child who has been told to pretend to fly, as the diminutive Warts makes a valiant effort to encircle him with his measuring tape. John opts for a lightweight mixture of wool, polyester and mohair ('You like lightweight, don't you, John,' says Brenda). 'Any preference as to how you'd like the trousers to fasten?' asks Mr Warts. 'Button or fly?' John looks ahead deep in thought, as if the question had been 'Beethoven or Brahms?' 'Button, I think,' he replies.

Brenda's bitterness over losing the house in Bloomington surfaces in a subsequent interview. By this time she has left the hotel and is living in a comfortable apartment in Redcliffe Square off the Brompton Road with a grand piano. Against all the odds, John is with her there for a trial period. There follows a surreal dialogue:

Brenda: We've been living apart for a year and a half. I left Bloomington in March 1980 because I was terribly, terribly upset. I was heartbroken. John's job was finished.
John: Meryl Streep's very good in this *French Lieutenant's Woman*.
Brenda: Is she? And I was heartbroken that this lovely home I'd made there was all broken up, and I ran away.
John: Well, you didn't run away.

Brenda: I did run away. Yes, I did. I packed my bags and I told you I was leaving, and I ran away.

John: Are we talking about Rubinstein? I remember him playing the D-minor Brahms in Liverpool.

Brenda: I was very happy on my own for about fourteen or fifteen months, but I found it so hard to find a flat for myself – a woman alone, it's impossible! [...] In addition to which John is very persistent. It's impossible to shake him off!

John: [very animated] Stephen Bishop played to Horowitz once!

Brenda is obviously uncertain about agreeing to have John back again and doesn't want him to get used to the idea. As soon as he says 'I think it's marvellous that we're together again' she begins to stress how temporary it is and how so many of their friends think it's a bad idea for them to be living together again. 'I wouldn't have thought it's any of their business,' says John, sounding hurt. Brenda changes tack and tells him how well he's doing at the Cheshire Home, but John is not to be put off. He's doing well, he insists, because he's back with Brenda.

Brenda: The psychiatrist doesn't seem to think so.

John: Well, he must be a bad psychiatrist.

Brenda: [sensing that John is on the back foot] In fact, he wants you back in the Cheshire Home.

John: [sullenly] Well, he can't force me.

Brenda: No, he can't force it, no. But he seemed to think it provided you with a certain stability that I couldn't provide.

After little over a month with Brenda John was returned to the Cheshire Home.

At this time John tried to earn a bit of extra cash by writing a series of articles entitled 'Thumbnail Sketches of Composers I've Met'. In one of these he tries to portray the influence that composers' families have had on their work. At the end of the article, no doubt thinking of the tattered condition of his own marriage, he writes rather poignantly:

Malcolm Williamson was, I feel, greatly helped and inspired both by his own Australian family, and by his American wife Dolly who vivaciously combined humour, charm and a creatively translucent personality (as was his). Brenda and I spent many a happy afternoon with Malcolm and Dolly and in all these cases the inspirational influence of a well-balanced family life and environment has also been a positive, enlightening and lightening force, helping these composers to find their freest expression.

At one point John writes 'composure' for 'composition' – a telling error that speaks to the importance of composition in balancing his life.

The Queen Elizabeth Hall concert in aid of the Mental Health Foundation comprised performances by John and Grace Kennedy (he played the first half; she sang after the interval). In *Coming Back* we see John coming off stage after his final piece – the solo version of Gershwin's *Rhapsody in Blue* – looking like a kid who's just won the candy trove. 'Lovely, lovely,' he says gleefully, his gaze briefly meeting the camera. Back in the green room he mixes drinks for the guests, who include Rodney Friend and Mrs Gulbenkian. Then Brenda arrives with Michael Kerr and the atmosphere in the room immediately changes. Everyone freezes. She stands bolt upright, holding her programme, and when John spots her he becomes agitated. He's afraid she might suddenly leave, so he comes dancing up to her in front of everyone – and all attention shifts to the centre of the room where Brenda has taken up her station. 'Yes, come and sit down . . . Come and sit down,' John beseeches her. Brenda advances upon him with a headmistress-like glare. 'If you want to sit down, SIT, because nobody else does.' John frowns and takes a couple of steps back; he seems to be pondering something. 'Yes, yes, good,' he mumbles to himself, hand on chin. The room falls silent. Then he comes forward again and says imploringly, 'Yes, I was trying to phone you yesterday . . . I was wondering where you were . . . Yes . . . Yes . .' Brenda declines to offer a response. There are embarrassed smiles among the assembled. When everyone has left we see John sitting alone backstage watching the second half of the programme on the closed-circuit TV. He smokes and nods to himself and applauds the screen when it's over.

The following month, in October, John returned to the orchestral concert platform with a performance of the *Emperor* Concerto with the RPO under Arthur Davison at the Fairfield Halls in Croydon. There was a message in the programme from the RPO welcoming him back and wishing him every success in the future. For the next few years – perhaps even for the rest of his career – John was caught in an endless succession of comebacks, his own Groundhog Day. It was hard to shake off the aura of yesterday's man. Now, with less pressure to practise and more time to compose, he tended to rely excessively on his memory or else play from the score. Generally speaking his musical eccentricities were given freer rein. At recitals he took to introducing the pieces in a quiet, meditative voice before he played them, almost as if he was having a conversation with himself. There were some big venues, of course, but John also had his fair share of hotels, schools and village halls. This didn't disconcert him in the least; he had always enjoyed what he saw as the informal and spontaneous nature of English music-making. When John Minchinton wasn't on hand to make sure he practised for the bigger occasions Graham Preston stepped in. Preston had a set of keys to the Minchintons' flat and would sometimes go over there with John. He once outraged Brenda by sitting down at the piano in Redcliffe Square and playing a Mozart Fantasy in front of John.

In addition to his succession of informal minders John had a warren of boltholes around the country where he could stay for a week or two when the heat in the kitchen got too much for him. There was something of the dethroned emperor about him as he went on progress from place to place, staying with those subjects who still held him in high honour. His hosts' wives would darn and clean his clothes, take his shoes to be repaired and make sure he took his medication. (Indeed, from Vera King in Aberdeen to Jan Cole in Ramsgate, John had a nationwide network of darners.) Wherever he went in public people recognized him. One day, as he walked in a little park near the Maudsley with Brenda's sister an old man approached and begged John to come to his house: it would, he said, be a great privilege to have John Ogdon perform on his piano. John was delighted to accept – and almost as honoured as his host.

One of John's favourite retreats was Elgar House, Keith Cole's Ramsgate home, where he could spend the days in Keith's music room composing and playing at leisure. Together he and Keith enjoyed improvising and working out musical ideas. When they took a break they'd walk around the harbour. Down by the sea John went very quiet. He would worry about Brenda, especially if he couldn't get hold of her on the phone. He tried to call her every day and always talked about her in glowing terms. Keith's wife, Jan, was shocked by the state of John's clothes: everything (including his concert gear) was worn, frayed, grubby, crumpled or scuffed. She bought him some new shirts and had his shoes mended. He never seemed to have any summer clothes, just suits, which weren't ideal wear for the beach. John would clamber up to bed quite early; Keith usually checked on him around eleven, taking the cigarette from his mouth if he'd fallen asleep, wiping the ash from his front and removing his taped-up spectacles. His clothes would be on the floor where he'd dropped them. While he was there John became part of the family. He used to play the piano for Keith's daughter when she was going through the pieces for her violin exam. He was also very friendly with their cat Gus and their tortoise Humphrey, for whom he always had a message at the end of his letters. When he was back in London John used to call Keith most weeks to discuss composition, and would play what he'd written down the phone for him.

John was readmitted to the Maudsley towards the end of April 1982 for having punched a fellow resident of the Cheshire Home. He'd been told to make his bed and keep his room tidy and had lashed out. He resented having to do such things for himself. When interviewed at the Maudsley about the incident he was deeply apologetic, but Gaywood wouldn't take him back. His mental state was deemed normal, so he was admitted as an inpatient on what was termed a 'social admission'. In his case notes it was observed that his problem was an immature and aggressive personality. By now he was back on lithium, together with Norpramin and Mogadon, and was taking Allopurinol for his chronic gout. The Maudsley, in conjunction with Basil Douglas, began looking for another hostel for him.

In his heyday John had shown unstinting hospitality to the

American harmonica player and composer Larry Adler. They had given a concert together at the Queen Elizabeth Hall in 1973; now, nine years later, Adler repaid John's kindness by forking out £1,750 to hire the Festival Hall for a repeat recital. It was a wonderful gesture. Ashkenazy also showed his esteem and affection for John, by giving a concert to raise money for Richard's school-fees fund so that he could keep his place at Eton. Brenda had by this time been appointed to the staff of the music department there, a move that further secured Richard's position. Richard was becoming an accomplished pianist himself and in his final term played the Tchaikovsky First Piano Concerto with the school orchestra under Graham Smallbone. In a letter to Ronald Stevenson John, who attended the concert, wrote that Richard had played the concerto 'really excellently'. He also mentioned that he had won an Exhibition to read Russian and Latin at Lincoln College, Oxford.

John spent seven months at the Maudsley between April and November 1982, but he came and went as he pleased and would go to Basil Douglas's house most days to practise. At the hospital he took part in occupational therapy and learned to cook pizzas and sponge cakes. There was a musical-appreciation group on Mondays and ward meetings every afternoon, at which people could talk about how they were getting on. He and some other convalescents set up a social club called the Agreeables with the aim of keeping in touch after they'd left. For the most part John shuffled peaceably around the ward, smoking and chatting to the other inmates. Visitors were few and far between. Sometimes he would become overactive and out of control but such episodes were relatively rare. The day after concerts Jessica Minchinton would turn up to collect John's clothes. She'd open his suitcase and out would come these enormous stinking-wet garments. She insisted that her husband request funds from the receiver so that John's concert clothes could be professionally laundered and ironed. On Bank Holiday weekends the Maudsley wanted as many people as possible to go home, so John would usually go to the Minchintons'. He'd call Brenda, asking if he could stay with her, but it never seemed possible. Brenda drove the doctors on the ward to distraction with her phone calls. She always had a view on what John ought to be doing and could deliver it in a destructive manner. One of the doctors had the impression that John was hiding from her. Enamoured as he was of the idea of living with Brenda again, John ignored the intolerable strain their relationship placed him under. Brenda admitted to a journalist from the *Daily Mail* that John was now beyond her care and talked of his need for full-time professional monitoring. On the other hand, she was careful to stress that his playing was completely unaffected by his illness. 'I feel the doctors have been wonderful to be able to preserve his genius,' she said.

Rob Daniel's *Coming Back* won Best Documentary at the 1982 Chicago International Film Festival. The last time Rob saw John was early that year when he drove him down to Hastings for a Sunday-afternoon concert. Rob popped his head round the dressing-room door before the recital to find John messing around with his clothes. While they chatted John picked up his glasses, which snapped in two along the bridge. He was going to be sight-reading one of the pieces in the concert so his specs were essential. A roll of Sellotape was located but the stuck-together bridge kept coming apart until Rob passed the tape round the frame several times in addition to fortifying the bridge. Finally John tried on the fully taped glasses and looked in the mirror. Though he bore a striking resemblance to a portly Ziggy Stardust, he just nodded and said, 'Hmm, yes, that'll work,' as they slipped forward again. The volume of tape was such that the glasses stood little chance of staying put. Moreover, John's habit of pushing them up on his nose in recital by the use of a 'third hand' presented an additional challenge. There was only one thing for it. Rob sat him down in front of the mirror and ran the tape around the back of his head to secure the glasses. Now not only did he have weird specs but he also had them taped to his head – and that's how he stepped out on stage. Many in the audience were doubtless there to witness just such a circus.

In late November a place was found for John at Clyde House near the Thames in Twickenham. The house was then part of the Richmond Fellowship, a charity founded by Elly Jansen in 1959, but the following year came under the supervision of the Fellowship

Charitable Foundation (also the brainchild of Jansen), founded with a view to providing long-term support for those who were unlikely to move on to fully independent living but required reduced care. It was an upmarket and enlightened halfway house, where individuals who had suffered a mental breakdown and been hospitalized could share in the daily running of the home in an atmosphere of brother-hood and mutual respect. Residents were encouraged to assess themselves and their fellows in a cooperative and non-judgemental spirit. To this end, regular group meetings were the lifeblood of the community. Residents had the friendly and discreet support of a full-time social worker who attended their gatherings, saw them individually and helped with things like budgeting, catering, repairs and nutrition.

John's fellow residents were well educated and many were from privileged backgrounds. In John's time these included two peers of the realm. One of them, another John, was the Fourth Earl Russell, eldest son of the philosopher Bertrand Russell, who had had a successful career in the United Nations before losing his mind in middle age. (He wrote his maiden speech at Clyde House with the help of Ogdon and one or two other whimsically minded residents, and so outlandish was it that it remains the only speech of modern times to go unrecorded by Hansard.) In February 1983 cameras were allowed in briefly to film John there for BBC's *Nationwide*, and the footage shows him in the kitchen, whisking eggs in his braces, while his well-heeled fellow inmates chat fitfully in the next room. John did his piano prac-tice at the Gothic villa at nearby Strawberry Hill, by permission of the owners, St Mary's College, in a beautiful high-ceilinged room with historical portraits hung on walls of crimson silk. (It would have thrilled him that Horace Walpole, the man who created the fantasy villa, wrote the very first Gothic novel, *The Castle of Otranto*, not far from where he was playing.) As a mark of his gratitude John gave a recital at St Mary's in aid of the Richmond Fellowship.

Raimund Herincx's old friend Howard Greenwood attended the Sunday-morning service at St Mary's one day and found himself unexpectedly face to face with John as the congregation turned to greet their neighbours with the sign of peace. John immediately said,

'Howard' and Howard said, 'John' – though the person before him was desperately changed from the man he'd last seen eight years before. His beard was tobacco-stained and his cardigan had at least a dozen cigarette burns in it – in fact, he looked like a tramp. After the service Howard took John to see where Alexander Pope was buried and they had a cup of coffee together in the church hall. John was very down about his career and said, 'Nobody wants me now. I'm finished.' Howard ran the Richmond Concert Society and offered to arrange a concert for him at St Margaret's Catholic Church. John readily assented, and on the night gave brilliant but undisciplined accounts of *Gaspard de la Nuit*, Schumann's *Carnaval* and Liszt's *Totentanz* for solo piano.

In January 1983 John played the Panufnik Piano Concerto with the BBC Symphony Orchestra with the composer conducting. The performance was recorded at Maida Vale and was broadcast on Radio 3 the following July. (This was the revised version of the concerto; John had also premiered the original work with the CBSO in 1962.) It was only when John failed to turn up for the start of rehearsals that Andrzej Panufnik learned he was living near him and his wife in Twickenham. Having called Basil Douglas and discovered John's whereabouts he asked his wife to pick him up from the hostel, where she found John in the kitchen doing the washing up. It seems he didn't have the money for a taxi but rather than contacting his agent had decided to stay put in the hope that he would be rescued. Camilla Panufnik was appalled to see his pianist's hands doing the dishes! At Maida Vale John didn't appear well prepared – though he did manage to improvise in the style of the composer, creating a sort of fantasia on the concerto. Andrzej Panufnik was quite shocked by the way his work had morphed in John's hands but went ahead anyway: partly out of fondness for the man and partly because he realized that John's general state precluded any kind of tightening up. John was, of course, an acknowledged master of improvising his way out of trouble. Martin Anderson recalls a recital in the mid-eighties at St John's Smith Square in which John was playing Beethoven's Op. 111 sonata, a piece he hadn't really played since he recorded it in 1963. He lost his way in the second movement but made up a section of completely convincing ersatz Beethoven until he remembered the music again. Anyone unfamiliar with the piece would have been unaware that anything was wrong. Not for the first time Ogdon the composer had colluded with Ogdon the pianist. As an encore at a recital at the Royal Naval College in Greenwich that same year John played Ravel's Concerto for the Left Hand, playing the piano part in his left hand and the orchestral part in his right!

It was in early 1983 that John first met the nephew who had been put up for adoption by his sister Ruth in 1948. John Lant, as he now was, had been brought up by a well-to-do, musical family in Edinburgh (Ronald Stevenson was a good friend of theirs) and after St Andrews University had become an osteopath. It wasn't until 1982, when he was thirty-four, that he decided to find out who his birth mother was; he and Ruth were reunited at the end of that year. He subsequently met John through Anne Diamond, who was doing a piece on the pianist for BBC's *Nationwide*. John Lant lived and worked in Cambridge and John was giving a recital at the Guildhall there. Diamond took the opportunity to interview them briefly together after the concert. After that the two men became friends and John Lant's house in Cambridge served as one of John's sanctuaries. He enjoyed visiting and playing the piano for his great-nephews and nieces.

It is interesting that when John came to write his 1-Act Opera, *Busoni and Egon Petri* in 1986, he depicted Petri as the illegitimate son of Busoni. The opening dialogue between the two men, which takes place in Busoni's music study in Berlin in 1903, suggests that beneath the surface platitudes John had thought quite searchingly about his own childhood and youth:

Petri: Ferruccio. Did you have an affair with my mother? Long ago? I have been quite exercised in my mind. Bitter, indeed!
Busoni: [thoughtfully] It was 20 years ago – an incandescent time. We *did strive* to have all interests at heart. At the time, we could see no other way.
Petri: It seemed to produce a strained, strange childhood; of course, one of great beauty and humour.

Busoni: We thought of you, every day; *that* I promise.
Petri: In my adolescence I despaired, I was distressed.
Busoni: [encouragingly] But you came through!
Petri: [optimistically] Yes. Friendship, travelling and seeing the world. These have all helped me.

In addition to fulfilling his concert engagements, writing music and wandering among his boltholes, John continued to do a bit of teaching. At the end of a recital at Leighton House for the Kensington and Chelsea Music Society he was approached by a young man called Mark Latimer, who in his teens had been a professor at the Royal College of Music. Latimer asked John if he could study with him and John readily agreed. They would meet at a funny little studio in St Albans Street off Piccadilly Circus and after lessons repair to a cafe on the corner. Mark didn't smoke at the time but John's tireless example inspired him to take it up. Soon he was travelling everywhere with the great man, turning pages for him and acting as all-round musical batman. For two years he followed him, like the baroquely eloquent Pistol in the train of Sir John – only this Falstaff kept his school of tongues firmly in his belly. Mark gave his services free, for the joy of it, and might have spoken Pistol's quixotic retort when Falstaff refused to lend him money, 'Why, then the world's mine oyster . . .' Mark provided John with another musical shelter in West Hampstead, where he shared a flat with his flute-playing girlfriend. There one day John began jotting something down on a sheet of paper, which after about ten minutes he handed to Mark. He'd written a piece for solo flute. On that same day, John gave Mark a dog-eared copy of J. B. Priestley's *The Good Companions*. Inside he'd written the words, 'Just like us'.

The apparent disinclination of musical London to take advantage of all John had to offer as a teacher is curious. None of the city's prestigious schools offered him a post. Less than a year after he returned to England John had phoned Sir David Willcocks – then director of the Royal College in London – to ask if there were any positions vacant in the foreseeable future, but had been brushed off by a secretary. In a 2007 Radio 3 interview the pianist and music writer Stephen Plaistow said, 'I think it's a great shame that the music business rather failed John in never providing him with a kind of pianist-in-association job or somewhere where he could have been very happy in a workshop environment, talking to students and exploring areas of the repertory with them.'

When he wasn't sleeping on Mark Latimer's sofa John sometimes stayed in Richmond with friends of Mark's, Tony and Anne Enticknap. They had a horrible little Gors & Kallmann upright and one night, after too many bottles of wine, they all tried playing it – Anne, Tony and Mark – but it was no good; it had no tone. Then John sat down at the keys and it was like a different instrument: the quality of sound was somehow transformed. It didn't matter how washed up or godforsaken the instrument; John always brought the most beautiful sound to the piano.

When Brenda moved to a two-bedroom flat in Harcourt Terrace in May 1983 it was reported that John had finally gone back to live with her. However, this was a fabrication to shift attention from John's hostel residency, which led many in the music world to conclude that he was still ill. John himself readily connived in the fiction because it gave life to his dearest wish – to be back with Brenda – and there is evidence that he felt ashamed of not having a home. In late 1982 Brenda had heard the Hitler historian and apologist David Irving talking about his schizophrenic daughter on Radio 4's *In the Psychiatrist's Chair*. She wrote to him, was invited to tea and the two became close friends. Irving was also pally with John and found work for Richard translating Russian. He later turned into a prominent Holocaust denier. A letter from Irving to Brenda on John's death refers to him in almost filial terms. Psychologically, it makes sense that apropos of Brenda's associations with men John was constellated as the son.

So, though he was still at the Richmond hostel, John addressed his letters from 'Flat 9, 65 Harcourt Terrace'. He did sometimes visit Brenda there during the day, and would practise at a nearby studio on the Brompton Road. Having two bedrooms meant that Brenda could now provide Richard with somewhere to stay during the school holidays. The *Mail on Sunday* ran a piece entitled 'Home ... the genius who came in from the cold' and talked of 'the beginning of the

reconstruction of Ogdon's shattered family life'. The article gave
notice of a forthcoming concert at the Richmond Theatre, to be
given by John, Brenda *and* Richard, to include music for two, four and
six hands. All of them played solo pieces, then John and Brenda played
Bizet's *Jeux d'Enfants* suite before the three of them finally sat down *en
famille* at the same piano to play pieces by Rachmaninoff. It was a real
riot and a tight squeeze. The purpose of the concert was to raise the
£4,000 needed to release the family's chattels from storage in Indiana.
'Ogdon family's brilliance shone', announced the *Richmond &
Twickenham Times* the following morning.

John's commitment to new music remained as bright as ever. He was
friends with the composer Christopher Headington, whose house in
Farnham, Surrey, he occasionally visited. Headington had been a
friend of Tolkien, another of John's literary heroes. John premiered his
Ballade-Image at the Farnham Maltings in June 1983 and wrote a piano
piece as a thank you for the composer's hospitality and 'the very real
delight' of his friendship, but only the dedication appears to have survived. He also played Headington's *Toccata* at the same recital. Around
this time he was programming works by other English composers,
such as Benjamin Dale, Arnold Cooke, Alan Rawsthorne, Graham
Whettam, Ronald Stevenson, Philip Cannon, Peter Maxwell Davies,
Alexander Goehr, Robert Elliott, Robert Simpson, George Lloyd
and Arnold Bax. He was also playing works by the modern Italian
composers Sciarrino and Dallapiccola and the Americans Benjamin
Lees and David del Tredici.

John returned to the Proms for the first time in eleven years on
13 September 1983, playing the Liszt E-flat concerto (which he'd
played at his Promenade debut in 1959) with the BBC Scottish
Symphony Orchestra under George Hurst. The concert was broadcast
live on Radio 3. He was greeted by the Promenaders with a long and
heartfelt ovation. There was a feeling in the air that everyone wanted
him to succeed, and he delivered a performance of real excitement.
Christopher Tennant of Basil Douglas Ltd went backstage afterwards
and bumped into orchestra manager Trevor Green; both had tears in
their eyes because it had been a triumph for John and one he

deserved – not by dint of his undoubted virtuosity but because of everything he had endured over the previous decade. People were applauding the man as much as the musician and it was a deeply moving occasion. The following morning Nicholas Kenyon declared that John's prodigious musicianship 'remained untouched – indeed if anything improved'. His playing, he said, was 'taut and lyrical' and his touch 'electric'.

John was not consistent (had he ever been!) and many critics commented on the impetuosity, recklessness even of his playing at this time. As for digital accuracy, Alfred Cortot's observation of Paderewski – that his wrong notes were 'a true commentary on the art of piano playing' – could equally well apply to Ogdon. One unashamedly virtuosic programme that he played many times in the UK that autumn (and took to Italy for a concert at the Teatro Sperimentale in Ancona) consisted of the *Hammerklavier* Sonata and Book 1 of Liszt's Transcendental Studies. After he played it at the Queen Elizabeth Hall, Dominic Gill in a damning review wrote that the few reminders that this was the uncommonly gifted pianist known in the 1960s were 'not powerful enough or frequent enough to sustain the illusion for very long'. The finale of the Hammerklavier, though 'genuinely affecting in its naked intensity', was 'a heart-stopping switchback, alternating terrifying memory-lapses and loss of control with sudden, unpredictable lightning-bolts of impressive command'. As for the Liszt studies, 'fumbled from page to blurred page, as Ogdon fumbled them, his foot glued to the sustaining pedal, they sounded like nothing more than a sequence of embarrassing pianistic gaffes'. Michael White in the *Guardian* seemed to agree and wrote of 'the greatness John Ogdon carries in his heart but can't seem to communicate'. Maybe John was simply communicating something different, which called for an altered kind of listening? His occasional jottings of the time could provide a clue, as well as a message to the critics:

Salt and sugar at a given degree will not dissolve. Tolerance is a fugitive virtue. In any kindergarten tolerance comes naturally. A communicative performance should contain improvisatory elements.

Tolerance, like interpretation, is in flux. TOLERANCE can allow unpredictable scores or unexpected events. Condition attempts to make emotion predictable. How much longer before we acquire the message of tolerance?

It was in the simplicity of his four encores from Bach, Mozart and Busoni that a truer spirit shone forth. 'The great, doubled hulk of Mr. Ogdon', wrote White, 'played them with the open-handed generosity of a child pulling presents from a Christmas stocking.' It was a reminder, perhaps, that John used complexity as a cover, but when he had the courage of his simplicity he achieved a rare level of enchantment.

When 1984 dawned Brenda moved from the rented flat at 65 Harcourt Terrace to another at No. 57 and John finally left the Richmond Fellowship to join her there. This was on the urging of Brenda's mother, who was unhappy at seeing the family split up and thought that being at home would be beneficial to John's state of mind. She sweetened the pill for Brenda by saying that she would look after John if Brenda couldn't cope – and indeed Mrs Lucas's home in Worcester had already been added to the burgeoning list of Ogdonian boltholes. Brenda was not alone in feeling that John's return to full civilian life was premature; those monitoring his welfare at the Fellowship also felt that he wasn't ready to leave the support system of the hostel. It was considered that he was acting from 'pressure rather than conviction' and the matter was raised with him to try to ascertain what his true feelings were.

What is certain is that John was re-entering an arena of financial stress. Brenda was unhappy with the Official Solicitor running his financial affairs. Dependent as she was on John's earnings, there never seemed to be enough money for her and Richard, as John's income was still patchy. She regularly lobbied Graham Preston, as acting receiver, to release more funds but all too often there were none to release. She once went to the Court offices in Chancery Lane to ask for some extra cash for Richard for the school holidays, and took John with her. Graham Preston explained that he had to pay £3,000 to the Inland Revenue and was not at liberty to draw from the small fund he had set aside for emergencies. Brenda was in no mood to back down, however, and decided to sit it out. John, sensing conflict around him, was squirming in his seat, while Mr Preston, who was now officially on his lunch hour, firmly but politely maintained his position. When John began glowering at Brenda, she decided to call it a day. Once out on the street something in John's eyes persuaded her to leg it down to Holborn, where she managed to flag a taxi before he could lay hold of her.

By now John and Brenda had lived separately for the best part of four years: the auspices for their reunion were not good.

12

THE BEAR AND RAGGED STAFF

Gifted with the high perception, I lack the low, enjoying power; damned, most subtly and most malignantly! damned in the midst of Paradise!

Herman Melville, *Moby-Dick*

The youngest of five children, he grew up in a literary household and loved to read from an early age. He was spoilt by his mother and siblings, including his brother Karl. His chain-smoking father was a writer with a nervous disorder who spent much of his time confined to his study. As a boy he loved the piano and began composing at the age of seven. He was sent to grammar school but was a fairly unremarkable student; only his gift for music shone brightly, and in this his early self-belief was unshakeable. Some would say his vision of himself and his artistic mission bordered on the grandiose. From an early age he had a taste for the fantastic and the macabre and was preoccupied with death. His addiction to literature was almost as great as his passion for music.

He had his first depressive episode following the death of the brother nearest to him in age, and from then on became obsessed with the thought of going mad. He married a pianist who was a great admirer of his musical genius. He thought of her and almost everyone else in his life in terms of music, and his career always came first. He was taciturn in company, sitting with bowed head and occasionally muttering to himself. There were brooding silences that made others uncomfortable, and he smoked incessantly. He was an eloquent writer on music, a generous critic and a champion of contemporary music who did much to establish the reputation of fellow musicians and composers. He adopted many masks and often wrote in the third person. As a teacher he was inscrutable and rarely said a word in class. He suffered his first nervous collapse in his mid-thirties, and made several suicide attempts. His wife was the last to discern the extremity of his state. At one point he requested psychiatric help for himself and was institutionalized. His name was Robert Schumann.

It is extraordinary that so many parallels existed in the lives of Schumann and John Ogdon. As mental illness consolidated itself in him, Schumann became more sentimental and – in contrast to his youth – developed a taste for the lowbrow. He was nagged by self-doubt and lapses in concentration, and his linguistic range narrowed. The same was broadly true of Ogdon, for whom everything was now 'marvellous' or 'lovely' or 'wonderful' and who often signed his letters 'Love from Brenda & John'. The size of his handwriting diminished over the course of his life, while in his compositions he turned for inspiration to popular culture, such as TV and radio programmes, and enjoyed making piano transcriptions of songs by Cole Porter, Jerome Kern, George Gershwin and Donald Swann.

Now that he was back living with Brenda John's rate of composition greatly increased. He wrote a Romance for Violin and Cello and a wealth of short piano pieces, including Six Poems after Scriabin and *Wonder-Visions of a Child*, a group of five pieces with the titles 'On a still pond at night', 'Swings', 'The Dolls' House', 'A Surreal Reality' and 'Cornflowers'. He wrote two piano sonatas, *Reminiscences of Scriabin* and *Reminiscences of Busoni*, and began work on a second piano concerto – or 'concertino', as he called it – in five movements (to be played without a pause). In February of 1984 he completed an oratorio entitled *A Voyage to Arcturus*, based on both the 1920 novel by David Lindsay and, as the title-page rather quaintly states, 'biblical quotations'. It is written for soprano, mezzo soprano, tenor and baritone soloists and SATB choir with pianoforte accompaniment. The work is dedicated firstly to fellow Nellie Houseley pupil David Chamberlain and the Mansfield Choral Society and, secondly, 'to Arthur Scargill and Mr. MacGregor in memory of the Miners' Strike'. The title page bears a quotation from his old composition teacher, Thomas Pitfield: 'Take nothing but pictures, leave nothing but footprints, kill nothing but time.'

David Lindsay was a composer as well as a novelist, and *A Voyage to Arcturus* contains a number of discussions about the nature and meaning of music. He took the title of his novel from a work of non-fiction by another David Lindsay, entitled *A Voyage to the Arctic in the Whaler Aurora* (Ogdon and whaling: the two are never far apart). The chapter called 'Swaylone's Island' explores through metaphor the destructive power of music, which in the terrible purity of its beauty can annihilate its hearers. It is as if the instrument (in this case a circular lake named Irontick) draws all feeling out of the performer, leaving nothing for his relationships. From Ogdon's notes and adaptation it is clear that he saw the novel as a religious work, and it is fascinating to see how he has woven in quotations from the Old and New Testaments. He transforms Oceaxe, a wild woman with three eyes and three arms, into Oceania, to whom he then applies the description from Book 12 of Revelation of 'a woman cloth'd with the sun, and the moon under her feet, and upon her head a crown of twelve stars' – only he writes 'seven stars' because he is thinking of the great red dragon with its seven heads, ten horns and *seven* crowns that stands before the woman to devour her child. All John's quotations, whether from the Bible or the novel, are evidently written down from memory; this fact in itself is an astonishing thing, as he ranges from Genesis to the Gospels to Revelation. *Voyage* is a religious book in the deepest sense because it is about the transformation of human consciousness. The new lands through which the hero Maskull journeys give birth to new ideas and new bodily forms and sensations (including new colours, such as 'jale' and 'ulfire'). The book is an adventure in consciousness, and John, with his cumbersome outer form, was the inner adventurer *par excellence*. At his death John left over 200 compositions in all, an astonishing feat for one so handicapped.

John and Brenda were now doing a lot more duet and two-piano concerts together. (This was good for Brenda because the fees could be paid directly to her instead of to the Court.) Some of these bookings came through Basil Douglas and others through Camerata Artists, an agency run by John Humphreys of the Birmingham Music School (now the Birmingham Conservatoire). Humphreys had recruited John at the end of 1983 to perform a concert at the BMS for Ethiopian Famine Relief, and this became the first of many engagements made under the aegis of Camerata. Humphreys was married to John's dear college friend Joan Taylor, and their home in Birmingham became another honoured bolthole and the scene of many a delightful musical soirée – with the two Johns playing pieces for four hands late into the night, accompanied on occasion by the violinist Josef Aronoff. As a memento of such sessions Ogdon wrote a set of three pieces for Humphreys and Aronoff, which Humphreys describes as 'terse, epigrammatic little pieces, not perhaps melodically memorable but well written and idiomatic'.

John would arrive in Birmingham with a black handbag full of pills. During the day he'd accompany Humphreys to the BMS, and while his friend taught John would sit around in the canteen eating cake with the students (one time he ate the whole of someone else's birthday cake). Humphreys did once take him to a singing lesson. He'd simply asked the teacher whether she'd mind being joined by an accompanist, so she was flabbergasted when it was John who came shambling in with cake down his front. John wanted to be (and enjoyed being) a part of whatever was going on. He implored Humphreys and Joan to take him with them on a Saturday morning trip to the DIY store and thought it absolutely wonderful – a real Aladdin's cave – taking naive delight in all the tins of paint and rolls of wallpaper. Of course nothing surpassed his enjoyment of new musical experiences. They took him to the Welsh National Opera to see Martinů's *The Greek Passion* and he made so many appreciative noises during the performance that the man in front turned round and asked him to shut up. It was, John wrote, 'a truly lovely opera'. In the interval people recognized him and came up to shake his hand.

His sojourns at the Humphreys' home were never without incident. Usually he would sleep in late but one morning Humphreys came downstairs to find John already at the kitchen table tucking into breakfast. There was the most extraordinary sound of breaking teeth, so Humphreys said, 'Look, John, what *are* you eating?' 'I hope you don't mind,' he replied meekly, 'but I got myself some cereal. It's delicious and quite unusual really.' Humphreys took a closer look. 'John,' he said, 'those are raw pasta shells!' Even then John somehow felt duty bound to work his way through them. As with music, so with food, he consumed everything. When he was brought the wrong dish in a restaurant (which seemed to happen frequently) it was for him a matter of total indifference.

Experienced pedagogue though Humphreys was, with years of gifted pupils under his belt, he marvelled at John's sight-reading ability and found that it presupposed 'a mighty intellect' – the gift of instantaneously integrating all the disparate musical elements of a piece (rhythmic, melodic, harmonic, stylistic) and making complete sense of them. He'd often treat John like a performing seal when he came to stay, putting up new and difficult pieces for him. 'Come on,' he'd say, 'see if you can work your way out of this one . . .' John was always up for the challenge. 'Oh, super, super!' he'd reply, his whole body infused with energetic glee.

John's abbreviated concert schedule and the fact of there being no piano in the small two-bedroom flat he now shared with Brenda meant that he was practising less. Composition, on the other hand, was unaffected, as John didn't compose at the piano. His lack of income told on his account at the Kensington Music Shop, where he purchased his composition paper and enjoyed looking through scores. He was forever writing to friends such as Ronald Stevenson requesting scores because he'd given his own away. He was also writing pitiful letters to provincial concert organizers, offering recitals for reduced fees.

In May 1984 a sentimental and inaccurate article written by

William Hickey appeared in the diary section of the *Daily Express*, entitled 'Sweet music again for Ogdon and Brenda' and describing the pair as living in renewed marital bliss. 'I'm feeling so much better,' a cheerful John was quoted as saying. 'We're both very happy now.' But not all was cake and blue sky: 'John is still badly in debt and is still unable to afford a piano,' wrote Hickey. Among those who read the piece was the philanthropist and art-lover John Paul Getty Jr, who was in the London Clinic being treated for drug addiction. He knew of Ogdon through their mutual friend Alistair Londonderry and that same day phoned Hickey with a message for the impoverished musician: 'Let him get a piano of his choice and make music. I'll pay – money's no object. He must have what he wants.' The following morning Hickey accompanied Ogdon to the Steinway showrooms off Wigmore Street, where he chose a small concert grand for £18,000 that he declared 'the most magnificent instrument I've ever played'. A further article, also by Hickey, appeared the next day announcing 'Getty's rich gift of music'. 'Money remains a problem,' Hickey noted towards the end. 'The couple share a small Kensington flat with their 19-year-old son Richard. "I don't know where we'll put the piano," said Ogdon, "but we'll manage."' For the time being it was kept at Steinway's and John went over there to practise.

A couple of months after these pieces were published Brenda went to see John's GP, Trevor Hudson, to discuss the possibility of John returning to the Richmond Fellowship. Their life together was already under very great strain and John's current acting receiver (number four) refused to pay their utility bills unless there was sufficient cash in the pot, meaning that gas, electricity and phone were often disconnected. After one particularly fierce row with Brenda he said, 'I'm glad you're not my wife.' As if life wasn't complicated enough, Brenda was now having a passionate affair with John's accountant. He had first approached her at the end of 1983, telling her how unhappy he was in his marriage. Brenda was keener than ever to get John's finances released from Court control – indeed, she had discussed the matter with Dr Hudson, who suggested that she consider forming an independent trust to take over from the Official Solicitor. She possibly imagined that the accountant would be a key ally in the fight ahead.

In September John toured Poland with the BBC Scottish Symphony Orchestra under Jerzy Maksymiuk. It was the first Western orchestra to perform in the country after the end of martial law. John was put under the care of a BBC secretary to make sure he got to concerts on time and didn't set fire to his bedclothes. The British journalists covering the tour found ways to describe his playing that camouflaged its vagueness and overreliance on the sustaining pedal. And yet the fog would lift now and then to reveal performances of mystic vibrancy, extraordinarily fresh and lucid. He was playing the Rachmaninoff Second Concerto, which was written as its composer was coming out of a severe depression. The whole piece is like a dam burst of deeply felt emotion after months of nullity and arid self-doubt. When John played it in the beleaguered city of Gdansk – a performance of magisterial sweep – he managed to open a door into the hearts of its long-oppressed people. 'We have no meat,' said one tearful woman after the concert, 'but we have had this.'

Back in Britain one of John's recital programmes that autumn, which he played at the QEH and elsewhere, comprised the three sonatas of Chopin (the first is rarely, if ever programmed) followed by Liszt's *Dante* Sonata as an encore. So much of John's playing in his final years sounded apocalyptic; in his hands even a boudoir piece like the Chopin G-minor ballade could seem like stars colliding. To adapt a line from *Moby-Dick*, he burst his hot heart's shell upon the keys. His programmes were unrelentingly heroic, one huge rough diamond pressed out after another, much as one imagines Anton Rubinstein to have played in his late forties.

In October 1984 John played the little-known Tchaikovsky G-major concerto, Op. 44, at the Usher Hall with the BBC Scottish. Barely containable in his skimpy-looking tails, his white and yellow tuft bobbing on a crumpled, oddly buttoned waistcoat, he tumbled towards the piano scattering music stands as he went. In place of a piano stool he sat on a small, delicate-looking wooden chair and next to him, identically seated, was his page-turner, a little lady, old and dry, with tiny wire-rim spectacles and a grey bun clinging to the back of her head. It was like an illustration from a fairy tale. The performance was wonderfully adventurous, with large helpings of Ogdon folded seamlessly into the Tchaikovsky. That night John stayed at the Edinburgh home of the secretary of the Godowsky Society and was presented with the ultimate sight-reading challenge, Godowsky's *Passacaglia* (on the opening theme of Schubert's Unfinished Symphony), which Horowitz said you needed six hands to play. Sorabji had been an admirer of the work and John admitted to his host that, although he'd never played it before, he had read through it in the early 1960s. Now, twenty years later, he flipped through it again, put it up on the piano and began to play. When he was halfway down the first page he nodded to his host to turn over, so that he was reading the second page while finishing playing the first, and thereafter remained a page ahead of himself throughout. His host was nonplussed, for John wasn't simply managing the notes: he was producing a meaningful and considered performance of an absolute devil of a work.

John resumed his recording career that October up at Snape Maltings, when he recorded William Alwyn's Fantasy Waltzes and 12 Preludes for the Chandos label. Alwyn and his composer wife, Mary, were there for the sessions, which John found enormously illuminating. He had first been introduced to Alwyn's music back in the late fifties by Denis Matthews and had been impressed with its 'lyrical melodiousness' (Alwyn was a poet as well as a composer). John certainly shared Alwyn's view that 'the very feel of the keys seems to bring renewed life through the fingertips'. Also around this time John met Chris Rice, a young recording engineer who had recently set up his own label, Altarus, dedicated to arcane and neglected piano repertoire. Rice was looking for someone to record Sorabji's *Opus Clavicembalisticum*. He had asked Ronald Stevenson, who declined categorically and told him: 'Ogdon is the man for the job!' John was predictably enthused by the idea of recording this great whale-hunt of a piano symphony, which had been beckoning to him since his student days. He was also given the opportunity to record some other, more accessible works in tandem with it and chose pieces by Busoni, including the *Fantasia Contrappuntistica*. Two weeks' worth of recording sessions was pencilled in for 1985.

After the Brighton bombing in October 1984 John wrote two short pieces, *In Memoriam Sir Anthony Berry* and *Elegie*, and before the year's end he finished *An American Sonata*, dedicated 'to my darling Brenda from John for Christmas 1984'. There were five movements to the piece: 1. 'Kansas Wheatfields'; 2. 'Elegy for Sam Barber'; 3. 'In an Old-time Dance Hall'; 4. 'Romance' (after hearing Ives's *The Alcotts*); and 5. 'Finale (Barn Dance of the Old West)'. It's an accessible and attractive piece – spacious and full of catchy, intricate rhythms – and in its way a tribute to some of the American composers who had most influenced John, in particular Barber, Copland and Ives. In the New Year he started work on a new opera in four acts entitled *A Garland for J. S. Le Fanu*. Le Fanu's work fell into neglect after his death in 1873, and John considered him a seriously underrated writer. For his skilfully woven garland of Le Fanu's work he chose three stories, and wrote the libretto himself. Act I tells the story of 'Madam Crowl's Ghost', Act II 'The Narrative of the Ghost of a Hand' – which is from the novel *The House by the Churchyard*, which influenced Joyce in *Finnegans Wake* – and Acts III and IV 'Carmilla and Laura', a Gothic novella. In the context of John's life, perhaps the most arresting theme that runs through all three stories is the haunting – and in one case death – of a child. One can see the particular appeal of the second story because it concerns a disembodied hand, a plump white hand that taps and knocks on doors and windows with an insistent, sinister beat. John's superbly dextrous and coordinated hands seemed like spirit hands, distant relatives at best of his large, cumbersome body. Vampire stories had always fascinated him and 'Carmilla and Laura' is one of the finest. The vampire, Carmilla, is deeply seductive and scheming; Laura is both her victim and her dearest friend and companion, so that what sucks her blood (or makes a ghost of her) gives her most pleasure. Again, the parallels with Ogdon's genius are obvious. In his notes at the back of the libretto John shows off his knowledge of film and film music. For instance, he states that a film was made of Le Fanu's novel *Uncle Silas* in 1946, starring Jean Simmons and Carleton Hobbs, with music composed by his old friend Alan Rawsthorne. John didn't finish the score until 1988, but in October 1987 Acts I and II were performed at the Civic Theatre in Mansfield with the singers of the East Midlands Music Theatre. It was part staged, with the singers in Victorian costume for 'Madam Crowl's Ghost' and eighteenth-century garb for 'The Ghost of a Hand', and featured one or two props, such as a child's pram. John accompanied the singers on the piano and was full of praise for the performance. At the end of the evening he was presented with a miner's lamp by the chairman of the Mansfield Choral Society.

Meanwhile Brenda sent John's completed opera, *The King of Alsander*, to Lord Harewood, managing director of the English National Opera, and they had a run-through at the Coliseum with John on the piano. The response was very positive. Mark Elder asked him to re-score it for chamber orchestra but John didn't follow this up: he never went back over pieces and so a valuable opportunity was missed. This quirky, attractive opera has yet to be performed.

These musical excursions were deeply congenial to John, but they weren't generating income. Moreover, what he did earn was being cancelled out by agents' fees, court fees, receivership fees, accountants' fees and solicitors' fees. Being a Patient of the Court of Protection was an expensive business. Following discussions with Alistair Londonderry, Getty stepped in once again and made a substantial gift to John through the Court so that he and Brenda could buy an apartment large enough to house the new Steinway. It is doubtful that Getty would have made this further contribution had not John's finances been under the care of the Court. It was at least a guarantee of sorts that his money would be spent for the purpose intended. John's accountant, egged on by Brenda, urged the Court to purchase not one flat but two, so that John and Brenda could live contiguously but separately, thus avoiding the tensions that were making life intractable when they occupied the same space. He had in mind a recently refurbished pair of flats, one in the basement and one on the ground floor of 18 Harcourt Terrace. The reasons he gave the Court for the purchase were two-fold. Firstly, a single flat would not be large enough to house both the Ogdons and John's new Steinway; secondly, by becoming substantial property owners they could guard against the inevitable fall in earnings that would accompany a future relapse in John's mental health. Of course, purchasing two flats instead of one would require a six-figure mortgage on the second property, but the Court was assured that this could be arranged. The two-flat solution won out in the end, in part because Getty offered an interest-free loan to help purchase the second flat.

John, one feels, played no part at all in the decisions that were being made to protect and sustain him; he was busy adding another 25 Preludes for piano to his corpus, this time 'dedicated with sincere gratitude to John Paul Getty'. John and Brenda's move into the two flats (John on the ground floor and Brenda in the basement) created a study in contrasting styles. Brenda lived plushly, with crystal chandeliers, opulent bathroom fittings, an attractive courtyard garden and John's Steinway; John, on the other hand, lived like a student in sparse surroundings, with no piano and no curtains, a battered old sofa, a coffee table, an ancient flickering wood-framed TV and his big green armchair. What books and scores he had sat in piles on the floor. Brenda's justification for taking charge of the piano was that John would go rampaging round his flat at night, making her ceiling shake, and could well have destroyed the instrument in one of his rages. It was true that he relapsed into chaotic behaviour when he didn't take his drugs, and he had already smashed a gorgeous Danish vase she bought in Copenhagen. Brenda's usurpation of the piano caused considerable anger among John's friends, especially when it became known that for the most part his use of it was limited to rehearsing duets with her.

Not long after the move John returned to Poland with the BBC Scottish. As well as his orchestral appearances he gave a recital of modern music at the Warsaw Festival, playing pieces by Busoni, Szymanowski, Boulez, Tippett, Stockhausen, Panufnik, Benjamin Lees and another sequence of twenty-five short preludes that he had written in 1983, entitled *A Record of Voyages with New Music Manchester*, dedicated to Peter Maxwell Davies. When he got back John had twelve concerts in October, more than he'd had in a very long time. Six of them were duo recitals with Brenda at music clubs in Newark, Plymouth, St Andrews, Gordonstoun, Glasgow and Hendon. Then he was off to northern Italy to give some recitals and take part in a Busoni symposium in Florence, where he gave a talk entitled 'Busoni and Schoenberg'. So flawless was his memory for matters musical that John did little or no research for such tasks. All he had to do was order his thoughts and jot down a few notes and he was set. The delivery would be seamless.

In the second half of 1985 John completed two of the three recording sessions for *Opus Clavicembalisticum* at the church of St Silas the Martyr in Kentish Town, a project that finally had the blessing of the composer himself. This was largely achieved through the auspices of the composer Alistair Hinton, one of the few with a direct line to Sorabji. Hinton attended all the recording sessions and his knowledge of Sorabji's score proved tremendously useful in navigating what was a musical minefield. They worked from the manuscript copy at Cape Town University (brought by Hinton) in tandem with a copy of Sorabji's publication proofs. Because Sorabji had no patience for proofreading he had corrected many things that weren't errors, thus making an already confusing score even less decipherable. John, with his uncanny ability to see both the wood and every single tree in it, was unfazed by the luxuriant, un-pruned tropical forest that stood before him. The misprints and mistakes were all part of the complex weave. One whole stave had the music printed with a treble clef when it should have been a bass clef; everyone present thought it sounded weird when John played the passage as printed. A look back at Hinton's copy of the manuscript score revealed a discrepancy of line change between the printed publication and Sorabji's original manuscript, whereby the bass clef had been omitted. As soon as this was rectified, despite the change of register and notes, John was able to play the passage perfectly – without even looking at it, let alone practising it. The fact that Sorabji didn't put many markings in his scores freed the performer to feel his way more deeply into the music.

Chris Rice, who at the time was only twenty-two, proved himself to be a highly skilful and sensitive producer. He seemed to know when to push John and when to hold back, and just what to say to get the best out of him. You had to read between the lines to understand what John wanted, because he never made it clear. Different shades of silence had to be interpreted. His impatience with repeating a passage might be shown in a smouldering look or a simple refusal to communicate. He'd never admit to completely screwing up a section; instead he'd fall silent for a while, then say, 'I could play it again, if you like.' On the whole there was no way of editing for accuracy between different takes, as John never played the same passage in the same way. Chris simply had to pick the version that best embodied the spirit of what John was after.

If one imagines *OC* as a sprawling Gothic cathedral, then John was constantly looking for new ways to understand the architectural lines or illuminate details of the carving. 'The way the fugues get progressively longer has a connection with building,' he commented after the sessions were over. He was happy to see where his spontaneous impulses at the piano took him – and if that meant changing something in the score, so be it. It might also mean drawing back again, as he would sometimes set off at a tempo that proved impossible to sustain. Generally speaking if something was musically satisfying he wasn't concerned about getting the notes exactly right. Chris never imposed his own ideas of how the music should sound; instead he discerned the path on which John was embarked and did his best to help him along it. John would always write Chris's suggestions faithfully on the score. Once, when Chris said 'This sounds as if it could do with a bit more aggro', John wrote in the margin, 'more aggro'.

For all the sessions John played on a Bösendorfer Imperial, with ninety-seven keys instead of the usual eighty-eight. His energy and concentration never flagged. Richard Black, who had the unenviable task of turning pages for John, marvelled at his sheer energy:

The fourth fugue and coda stretta comprise some 50 minutes of music, fantastically difficult. At the third set of sessions (in March 1986), he played this section straight through four times in succession, with hardly a pause. The listeners appeared to have reached exhaustion; Ogdon might just have played a Clementi Sonatina. Never have I felt so strongly that the piano had become a part of the pianist.

John's weight appeared to fluctuate a great deal over the days, as if the moon exercised an inordinate influence over him. At his biggest his suit jacket would be extremely tight but this didn't impede his movement. It helped that he was naturally still at the piano and never raised his arms for extra force; keeping his hands close to the keyboard at all times, he knew exactly how much weight to apply and where. Alistair Hinton noticed that John would typically end the day a lot more energetically than he began it, and this may have had as much to do with the peculiar Oriental nature of the music as with the sweating out of drugs.

As was the case with most people who entered John's life, Chris Rice ended up as an unofficial minder, driving him around and generally keeping him company. Being a bit of a handyman, he even put up a small breakfast bar in the kitchen at Harcourt Terrace, which Six-Pie promptly leaned on and broke. (Chris returned another day to reinforce it.) Someone else taking John around at this time was the writer William (Bill) Humble. Brenda's book *Virtuoso* had been optioned a couple of years earlier and Humble had begun work on the screenplay. At their first meeting, at Brenda's flat, John was hovering in the passageway. 'It's a great honour to meet you, Mr Humble,' he said, emerging from the shadows. 'I saw your *Churchill: The Wilderness Years* and much admired it.' They got to talking about his current research on *Virtuoso*, but about ten minutes into the conversation John said again, 'I saw your *Churchill: The Wilderness Years* and much admired it.' He said it three times in all. He had learned certain social formulae but couldn't judge what was appropriate and what wasn't; consequently he could overdo the compliments. When Bill offered him a little cigar, John took it, put it behind his ear and lit up a cigarette.

Bill found the most interesting thing about John to be his relationship with Brenda, whom he described as 'a coiled spring'. He felt that the two-flat arrangement was like a sitcom, only the humour was black. Brenda used to go up onto the street with a tray to take John his meals. One day she phoned Bill in quite a state – apparently because John had just torn the telephone out of the wall, and thrown it at her. She had run down the street with him pounding after her and stopped a car to get help. John was mild-mannered for the vast majority of time but then something would change in the eyes. Brenda, though, rarely heeded the warning signals. In company she would bait him, almost as if she craved that moment of danger. For the most part, he would submit like a chastised child. 'John, your flies are undone!' she'd shout across the table. 'Oh, sorry, Brenda,' he'd reply with bovine docility. Or, 'You're impossible, John, aren't you?' to which the response would be, 'Oh, yes. Yes, I am.' She was easily irritated by the adulation accorded him after concerts, when he'd do his big-bland-cuddly-bear act, and her aggression had a jealous edge to it. In a way she was Salieri to John's Mozart, only they happened to be married.

John gave a number of solo and duo concerts in Moscow, Kiev and Leningrad in January 1986. The following month he stepped in at the last minute for the Czech-American pianist Rudolf Firkušný at the Brahms Festival in Gothenburg, a concert recorded by Swedish Radio. The conductor was his old friend James Loughran. At rehearsal John looked up and said, 'Which concerto is it, Jimmy? One or two?' After Sweden he was back in Birmingham for a lunchtime recital at the Birmingham and Midland Institute. The morning of the concert John Humphreys showed him a sonata that one of his students, Colin Decio, had recently composed. John was so impressed with it that when he was introduced to the young composer he said, 'This is wonderful, Colin. Can I play it at my recital today? It would be an honour for me to play it.' So he and Colin sat down together and went through it. The sonata had been written following the failure of Colin's marriage and a great deal of raw feeling had gone into it. He mentioned this to John, who winced sympathetically. John's programme was rather large that day and it was ultimately decided that he should play only the waltz-like final movement of Colin's piece. According to Decio, John played it 'with unbelievable sensitivity and consummate skill', and called him up onto the stage to take a bow. Whenever John saw Colin after that he would mumble, 'Wonderful sonata! Wonderful sonata!' It took Colin a while to realize what a gift John gave him that day.

One of the Busoni pieces John had recorded for Altarus the previous year was the *Fantasia Contrappuntistica*, an extended fantasy on the final, incomplete fugue from J. S. Bach's *Art of the Fugue*. It is deeply mysterious music and John was very much at home in its fluid, geo-metric depths. Where others might see a kind of anarchy, John divined structure. He had always been struck by Louis Kentner's statement that 'architecture is frozen music', which he saw as a useful base for com-position. In a commentary on the *Fantasia Contrappuntistica* he noted that its 'accumulating grandeurs' were inspired by the Palace of the Popes in Avignon. John formulated a number of new ideas about the piece while playing it in concert. After a performance at the Queen Elizabeth Hall, described by Chris Rice as 'absolutely devastating', he expressed a strong desire to record it again. It was a darker, scarier account than the first with some interesting textual variations. He gave the B–A–C–H fugue, for instance, a more austere, uncluttered texture. Of the first recording, Calum MacDonald writing in *Tempo* doubted whether Ogdon had ever made a greater recording. 'He unleashes the *Fantasia*'s volcanic, intimidating power,' he wrote, 'but also discovers an almost sensuous sweetness in some of the quieter passages. It is an awe-some display of pianism.' John's recordings of Busoni, Dohnanyi, Ogdon, Liszt and Sorabji for Altarus in 1985 and 1986 prove that, given the right conditions and level of sympathy, he could still give performances to rival his best from the 1960s and early 1970s.

John gave fifty-five concerts in 1986, but only thirty-nine of those were solo engagements; the remaining sixteen (almost 30 per cent) were duo concerts with Brenda. Although he enjoyed travelling with her, there was considerable tension in rehearsals and the underlying aggression he felt would often surface. Brenda made the musical decisions, and John was relegated to the bottom of the piano while she performed heroics in the upper registers. In her search for per-fection she frequently stopped the playing to ask for a particular passage to be repeated as John sat there fuming. His minder would sometimes intervene, suggesting coffee or cigarette breaks to calm things down.

Even solo concerts could be burdensome to him at this stage of his career, especially if he had to travel alone. He would find ways to wriggle out of his commitments, which usually meant disappearing. Having repeatedly absconded, he was eventually traced to a second-hand bookstore in Piccadilly that had become a favourite concert-day hideout; he liked to 'get his fingers grubby' leafing through old paperback novels. Once, when he was meant to be giving a recital in Birmingham, he turned up in Richard's rooms at Oxford, much to his son's astonishment. Richard phoned Brenda, who told him to put John back on the train to Birmingham. This he did – but John got off at the next stop, crossed over to the other side of the track and returned to London. It transpired that he'd been nervous at the thought of playing Mozart's Sonata in A minor, a work of veiled despair written at the time the composer's mother was dying.

In addition to the Altarus sessions, John recorded two CDs for John Boyden on the Pickwick label. These were pieces by Chopin, including the third Sonata in B minor, and the classic Beethoven trinity of *Moonlight*, *Pathétique* and *Appassionata*. Jeremy Siepmann found himself greatly moved by the Beethoven, which emerged 'as *experienced* rather than performed' and reminded him of descriptions of Beethoven's own improvisations. In Ogdon's hands 'the tragic stature' of the *Pathétique* had never seemed clearer to him, while his account of the *Appassionata*, though outwardly conventional, managed to be 'among the most involving and exhausting' he had ever heard. John Boyden, like John Ogdon, believed in performance over digital accuracy, even in the recording studio, and egged him on to follow his instincts. John always called him 'Sir' and took his suggestions as absolute instructions. When he said to him of a certain passage in the *Appassionata*, 'this has got to come out of nowhere', John seemed deeply impressed. Later on, when they were discussing another passage, John Boyden noticed that Ogdon had written on the score in pencil, 'come out of nowhere'. At the time of the session John had just been to see Harrison Birtwistle's new opera, *The Mask of Orpheus*, at the Coliseum, and he and Boyden got to chatting about it:

Ogdon: I went to see Harry's opera last night.
Boyden: Really. What was it like?
Ogdon: Well, the first forty minutes were wonderful.
Boyden: What happened after that?
Ogdon: I don't know. I left.

John found it excruciating to say he didn't like something.

Aside from his production outfit Boyden had set up Finesplice, the first company in Europe dedicated to digital post-production. It was located in Staines, near Heathrow airport, and it was here that he brought John and Brenda to listen to the master of the Beethoven. John sat immobile and absorbed, working his way through a packet of mint humbugs, which he kept pressing upon the other John. Brenda was bowled over by the *Appassionata* and exclaimed, 'How does *that* [pointing to the speakers] come out of *that* [pointing to John]?' Of the final movement Boyden said, 'It was like some crazy, raging monster and brought the work to a colossal stature. It wasn't perfect, but it was awesome.'

John gave one of his epic programmes at Shrewsbury School in May, playing both books of the Brahms Paganini Variations in the first half and the *Appassionata* and Liszt B-minor sonatas in the second. John Humphreys and his wife drove John and Brenda to Shrewsbury, with John smoking the entire journey and Brenda demanding that they stop the car and John throw his cigarette out of the window. He would obey meekly, but then light up again fifty yards down the road, and so it went on. Shrewsbury's head of music, Andrew Auster, was there to greet them and took them to the Lion Hotel, where Brenda had requested separate rooms. At the recital John shuffled onstage, took a bow, sat down, looked down, thought a while, stood up again and disappeared into the wings. Auster ran backstage to ask what the problem was. John had noticed that his flies were undone and needed some help doing them up. Brenda, sitting with the Humphreys, said, 'Oh God, hopeless! Can't take him anywhere.' John's clothes were always playing tricks on him. At another comeback recital, at the Birmingham School of Music, he somehow managed to get stuck behind the piano as he got onto the stage and ripped his waistcoat down the middle, so that when he bowed to the audience it swung apart like two flags. Unfortunately for the waistcoat he gave six encores that evening, so there was much flapping amidships. After the sixth John Humphreys said to him, 'You're going to have to stop playing or people are going to miss their last bus home.' John was terribly apologetic.

*

About a month after Shrewsbury John and Brenda played a duo concert in Carlisle, arranged by John Humphreys. As their return train
drew in to Euston Station John was fast asleep, so Brenda leaned over
and shook him: 'Come on, wake up, go and get the cases!' John rose
obediently, if a little heavily, to his feet but then suddenly swung
round and hit Brenda hard in the side, sending her reeling down the
carriage. She fell backwards and was picked up by two other passengers. Minutes later, as they walked down the platform and drew level
with the engine, John made another lunge at her – as if to push her
under the train. This time she avoided contact. There were many witnesses to the incident; indeed, many passengers had recognized John
as the train left Carlisle and had requested autographs. Brenda wrote
to the Court with details of the attack, though she didn't press charges
on this occasion. However, with plans already in place to find a travelling companion for John, she did recommend that this should be a
fully trained mental nurse – preferably a strongly built male. She also
asked the Court to pay her doctor's and physiotherapist's bills. Shortly
after the incident John Humphreys visited Brenda at Harcourt Terrace.
No sooner was he through the door than she removed her blouse to
show him the black bruises on her arm and side. Now, for the first
time, Humphreys realized what a terrible violence there was in John,
waiting to be unleashed.

Earlier that month Brenda had tried to book John into Dulas
Court, the Musicians Benevolent Fund home in Hereford. She
wished to have a complete break from him, but in the event he
ended up staying with her mother and sister in Worcestershire. John
was incapable of looking after himself and, despite the two-flat
arrangement, Brenda began to feel that she was running her own private mental hospital at Harcourt Terrace. She was understandably
fearful of John's violent outbursts and had iron bars fitted on the front
window of her basement flat, a steel plate on her front door and a
panic button by her bed that connected to the local police station.

In April 1986 John's accountant was appointed as acting receiver
number six (there would be eight in eight years). He undertook
the role against his better judgement, knowing that it would be a

time-consuming and thankless task – and his on-going affair with the
wife of the man he was serving complicated matters to a nightmarish
degree. Around this time it was decided that John would switch from
Basil Douglas Ltd (which was winding down) to Kaye Artists, a management company run by Nina Kaye. The original introduction had
been made by John's friend Barry Tuckwell, himself a Kaye artist, and
Brenda wholeheartedly advocated the move. It was an uncontroversial
decision approved by the Court: Nina was very well thought of in the
business and had a reputation as a tough negotiator who got good
money for her artists. Her roster of musicians included Anne-Sophie
Mutter, Julian Lloyd-Webber, Evelyn Glennie, Rosalind Plowright
and Christopher Warren-Green. Once she'd written more than 400
letters to promoters and concert agencies on John's behalf, it became
clear to Nina that there was considerable nervousness about engaging
him because of the numerous missed concerts of the previous year. She
realized that the only way to rebuild trust in John was to hire a full-time
minder to travel with him to venues, make sure that he was properly
fed, had the right music, didn't wander off and got home safely afterwards. She was also conscious of the fact that he should be doing a
maximum of forty to fifty concerts a year. All in all he required very
careful handling, but with the right management it would be possible
to structure a lovely career for him again because there was still enormous warmth towards him among the music-going public.

For the role of minder Nina's brother-in-law Malcolm Singer, head
of music at the Menuhin School, recommended Virginia Renshaw,
the ex-wife of the school's former principal. Virginia was a musician
of around forty years old who had studied cello at the Royal Academy
and was delighted to accept the job. Brenda, meanwhile, was dead
against the idea – though her objections to the Court were couched
in financial terms. She said that John could not afford to pay £8,000
per annum (excluding travel) to Mrs Renshaw; after all, Chris Rice of
Altarus had offered his services for free. Brenda wrote to advise Nina
Kaye that John had already invited Chris to be his travelling companion. On the heels of this John wrote one of his sad, coerced-seeming
letters, affirming Brenda's position and denying that he'd received
written confirmation from his accountant of Renshaw's appointment:

'Please do not harass me on this subject, otherwise I will be upset, and unable to function – thus my playing will suffer.' A couple of months later Brenda wrote to the Court, signing herself 'John Ogdon' and demanding a hearing so that he could appeal against the accountant's decision to appoint Mrs Renshaw. Another letter to the Court, this time signed by John, asked for his own monthly allowance to be increased from £60 to £100, for Richard to receive £160 per month while studying at Oxford and for Brenda to receive £800 per month for a trial period of six months. Meanwhile John's accountant proposed to the Court that an overdraft facility of £10,000 to £15,000 be arranged with the bank, secured by means of a charge over one or both of the Harcourt Terrace flats, so that any short-term increase in expenditure could be covered.

The pressure of being caught in the middle of this financial wrangling was too much for John and he suffered a relapse. There were incidents of self-harming and he ended up in hospital. It's a wonder that Brenda didn't join him there, given the tensions and complexities of her life at the time. Now that Virginia had (as she thought) been appointed over her head, Brenda also turned against the idea of Nina handling John's career and began to court John Boyden to take over John's management through his company, Manygate. In September 1986 she threw a lavish fiftieth-birthday party for Boyden. A champagne reception at Harcourt Terrace, at which John played 'Happy Birthday' on the Steinway, was followed by dinner in a private room at a restaurant in the Hollywood Road. There was even a cake in the shape of an old-fashioned gramophone, with a big horn made of icing. Boyden knew almost no one there but did recognize John's accountant, who was blanching at the extravagance he was witnessing. 'Brenda,' says Boyden, 'was a fantastic organizer and manipulator in her determination to achieve what she wanted to achieve. She was like an arrow: straight.'

The following month John's accountant wrote a furious letter to Brenda and John, berating them for their ingratitude and continuing profligacy:

I am constantly being telephoned by your creditors seeking the settlement of their outstanding accounts. I very much resent having to fend these people off when, after all, they have the right to be paid. I feel your action in incurring debts, in taking services, in purchasing items for which you know you cannot pay is all totally wrong. I have never ever come across such needless extravagance before and in my accountancy practice we have over 600 clients, many of whom are in the acting and music professions where it may be said their earnings tend to fluctuate from feast to famine. None of these clients would deliberately spend money they do not have, relying on others to fend off their creditors. You have no right to behave with such wanton disregard for the financial consequences you put in motion.

He also threatened legal action for slander in the event that they ever again malign him and his accountancy practice, and made clear his impatience with complaints about Virginia Renshaw and Nina Kaye. The letter concludes with a warning that if he were to resign as acting receiver the consequences would likely be a new financial policy implemented by the Court to settle all outstanding debts – which would mean the sale of one of the Ogdons' flats. It is extraordinary to consider that the man writing this letter was in a compulsive sexual relationship with the object of his fury. Brenda retaliated by advising the Court that any proposal to sell one of the flats would lead her to take out an injunction against John Ogdon followed swiftly by an action for divorce.

When the Ogdons had gone to see the movie *Amadeus* on his forty-eighth birthday, John had written a short instrumental sonata entitled *Character Sketches of Mozart's Friends & Acquaintances inspired by Milos Forman's film* Amadeus, which he then transcribed as a piano duet for him and Brenda. He also worked on a similar piece for four hands, which used quotations from all four Rachmaninoff Piano Concertos and his *Rhapsody on a Theme of Paganini*. Nina Kaye, however, did not book duo concerts for Brenda and John as she didn't want to deal with Brenda. These bookings now came in through Brenda's agent, Terry Slasberg, and it seems there were quite a few in the Channel Islands and the Isle of Man, where the Court order was not in force.

The switch to Nina Kaye represented a significant break with the past for John. Hers was a more modern and professional kind of representation, and her insistence on a full-time minder marked a turning point in his relationship with Brenda. Apart from a few spells when those looking after him were away or had resigned, his care was no longer in Brenda's hands. They came together professionally to rehearse and perform in duo concerts, and formally for certain social occasions, but that was it. John nonetheless continued to profess his devotion whenever Brenda's name came up. He preserved a certain image of her – like a rose in crystal – that no amount of suffering could deface. The marital break was symbolized in rather macabre fashion by the removal of all John's teeth, which were badly rotted after years of neglect and resembled the keys of a very old piano. Brenda took him to King's College Hospital for the operation but he got cold feet and made a run for it down Denmark Hill. He had to be coaxed back in. When he walked out again it was with a brand-new set, all white and even.

Virginia Renshaw's first major trip with John was to Poland in September 1986, where he had concerts in Bydgoszcz, Katowice and Warsaw. On this occasion she hadn't packed his case for him and discovered in Warsaw that it was practically empty. Even buying basic things like toiletries (or belts) in Poland at that time was problematic, but John never complained and wasn't bothered by his sparse wardrobe. They never did find a way to keep his concert trousers a-hoist, though there was much head-scratching among the Poles (even the conductor came and had a look at them); in the end he just held them up. John's mood lightened greatly when he was abroad and he took a keen pleasure in meeting people and seeing the sights. He was the soul of courtesy to any member of the public who approached him and would kiss the ladies' hands. John had been asked to play Paderewski's Piano Concerto in A minor, Op. 17, as part of the Bydgoszcz Festival. The music arrived at Harcourt Terrace about two weeks before the tour but John was not given access to the piano in Brenda's flat, so by the time he and Virginia set off for Poland he had done no more than look through the score. At the Paderewski Concert Hall in Bydgoszcz, which has one of the finest acoustics in Europe, there was a crummy old upright in the green room. Virginia told him he had thirty minutes for a quick pre-rehearsal run-through but he wasn't in the least concerned. 'No, it's OK,' he said. 'I don't need it.' During the performance itself, with the Pomeranian Philharmonic under Mieczyslaw Nowakowski, Virginia turned the pages and John played the piece as if he'd been performing it all his life. This was Virginia's first experience of his transcendental level of musicianship. She noticed, too, that he had an extraordinary capacity for generating warmth in others, and this warmth enveloped everyone in the hall so that you felt you were part of a very special atmosphere. This cordiality flowed from John's musical integrity, a quality that was very much on display when he and Virginia battled their way through snowstorms to reach Rhyl Town Hall in North Wales for a recital one January night. Only three people turned up because of the blizzards, but John performed as if he was playing to a packed Festival Hall.

Brenda's jealousy towards Virginia bubbled under the surface until, over the course of time, her opposition became more overtly hostile. She accused Virginia of coming into her home and treating her like a second-class citizen, but this was to ignore the fact that she and John had separate homes now (an arrangement Brenda had pressed for) and that Virginia's sphere of operation was John's flat, not Brenda's. In fact few of Virginia's tasks directly involved Brenda. She did have to remind local shopkeepers not to allow her to run up bills on John's credit, and was meant to curb Brenda's spending on tour with John – though conflict here was pre-empted by Brenda's refusal to allow Virginia to accompany them. Relations were not helped when Kaye and Renshaw attempted to set up what John called a 'secretariat' in his flat – an office for Virginia, which would have meant co-opting the spare bedroom. The plan was quickly scotched by an indignant Richard.

Nina Kaye was not insensitive to the financial pressures that the Court order exerted on Brenda, and could appreciate her hunger for the grand life. One summer, therefore, she organized a tour on a cruise liner with both Brenda and John performing in order that they could have a holiday together in opulent surroundings and earn some money at the same time. They were given cash to spend so they could live it up a bit and dine with the captain. A week before they were due to set sail Brenda announced that she had lost her wedding ring and couldn't possibly share a cabin with John Ogdon without one: it would look as though they were living in sin. The Court gave her permission to buy a replacement but instead of a simple band she bought a £500 white-gold beauty.

Virginia made sure that John ate proper meals instead of subsisting on black coffee and cigarettes. When she arrived in the mornings she would cook breakfast for him. If he was still in bed she would simply tell him to get up and he would obey immediately. Usually, though, he would be slouched in his big green chair, haphazardly dressed and puffing away. She cleaned for him, made sure he was presentable and occasionally bought him new clothes. They made trips to the cinema and to various parks to feed the ducks, and enjoyed sampling Chinese restaurants. Much of her job involved simply keeping him company. John didn't really have normal conversations; he wouldn't discuss a film he'd been to see with her or talk about his life and feelings. There was an inwardness to him that was bigger and more compelling than any outward commerce. So being with him often meant sitting in silence. Occasionally he would bring out a tiny, crumpled photo of Annabel from his wallet and show it to Virginia. He was absolutely devoted to his daughter and delighted that she had now moved back to England.

In November 1986 John was due to begin a two-week tour with the Danish Radio Symphony Orchestra, beginning in Denmark then moving on to Scotland and England. When Virginia arrived to take him to Heathrow he was nowhere to be seen. She made urgent enquiries among the local shopkeepers and then, on Brenda's suggestion, tried the psychiatric unit at St Stephen's Hospital in the Fulham Road. There she found John trying to admit himself as an outpatient. He hadn't taken his drugs, probably because he didn't want to do the tour. Virginia managed to persuade him to go home with her and then got him ready for the airport. Hours later they were sitting waiting to be called to the gate when John sprang up and pulled Virginia so hard after him that she didn't have time to pick up her handbag. As he dragged her across the airport and down into the underground station she looked desperately around at everyone, not quite sure how to signal for help without alarming John further. Finally an airport detective offered assistance. He took them to a special room, got John to take his medication and kept them there until the plane was fully boarded then whisked them on. From that moment John was perfectly content and calm and loved every minute of the tour, making friends with members of the orchestra, the conductor David Shallon and the orchestra director. He played the Grieg and Rachmaninoff Second concertos on alternate nights, and according to Virginia each performance was a completely new experience.

The year of John's fiftieth birthday, 1987, was heralded by his appearance on the January cover of *Classical Music* as well as by an exhibition at the British Music Information Centre in London to celebrate his contribution to twentieth-century British music. He was interviewed by the magazine's editor, Keith Clarke, who was much taken with Ogdon's still-youthful enthusiasm for the music of his contemporaries. An unusually loquacious John kept getting up from his chair to pull scores out of a cupboard. One that had a particular hold on him was *Kemp's Nine Daies Wonder* by Trevor Hold, a poet and composer who had a special affinity for the work of John Clare. 'It's a tremendous piano piece about a friend of Shakespeare who dances from London to Norwich in nine days and is welcomed by the mayor,' he enthused. On the other hand John's illness had rekindled his interest in the classical composers, at whom he looked with fresh eyes.

I think it made me look more closely at the meaning behind the notes. I found that I had much more devotion to the music of Bach and Mozart than formerly. Bach does seem to be a marvellous river from which all things flow and I love to play Mozart too. I had the honour of studying with Denis Matthews who is a noted Mozart person. I think the wonderful unexpectedness and the written grace of Mozart is something most unusual.

The written grace of Mozart: what a wonderfully felicitous phrase! Has the gift of Mozart to the world ever been better described? John also talked about a new piece he was writing for two pianos: 'It's a sketch on St Dunstan and the devil, which Malcolm Williamson did an opera on. It's a lovely story about how the devil wants to destroy the people of Maidstone in Kent and they turn the clocks back an hour so that he mistakes the time. Somebody tweaks his nose with hot tongs and off he goes!'

On 27 January a surprise party was held for John at Steinway's, organized by Kaye Artists. Nina Kaye and Virginia Renshaw knew that John had written a string quartet, so they arranged for Jagdish Mistry and his quartet to come and play it for him and his guests. It was a tremendously meaningful moment for John and he was visibly moved. In addition Ronald Stevenson had written a piece for the occasion, which John half sight-read, half improvised. The piano didn't have a music stand so Virginia had to hold the pages for him; they were very long so this was quite a challenge and rather than turning them over she simply tossed them to the floor. John was completely unfazed by the chaos. After the musical interludes he was presented with a cake in the shape of a piano. It was hard to believe he was only fifty: his ashen hair and bent-over frame bespoke a man of seventy. Brenda had arrived separately, though she and John acted as if they were a couple while the party lasted. When they returned home, however, Brenda disappeared down to her flat with the cake, while John sat upstairs with Virginia.

During the 1980s John had got to know Miron and Carola Grindea, Romanian Jewish refugees who had been in England since 1939. Miron, a true intellectual, was the editor of an international journal called *ADAM* (Art, Drama, Architecture and Music) for which John wrote his series of articles on composers he'd met. Carola Grindea was a pianist, art collector and pedagogue who taught at the Guildhall School of Music and founded the European Piano Teachers Association (EPTA) and the Society for the Study of Tension in Performance. They had known Picasso, Jean-Paul Sartre, Jean Cocteau and others, and their London home was still an artistic hub. Carola had approached John about doing an interview for EPTA's *Piano Journal* to celebrate his fiftieth birthday. On Carola's arrival at Harcourt Terrace, Brenda (who didn't usually come to John's flat) suddenly appeared and announced that she was going to sit in on the conversation. When the interview broke off for tea Carola became intrigued by the one oil painting John had on his wall. John said it was given to him when he had performed a concert in Romania and told her the name of the painter. 'Gosh,' exclaimed Carola, 'he's quite a well-known artist now. It's probably a valuable picture.' Barely five minutes into the restarted interview Brenda got up, took the picture off the wall and withdrew to her apartment with it. The next day a large photo of herself filled the space on the wall.

At the beginning of February Brenda wrote to her lawyer about a further Court hearing. It is clear from the letter that she was applying pressure to have John's representation switched from Nina Kaye to John Boyden. She does not specify the reason but her final sentence provides a clue. She says she hopes the hearing is before the end of February 'because I am not prepared to tolerate Mrs. Renshaw after the end of this month'.

There were two big birthday concerts for John in February. The first was at the Festival Hall, where he played his own piano concerto and the Rachmaninoff *Rhapsody on a Theme of Paganini* with the LPO under John Lubbock. The concert had been John Boyden's idea and was arranged through Manygate Management. Boyden got the necessary sponsorship from Pickwick, which was going public and needed a big event to invite City people to. There was a lavish programme with written congratulations from Steinway's, Rothschild's, EMI and John's publisher, Chappell's, as well as messages from Ashkenazy, Peter Donohoe and John Lill. After the concert was a reception at which John was presented with a solid-silver dish by Pickwick chairman Monty Lewis. A very riled John Drummond came up to John Boyden, pointed to the other John and said, 'You should be ashamed of yourself, parading this lunatic.' Yet the concert was given a tremendous ovation, in both the hall and the newspapers.

The second concert, two weeks later, was put on by the Park Lane Group at the Queen Elizabeth Hall and was entitled 'John Ogdon and Friends'. John played in every piece but one and carried out every pianistic function. He started and finished with solo pieces, Percy Grainger's transcription of Tchaikovsky's *The Waltz of the Flowers* and

Liszt's Mephisto Waltz No. 1; he accompanied the soprano Elizabeth Harwood in Schubert's *The Shepherd on the Rock* (with Richard Hosford on clarinet); he played excerpts from Bizet's *Jeux d'Enfants* for four hands with Brenda; he joined Barry Tuckwell and Rodney Friend in Brahms's Horn Trio in E-flat major, Op. 40; he was also the accompanist in Debussy's Sonata for cello (with Raphael Sommer) and Maxwell Davies's Sonata for trumpet (with John Wallace); finally, he played Lutoslawski's Paganini Variations for two pianos with Tamas Vasary. John Wallace had sent John the music of Max's Op. 1 Sonata for trumpet in advance of the rehearsal, but he hadn't opened it: it remained in its sealed brown envelope when he turned up for the rehearsal and there were no marks on the brand-new copy from Schott's when he took it out. He had last performed the piece in 1956 yet clearly remembered it some thirty years later, for he played it note and rhythm perfect − despite the fact that it has no bar lines, its rhythms are serial and asymmetric and it is very complex and fast. Wallace was astounded by the effortless manner in which John reeled it off. The one piece John didn't perform was his own sonata for unaccompanied flute, which he had composed specially for the occasion (he lost the score of the one he'd written previously). This was played by a young flautist, Rachel Brown, who described the piece as a 'fantasy trip' in five movements. John liked her performance so well that he asked her permission to dedicate the sonata to her. As a tribute to John all the artists gave their services free. After the concert there was tea and birthday cake at the QEH. For John, it had been like old times, rehearsing at Rodney Friend's house in Notting Hill and sitting round Barry Tuckwell's kitchen table with his old music chums.

John was feted everywhere that birthday year, as if on a kind of royal progress. In the street people would come up wanting to talk to him, or would shout out, 'Good luck, John!' They invited him into their homes and gave him food or gifts, and restaurants wouldn't hear of him paying for his meal. Everyone had read his story and knew who he was. At home things were less charmed. As spring turned to summer Brenda's tolerance of Virginia Renshaw reached the zero mark and she wouldn't allow her near John's flat. She and John had to meet at a prearranged place (to which he was sent in a taxi) and go on to engagements from there. She was no longer able to cook for him and make sure he was taking his medication. John was powerless to object or assert his will in these situations; the way he protested was by harming himself. At his last Promenade concert in July 1987 the girl from Kaye Artists who was looking after him was beside herself because John was in the green room at the Albert Hall cutting his hands with a razor before he was due to go on. She thought the concert would have to be cancelled. But John did go on, playing the Shostakovich Concerto for piano, trumpet and strings – and by all accounts playing it stunningly. Eventually the inevitable happened and Brenda issued an ultimatum: if Virginia continued in her role as minder then John would never play again! It put the agency in an impossible situation. Nina wrote to the Court, saying that she couldn't manage John without Virginia and that the key to his successful comeback was having a minder and keeping Brenda out of his professional life. Virginia's position had finally become untenable, though, and she relinquished it that September.

On her last day Virginia was to drive John to Birmingham to give a lunchtime concert at the BBC Studios at Pebble Mill. When he emerged from the taxi at their meeting place she was horrified to see that he had slashed both sides of his face with a razor blade. She rushed to the nearest chemist and bought some plasters to stop the bleeding. In Birmingham they were met by Denis Matthews, who was deeply upset to see the state of his old friend.

Nina Kaye remained John's agent for a further six months. Initially an American student was employed to look after John, but when he fell ill one of Nina's other pianists, Philip Fowke, recommended a young musician friend of his. Alex Durston had studied violin at the Guildhall and was considering entering the priesthood. Like John, Alex was a heavy smoker; the two enjoyed a relaxed relationship and spent a good deal of time sitting in the flat smoking cigarettes and drinking gallons of coffee. There was never any food there, except perhaps cereal, so they would visit a cafe in the Fulham Road for meals. By this time John had an upright piano on loan but Alex had to be quite cunning to get him to practise for concerts. He couldn't simply ask him to practise, so he'd say things like, 'The Liszt Sonata is a really interesting piece . . .' – knowing full well that it was on John's recital programme that evening – and they'd begin talking and John would get up and play passages from it.

As always with John things were a mixture of the comical and the sublime. When Alex arrived at John's flat one morning to set off on a Swedish tour Mr Butters the driver was already waiting outside to take them to Heathrow. Alex knocked on John's door but there was no reply. When eventually the door opened there stood John in his striped pyjamas. Alex reminded him with some urgency that they had to get to the airport in forty minutes. John looked at him rather sheepishly. 'I don't think I can go, Alex,' he said. 'I think I've had a psychological relapse.' Alex had to bite his lip to stop himself laughing at the absurdity of John's pronouncement – John hadn't relapsed; he simply didn't want to go on tour. Fortunately the agency was able to change the flights to the following day, by which time John was in a more positive frame of mind.

In Stockholm they met up with Sir Alexander Gibson and the violinist Manoug Parikian, who were performing the day after John. On the evening of his recital they came backstage to wish him well. Alex was flipping through a copy of the programme when he noticed that the first piece was listed as Liszt's Don Juan fantasy, which hadn't been on John's schedule at all: he was due to open with the Chopin F-minor fantasy. Not wanting to disturb John unnecessarily he sought advice from Gibson and Parikian, who suggested he ask John before having any announcement made to the audience. By this time the first bell was sounding and John was pacing up and down deep in thought. When Alex explained the situation he stopped in his tracks and said simply, 'I'll give it a go.' In fact he played it as if he'd been practising it all week. Alex, standing nervously in the wings, found himself weeping as the music poured forth. It was, he says, an overwhelming experience.

Looking back, Alex feels that John's loneliness was made more acute by a great capacity for love that he was unable to express. Apart from his cleaning lady, who came most mornings, John was still not seeing anyone much, and to those who did come it could prove a slightly surreal experience. When David Ferre, who was writing a biography of Andrzej Czajkowski, turned up to interview him John opened the door wearing two ties and was painfully reticent. To remedy John's seclusion Alex tried to arrange a visit from two of his best friends at the time, both pianists who admired John's playing. John was most agreeable to the idea but, in his guileless manner, must have mentioned the plan to Brenda because she put a stop to it. More than that, she reported Alex to Kaye Artists for unprofessional conduct. He was extremely hurt, as he had always done his best to be polite and accommodating to her. Now, after three months in the post, he gave his notice to quit.

John had many carers coming in over the next eight months, sometimes round the clock. The procession included Angelo, Dilys (day nurse), Mohammed (night nurse) and Louise, but nobody stayed for long – partly because the agencies from which they came were never fully paid. The many grocery lists John has left us on the back of envelopes, as well as the unpaid account of almost £900 he left at his death, attest to the fact that he was a regular shopper at Economic Foods on the Earl's Court Road – or that Brenda was, for those who saw Six-Pie's fridge say that it was as bare as Mother Hubbard's cupboard. Three packets of Rothman's Special and three boxes of matches were always near the top of his list, with coffee, sugar cubes and Hobnob biscuits close behind. Sometimes Richard would stay at the flat and might cook supper for John or watch a film with him, with John in his big green chair. They didn't have any deep and meaningful chats but John enjoyed having him there and Richard would feel guilty when he had to say goodbye, as John could cut quite a desolate figure. As Melville wrote of Ahab, 'He lived in the world, as the last of the Grisly Bears lived in settled Missouri.'

In February 1988 the Official Solicitor came under further pressure to hand over John's management to John Boyden's Manygate agency. In another letter to the Court Brenda claimed that Nina Kaye was 'actively seeking to destroy John's career' by ignoring engagements that were coming in for him. (This was of course vigorously denied by Nina, who had simply been anxious not to overwork John.) John's accountant, who had backed Nina's approach, applied to be discharged as acting receiver and Ken Barnes (a Manchester accountant who was in partnership with Brenda's cousin) was appointed in his stead. There was thus a general changing of the guard in John's professional life, and this he marked with a bizarre speech addressed to the Master of the Court headlined 'Background to Change of Agent'. First he apologized about the fact that the last time he had attended the Court, back in 1986, he and Brenda 'had had an accident at the end of a concert tour' (meaning the assault at Euston Station). Then, because he thought it might be helpful, he began a lengthy summary of different pianistic traditions, including those of England, Russia, America, France, Germany and Italy, according a paragraph to each. He praised the 'undying dedication of Yehudi Menuhin, Georges Enescu, Busoni, Manuel de Falla, Ralph Vaughan Williams and Vladimir Ashkenazy (himself the beginner of a new piano tradition)' in helping to take music beyond frontiers and make it an international language. In conclusion he said he thought John Boyden was the right person to manage his affairs because 'as a person who was precocious as a child, I should think I need masculine guidance'.

John Boyden had set up Manygate because he wanted full control of the record-making process, including management of the artists themselves. Synergy was his watchword, and his great lure to artists was the promise of an active recording career. With his highly successful Classics for Pleasure and IMP labels, he had a proven track record. Jamie Thomson, a former actor, was put in charge of Manygate, which never lost its reputation as an oddball, buccaneering company that pulled off slightly dodgy coups, such as the world premiere of Beethoven's Tenth Symphony. Boyden himself played the role of imperator and when he arrived at the office in Battersea once a week all the employees would throw their caps in the air and shout, 'Hurrah!' They presented him with the week's problems and he would pronounce on them, Solomon-like, and then depart. Bringing in John Ogdon was his personal masterstroke, and he was of the opinion that Nina Kaye had got it wrong in trying to tell the world that John was fully recovered and back to his old self. It was decided that Manygate, on the other hand, would present John as he was, warts and

all, as a brilliant, troubled, eccentric artist whose recitals were increasingly *sui generis*. This approach worked for recitals but orchestral
concerts, with the extra costs involved, were a different matter.
Manygate didn't secure dates with major orchestras for John, perhaps
because he was deemed unworthy of the risk. By dint of his idiosyncrasies John in some respects fell casualty to the corporate mentality
prevalent in the classical-music world at that time. Money passed
through very few hands – including those of the BBC and the Arts
Council – and such bodies dictated a public taste that was perceived to
cater to a standard of competent inevitability.

At Manygate John was under the care of Alexander Waugh (grandson of Evelyn), a pianist himself and a big fan of English music whose
good manners and conciliatory demeanour had landed him the job of
agency front man. He it was who dealt with the artists and complicated people like Brenda. With Manygate Brenda regained the
influence she'd had to relinquish during the Basil Douglas and Nina
Kaye years, and lost no time in persuading the company that John was
ready for a full concert schedule. She transacted business relating not
only to her duo with John but also to John's solo career and was on
the phone most days to discuss, in a rather tense way, what was next.
Because she wanted to play so badly but couldn't get solo dates Brenda
also constantly agitated for two-piano and duet engagements, and in
the end essentially told Manygate, 'You can't have John unless you take
me.' Consequently Waugh found himself offering promoters John
and Brenda for half the price of John alone – which wasn't good business at all. Nevertheless Brenda was happy with this arrangement,
not least because she could be paid directly for duo dates. She and
John even resumed recording together; the result was a CD set of the
complete two-piano works by Rachmaninoff for ASV.

Alexander Waugh was frequently over at Harcourt Terrace as there
was nearly always some sort of crisis going on, usually with money at
its root. He took the view that Brenda was unbalanced and very
highly strung, and that she had suffered a great deal herself. There
was, however, a kind of sweetness to her. According to Waugh, she
liked to be spoiled and fussed over and when she was she had a
beaming smile, like a child. Brenda was, on the whole, extremely

frustrated with her life. She was all about appearances and no longer had the money to keep them up or live in the manner to which she felt entitled. The crises were precipitated as a means of voicing her discontent. Waugh found that the tension she generated got under his skin, and he had to fight hard to keep calm, listen to what she had to say and then find a solution. Everything with her *started* at a very high pitch.

With *Virtuoso* having finally been taken up by the BBC, the script had been approved by John and Brenda in autumn 1987 and in the summer of 1988 filming began with Alfred Molina playing John and Alison Steadman as Brenda. John recorded all the solo playing for the film and Brenda joined him in the two-piano pieces. There were nine sessions in all, over the course of three weeks, and John got to visit various of the sets. He had also begun his recordings of the complete solo piano works of Rachmaninoff for Collins Classics and was doing a set entitled 'Popular Classics' for Pickwick. The Rachmaninoff recordings were sadly beneath his best; the playing is frequently blurred, there are cascades of wrong notes and behind it all a kind of effort of despair and deep vulnerability. Despite some beautiful and powerful playing, especially in the Preludes, they provide a painfully raw catalogue of his mental struggles. He was also preparing for his mammoth recital of Sorabji's *Opus Clavicembalisticum* at the QEH, for which he received every kind of superlative – and rightly so. This was a gargantuan performance, in which whole chunks of the score would appear before him like news flashes that had to be processed in the blink of an eye. John's musical personality was enormous, his everyday nature elfin and unformed, and people were constantly trying to marry the two – sometimes to comical effect. After the *OC* concert John received a letter from the artist Polly Hope, who had been in the audience. 'I feel you are too important a personality to be constrained inside a tail coat,' she wrote. 'Why not a rather grand, but sombre robe such as Liszt used to wear? I would be happy to make you one. During fittings you can play on my well-tempered Steinway.' The thought of Six-Pie in a grand and sombre robe is too farcical for words; he would surely have found a way of either tripping over it or setting fire to it as he paced and puffed in the wings!

Among the names on the Manygate books were cellist Felix Schmidt and the Serbian violinist Mateja Marinkovich, but John, even in his ruined pomp, was the agency's trophy artist. When they took over his management John owed £40,000 in taxes. John Boyden made it a priority to release him from this debt, which resulted in him being marketed more aggressively than he had been at either Basil Douglas or Kaye Artists. Some would say he was pushed too hard. However much John earned, though – and he earned more than £17,000 in the course of one month at the beginning of 1989 – the money never seemed to filter down to him. He was given an allowance of £103 a week, of which he had to pay £50 to his cleaner. Given that he spent over £30 a week on cigarettes, this left just £23 a week for food and taxis. John always had to have £20 in his pocket, otherwise he'd get agitated, and on no account could the cigarettes be allowed to run out. He was always writing little notes to himself, as if instructing another person. For instance he wrote a list of the payments that he was due and then told himself to tick them off (neatly!) when he had received a copy of the payment advice from Manygate notifying him that they had sent the funds to the acting receiver. He then added: 'I would like a written confirmation from Manygate Management that this is a matter of normal business practice. It is your money – you have earned it – Good God!' Some of his notes were like little pep talks to himself, such as 'keep to the point of raising money for the French Record' and 'make eye to eye contact with John Boyden about the French records'. 'Can we get the Court Order rescinded,' he asks elsewhere, 'as I feel I could control a budget?' Others were exhortations to himself, for instance to learn Alistair Hinton's Third Sonata, of which he thought very highly, or the Otto Luening Sonata.

Both Brenda and Richard Ogdon were keen to have John released from the Court Order. The basic plan was to take out a large loan secured on the two flats to pay off all outstanding debts and then have John's mental condition reassessed. However, unless Richard, who worked at S. G. Warburg merchant bank, was intending to assume control of the family budget, it was surely reckless to imagine that John was ready for any such responsibility. Budgets meant only one thing for him: stress. Alistair Londonderry saw John and Brenda infrequently in the late 1980s. Over lunch one day at an expensive restaurant in Knightsbridge, to which the Ogdons had invited him, Brenda turned to John and said, 'You know we can't afford this, John', whereupon Alistair reached for his credit card.

Alexander Waugh would call John to discuss the repertoire for his upcoming recitals and ask him what he wanted to play. 'Oh, hmm, we could try some Beethoven,' the Og would venture. 'Do you want to play some Scriabin?' 'Oh, yes! I like Scriabin. I could play some Scriabin, Alex.' 'Well, what would you play?' 'I like the Fifth Sonata. It's a wonderful piece.' It was all very random and fanciful and by concert day he'd have forgotten what he was meant to be playing – but whatever it was he'd pitch up with his great ramshackle body and play it.

It was Manygate that arranged for John to have a rented upright piano for the top flat. It was by no means a great instrument (Alexander Waugh describes it as 'real honky-tonk shit') but he could do his basic practice on it. There was a vague plan hatched at Altarus for John to record a selection of Sorabji's Transcendental Etudes, of which there are 100. When Waugh was at Harcourt Terrace one day the photocopied score arrived from Alistair Hinton. The music was handwritten on four staves and fairly illegible but they put the sheets up on John's upright and he raced through them. Waugh couldn't tell if every single note was in the right place but it sounded absolutely phenomenal. John's fingers were everywhere at once and sweat was running off his face. With his eyes drilling into the score he looked like a wartime decoder cum bomb-disposal man desperately searching for the correct combination to avert an explosion. When he'd finished the first étude he stopped and there was a silence. Then he turned to Waugh and said in his goofy drawl, 'Is that alright, Alex?'

John Boyden's son, Matthew, was another regular visitor at the Ogstead and sometimes travelled to concerts with John. All too often he found himself talking to him as if he was a fool or a child – everybody did. He was able to step out of this register only when he read Sherlock Holmes stories to him as he sat in his big green chair. John revelled in the gratuitous intelligence of Conan Doyle and could comment perceptively on the writing; and when he was amused he had a batting eye. People wanted to be associated with John's genius but relating to him as a man was hugely uncomfortable territory. Ever since the Tchaikovsky prize he had been a sort of totem, which people garlanded then forsook. According to Matthew, he was 'probably the most patronized man of the twentieth century'.

If he wasn't doing anything John would sometimes turn up at the Manygate office and ask if he could help. The girls would give him some envelopes to stuff and Matthew would be dispatched to buy Hobnobs, which John would then sit chain-eating until the whole packet had disappeared. One day they looked down to see him walking across the courtyard in his trademark frosted glasses – only his hair and beard were blue! 'John, why have you got blue hair?' they asked. 'Oh,' he said, 'is it blue? B ... B ... Brenda dyes it. She doesn't like the nicotine.' This particular dye job had gone south, it seems, leaving him wandering around London like the wife-murderer of the old tale.

At other times, if he had been 'naughty', John would be locked in his apartment so he couldn't try to enter the basement flat by force. In August 1988, however, John, who had tremendous upper-body strength, did manage to smash his way into Brenda's flat. She pressed her panic button and the police arrived *prestissimo* to calm things down. The British Nursing Agency was asked to send a professional nurse, and one arrived in the form of a young man in his early twenties called Dennis Ridewood. When Dennis reached the Ogdons John was melancholic and sat puffing on a cigarette (which was taboo in the basement flat) and Brenda was shrieking that he had tried to kill her. Dennis suggested that Brenda make herself a cup of tea while he took John back upstairs. Dennis was not a live-in nurse but became John's carer almost for the rest of his life and did from time to time spend the night at John's place, usually if they had to be off to an engagement early the next morning.

Always a glutton for pianistic punishment, John gave a second performance of *Opus Clavicembalisticum* at Skinners' Hall in the City of London as part of the Cornhill Festival of British Music that November. The day before the concert he and Brenda were practising at Steinway's for a duo recording of transcriptions of Ravel and Debussy. During a short break in their rehearsal she tried to get him to take his lithium, whereupon he swung at her without warning, shouting, 'Don't you understand how I feel when I have to take these pills?' Then he hit her in the face, smashing her glasses – shards from which narrowly missed her eye. Brenda's injury required thirteen stitches. Doctors at the Wellington Hospital told her she was lucky not to have lost an eye, and a policeman visited her bedside to ask if she wanted to press charges. She declined, but the following month a writ for damages was issued against John in the Civil Courts. When Ross Benson of the *Daily Express* called John about it for a piece he was writing in his gossip column, John would say only that 'There's been a bit of a spat'. And when Dennis asked what had happened he said he'd gone to turn the page, Brenda had leaned forward and his hand had accidentally caught her glasses!

In the autumn of 1988 Gerald Fox, son of the concert pianist Joscelyn Steele, was interviewed for work at LWT's *South Bank Show* and made his calling card a film about John Ogdon. Melvyn Bragg was taken with the idea and immediately found him a slot. Filming started pronto, in January 1989. Fox saw the film as an opportunity to present a portrait of Ogdon the musician that focused on his championship of English music. There were interviews with Peter Maxwell Davies, Alexander Goehr, Robert Simpson and Malcolm Williamson among others. The filming with John himself was done mainly at Harcourt Terrace and took three days. Footage shows him playing on the upright in his flat and on the Steinway down in Brenda's. On the upright he played from memory part of a sonata he'd composed when he was fourteen as well as sections from *Opus Clavicembalisticum*; in his brief comments about the piece he discussed its apocalyptic ending. The piano was awful. Even John, who was extremely tolerant of bad pianos, said to Chris Rice, 'It is a bit of a thing, isn't it?' On the Steinway he played a section from the first movement of the Tchaikovsky Concerto, and spoke about how his playing had been influenced by Ashkenazy's. He was joined in the basement flat by Peter Maxwell Davies as they reminisced together about their student days and he played the first piece from his friend's Five Little Pieces,

Op. 27. He talked about the influence of cinema on his composing and played from his *Kaleidoscope on Cinema*, a set of pieces inspired by iconic lines from some of his favourite films. He wrote a number of 'Kaleidoscopes', twelve in all, including one dedicated to Karl Ogdon that contains pieces based on themes composed by his brother. The idea of short, semi-improvised pieces that resemble oscillating images is clearly one that appealed to him. In fact, the kaleidoscope is a good image for how John viewed the world: not as cause and effect but as a series of shifting patterns. Another sequence featured John sight-reading Bob Simpson's *Variations and Finale on a Theme of Haydn* under the approving gaze of the composer.

Behind the scenes John and Brenda were chugging down the Diet Coke and during his main interview John kept trying to light cigarettes and had to be told to put them away. His eyes look trapped under the gaze of the camera and terribly troubled (both menacing *and* hurt); Brenda, meanwhile, is wearing big glittery white, tinted glasses to hide the stitches around her eye. She paints a vivid picture of John and herself on a merry-go-round of concerts and parties during their golden years.

It was decided that a fourth day of filming would be done, based on an unusual idea. John used to enjoy turning the sound down on the TV and using the images as a focus for his improvisations. He'd even accompany the weather forecast. Gerald Fox knew that John had been planning a major orchestral work based on *Moby-Dick*, so he suggested that he improvise to the closing sequence of John Huston's 1956 movie to show how he might work on a new composition inspired by the story of Captain Ahab's pursuit of the white whale. John was naturally enthused by the idea and there was a whole new energy and excitement to his personality that day. His old TV was set up at the end of the keyboard and he was off, playing and commenting on the film as he went. We see the sweat breaking out on his brow as he hammers away at the keys, head skewed towards the screen. Afterwards he stays at the piano, puffing away and flicking his ash into a teacup balanced on the keys. Finally he pulls together all the ideas he's had during the improvisation into a suite for piano, and with that the show ends. 'Well,' he says, 'in the piece I'm going to play I've tried to coordinate the different impressions I had of the film of *Moby-Dick* in its closing scene – the beauty of the seagulls, the whiteness of the whale, the monomania of Captain Ahab and the evident distress of his crew as their voyage reaches a tragic end.' After Fox's film was aired on ITV in March 1989 Manygate brokered a deal with the National Film Theatre whereby John would attend for a concert fee and busk to silent pictures, such as *The Four Horsemen of the Apocalypse*. John died before this arrangement could come to fruition.

Very many incidents in John's life – especially during the later years – had the quality of parables. He gave his last Wigmore Hall recital at the end of January 1989. In addition to Beethoven's *Moonlight* and *Pathétique* Sonatas he played a couple of Rachmaninoff transcriptions and that composer's final piece for piano, the *Variations on a Theme of Corelli*. Brenda had told Dennis that John should not attend the function after the concert but should come straight home. There was no £20 note in his pocket that day; he and Dennis had only £10 between them, which meant they didn't have enough for cigarettes *and* a taxi. Dennis smoked as well, so it wasn't much of a choice: they decided to buy cigarettes and go home on the tube. It had been a long day and neither of them had eaten. Many of the people at the underground station had just been to John's recital and couldn't believe their eyes when they saw him getting on the train. There was a general press, with many asking for his autograph, which Dennis eventually had to disperse. When he picked up the cigarettes at the corner store Dennis bought half a dozen eggs and a couple of potatoes to make egg and chips, but at home he discovered that they had no cooking oil and no salt. A number of Brenda's plates and cutlery were up in John's flat from the *South Bank Show* filming and he decided to wash them up and take them downstairs so he could ask her for some oil and salt while he was at it. According to Dennis, Brenda flatly denied his request and accused him and John of doing nothing but 'take, take, take', so he beat a hasty retreat. All seemed lost until John remembered there was a little margarine in the back of the fridge and they made do with that. A few months later, at a fancy restaurant in

Mexico City, Dennis commented on what a fabulous dinner they were enjoying. John looked up with a little smile and said that the best meal he'd ever had was the egg and potato Dennis had cooked that night after the Wigmore Hall.

The day after the recital there was a preview screening of *Virtuoso* at the BAFTA Centre for press and selected guests, including the actors. During the film there was a lot of nervous laughter from Brenda as she watched Alison Steadman's shrill, brass-plated portrayal of her. During the scene about her spending the money from the Musicians Benevolent Fund on a fur coat the house erupted. Dennis, who sat between the Ogdons, couldn't bring himself to look at Brenda, but John was giggling away in his seat. When it was over Brenda apparently turned to screenwriter Bill Humble and said, 'Alison Steadman's much nicer to John than I ever was!' On the phone the next day she told Michael Kerr, 'Actually, it was very good. They got my hair right, they got my clothes right; they even got the wallpaper right.' But when the film went out on BBC2 some of the reviews made the inevitable comparison with Steadman's portrayal of Beverly Moss and said that Brenda had been portrayed as a monster, which had certainly not been Humble's intention. Brenda then went on *The Late Show*, again in huge tinselly glasses, and protested at the characterization of her. She said she had been made out to be 'the baddy': for her the film enshrined the perspective of the Schurmanns and others in the music world who were unsympathetic towards her.

Much of the film must have made uncomfortable viewing for both Brenda and John – for instance the scene in Dr Michael Johnson's office in which Brenda says she hasn't got time to wait for the lithium to work. 'For better or for worse I married a great pianist,' she says, raising her voice. 'Take that away and there's nothing left!' Like the book, the film ends on an upbeat note – only here it is rather later in their story. We see John and Brenda talking in the kitchen of the Richmond Fellowship about getting back together again. 'I'm impossible, and you certainly are,' says Brenda. In the final sequence they walk on stage together at the Wigmore Hall and begin playing Rachmaninoff's Suite No. 2. It's quite an affecting moment as the unity and harmony they have vainly sought in marriage is for a brief moment brought to life by the music.

John was certainly enjoying all the attention and there was a gala air – maybe in retrospect a valedictory air – to everything he did. In February he was a prominent part of Larry Adler's 75th Birthday Concert at the Royal Albert Hall, at which Malcolm Arnold was guest conductor. John, in an echo of his childhood, partnered a pianola in a two-piano piece (with Adler joining in on the harmonica). A party afterwards at Stringfellow's found John in bubbly form. Usually Brenda vetoed his attendance at such things: it was straight back home with strict instructions not to watch the night-owl movie on TV. He would sit in his big green chair and ruminate. He often found it hard to get to sleep and would pace around the flat. Sometimes when they were on the road Dennis would hear him at 3 a.m. having conversations with himself and giggling. This would be a sign that he was entering a manic phase, and Dennis might give him an extra 25mg-tablet of Melarill to calm him down. In addition to the lithium and Melarill, he was taking Tenoret for his high blood pressure and nitrazepam to help him sleep. Lack of sleep, no exercise and very poor diet (nicotine, pots of strong sugary coffee and one meal a day of the boil-in-the-bag variety) contributed to John's mood swings and fuelled the undiagnosed diabetes. John appeared very ill the night that he and Brenda performed at a televised benefit concert at the Royal Festival Hall in aid of the Orphans of Armenia: he was pasty, sweaty and confused-looking.

At the end of March John and Dennis flew to Bern for a couple of concerts with the Berner Symphonieorchester under another Manygate artist, Peter Maag. The concerto had been changed at John's request from the Beethoven First to the *Emperor*, which he knew much better. At the first rehearsal John couldn't find the music; and, though he said he could manage without it, Maag – who was generally known to be somewhat hot-headed – reportedly made no effort to hide his displeasure. He kept stopping John in the final movement, saying he was playing too fast. At the break John and the conductor shared a dressing room. Dennis got John a coffee and an orange juice and made sure he had a cigarette, but when Maag directed Dennis to do the same for him John jumped up off his chair. 'Dennis works for me,' he shouted. 'If you want someone to run around after you, find your own assistant!' It was a rare display of self-assertion on John's part and one that clearly rattled the conductor. The second half of the rehearsal had a real edge to it – though this time it was the first violinist who complained about John's playing. For any conductor working with him for the first time John at this stage in his career could be quite a scary proposition. He didn't appear to be connecting with the other musicians; he went off at his own pace while the orchestra scrambled to keep up.

Being abroad provided rare opportunities for John to have some spending money, as the local concert organizers would give him and Dennis £200 cash for incidentals. In Bern they had a pleasant evening after the first day's rehearsal, and ended up at the casino after dinner. They didn't discuss the incident with Maag; if anything Dennis sensed that John felt exhilarated from having put his foot down. Any such sense of abandon proved short-lived, however. Early the next morning Dennis got a call from Alexander Waugh: the promoter had contacted him to say that John had played erratically at rehearsal and was patently unwell; reluctantly, they had decided he was unfit to play at that night's concert. Waugh told John the news himself. John spoke very slowly on the phone, holding his anger in. This had never happened before in his career and must have been a humiliating blow. At John's insistence they flew home that evening. Dennis recalls John being in a very melancholic mood on the train to Zurich. He said nothing, just sat looking blankly out of the window as he pulled on a cigarette. Finally, as they were going through the Alps with the snow peaks visible in the distance, he looked up and said wistfully, 'It's a bit like *The Sound of Music*. They escaped *to* Switzerland, we're escaping *from* it.' With that the ice was broken: he lost his glazed look and they felt comfortable enough to order their food on the train. Back in London there was a big hoo-ha. Brenda was outside on the street and Waugh was there wanting to know exactly what had happened. Dennis and John were flying out to Mexico the following week, so Dennis quickly excused himself and returned home to rest.

John and Dennis had a very relaxed two weeks in Mexico, and John in particular was glad to be shot of the tensions in London. There was another little contretemps with the conductor, this time John's old friend Jorge Velazco, but with no serious consequences. He wanted John to play his own concerto from the score rather than from memory, and tried to engage a page-turner, but John was having none of it. There was a fuss in the dressing room before the concert, but in the end John had his way and performed the piece as only he could. In Mexico City John took to holding court in the foyer of the Hotel Royale, where they were staying. There was a grand piano down there and he used to play for his hosts and their guests as well as for the university students. He had a stream of beautiful and wealthy Mexican women after him and there were flirtatious lunches at the hotel restaurant. Dennis remembers one of these middle-aged belles saying to John, 'You must be a god, the way you play your music.' He chuckled at this and gave his shy little smile. When he wasn't soaking up the adulation he used the informal gatherings in the lobby to talk in detail about the pieces he'd played. There were sightseeing expeditions, including one to the pyramids of Teotihuacan thirty miles away. John was treated like royalty; if he expressed a desire to see something, then it was as good as done. He seemed remarkably au fait with Mexican culture, too. He had a radio interview during the first week and when the topic of conversation strayed from music Dennis was astonished to find John talking fluently and in some depth about contemporary Latin American politics!

There was a scramble after Mexico to get their visas for Moscow. John, as chief Tchaikovsky merchant, had been invited as the cultural lynchpin of an Anglo-Soviet business summit. They were given rooms at the Hotel Moskva on Red Square and John was wheeled about like a statue of Marx and accorded a similar veneration. He was taken to schools and museums (including the Museum of Musical Culture), and when he gave an impromptu recital at a British Chamber of Commerce event everyone stopped to listen. There was a TV interview before his performance of the Tchaikovsky Concerto at the Great Hall of the Moscow Conservatory, and the concert was recorded by an old gramophone-style machine that was whirring round backstage. Afterwards the British Ambassador Sir Rodric Braithwaite gave a dinner at the Embassy in John's honour, which was attended by the business delegates. John, who had no small talk, chatted away about Russian composers as if they were cousins and uncles from Mansfield.

After Moscow came Glasgow, where they joined Peter Maxwell Davies for a tour with the Scottish Chamber Orchestra. John liked to be on the go and preferred it when life wasn't rigidly scripted. He certainly had more energy when he was working; the company stimulated him and he rarely tired, even on two to four hours' sleep a night. However, he was never very keen to haul himself out of bed in the morning and he sometimes required prompting. He'd throw on his dirty clothes, with the buttons in the wrong holes, his hair unbrushed and his beard adrift, but was happy to let Dennis straighten him out a bit. The two men had grown fond of each other. On their way to Hull shortly after the Scottish tour, Brenda sent Dennis to buy something at the station and he missed the train. John was in a state of high anxiety and at Hull City Hall refused to change into his concert clothes until Dennis had been found. After the concert a girl came up to him who had last met him at a performance in 1972, when she was twelve years old. John not only remembered her name but was also able to recall the concerto he had been playing that day.

Later the same month John and Brenda appeared on *Wogan* on BBC One with Sue Lawley. Either side of the interview John and Brenda played the first and last movements of Darius Milhaud's Suite for two pianos, *Scaramouche*. There had been the usual hullabaloo leading up to the show, with John's nerves tested by the number of rehearsals called by Brenda. Her own nervous intensity was soothed by a trip to Harvey Nichols, where she bought an expensive pair of white silk gloves. 'What do you think of these, Dennis?' she cried, unable to hide her delight. John, meanwhile, had hired a suit from High and Mighty. On Brenda's insistence, a Jag was ordered to drive them to the studio. The interview comes across as an excruciating experience for John, who was moving his mouth very strangely as if he was having trouble with his teeth. With Lawley probing some of the more sensitive areas of his life, he looks and sounds in his responses like a brainwashed victim of Stalin. Brenda too is put in the spotlight. 'Are you still afraid of him?' Lawley asks her at one point. 'He's sitting right here!' gasps Brenda, gesturing towards the crest-fallen John, who looks physically ill: the loss of weight and muscle bulk brought on by diabetes is all too evident. A number of his replies have that trademark Ogdonian inconsequence. ('Can you still remember the day of the Tchaikovsky Competition finals?' asks Lawley. 'Yes, I can,' replies John. 'It was quite cold weather . . .') When Lawley quizzes Brenda about the electric-shock treatment John becomes visibly disturbed and interrupts to say, apropos of nothing, 'I think Brenda's tremendous musicality didn't really come out in the film, personally.' He is, as ever, deeply apologetic about his suicide attempts.

Three weeks later, again with Sue Lawley, John recorded his *Desert Island Discs* for the second time. Unlike the 1967 programme with Roy Plomley, when he chose no piano music at all, this time five of his eight records involved the piano. His choices were surprisingly tra-ditional and comprised two pieces each by Rachmaninoff and Debussy as well as selections from Britten, Walton, Mozart and Liszt. There was no Busoni, Scriabin, Alkan or Sorabji, and no work by his Manchester contemporaries. He chose William Walton's Symphony No. 1 as the piece he'd take with him to the desert island if he could only take one record 'because we knew them [the Waltons] so well'. Earlier in the programme he'd said, 'I feel the piece takes one back to the year of 1935. You can feel the tension in it of armaments races building up.'

At the end of May Richard got married. It was a happy occasion for John and he played Chopin's F-minor ballade at the reception. The disappearance of his top hat after the wedding was less felicitous and was followed by a draining inquisition that had John and Dennis dreaming of the road again. According to Dennis, Brenda wasn't con-tent unless she was stirring things up. As a result, they appeared to live in the shadow of a constantly looming calamity. In June John and Brenda were to take a much-needed holiday in Sardinia, the necessary funds having been made available by the acting receiver. But, on the night before they were supposed to leave, Brenda suddenly decided that she didn't want to go with John. She worked herself into such a state about it that Dennis, who was staying the night at John's flat to help him get ready the next morning, had to call Annabel to come over and calm things down. By this time John too was getting worked up. Annabel spent the night at Brenda's flat and it was she who ended up accompanying her to Sardinia.

With Dennis also going abroad for a few days and Richard on honeymoon, John was left to shift for himself in London. Fortunately, he was rescued by the Sorabji crew, who had hatched a plot to get him his own grand piano – and not just any old grand piano, but Sorabji's. When the composer had gone into a nursing home, not long before his death, Alistair Hinton had been charged with arranging the disposal of the larger contents of his house. One of his two grand pianos, a 1921 Model B Mason & Hamlin, had been taken to Bath Piano Workshops for some restoration work and it was this piano that was earmarked as the ideal instrument for John. Sorabji died in October 1988 and early the following year Hinton had called John to ask if he'd like to go down to Somerset to have a look at the instrument with a view to having it on permanent loan. John was driven down by Chris Rice and tried out the sixty-eight-year-old piano, declaring himself delighted with it. At the time Brenda had objected, saying it would make too much noise. Now, with her away in Sardinia, John's associates swung into action and had the piano brought up and installed in his flat next to the bay window, so that by the time Brenda returned it was a *fait accompli*.

During the hot and humid summer of 1989 John played with the windows open. One of his neighbours, Christopher Buxton, wrote to Brenda after John's death:

> For us who live and work across the street, it has been a particularly poignant summer. During the last two or three months, John opened his windows in the warm sunshine. So there were the magical days when his wonderful music playing flowed out across the street and into our open windows. I came out the other day and sat by your steps listening to part of the Beethoven Fourth

piano concerto played with such triumphant freedom. I shall always remember this summer for that reason.

If Manygate was doing a good job for John then the money wasn't reaching him. His clothes were grubby, he had no social life and for nourishment made do with a piece of white fish running out of a bag. Nearly all those around him treated him like a child who was either too fragile or inept to be consulted about his own life. John may not have been able to do up his shirt buttons correctly or tie his laces but he certainly knew what was going on. Many thought that he was being overworked and exploited again; he certainly failed to reap the rewards of all the TV work he did in the last year of his life. Moreover, the Court of Protection was, if anything, a complicating influence, especially now that Ken Barnes was in the saddle.

At the beginning of July 1989, in an extraordinary volte-face, Brenda took John into the offices of Nina Kaye on the King's Road to request that he be taken back. It is hard to see how she could make this bid without at least acknowledging her mistake in having persistently petitioned the Court to have John's management moved to Manygate. In fact Nina Kaye wasn't in the office when the Ogdons turned up but later wrote to Brenda expressing considerable surprise at her request and refusing it point blank.

> During much of the two years we worked for John, you continually asked the Receiver [John's accountant] to change John's representation to Manygate Management, which he refused to do. [He] then resigned his post and the new Receiver was instructed to change the agents to Manygate, as per your request. I am sorry to learn that this new arrangement has not worked out to your satisfaction, but regretfully we cannot repeat the efforts we made two years ago to help John's career.

Brenda replied that she did nothing of the kind and demanded to know where Nina had got her information. She claimed that she only ever asked for the duo to be represented by Manygate, never John's solo representation. If John's accountant had given Nina 'this 'misinformation', she wanted to know why. However, Brenda's correspondence and the letters John wrote would appear to render any such denial on her part untenable.

Also at the beginning of July John went to St Silas's to record an all-Liszt programme for Altarus. It was a concession to Manygate, who wanted something more mainstream after all the Busoni and Sorabji. John was so obviously unwell, however, that Chris Rice terminated the session and called a cab. 'Why don't we do this another day?' he said, and there were no objections. That other day never came. Chris was sad to see that there was no one looking out for John, no one to say, 'Sorry, he's not well enough to play.' With almost £2,000 owed in outstanding invoices Dennis was now gradually and reluctantly withdrawing his services and seeking other work. Before he finally resigned, in mid-July, he wrote to both the acting receiver and John's GP expressing his fear that 'a subsequent downward spiral of events' would be inevitable were he to be compelled to hand in his notice.

On 8 July it was Matthew Boyden, not Dennis, who accompanied John down to Exeter to play the *Emperor* Concerto with the Exeter Symphony Orchestra under David Cawthra. The concert, which was held at the new Plaza Leisure Centre, was sponsored by Peugeot – so when John walked onto the makeshift stage in his summer concert gear he was confronted by a number of parked cars, which seemed to disorient him. He walked up to one of them and for a moment it looked like he might try one of the doors. Then, in the long tutti section of the *Emperor* shortly after the opening, Matthew noticed that he had fallen asleep, so he leaned forward over the stage and tugged on his jacket. John woke abruptly – and came in perfectly on cue – but it was a close-run thing. He was bemused for a second or two but once he realized where he was and what he was playing his musical instincts took over.

John's final performance was given two weeks later, on 23 July – his twenty-ninth wedding anniversary. The concert was entitled 'The Great Romantics' and, like his first London concert thirty-one years before, was sponsored by the Park Lane Group. When John was rehearsing at the Queen Elizabeth Hall the chair of the PLG, John Woolf, asked the technical staff if they could alter the lighting so that it was more sharply focused on the piano. The lighting man climbed out onto the rigging over the stage, and while he was there all the lights suddenly went out; there was total darkness for four or five minutes. John continued playing, and when Woolf went down onto the stage from the lighting box to apologize he said, 'Oh, did anything happen?'

In the first half of the recital he played Chopin's G-minor ballade, Balakirev's *Islamey* and the Paganini Variations of Brahms, while the second half was devoted to Liszt: the *Dante* Sonata, the Transcendental Etudes Nos. 1–4 and the Mephisto Waltz No. 1. It was largely music instilled with the devilish virtuosity of Paganini. Music containing demons to unlock and unleash appealed to John because it released something in him. His late virtuosity reminds one of Stravinsky's vision of the maiden who danced herself to death in a circle of seated elders. Given that it was his wedding anniversary, the last programmed piece John ever played was profoundly significant. Liszt based his Mephisto Waltz not on Goethe's *Faust* but on the version written by another German poet, Nikolaus Lenau, who died in a mental home at the age of forty-seven. The particular episode on which Liszt zeroes in is 'The Dance in the Village Inn', in which Faust and Mephistopheles wander into a village tavern where wedding celebrations are in full swing. Mephistopheles grabs a violin from one of the band and whips the dancers into a frenzy with the unbridled passion of his playing. Faust picks out an alluring wench and, guided by the Devil's searing tune, dances with her out into the open and into the wood where they are 'swallowed by the roaring sea of lust'. True marriage, one could say, is usurped by the demons of art and human intimacy sacrificed to artistic passion.

The *Evening Standard* critic described the concert as 'an evening of almost relentless transcendentalism', adding that 'if some of those flying semiquavers went slightly astray, they hardly counted among such cosmic displays of Romantic virtuosity'. Professor Cyril Ehrlich wrote of the concert after John's death, describing his 'restless energy, urgent irresistible communicativeness, and wondrous beauty of tone'. He recalled Ogdon's own words to describe Liszt's piano writing – 'sulphuric fitfulness' – and said that no phrase could more aptly describe his playing on that 'sad and glorious evening'. In the latter part of his career John's idol Busoni had limited his concert repertoire to a few Beethoven Sonatas and Bach pieces, the Liszt Sonata and the Ballades of Chopin, and played them 'in the spirit of a seer and a visionary'.

A couple of days after the concert John fell ill with a chest infection. He had recently moved to an NHS doctor from a private GP because the receiver was cutting costs and had insisted he get his lithium on the NHS. That Friday Brenda, who was now looking after him, took John to see his new doctor in Cornwall Gardens. It was a swelteringly hot day and he was having difficulty breathing. Having asked if he'd ever been diagnosed with diabetes, the doctor enquired if there was a history of ill health in his family – to which he replied, 'No, everybody's fine.' She requested a urine sample but John was unable to pass water. He already had an appointment at the Brompton Hospital for a chest x-ray the following Monday and the doctor told him to keep it. She asked him also to return to her for some blood tests. When he and Brenda got home he refused all food and lay down on his bed. Brenda phoned John's old GP, Dr Hudson, who said he'd come on the Sunday. The next day John was visited by his daughter, Annabel. Though still not eating, he was sitting in his big green chair and described himself as feeling 'a bit woozy'. Annabel didn't think too much of it as he was drinking coffee and puffing on a cigarette. She managed to persuade him to go for a walk up Harcourt Terrace but he clearly wasn't himself and shuffled along very slowly. He had never been one to complain or ask for help and now – when most people would at least be saying how desperately ill they felt – he kept silent. When Brenda went up to see him late that evening he was sweating very heavily, and she helped him into his pyjamas. On Sunday Dr Hudson did no more than prescribe paracetamol and recommend plenty of fluids. According to Brenda, he seemed fascinated by John's new piano and asked several questions about it (in more ways than one the piano *was* John's body, so the doctor's intuition was working well). Brenda was extremely worried by now, and confused by the doctor's response, but decided to wait it out until the next morning, when John would have his chest x-rays.

In the morning, however, Brenda found him slewed across his mattress, which had fallen off the bed and onto the floor. He was in a semiconscious state, unable to speak, and his eyes were rolling. The telephone had come off the bedside table and was under the mattress; she had to pull it out to call 999. He may have been trying to call her when he fell out of bed. The bed was a flimsy mock-brass affair whose bolts were always needing to be tightened, so it may be that the whole structure had collapsed. The ambulance was there in fifteen minutes and by 9 a.m. he was at Charing Cross Hospital. He was in a diabetic coma, had a serious lung infection and was suffering from kidney failure. He was given insulin and intravenous antibiotics and was gradually rehydrated. There were plans to put him on a kidney machine if his renal condition showed no improvement, but during the night the infection in his lungs spread to his bloodstream, causing septicaemia and, ultimately, a complete systems failure. He had fought gamely – his heart read strongly on the monitor and his family could see his eyes responding to their desperate encouragement – but the hospital doctors said he'd been admitted too late. He died around 8 a.m. on the Tuesday. It was 1 August, Herman Melville's birthday. John was fifty-two.

The funeral took place the following week at St Luke's Church, Redcliffe Square. Chris Rice brought a PA system and played the last section of John's recording of Busoni's *Fantasia after J. S. Bach*, written on the death of the composer's father, and with it John's presence entered the church far more potently than it had with the entry of the coffin. Many marvelled at how small the coffin was, as if the large body with which John had been so uncomfortable in life was nothing but a mirage. John Boyden was heard ranting to a journalist from the *Evening Standard*. 'It's a disgrace,' he stormed. 'Where is musical London?' John Lill and Moura Lympany were there, as were the composers Ronald Stevenson, Alexander Goehr and Graham Whettam, and the conductor Wyn Morris, but no one came from the BBC, the Arts Council, the South Bank or the British Council. The truth is that John was a non-person in the 1980s as far as the Establishment was concerned. The paper printed Boyden's views and the next day he received a call from Brenda, who was blowing rivets. 'How could you say such things?' she cried. 'It wasn't true.' She thought it looked bad for John but Boyden assured her that the people who looked bad were the people who had ignored John.

John's anonymity, though, was more profound than the cold shoulders of musical London could possibly imply, and there was a sense in which no one at that church remotely knew him, for he had lived inwardly to an extreme degree – like Ahab brooding over the whale – that all judgements are in the end impertinent.

'Oh, Starbuck! it is a mild, mild wind, and a mild looking sky. On such a day I struck my first whale [. . .] Forty years ago! Forty years of continual whaling! forty years of privation, and peril, and storm-time! forty years on the pitiless sea! for forty years has Ahab forsaken the peaceful land, for forty years to make war on the horrors of the deep! [. . .] But it is a mild, mild wind, and a mild looking sky; and the air smells now, as if it blew from a far-away meadow; they have been making hay somewhere under the slopes of the Andes, Starbuck, and the mowers are sleeping among the new-mown hay.'

Afterword

EXONERATED

Everything that is sacred and that wishes to remain so must envelop itself in mystery.

Stéphane Mallarmé

John loved all kinds of mystery, from Edgar Allan Poe to Agatha Christie, and the word (transformed by his slight lisp to 'myth-tree') was often on his lips. He was himself an enigma; no one I interviewed for this book claimed to have pierced beneath the surface of this most evasive and self-contained of men. Even had he been alive today, I doubt I would have come away any the wiser. It is not my place to pluck out the heart of the mystery that was John Ogdon, but I hope that this book has laid bare something of the strange deeps in which he toiled – and soared.

John's *Desert Island Discs* was first broadcast a few weeks after his death and contained this amusing exchange with Sue Lawley:

Lawley: You told us at the beginning that you'd like your luxury to be a piano. Perhaps you'd tell us what kind of piano?
Ogdon: Yes, I'd love it to be a Steinway, perhaps a Steinway upright. I think that would be wonderful on a desert island.
Lawley: What! You'd prefer the upright to a grand?

Ogdon: No, a grand if possible.

Lawley: You just have to promise not to live under the grand, because then it would be of practical use, you see. It would be a shelter.

Ogdon: [unable to contain his laughter] Yes, yes, I promise not to live under it. [Huge guffaws of gleeful laughter from John]

John, of course, had been using the piano as a shelter all his life; his soul had made its nest under its shiny black eaves very early on. By concealing his soul inside the piano he was able to buy himself a measure of immortality, but at what cost? It protected him, laved his wounds, won him applause, but in return he could never fully enter the warm world of humanity and enjoy its intimacies. It was a Faustian bargain, but negotiated unconsciously.

John talked of experiencing withdrawal symptoms if he didn't touch the keyboard at some point during the day. It was something akin to what the French call *le délire de toucher* (delirium of touch), whereby a patient feels a compulsive desire to touch certain objects. Such fetishes have their roots in emotional deprivation. The Chinese pianist Lang Lang refers to the piano as 'home sweet home' and claims that when he is tired simply touching the keys refreshes him. Clearly for many top instrumentalists a displacement occurs early in life between a parental figure and their chosen instrument, the latter becoming the more vital and reliable source of comfort. More than this, it becomes their primary means of self-expression, without which they feel lost. ('I miss my cello!' sobbed the six-year-old Jacqueline du Pré during a family holiday on Dartmoor.) In a sense a union takes place: they become wedded to their instrument. Bruno Walter's 'half piano, half man' musical centaur is relevant here. For child prodigies such as Ogdon the displacement happens so early in life that it remains largely unconscious and itself becomes impossible to displace. As with most marriages, a love–hate relationship evolves.

The instrument acts as an agent of order. Those who suffer from schizoid problems, as Ogdon surely did, tend to feel the threat of confusion and disorder more acutely than does the general run of mankind and hence develop the urgent need to reorder the world through a system of meaning that is secure. Music created this kind of order for Ogdon. The piano was his protection against chaos because it did what he wanted and responded in the way he expected; it didn't turn round and say, 'No', or, 'What do you mean?'

When we talk of supernatural possession it is usually in the context of madness rather than inspiration but there is no clear boundary between the two. Whatever form possession takes there is a high price to pay for trafficking with the divine. When Prometheus stole fire from the gods he was chained to a rock and an eagle feasted on his liver. Ogdon, as a man who lived and breathed music and was a channel for musical ideas, hardly lived in the finite world of concrete objects. Of all the arts music has the most direct link to the unconscious; the feelings it evokes are archetypal rather than individual. As such it brings with it a danger of what psychologists call 'inflation' (the exhilaration experienced when a person identifies with the numinous powers working through him or her), not to mention the depression that inevitably follows. Orpheus, the archetype of the inspired musician, lived in a world of musical enchantment that kept him sealed off from the concerns and attractions of everyday life. His 'punishment' was to be torn limb from limb by the Maenads, wild women who followed Dionysus, a god whom Orpheus in his single-minded pursuit of his art had failed to honour. In many ways manic depression mimics and exaggerates the natural swings of the creative process. Additionally, in John's case, the inflation (or mania) could be seen as a consequence of the overvaluing he received as a child, and the depression an outgrowth of the lack of human warmth.

When asked by Sue Lawley what book he would like to take to the desert island John replied, in that hesitant way of his, 'I thought I might take The Moonstone of Wilkie Collins.' The way he said it, it sounded as though he wanted to take the stone itself rather than the book. It might seem strange that John should have abandoned his beloved white whale for a huge Indian diamond, but his choice did at least prove that he wasn't mono-symbolic. John himself was a rough diamond, of the kind that comes along once in a blue moon. His wonderfully natural and spontaneous approach to the piano reminds one of Art Tatum, who, like John, learned from his mother's collection of piano rolls. John's innate talent was as sensational as Tatum's, including the fabulous memory, but his sight-reading was something else altogether – a truly unearthly ability. It's as if it wasn't a pair of human eyes looking at the music. He seemed to have access to areas of mental processing closed to the vast majority of people. Once, after a BBC recording session at Maida Vale, Bob Simpson pointed to two pianos standing side by side and jokingly suggested that John play the opening of the *Hammerklavier* Sonata (the piece they'd just been working on) on both pianos at once. 'Hmm, that's a very interesting idea,' said John, then sat down between them and began to play. Though his right hand was playing the bass notes and his left hand the treble, he didn't falter. In fact he simply kept playing until someone asked him to stop.

There may have been a touch of Asperger's about John's facility. He wouldn't have been the first famous musician to have this condition. One thinks of Prokofiev, Janacek, Satie and Britten, to name just four. With Asperger's, however, there is a rather cold, dissociative manner of regarding both oneself and others; while John did maintain a quirky distance from his feelings – as if he wasn't quite sure that he was in fact himself – he did generally respond very warmly to people, often casting an undeserved mantle of glamour over those with whom he came into contact. It was perhaps an idealistic rather than a human warmth, but who could argue with Peter Donohoe when he said of Ogdon's playing, 'His gentle and generous personality shines through music of all styles.' If John demonstrated something of the narcissism often associated with autism in its various forms, it was at least not of the nasty pathological type; nor was it based on pride or egotism. There was no vanity there at all: he knew his gift was his only in so far as he shared it – and share it he did, on a gargantuan scale. One of his favourite and oft-quoted sayings was Stravinsky's line, 'I am the vessel through which *Le Sacre* passed.' Music being the most oceanic and untrammelled of the arts, it makes sense that many of its finest exponents have been overwhelmed by the unconscious. John himself, one feels, lived at a tremendous depth. The notice of his death in the *Swanage & Wareham Advertiser*, entitled 'Death of a master music maker', was placed next to an article with the headline 'Mystery of Swanage's deep water monsters'. The disciple of *Moby-Dick* would have approved!

When John was in his prime the sheer hugeness of what he was stating at the piano was almost too much. There was a rage to his genius that in its intensity reminds one of Beethoven (another artist cut off from intimate contact with his fellow human beings); and, despite his passion for Busoni and Sorabji, it was in Beethoven that John revealed his deepest musical insights. This rage, it seems to me, was a kind of exorcism, and what was being driven out were the war demons that had lodged themselves in both his father's psyche and his childhood home. Anyone who has heard John's 1967 recording of Liszt's *Funérailles* will know what it sounds like when grief and fury contend which is the mightier.

Many great pianists have been visited by nervous breakdown – one thinks of Horowitz, Arrau, Van Cliburn and Terence Judd among twentieth-century examples – but John was perhaps the only one who was universally loved by his colleagues and whose life told in such bold relief the parable of the innocent and exploited artist. Even here, though, the watchword must be caution. John's genius (in the original sense of his tutelary spirit) kept him in thrall to the piano. *It* did the exploiting. Moreover, he was the archetype of the artless prodigy, onto whom we love to project our fantasies of lost innocence. It is too easy to deify him while demonizing all those who attempted to bring order to his life or to express the will that he appeared unable or unwilling to exercise. Whatever their faults, those around him cannot be held responsible for the path that John trod.

John's relationship with Brenda is at the heart of his story. On one level it was an alchemy of two souls that lacked self-awareness and were drawn together by deep-seated need, each appearing to the other as a kind of deliverer. As such it had a strong feeling of fatedness about it. In an interview with Sandra Parsons for the *Today* newspaper three days after John died, Brenda said, 'John and I were bound together, and it was he who chose me. John Ogdon decided he was going to marry me and there was nothing I could do about it.' She was, of course, marrying two people: the masterly and authoritative artist and the lost and wayward child. She looked up to the one and recoiled from the other. She recoiled from the other because she too possessed elements of that lost and wayward child, and feared the feelings of weakness and vulnerability that came with it. From an early age she had shared John's ambition to be a world-class concert pianist but lacked his extraordinary talent. She had plenty of executive skill, but was careful and tightly controlled – the very opposite of John, in fact, who at the keyboard was free and fearless, reckless even. She brought order to his life; he brought chaos to hers. Being part of John's shining talent became a compensation for the loss of her own career and she grew to identify closely with him, as if he was a perfected image of herself. Neither could satisfy the emotional needs of the other, but neither could they release each other for a different kind of life.

On another level, their relationship is the story of a single soul: John's. Brenda embodied those repressed elements of John's psyche that had fallen into shadow, such as will, order and the aggression needed for everyday life. He was reunited with these lost drives through her but, because he wouldn't recognize them as his own, they appeared in a destructive form, as outside aggressors. He was nagged, needled, driven and bullied, but only because he took such pains to repress all that was dark and ugly and inferior in himself. Gentle, humble, accommodating John got others to express his shadow for him. This wasn't a conscious process, far from it. Ultimately we each must take responsibility not only for what we do but also for what is done to us – in some sense regardless of our capacity to do so. It is a necessary part of the energetic orbit we create for ourselves. The people who enter our lives, the events that happen to us, all act out the drama of the individual soul. The fact that neither John nor Brenda took responsibility for themselves reduced their marriage at times to a battlefield. There is no blame or judgement here, simply an observation of what happened.

Even today many people demonize Brenda because they want to cling to an image of John as pure and childlike. That was certainly an element of his character but of course he had demons aplenty of his own. Brenda was made to carry those demons because John was at such pains to present himself as a mild, courteous, compliant character. She alone lived on the edge of the volcano and witnessed the violent, destructive side to his character that he kept hidden from the world. Even those who have felt bitter towards Brenda acknowledge the protective role she played for a good many years. Peter Maxwell Davies wrote to her on John's death: 'You stood by John through all those awful years, with huge courage and loyalty – something I can imagine few other people – perhaps nobody – ever doing.' There were many such tributes.

People ask if John was neglected in the final years of his life. Some even suggest that he died of neglect, but this is a failure of perception. It is the wrong question, based on the wish to find a scapegoat for his suffering. John's enormous mental stamina, which meant he could play the piano brilliantly even under severe mental and physical stress, masked the fact that he was much sicker than people knew. He neglected himself and the years of mental illness robbed him of any real survival instinct. The image of the metamorphosed Gregor Samsa in Kafka's chilling tale of mental breakdown springs to mind, though it is an almost unbearably harsh symbol for John's life. Here we see Gregor, finally ignored by his family – who are baffled by his transformation and see in him only a monstrous insect – shuffling around his room in a filthy, unkempt state. Made callous by his painful sensitivity, only the sound of his sister playing the violin can draw him out of his inner morass. When he finally dies he is called 'the thing' and is swept up by the charwoman's broom. The rest of the family can't help but feel a new lease of life at his going. Manic depression can be a deadly disease and John's lack of self-assertion meant that he was moved around by others like an object. 'John's tragedy,' says Brenda, 'is that he was too easily bullied.'

There was always something wrong with John's body. He was overweight, had gout, short sight and bad hearing and of course for sixteen years had to contend with a battery of powerful drugs that would have prevented most people from playing at all, let alone at the top of their profession. His early death must also be seen in the context of his early start. He may not have been put on the concert circuit as a child but he nevertheless pushed himself relentlessly from an early age. Busoni, who did go on the circuit as a boy, felt old and spent at thirty-nine. John was grotesquely overworked but there was no harsher taskmistress than his own genius. 'He was very brave, the way he coped with everything,' says Brenda. 'He was carrying that body around, was very heavy, on pills, and always expected to perform. He was a lonely person. God knows what went on in his head. It's quite moving really, looking back on it.'

Though John was clumsy, shy, awkward, self-conscious and burdened, through the piano – his second (purified) body – he was transformed into a supremely self-confident, coordinated, adroit and spontaneous being. What he overcame to share his gift of music with the world would daunt even the most courageous of souls. On the day after John's death the conductor Edward Downes, a fellow champion of English music, gave a concert at the Albert Hall. In introducing Richard Strauss's tone poem 'Ein Heldenleben' ('A Hero's Life') Downes told the audience that he was dedicating the piece to John Ogdon.

There was a heartfelt roar of approval.

ACKNOWLEDGEMENTS

It was Richard Ogdon who asked me if I would write the life of his father, as he felt that John's contemporaries were beginning to pass away and valuable memories were passing with them. It is to him that my first thanks must go for his unwavering support, both as friend and sponsor, and to his mother Brenda, John's widow, who accorded me four interviews – reliving some harrowing experiences in the process – and was generous throughout with her time and gave me access to written and broadcast records. (*Virtuoso*, her book with Michael Kerr, to which I am indebted, is a moving memorial of Brenda's relationship with John.) The family quartet was completed by daughter Annabel, who agreed to be interviewed and supplied further information by email.

I am also grateful to John's other surviving family members, in particular to his eldest sister Philippa, who lives in Australia and is now 91 and her daughter Delia O'Hara, who arranged for me to speak to her mother by phone and gave me access to family photographs; to John's sister Ruth who wrote me a number of letters from Manchester in answer to my enquiries and her son John Ogdon Lant, who took time from his busy medical practice to be interviewed; and finally to Gwen Ford, the widow of John's brother Karl, who spoke to me from her home in the suburbs of Melbourne, and provided me with articles about John's Australian tours of 1964 and 1975. She died while this book was being written.

Special gratitude goes to John's childhood muse and benefactress Marjory E. Wood, whose book *The Young John Ogdon* was an invaluable resource for John's early years. Even at 96 she was happy to answer my questions from her home in North Carolina and was delighted with my description of her as John's 'fairy godmother'. Her sons James and Philip Kasen were also a welcome source of help and encouragement.

A big thank-you to all those who agreed to be interviewed and who, in addition to their time, provided me in many instances with printed materials, invaluable leads and heartwarming hospitality. They are Ronald and Marjorie Stevenson, Gerard and Carolyn Schurmann, John and Joan Humphreys, Alistair Londonderry, Alexander Goehr, Sir Peter Maxwell Davies, Sir Harrison Birtwistle, Sir Ernest Hall, Elgar Howarth, Rodney Friend, David Wilde, Keith and Jan Cole, Robert Elliott, John McCabe, Arthur Butterworth, Daniell Revenaugh, Dr Raimund Herincx, Howard Greenwood, John Woolf of the Park Lane Group, Peter Shahbenderian, Vladimir Ashkenazy, Abbey Simon, John Lill, Philip Fowke, Gordon Fergus-Thompson, Stephen Hough, Susan Starr, Roy Bogas, Alan Schiller, Mark Latimer, Mark Tanner, James Loughran, John Carewe, James Blair, Lawrence Foster, Barry Tuckwell, Charles Webb, Menahem Pressler, James Tocco, Gilan Corn, Karen Shaw, Henry Upper, Michael Duff, Alfonso Montecino, Clipper Erickson, Edna Chun, Andrew Axelrod, Angela Simpson, Bryce Morrison, Terry Harrison, Jasper Parrott, Martin Campbell-White, Brian Masters, Michael Kerr, Humphrey Burton CBE, William Humble, Gerald Fox, Harold Taylor, Colin Decio, Nigel Scaife, Joy Hancox, Christopher Tennant, Maureen Garnham, Nina Kaye, Virginia Renshaw, Jane Krivine, John Boyden, Matthew Boyden, Alexander Waugh, Alex Durston, Dennis Ridewood, Tony Palmer, Robert Pike Daniel and his wife Violetta, Martin Anderson, Stephen Plaistow, Graham and Brenda Preston, Christopher Bishop, Brian Culverhouse, David Mottley, John Pattrick, Alistair Hinton of the Sorabji Archive, Chris Rice, Richard Black, Janet and Terry Grotefeld, Francis and Helen Bullock, Mrs Jaqi Fielding, John le Carré, the Hon. Simon Eccles, Clive Barda, Jessica Minchinton, Dame Cleo Laine, Lady Camilla Panufnik, Lord Harewood, Andrew Auster, Murray St Albans, David and Brenda Chamberlain, Millicent Round, Tony Barton, Michael Hayes, Raymond Clark, Keith Beastall, Professor Michael King, Dr Gerald Libby, Dr Michael Johnson, Lady Tuema Pattie, Lord Armstrong of Ilminster, Judy Arnold, David Ferre, Nadia Lasserson, John Harvey, Andrew Reekie and Julian Gallant.

The staff of the Royal Northern College of Music was unfailingly helpful and resourceful on my behalf, in particular Mary Ann Davison, whose prompt and stellar service saved me endless time and trouble: my grateful thanks to her and her team. Jeremy Ward and Rachel Kneale of the Manchester Grammar School Archives, Kenneth Dunn of the National Library of Scotland, Trisha Hayes of the BBC Written Archives, Rob Hudson of the Carnegie Hall Archives, Philip Bantin and Bradley Cook of the Indiana University Library, Silvia Torresin of the Fondazione Concorso Pianistico Internazionale Ferruccio Busoni, Paul Collen of the Royal College of Music's Centre for Performance History, Bridget Palmer of the Royal Academy of Music, Paula Best of the Wigmore Hall Collections, Ann Edgcombe of the Mansfield Historical Society, Elly Jansen of the Fellowship Charitable Foundation, piano pedagogue Juan Wang and independent researchers Susan Clitheroe and Joanna Brook all provided me with friendly and efficient assistance on numerous occasions, as did the staff of the Bury Archives, Greater Manchester, the Nottingham County Archives and the Mansfield Library. The chapter on the Tchaikovsky competition benefited greatly from Christine Barnard's excellent Russian translations as well as the assistance of Maria Kholkina, Press Manager of the Tchaikovsky Competition, while Angus McGeoch made sense of German, French, Italian and Swedish reviews for me. I am also grateful to Dr Dele Olajide of the Maudsley Hospital for releasing John's admission and discharge records and to the Australian Broadcasting Corporation for making available recorded interviews from the 1960s and 1970s.

Very special thanks must go to Lisa Wilson, who ably assisted me with the early research and filmed and helped conduct a number of the interviews; to Sally Mosher, who explained so much I didn't understand of music and musical theory; to Simon Abbott for his encouragement and advice at our breakfast summits on Holland Park Avenue; to Susie Sanders and Simon Horton for their insights into the psychology of the story; to Adrian Stott for acting as an inspired sounding board for my ideas throughout the project; to Robert Warwick for digging up rare recordings for me; and to my mother Rosemary Exmouth for inviting herself to stay in order to join battle with (and subdue) the chaos that was my filing system.

From contract to publication is a long, twisty path for any book and those who shepherd it along the way and sweep the mines from the road perform a heroic task. A special thank-you to Mike Jones of Simon & Schuster, who took the book on and has been a wonderfully relaxed yet focused helmsman throughout; to my agent Peter Robinson and his assistant Alex Goodwin for their diplomacy and flawless counsel; to Martin Soames of Simons, Muirhead & Burton for his scupulous legal advice; to Karl French who suggested ways that the original leviathan of a text could be cut; and to my editor Monica Hope, who performed the necessary surgery so elegantly and seamlessly, with such deep understanding and good humour, that there was no pain involved: the text flourished under her knife.

My final thanks are to John himself, not only for the gift of music he shared with us all, but for the vast train of goodwill he left in his wake, which made my undertaking a pleasure as well as a privilege.

BIBLIOGRAPHY

Andry, Peter. *Inside the Recording Studio*. The Scarecrow Press, Lanham, Maryland, 2008.

Bertensson, Sergei & Jay Leyda. *Sergei Rachmaninoff, A Lifetime in Music*. Indiana University Press, Bloomington, 2001.

Bowers, Faubion. *The New Scriabin*. David & Charles, Newton Abbot, 1974.

Busoni, Ferruccio (Rosamond Ley, tr.). *The Essence of Music and Other Papers*. Dover Publications Inc., New York, 1965.

Collins, Wilkie. *The Moonstone*. J. M. Dent & Sons, London, 1947.

Copland, Aaron. *What to Listen for in Music*. McGraw-Hill Inc., New York, 1939.

Crimp, Bryan. *Solo: The Biography of Solomon*. Appian Publications, 1992.

De Schloezer, Boris. *Scriabin, Artist & Mystic*. Oxford University Press, 1987.

Du Pré, Hilary and Piers. *A Genius in the Family*. Vintage, London, 1998.

Fenby, Eric. *Delius as I Knew Him*. G. Bell & Sons Ltd., London, 1936.

Fowles, John. *The Magus*. Jonathan Cape Ltd., London, 1966.

Garnham, Maureen. *As I Saw It: Basil Douglas, Benjamin Britten and The English Opera Group, 1955–57*. St. George's Publications, London, 1998.

Goehr, Alexander. *Finding the Key*. Faber & Faber, London, 1998.

Golding, William. *Lord of the Flies*. Faber & Faber, London, 1954.

Graham, J. A. & B. A. Phythian, eds. *The Manchester Grammar School, 1515–1965*. Manchester University Press, 1965.

Greenwood, Howard. *All Kinds of Musick: The First 40 Years of the Richmond Concert Society*. Ashwater Press, Twickenham, 2002.

Grubb, Suvi Raj. *Music Makers on Record*. Hamish Hamilton, London, 1986.

Harewood, Earl of, ed. *Kobbé's Complete Opera Book*. Putnam & Co., London, 1983.

Kafka, Franz. *Metamorphosis and Other Stories*. Penguin Books, London, 1981.

Kalsched, Donald. *The Inner World of Trauma*. Routledge, London, 1996.

Kennedy, Michael. *The History of the Royal Manchester College of Music, 1893–1972*. Manchester University Press, 1972.

Laing, R. D. *The Divided Self*. Tavistock Publications Ltd., London, 1960.

Lawrence, D. H. *Studies in Classic American Literature*. Martin Secker, London, 1933.

Le Fanu, J. Sheridan. *In a Glass Darkly*. Peter Davies, London, 1929.

Le Fanu, J. Sheridan. *Madam Crowl's Ghost & Other Stories*. Wordsworth Classics, London, 1994.

Lindsay, David. *A Voyage to Arcturus*. Methuen & Co. Ltd., London, 1920.

Logan, George M. *The Indiana University School of Music, A History*. Indiana University Press, Bloomington, 2000.

Lucas, Brenda & Michael Kerr. *Virtuoso, The Story of John Ogdon*. Hamish Hamilton, London, 1981.

MacDiarmid, Hugh. *The Company I've Kept*. Hutchinson & Co. Ltd., London, 1966.

Macdonald, Hugh. *Skryabin*. Oxford University Press, 1978.

MacDonald, Malcolm. *Ronald Stevenson*. National Library of Scotland, Edinburgh, 1989.

Mach, Elyse. *Great Contemporary Pianists Speak for Themselves*. Dover Publications Inc., New York, 1991.

Magee, Bryan. *Aspects of Wagner*. Alan Ross, London, 1968.

Masters, Brian. *Getting Personal*. Constable, London, 2002.

Matthews, Denis, ed. *Keyboard Music*. Penguin Books, London, 1972.

Melville, Herman. *Moby-Dick*. Penguin Books, London, 1978.

Miller, Alice. *The Drama of the Gifted Child*. Perennial, London, 1997.

Montparker, Carol. *A Pianist's Landscape*. Amadeus Press, Portland, Oregon, 1998.

Newman, Ernest. *The Man Liszt*. Cassell & Co. Ltd., London, 1934.

Ogdon, Howard. *The Kingdom of the Lost*. The Bodley Head, London, 1947.

Orga, Ateş. *Beethoven, His Life & Times*. Midas Books, Tunbridge Wells, 1978.

Perry, John Weir. *The Far Side of Madness*. Prentice-Hall, Englewood Cliffs, New Jersey, 1974.

Plaskin, Glenn. *Horowitz*. Macdonald & Co., London, 1983.

Poe, Edgar Allan. *Selected Tales*. Penguin Books, London, 1994.

Rapoport, Paul. *Opus Est: Six Composers from Northern Europe.* Kahn & Averill, London, 1985.

Rimm, Robert. *Hamelin and The Eight.* Amadeus Press, Portland, Oregon, 2002.

Ross, Alex. *The Rest is Noise: Listening to the Twentieth Century.* Fourth Estate, London, 2008.

Sacks, Oliver. *Musicophilia: Tales of Music and the Brain.* Picador, London, 2008.

Schonberg, Harold C. *Horowitz, His Life & Music.* Simon & Schuster, New York, 1992.

Schonberg, Harold C. *The Lives of the Great Composers.* Abacus, London, 1998

Schonberg, Harold C. *The Great Pianists.* Simon & Schuster Paperbacks, New York, 2006.

Shaw, Otto L. *Maladjusted Boys.* George Allen & Unwin Ltd, London, 1965.

Sorabji, Kaikhosru. *Around Music.* The Unicorn Press, London, 1932.

Sorabji, Kaikhosru. *Mi Contra Fa.* The Porcupine Press, London, 1947.

Stevenson, Ronald. *Western Music: An Introduction.* Kahn & Averill, London, 1971.

Storr, Anthony. *The School of Genius.* Andre Deutsch, London, 1988.

Storr, Anthony. *The Dynamics of Creation.* Penguin Books, London, 1991.

Storr, Anthony. *Music and the Mind.* HarperCollins, London, 1997.

Styron, William. *Darkness Visible.* Vintage Books, London, 2004.

Taylor, Harold. *The Pianist's Talent.* Kahn & Averill, London, 1979.

Taylor, Ronald. *Robert Schumann, His Life & Work.* Granada, London, 1982.

Van Der Post, Laurens. *Journey Into Russia.* The Hogarth Press, London, 1964.

Walker, Alan, ed. *Franz Liszt, The Man & His Music.* Barrie & Jenkins, London, 1970.

Wightman, Alistair, ed. & trans. *Szymanowski on Music.* Toccata Press, London, 1999.

Wilkinson, Anthony. *Liszt.* Macmillan, London, 1975.

Wood, Marjory E. *The Young John Ogdon.* Morris Publishing, Nebraska, 1999.

Zamoyski, Adam. *Chopin, Prince of the Romantics.* Harper Press, London, 2010.

INDEX